VK
549
.W55
1992

Williams, J. E. D.

From sails to
satellites.

$35.00

DATE			

WITHDRAWN

BAKER & TAYLOR

From Sails to Satellites

Edmond Halley, scientist and navigator.

From Sails to Satellites

The Origin and Development
of Navigational Science

J. E. D. Williams

Oxford   New York   Melbourne
OXFORD UNIVERSITY PRESS
1992

Oxford University Press, Walton Street, Oxford OX2 6DP
Oxford New York Toronto
Delhi Bombay Calcutta Madras Karachi
Petaling Jaya Singapore Hong Kong Tokyo
Nairobi Dar es Salaam Cape Town
Melbourne Auckland
and associated companies in
Berlin Ibadan

Oxford is a trade mark of Oxford University Press

Published in the United States
by Oxford University Press, New York

A catalogue record for this book is available from the British Library

Library of Congress Cataloging in Publication Data
Williams, J. E. D.
From sails to satellites : the origin and development of
navigational science / J. E. D. Williams
p.   cm.
1. Navigation—History. I. Title.
VK549.W55 1992 623.89'09—dc20 92-8456
ISBN 0-19-856387-6

Photoset by Rowland Phototypesetting Limited
Bury St Edmunds, Suffolk
Printed in Great Britain by
Butler and Tanner Ltd, Frome, Somerset

Author's Preface

✠

THIS book is not a product of scholarly research; it is a by-product of fifty years of promiscuous reading in pursuit of pleasure. I am indebted to more writers than I can remember. There is no bibliography. The List of References is limited to sources quoted directly or mentioned in the text, or else answers the question 'where did he get that story from?' in the cases where it is most likely to be asked. Some sources are quoted because they are authoritative, others because they are apt and expressive. Wherever possible reference has been to papers published in the *Journal of Navigation*. The 20 000 pages or so of the first 44 volumes (1948–91) give a fascinating picture of the development of both the philosophy and technology of navigation since the Second World War. They also include many historical papers by some of the most distinguished historians of navigation of our times. I am grateful to the Council of the Royal Institute of Navigation for permission to reproduce material from the *Journal*.

I am grateful to the following who have reviewed in draft the section of the book to which their expertise is relevant, or who have assisted with advice or information: Professor V. Ashkenazi, Professor C. A. Bates, J. H. Beattie, W. F. Blanchard, Rear Admiral R. M. Burgoyne, Dr D. E. Cartwright FRS, Sir John Charnley, Cdr A. E. Fanning, Cdr D. Howse, Professor J. F. Kemp, B. Kendal, J. B. Parker, C. Powell, Dr J. Preston, Cdr M. W. Richey, S. G. Smith, Cdr D. W. Waters. Any errors or solecisms which have survived their wise counsel are entirely my responsibility.

I am also grateful to P. Fitzgerald and Dr K. Lippincott for assistance and advice in the selection of photographs of material in their care. A full list of acknowledgements for photographs reproduced in this book appears on p. 303.

In the matter of names of which more than one version exists I have tried to follow most common English usage, although this leads to many anomalies: for example, Leonardo *da* Vinci, but Leonardo *of* Pisa, a few miles down the road. It is said that Oxford University Press sets the standard for the presentation of the printed word in the English-speaking world; working with it has been a rewarding experience, and the publisher's editing has improved the quality of the book.

Piazzano   J. E. D. W.
February 1992

Contents

✠

INTRODUCTION

✠

THE proliferation of weapons of mass destruction during the 'Cold War' made superior military navigation—the ability to deliver one's weapons and frustrate the delivery of the enemy's weapons—literally priceless. Since then, the Gulf War has demonstrated the feasibility of weapon navigation systems of a precision to permit the maximum damage to the enemy in economic, strategic, or tactical terms with the minimum loss of lives, buildings, and other artefacts the user of the weapon desires to save. Modern navigational science has not only revolutionized the conduct of war; it has transformed its aims and objects. Only in modern times has navigation been central to warfare and defence; but it has long been a major spur to scientific discovery. Until the early twentieth century trade was usually the motive although competition frequently took a military form. In our own times it has been the needs of defence and warfare which have powered and funded the development of navigational science.

For many centuries men successfully navigated long voyages without science or even formal reckoning, often without knowing or caring where they were for much of the time; but fifteenth-century voyages of exploration saw a more formal reckoning and a glimmering of scientific method. As a separate matter, the discovery of the new world created a need to know where the new places were, initially for political and military reasons rather than for navigation. The latitude is easy, some of the ancient Greeks and medieval Arabs could measure it quite accurately, but the longitude requires the science and the engineering of a civilization which only began in the seventeenth century with the evolution in Europe of powerful new methods of thought about the physical world.

The Great Pursuit of the Longitude lasted for more than two centuries, and, before the industrial age, was a major spur to science. The Pursuit was joined by several kings and some of the greatest scientists that ever lived. It was the reason for founding both the French Royal

Academy of Sciences and, in England, the Greenwich Observatory. The problem proved much more difficult at sea than on land.

The longitude problem solved, science moved on to other things. Navigation became a backwater benefiting little from the nineteenth-century transformation of civilization by science and engineering through the railways, electricity, the telegraph, and machines of every kind. In the Victorian era there is little evidence of navigation as a driving force behind scientific discovery.

Then, on 17 December 1903, the Wright brothers flew an aeroplane. However boundless the possibilities of aeronautical engineering after the engineering achievements of the previous century, the aeroplane suffers from a defect which might have seemed fatal. It cannot heave to. It can only go forward at high speed for a few hours, and then it must stop—either catastrophically or by rigorous adherence to a trajectory which touches no obstacle and is tangential to a flat, level, smooth surface in a direction consistent with the surface wind. In the matter of how to conduct an aeroplane through cloud to a safe landing, navigational science in 1903 was as silent and as helpless as it had once been in the matter of longitude. A pilot cannot even fly straight in cloud by magnetic compass alone, still less, before radio direction-finding, know which way to go.

The aeroplane is fast, small, unnatural, and inherently dangerous. The greatest challenges to system designer and navigator alike in the twentieth century have been in aerospace, even in classical systems. From 1910 nearly all important advances in magnetic compasses have been inspired by the aeroplane. From 1919 the airman's need for astronomical navigation led to a new methodology which was eventually adopted by seamen. There was nothing in the history of marine radio to compare with the routine automatic landing in fog of airliners with hundreds of passengers aboard. The distribution of resources is such that the cost of operating the world-wide system of aeronautical radio beacons (point-source aids) is about eighty times that of operating the marine system. When the submarine's strategic potential as a covert launcher of nuclear weapons was realized, it too became an important prime mover in navigation.

It seems a strange and wonderful thing that, the day the first aeroplane flew, the thoughts of Stone in the US and Bellini and Tosi in Italy were already turning to radio direction-finding; while in Germany Anschütz-Kaempfe was developing the first gyrocompass (with the submarine problem in mind) and Hülsmeyer was preparing to file the first radar patent. Instead of marvelling at the extraordinary confluence of aerodynamics, the internal combustion engine, radio direction-finding, radar, and the gyroscope, we might wonder that it ever happened at all. A dozen generations earlier, science and engineering had not been much more developed than in some earlier civilizations. What was the device of Christian Europe which led in only ten generations from the days of Galileo and Kepler to the aeroplane and radio?

The landing of men on the moon only 66 years after the first aeroplane flight can hardly be described as an anticlimax; but after the wonderful events with which the twentieth century began there seems a certain inevitability about navigation's development thereafter.

The development of radar, inertial navigation systems, lasers, computers, and the rest are exciting stories; but they have the quality of majestic marches rather than astounding leaps.

In 1948 Sir Robert Watson-Watt, sometimes called 'the father of radar', daringly asserted 'Radio systems are now primary, and the celestial arts secondary, parts of navigation.' They were only so for a moment. Soon it was heat sensors which guided anti-aircraft missiles, magnetic fields which betrayed the presence of submarines, and inertial navigation systems which navigated and steered airliners above the ocean and submarines beneath its surface. None of these are radio systems; and even more esoteric ideas are bubbling. However, incredibly accurate fixing by signals from navigation satellites originally developed for nuclear submarines are making Watson-Watt's assertion valid again, except in respect of some weapon-delivery systems.

There are several strands to this tale. One is the way the needs of navigation have sometimes led and directed scientific discovery; another is the way navigation has adapted—and often failed to adapt—contemporary science, mathematics, and engineering to its needs. There is the development of physics and the belated application in the twentieth century of mathematical rationalism and scientific method to the practice of navigation itself. Thirty volumes would scarcely contain an account of all the events and ideas woven into this complex tapestry which the writer seeks to illuminate anecdotally.

CHAPTER ONE

Geography to Magellan

✠

'THE first and most principall thing for any seafaring man or traveller is to know what Part of the Earth ye meaneth to go.' Thus wrote William Bourne[1] in 1574. That may seem trite now; but the words would not have been written in any earlier time. They imply a shared general knowledge of the *Parts of the Earth*. The attainment of that knowledge took two thousand years of exploration, mathematics, and astronomy, repeatedly lost or forgotten, and then found again or rediscovered.

The final chapter started on 6 September 1492 when Christopher Columbus sailed west from the Canaries in the faith that Japan lay about 4000 kilometres[2] ahead. After logging about 6000 km he discovered the Bahamas, cruised the Caribbean during the winter, and returned early in 1493 with the news that he had claimed the Indies in the names of 'the Catholic Sovereigns', Ferdinand and Isabella of Aragon and Castile. On this and subsequent voyages to the area Cathay, the Indies, or Japan always lay beyond the next headland but one. The notion of sailing west to reach the east did not originate with Columbus. The idea had been mooted among the ancient Greeks and revived in medieval times, and again most recently by the contemporary Florentine scholar Paolo Toscanelli. The ideas particular to Columbus derived from a thorough study of Marco Polo, a fragmentary and second-hand knowledge of Greek science in antiquity and of medieval Arabic science, both of which he misinterpreted, and a writer of apocrypha. Columbus owes his place in history to his courage, resolution, and audacity rather than to his insight, intellect, or erudition.

Columbus was born in Italy during that second period of Italian greatness which they called the *renascimento* or *rinascenza*, which the French translated as *renaissance*—a word the English then made their own, to mean the rebirth of art and learning. One feature of the Renaissance is artfully exhibited in the Uffizi in Florence. One tramps through rooms of late medieval paintings. Morning twilight is scarcely visible at first; then suddenly one is in the

Botticelli room, and all is light, beauty, and wit. Some aspects of the Mediterranean scene in 1492 are listed in the adjacent Table.

Another feature of this questing and questioning age was the Portuguese exploration of the African coast. There was a good commercial reason for their search (and that of Columbus) for a sea route to the Far East. Christians had acquired a taste for eastern spices. Moslem kingdoms bestrode the trade routes and profited exorbitantly. A bale of beans which sold in the Spice Islands (the Moluccas) for one ducat sold in the London market for 105 ducats.[3] Gradually the Portuguese groped their way around Africa (Fig. 1.1).

They might have been less timid if they had known they were merely backtracking a Phoenician voyage two thousand years earlier. According to Herodotus, in the days of the Pharaoh Necho II (c.600 BC), the Phoenicians claimed to have circumnavigated Africa from the Red Sea, sailing via the Cape of Good Hope and the Straits of Gibraltar back through the Mediterranean to the Nile Delta[4] (see Fig. 1.1). We may believe their story for the very reason that some of the ancients did not. For they claimed that 'as they rounded Libya [meaning Africa] they beheld the sun on their right hand' [i.e. to the north]. Plutarch tells us[5] that in 324 BC, when Alexander the Great met with his admiral Nearchus in the Persian Gulf after their return from India, 'He resolved himself to sail out of the mouth of the Euphrates with a great fleet with which he designed to go round by Arabia and Africa and so by the Pillars of Hercules into the Mediterranean.' The plan was abandoned; but even if, like Flavius Arrianus (a more scrupulous biographer of Alexander), we doubt the story, it shows at least that Plutarch, writing in the first century AD, had a clearer idea of African geography than any West European had in, say, AD 1400.

This is not to say that geography is a European invention. Written sailing directions which were really fragmentary geographical descriptions of the shores of seas and navigable rivers are said to have existed in China in 2000 BC. During the Tang dynasty (seventh century AD to the beginning of the tenth) such sailing directions were extended from Korea around to East Africa and the Persian Gulf.[6] The earliest known Greek sailing directions, the *Periplus of Scylax of Caryanda*,[7] are thought to be of the fourth century BC.

Greece in Alexander's day was as brilliant intellectually as Florence was artistically in the days of Columbus. The Greeks plotted the position of the planets against the fixed stars and wondered, as men have done since they were men, at the motion of these 'wanderers'. Earlier civilizations had collated data on apparent planetary motion; but the Greeks were the first to apply mathematical reasoning to the question 'What does the evidence of our eyes mean?' Heraclides in the fourth century BC conjectured that the inferior planets revolve around the sun and that the earth rotates. In the next century Aristarchus taught that the earth not only rotates on its own axis but revolves around the sun like the other planets. His system was essentially that which Copernicus proposed nearly two thousand years later. Naturally Aristarchus was accused of impiety for 'putting in motion the hearth of the universe', just as Galileo was in AD 1633. It seems he later recanted. As Durant remarked in 1936 'Perhaps a distaste for hemlock moved him to be the Galileo as well as the Copernicus of the ancient world.'

6

The Southern European scene in 1492

In Spain
The Castilians captured Granada and ended Islamic governance in Western Europe.
In Italy
Rodrigo Borgia became Pope Alexander VI. Lorenzo *Il Magnifico* died, and Savonarola sought to create the City of God in Florence.
Some Florentine birthdays
Botticelli was 48. Leonardo da Vinci was 40. Amerigo Vespucci was 38. Machiavelli was 23. Michelangelo was 17.

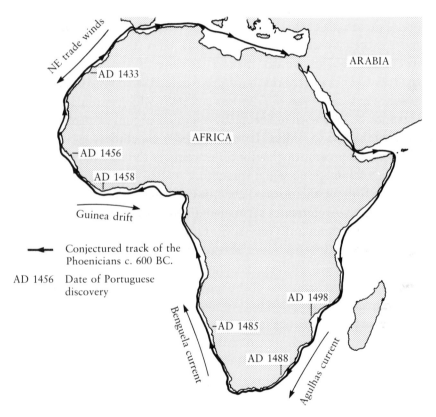

FIGURE I.I
Sixty-five years of Portuguese exploration of the African coast and a Phoenician voyage 2000 years earlier.

Some of the flavour of Greek mathematics in the third century BC is conveyed by the following exquisite little proposition of Archimedes[8] (see Fig. 1.2). To prove that, if A is the area of a circle, R its radius, and S its circumference, $A = \frac{1}{2}RS$. If A does not equal $\frac{1}{2}RS$ it must be more or less than $\frac{1}{2}RS$. Suppose it to be more. Then $A = \frac{1}{2}RS + e$, where e is some definite amount. Inscribe in the circle a regular polygon of area P. It is easy to show that

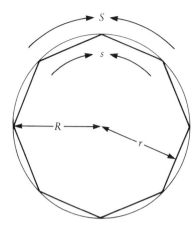

FIGURE I.2
The proof of Archimedes.

$P=\frac{1}{2}rs$, where r is the length of the perpendicular from the centre of the circle to any side of the polygon and s is the sum of the lengths of all its sides. By doubling and redoubling the number of sides of the polygon we can make P as close to A as we please, although it will never quite reach A. Eventually we reach a stage where $A = P+f$, f being a number smaller than e. Thus $\frac{1}{2}RS + e = A = \frac{1}{2}rs + f$, so $\frac{1}{2}rs > \frac{1}{2}RS$; which is impossible, since $S>s$ and $R>r$. Thus A cannot be *greater* than $\frac{1}{2}RS$. By a similar argument Archimedes then proves that A cannot be *less* than $\frac{1}{2}RS$. Thus, he triumphantly concludes, $A = \frac{1}{2}RS$.

This is a most consequential ratiocination; it introduces the idea of convergence: the study of the limiting value of something when something related tends to infinity or zero without quite getting there. Without this idea science must remain for ever primitive. In this and several other propositions Archimedes seems tantalizingly close to the calculus developed by Newton and Leibniz two thousand years later. Of course, by modern standards of analysis the proof of Archimedes is invalid, since it contains unconscious appeals to intuition. But such matters were not settled until the general restructuring of the logical foundations of mathematics in modern times; and one of the most powerful tools then used was a refinement of this idea of Archimedes.

Greek astronomy and mathematics had no immediate influence on Greek navigation. The Greeks steered by the stars much as Columbus did; but one requires neither the daring imagination of Aristarchus nor the subtle intellect of Archimedes to do that. However, Greek astronomy and mathematics did lead directly to Greek geodesy, which is central to the subject of this chapter. Eratosthenes, a friend of Archimedes, was, as far as we know, the first to make a fair determination of the circumference of the earth. At Syene (Aswan) one could see the sun reflected in the bottom of a well at noon on a certain date. At Alexandria at noon on the same date the zenith distance of the sun was a fiftieth part of a circle (7.2°). A camel-train took fifty days from Alexandria to Syene. Assuming that the camels travel 100 *stadia* a day; that the sun is so far away that its beams may be assumed to be parallel; and that Syene is due south of Alexandria (it is south-south-east), the earth's circumference is 50 × 50 × 100 = 250 000 *stadia* (see Fig. 1.3). Eratosthenes later refined the calculation to 252 000 *stadia*.

In the next century Posidonius interpreted the observation that Canopus, a bright star of

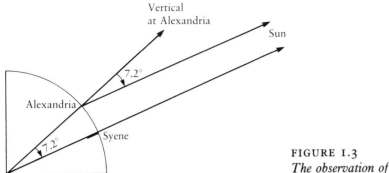

FIGURE I.3
The observation of Eratosthenes.

the southern hemisphere, was barely visible on the southern horizon at Rhodes but attained an altitude of 7½° at Alexandria as meaning that the arc of the earth between them is 7½°. In fact it is less than 6°, and they are not on the same meridian. Posidonius estimated the baseline as 3750 *stadia*, deducing this figure from sailing times between the two ports—the first but not the last dependence of geodesy on navigation. Thus the circumference of the earth is 360/7.5 × 3750 = 180 000 *stadia*.

Some historians have ascribed an accuracy to Eratosthenes which would be phenomenal given the crudity of his method of estimating the baseline; but more prudent writers note the uncertainty of the length of the *stadion* of Eratosthenes. A *stadion* was 600 Greek feet, and also the length of the foot-race course in the stadium (which derived its name from the measurement). They both varied with time and place, as the mile and the league have in more recent times. Anywhere within the possible range of uncertainty for the *stadion*, however, the Posidonius figure for the earth's circumference is far too small. The Eratosthenes figure, on the other hand, may have been quite close to the actual circumference of about 40 000 km.

Eratosthenes also conjectured that the earth is ellipsoidal, and measured the obliquity of the ecliptic as half the difference between the noon altitude of the sun at the summer and winter solstices (see Fig. 1.4). He speculated that one could sail westward from Spain to India were the extent of the western ocean not an obstacle—the proviso that Columbus, many centuries later, was so wilfully to reject.

The Greeks also sought to determine position on the earth. Latitude was easy. Pytheas (*c*.300 BC) found the latitude at a gnomon in his home town Marseilles with an accuracy of perhaps a quarter of a degree by measuring the length of its shadow at noon at the equinox (see Fig. 1.5). The latitude known, the gnomon may be used to find the declination of the sun at other times of the year by measuring the length of its shadow at noon. With a table of the declination of the sun against date, the latitude of any place can be found at any date by measuring the length of a gnomon's shadow at noon. Pytheas claimed that he followed this procedure when he rounded Spain, circumnavigated Britain, and reached Thule, where the summer solstice is the arctic circle, meaning that at the summer solstice the sun is on the horizon at midnight.

In about 225 BC Eratosthenes produced a map based on the observations of Pytheas and

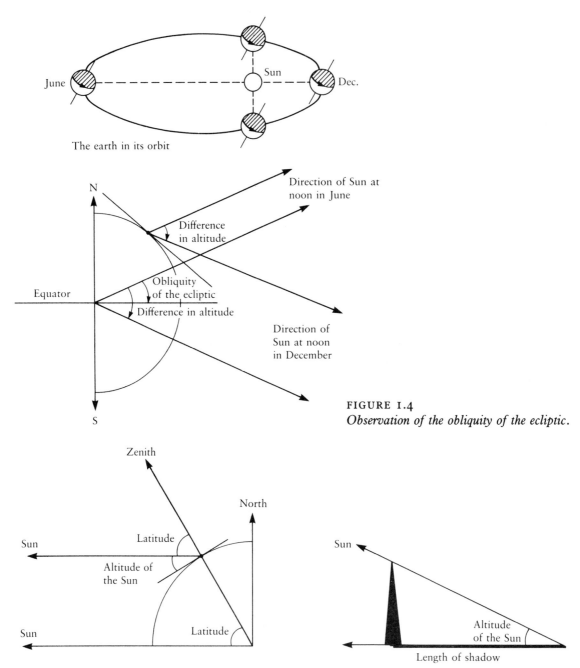

The earth in its orbit

FIGURE I.4
Observation of the obliquity of the ecliptic.

FIGURE I.5
Latitude by noon altitude at the equinox.

others which is outlined in Fig. 1.6. Astronomical observations provided the latitude, that is to say the *northing*, of places; but he had no effective knowledge of their *easting*, the relative orientation of places in an east–west direction. In the second century BC Hipparchus pro-

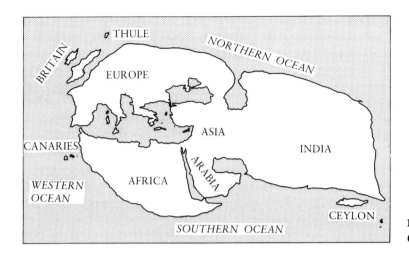

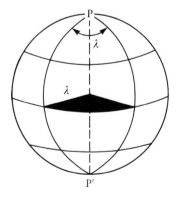
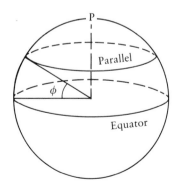

FIGURE 1.6
Outline of the Eratosthenes map.

posed the system of latitude and longitude shown in Fig. 1.7, which we still use today to specify position on the earth (subject to refinements because the earth is not an exact sphere). The parallel of latitude are small circles centred on the earth's polar axis. The meridians are great circles (centred at the earth's centre) passing through the poles and the difference of longitude between any two places is the angle between the planes of their respective meridians. Latitude and longitude are very different in nature. The latitude of a point is the complement of the curvature of the earth between it and the pole. Unless the position of the pole on the earth changes, the latitude of a point is fixed forever. Unless the earth's axis wobbles, the plane of the parallels and the equator is fixed; but the plane of every meridian rotates once a day, and nature provides no prime meridian. Strictly speaking, we can only speak of the *difference* of longitude of places. The length of a unit of longitude equals that of a unit of latitude at the equator, declining to zero at the poles in proportion to the cosine of the latitude —but that trigonometrical function had yet to be invented (see Chapter 3).

FIGURE 1.7
Latitude (ϕ) and longitude (λ).

At the beginning of astronomy the stars were visualized as being fixed in a vast celestial sphere rotating around the earth in a little less than 24 hours (the sidereal day is 23 hr 56 min. 4.091 sec.). The sun, moon, and planets were visualized either as fixed in celestial spheres of their own, or as moving in a systematic way about the celestial sphere in which the stars are fixed. The latter concept is the basis of astronomical navigation, although it has had no relation to our perception of the geometry of the universe for some centuries. The coordinates in the celestial sphere corresponding to latitude and longitude on the earth are declination and hour angle.[9] The prime meridian is that which passes through the *first point of Aries* (♈), the position of the sun at the vernal equinox when, following the ecliptic in its annual orbit of the celestial sphere, it crosses the celestial equator northbound (see Fig. 1.8). At the point vertically above the observer (his zenith) the declination equals his latitude; but the hour angle of the zenith depends on the date and time, because of the rotation of the celestial sphere. Hence one can determine one's latitude and hour angle by astronomical observation, but not the longitude, unless the hour angle of some standard meridian on earth (that is to say the date-time on that meridian) is known.

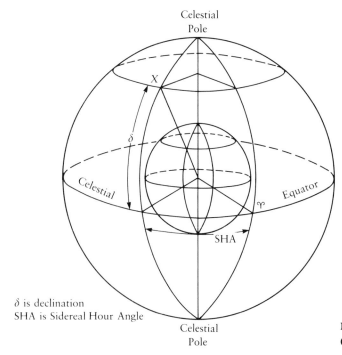

δ is declination
SHA is Sidereal Hour Angle

FIGURE 1.8
Coordinates of a star in the celestial sphere.

Hipparchus proposed to determine the difference of longitude between two places by determining hour angle at both places simultaneously at the moment of an eclipse. Variations on this notion were to reverberate through the centuries until there were accurate and reliable chronometers at economic prices. The principle Hipparchus sought was sound; the difference of hour angle of the zeniths of two observers at any moment is always equal to their difference of longitude. The difficulty is that the moon is so close to us that observers in different places see the moon in a different place relative to other heavenly bodies. Observers in different places therefore do not see a solar eclipse at the same moment. In some places the sun may not be eclipsed at all. The problem of the moon's parallax when determining longitude from the place of the moon in the celestial sphere was not solved until the eighteenth century; and the solution was never satisfactory. The difficulty with a lunar eclipse is different; the time of onset of the earth's shadow on the face of the moon is the same from wherever it is seen. The difficulty is in timing it precisely.

In about AD 150 Claudius Ptolemy's *Geographike Huphegesis* sought to apply the ideas of Hipparchus. The work discusses the mathematical principles of cartographic projection of a spherical world and lists the position of thousands of places; there are regional maps and the famous world map. The Eurasian continent is shown as extending through 180° of longitude. Ptolemy talks of using the method of Pytheas for finding latitude and that of Hipparchus for finding longitude; but, as we know, the latter does not work in practice. He seems to have relied, directly or indirectly, on travellers' tales; but, as one of Ptolemy's own main sources, Marinus of Tyre, put it, 'merchants care little for exploration, and often through boasting exaggerate distance.' In modern terms the positions established for places were not fixes, but dead reckoning positions supported by a few latitude observations. Unfortunately, Ptolemy also adopted the Posidonius figure for the size of the earth, not that of Eratosthenes.

The world map which was to become so influential from the fifteenth century is shown in Fig. 1.9, but its provenance is now suspect. The earliest extant copy is of the twelfth century. Although Ptolemy's map is epochal, in that it gives the latitude and longitude of places, however incorrectly, its enclosure of the Indian ocean was ridiculous. As has already been noted, Plutarch, a few generations earlier, had been aware of the circumnavigability of Africa. The representation of the Mediterranean, on which Ptolemy had his best data, illustrates the consequences of being unable to measure the longitude. The general shape is remarkably

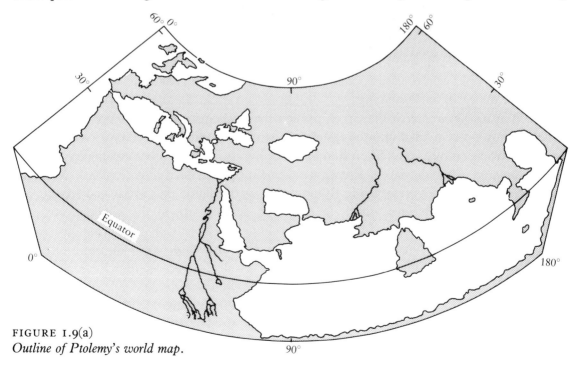

FIGURE 1.9(a)
Outline of Ptolemy's world map.

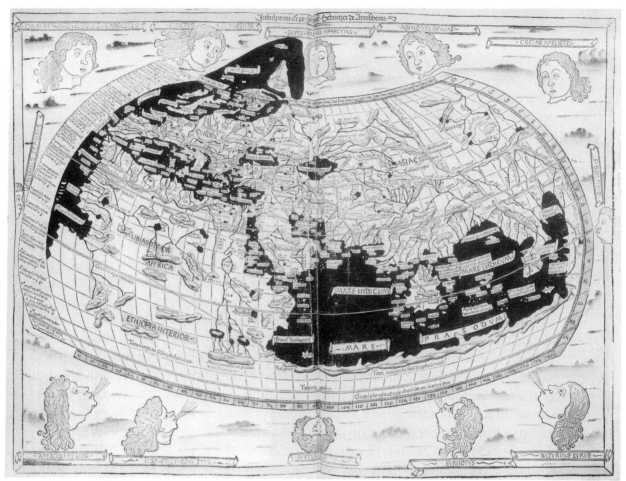

FIGURE 1.9(b)
A fifteenth century version of Ptolemy's map.

accurate; but it is elongated in agreement with the dictum of Marinus and its extension in longitude is 50 per cent too great, consistent with this elongation and the underestimation of the size of the earth by Posidonius.

The Romans never shared the Greek passion for mathematics and astronomy. When the Roman empire was divided into the eastern (Byzantine) empire, centred on Constantinople, and the western empire, centred on Rome, it was Byzantium which became the custodian of Greek thought. After the fall of Rome, western Europe declined into the Dark Ages; but some Greek knowledge, preserved in Byzantium, was translated into Syriac and Arabic, and diffused through the Islamic world. In the ninth century AD, in the Baghdad area, the methodology of Eratosthenes and Posidonius was improved by actually measuring the baseline with rods instead of relying on how far a camel-train or a ship moves during a day. The result, that the length of one degree of latitude is 56⅔ miles, is very accurate if, as is believed, the Arabic mile of the time was about 1950 metres. The figure became a fixture of Islamic science, was well known to Columbus, and was not materially improved for many centuries.

Gradually the ancient learning returned to Europe. Contact with the Moors in Sicily and Spain was one route; the Crusades and Venetian and Genoese trade with the Byzantine and

14

Ottoman worlds were others. Some works of writers as diverse as Euclid and Aristotle reached the Western world by translation into Latin not from the Greek, but from Arabic and Hebrew. Most of all, it was the result of what I have called the questing, questioning spirit of the age and—in Italy at least—the surplus wealth necessary to sustain art, science, and philosophy. From 1439 Cosimo de' Medici, probably the wealthiest private citizen in Europe at the time, had lured Greek scholars to Florence, financed the translation of all known works of Plato into Latin, and sent his agents scouring the world for manuscripts.[10] His personal library, open to all scholars, amounted to 10 000 works of Latin and Greek authors.

Much of the recovered learning was second- and third-hand. The story that Pytheas reached Thule comes to us from Strabo, who quotes a lost work of Posidonius which quoted a lost work of Pytheas. Our credulity is strained because Strabo says that Pytheas, who lived centuries before him, was a liar. In the fifteenth century, in a world where all literate men read Latin but few could read Greek, translations of the good, the bad, and the indifferent were received avidly, uncritically, and credulously. Greek conjectures were accepted as scientific theories, and Greek legends as facts. In all this conglomerate of gold and dross the map of Ptolemy made an important impact. The *Geographike Huphegesis* was translated into Latin in 1409. The world map was redrawn and printed in 1477.

The first mistake which Columbus made was to treat the established Arabic figure of 56⅔ miles to each degree of latitude as meaning Roman or Italian miles of about 1480 metres, reducing the size of the globe by a quarter and making the Arabs agree roughly with Posidonius (and thus with Ptolemy), if we take the *stadion* to be one-eighth of a Roman mile. This was not the mistake of a well-read man. By contrast, Compano da Novara, mathematician and physician to a thirteenth-century pope, tells his readers that the length of a degree of a meridian is 81 geometric (little sea) miles, 68 Italian miles, or 56⅔ Arabic miles, which is not grossly in error. On his wrong assumption Columbus calculated that, at the latitude he would cross the Atlantic westbound, the length of a degree of longitude would be 50 Roman miles. The ratio corresponds to the cosine of 28°, the latitude at which Columbus proposed to sail —so he could get things right sometimes. If Ptolemy is right and Eurasia extends 180° to the east, the western ocean is also 180° wide—170° if he starts from the Canaries. Even so, 8500 'miles' was an impractical voyage without fresh food or water. Ptolemy must be shown to have grossly underestimated the extension in longitude of Eurasia. In fact Ptolemy greatly overestimated it. Beijing is only 125° east of Lisbon.

Help was at hand. Among the books of Columbus which have been preserved is a Latin version of the travels of Marco Polo. Marco Polo does seem to describe lands to the east of those known to Ptolemy; but there is no thought of latitude and longitude in these travellers' tales. Marco Polo's usual unit of distance is the travelling day. The most important of the rare cases in which Marco Polo uses linear units of distance is the statement 'Cipangu [Japan] is an island far out to the eastward, some 1500 miles from the mainland.'[11] In fact the distance across the Korean Straits is scarcely 150 Roman miles. Someone had added a zero; but Columbus must have seized on the figure to reduce the distance he must sail westwards by 1500 of his miles. The voyage is still too long. The Asian mainland must be extended further east.

Paolo Toscanelli was one of the few scholars of the time to accept Marco Polo's picture of Asia. His views, supported by a map showing the Chinese city of Quinsay [Hangzhou] to be 9000 km west of Lisbon, with a convenient re-victualling point at the legendary island of Antilla, were known to King Afonso V of Portugal by 1474. The king was unimpressed; but Columbus eagerly corresponded with Toscanelli. Then there was Marinus of Tyre (already mentioned). His treatise is lost; and one of the most important references extant is that of Ptolemy himself. No matter: Columbus seems to have decided that the Asia of Marinus extended 45° further than that of Ptolemy, and that Marinus was right. Thus we have:

Extension of Eurasia according to Ptolemy	180°
add for Marinus	45°
add for Marco Polo	28°
add for easting Asia to Japan	30°
add for westing Europe to Canaries	10°
add for luck	7°
	300°
westing Canaries to Japan	60°
	360°

60 × 50 = 3000 Italian miles, say 4400 km.

In fact, from San Sebastian de la Gomera, where Columbus weighed anchor in the Canaries, Tokyo lies 157° to the east, not 60° to the west. The error is more than a third of the circle.

Another book in the possession of Columbus which was preserved is a well-used copy of Pierre d'Ailly's *Imago Mundi*, published in 1410, which may be useless as geography but gives a spurious respectability to this farrago because d'Ailly was a cardinal. He misquotes Aristotle (who in the Christian hagiography of the period was the pagan nearest to the right hand of God after Plato) as saying that the sea between Spain and India could be sailed in a few days. According to the *Apocrypha of Esdras* the earth is six parts land—which fits very nicely if the division is longitudinal. St Ambrose is quoted as having a high opinion of *Esdras*. All the best people, it seems, were on the side of Columbus. In fact there were others of his mind. The oldest globe extant is the Nuremberg globe of Martin Behaim, the German geographer, made coincidentally in 1492. It resembles the world which Columbus envisaged, with a tasteful arrangement of legendary islands in the western ocean. The coincidence has led to speculation that Behaim and Columbus had a common source—Toscanelli perhaps.

Columbus took his ideas to King John II of Portugal. He was politely received; but these ideas were second-hand goods, which the king's late father had already declined from Toscanelli. Moreover, any examination of Columbus must have established that Portugal had more erudite scholars and more skilful navigators than Columbus. Whatever the merit of his ideas, they certainly had no need of the man. Nor any need of his ideas, if we are to follow

Facsimile of Martin Behaim's globe, 1492.

Ian Cameron,[12] who quotes King John in 1484: 'The king of Portugal has information regarding the western lands more positive than the visions of the Genoese.' In 1486 he gave a charter to Fernão Dulmo for colonization of the islands and *mainland* to the west.

Columbus liked a passage from Seneca's *Medea*[13] 'There will come a time when . . . a new sailor . . . shall discover a new world, and Thule shall no longer be the last of lands.' Columbus may not have been the sailor the enchantress had in mind. The Vikings, Norsemen, and even Irish monks had explored the Atlantic. The *Navigatio Sancti Brendani*, written in the ninth century, may be interpreted by those so inclined as evidence that Irish monks ranged in their curraghs from Jan Mayen island in the north-east to Jamaica in the south-west. The debate whether the 'Vinland' of the Norsemen was Massachusetts will no doubt be perpetual. Wherever it was, two Nordic chroniclers record that the Irish were there before them. It has been hypothesized[14] that Bristol seafarers discovered some part of North America before 1492. An intriguing feature of the globe which Gemma Frisius and Mercator (see Chapter 3) produced in 1537 is a strait between Canada and Greenland bearing in Latin the words 'John Scolvus the Dane was here about 1476'. There are other references to this pre-Columban navigator in north-western waters. To the men of the north the Atlantic never was the vast ocean that it was to the southerners. From Norway to Canada, via the Faroes,

Iceland, and Greenland, one is never far from land, however inhospitable. Leif Ericsson reported a land-mass to the west of Greenland about AD 1000.

Finally, there was commerce between Scandinavia and Portugal, and not improbably co-operation and sharing of information. The pretensions of Columbus may well have raised a secret giggle among the confidants of King John. Sadly, the achievements of the northerners, however heroic, are not in the mainstream of those cultural developments which form the provenance of navigational science. Columbus *was* in the middle of it.

Later, the ideas of Columbus were rejected by Spain, on the advice of *savants*; but *their* quality is suggested by their use of St Augustine to confound Columbus. The notion that a great theologian is necessarily an arbiter of geography is medieval, and alien to the spirit of the Renaissance. Whether Isabella sensed the inadequacy of the wise men of Spain, had intelligence of secret Portuguese knowledge, or relied on feminine intuition, is irrelevant. She acceded to the request of Columbus and persuaded Ferdinand to do so. The long search of Columbus for Asia failed. Years later he complained to Ferdinand and Isabella, 'neither reason, nor mathematics, nor maps were of any use to me'. Reason and mathematics rarely help to prove that false is true.

Not unnaturally they called America after someone else. Amerigo Vespucci, like Leonardo da Vinci two years earlier, was born the son of a notary of Florence. When Ferdinand and Isabella unleashed Torquemada on his fellow Jews, Italian bankers took their place. The Medici sent Amerigo Vespucci to Spain. Later, he became a navigator of the highest distinction, in the service, at different times, of both Spain and Portugal. While Columbus, still cruising the Caribbean, was consoling himself for the absence of Asia with the discovery of the Garden of Eden, Vespucci was exploring the east coast of South America about as far south as the estuary of the river Plate (35° S), and even some way down the Patagonian coast, if his own claims are to be believed. He thus proved in 1502 that this was a massive new continent, not an adjunct of Asia. The new continent was called *Terra America* in his honour by Waldseemüller in 1507; and the name stuck. The extension of the term many years later to North America was unreasonable. When John Cabot planted the English flag of Henry VII on what is now Canadian soil in 1497, Amerigo Vespucci was still the manager of the Seville branch of the Medici bank.

There have been so many epic voyages of exploration, some half-forgotten, and many doubtless entirely forgotten, that one hesitates to call any of them the greatest; but if any deserve that epithet it must be the last voyage of Magellan. Ferdinand Magellan was born into the lesser Portuguese nobility in 1480, and at an early age entered the service of his king, Manuel I, the successor to John II. In 1505 he sailed with the Portuguese fleet for India, and remained in the east until 1512. During this period the Portuguese broke the Arab domination of the Indian Ocean and gained control of the Malacca Straits. Magellan participated in these events, and may have been on the first Portuguese expedition to the Spice Islands themselves (125° E) in 1511.

Back in Lisbon, Magellan twice sought advancement from his king; and twice he was spurned. Magellan took his dudgeon to Spain, then ruled by Charles I,[15] to whom Magellan proposed a circumnavigation of South America to reach the Spice Islands by sailing west that was reminiscent of the original proposal of Columbus to Ferdinand and Isabella thirty years earlier. The king accepted, and provided five vessels for the expedition. After probing the Plate and other estuaries down the east coast of South America (the simple test to distinguish a river estuary from a through passage is to taste the salinity of the water) Magellan entered the strait which now bears his name on 22 October 1520. On 28 November they entered the ocean they called the *Pacific*. On 6 March 1521 he landed at Guam, after 99 days at sea without fresh food or water. Magellan was killed in a pointless affray with natives in the Philippines. As those islands are to the west of the Moluccas, the claim made on behalf of Magellan that he was the first man to circumnavigate the globe relies on the questioned fact that he was on the expedition to the Moluccas ten years earlier.

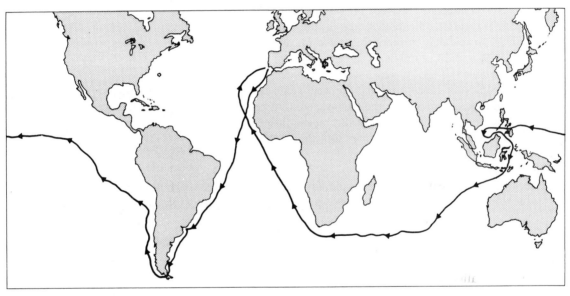

FIGURE I.10
Voyage of the Victoria *1519–22.*

Only one of the original fleet of five vessels returned to Spain. Sailing west, the *Victoria* thus became the first vessel to circumnavigate the globe (Fig. 1.10). It arrived under the command of Sebastian de Elcano, originally master (navigator) of a different vessel in the fleet, who had mutinied against Magellan early in the voyage. So it was Elcano whose arms were augmented with a globe inscribed 'Primus circumdedisti me' (you were the first to encircle me).

Only thirty years after Columbus had sailed west, his head full of the muddled notions of the ages, men knew, in broad outline at least, what were the Parts of the Earth. Men had sailed incomparably vaster distances over open sea than ever before. Geography was transformed, and the old ways of navigation were not good enough. There was a profound implication. The wisdom of the sages of ancient Greece had been unquestioned; but their geography was now seen to be wrong. Real science could only begin when the ancient wisdom was dethroned, and men extended their exploration to the world of ideas; that process is the subject of Chapter 4.

Notes to Chapter 1

1. In *A regiment of the sea*. Taylor (1960) described this book as 'the first really English seamen's manual'. A man of many parts, Bourne was also a port-reeve and an innkeeper.
2. The use of the metric system may seem a metachronism, but there have been so many miles, ranging from the 'geometric' or 'little sea mile' of about 1250 metres used in the thirteenth century *Compasso da navegare*, through the Italian or Roman mile of about 1480 m used by Columbus, the English statute mile of 1609.344 m, the modern international nautical mile of 1852 m, to the medieval Arabic mile of more than 1900 m, that the term *mile* in this context would confuse us as much as it did Columbus.
3. Cameron (1965).
4. The Phoenicians' cousins of Carthage went some distance around Africa in the opposite direction. Carthaginian settlements on the Atlantic coast of present-day Morocco are thought to date from the same period. It has been said that in the fifth century BC the Carthaginian admiral Hanno settled points along the coast down into the Gulf of Guinea.
5. In John Dryden's translation.
6. Sun Guang-Qi (1989).
7. According to Herodotus, Scylax explored as far as the Indus in about 515 BC; but the *periplus*, which describes Mediterranean coasts, is thought to be a later work. The oldest surviving codex is estimated to be twelfth century.
8. The first proposition of *The measurement of the circle*.
9. The terms *celestial latitude* and *celestial longitude* are reserved for a system of coordinates in which the ecliptic replaces the equator.
10. The dominance of the Medici bank was due in part to the bankruptcy in an earlier generation of leading Tuscan bankers who had loaned Edward III of England and other sovereigns more than their kingdoms were worth with an incontinence reminiscent of leading British and American bankers lending to Third World sovereign borrowers in the 1970s.
11. In Ronald Latham's translation.
12. Cameron (1965).
13. Castlereagh (1971).
14. Francis Bacon, writing in 1622, accused Columbus of suppressing information on the earlier discovery of America, being 'desirous rather to make his Enterprise the Child of his Science and Fortune rather than the follower of a former discouerie'.
15. Charles I of Spain, that is; he is better known as the emperor Charles V (imperial coronation 1520).

CHAPTER TWO

Numerate Navigators Without Science

✠

IF one knows the direction followed on each tack and the distance run along it, one can estimate one's position relative to the departure point. If one knows the bearing and distance of the destination from the departure point, it is easy, as Fig. 2.1 shows, to determine the direction to take and the distance to go. This process has been called *Dead Reckoning* (DR) in English[1] at least since 1580.

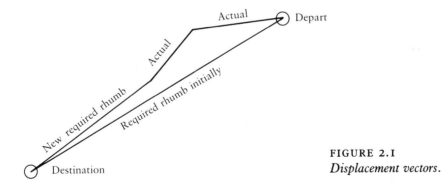

FIGURE 2.1
Displacement vectors.

There are three conditions precedent to DR: first, the means of knowing the direction sailed and the distance run on each tack; secondly, charts and/or pilot books correctly showing the relative orientation of places; and thirdly, navigators sufficiently literate and numerate to read numbers and the names of places, to use scales and dividers, to measure direction,and to multiply, add, and subtract. These conditions began to emerge in the Mediterranean in the twelfth century, but one cannot be too precise. Before the fifteenth century our sources are scholarly travellers who sought to describe marine practices which they may have misunderstood, rather than the navigators themselves.

It is unsurprising that the Mediterranean should be the place. Out of sight of land, without the sciences of hydrography and tidal prediction, no navigator can estimate the movement of the sea relative to his land-based DR system. Off the Atlantic coasts of Europe the ebb and flow of the tidal stream often exceeded the speed of a medieval ship through the water, and DR was of little use.[2] In the Mediterranean, currents are light in most places. As Homer knew, the great exception is the strait between Scylla and Charybdis—the Straits of Messina. DR is seen to work in the Mediterranean. The sea has always been much trafficked; its many hilly islands and, in season, excellent visibility, enabled an accurate picture of the relative position of places to be drawn over the centuries. The Mediterranean is extended in longitude rather than latitude. The curvature of the earth could be (and was) ignored. One managed without the concept of latitude and longitude. Finally, it was in the Mediterranean that the Christian world had contact with more numerate civilizations.

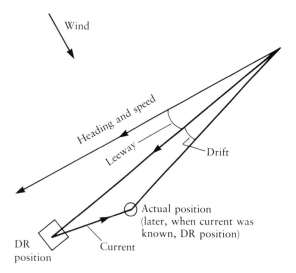

FIGURE 2.2
Leeway and drift.

Log lines and other devices for measuring speed or distance run through the water are not known to have been used until the sixteenth century, and were little used even then.[3] Speed and leeway (Fig. 2.2) were estimated visually, presumably with the surprising accuracy some yachtsmen demonstrate today. If the sea is not too rough and the helm is steady, one sees leeway as the angle between the wake and the reciprocal of the heading. For thousands of years men had steered in open seas by the sun and the stars when the sky was not overcast. The great development of the twelfth century as far as the first precedent condition is concerned was the introduction of the magnetic compass, which provided more accurate orientation and performed when the sky was overcast.

The attractive properties of lodestone were known in ancient times to the Greeks, the Chinese, and presumably other civilizations wherever this iron oxide (Fe_3O_4) occurs naturally; but the realization that a freely pivoted or floated iron needle after being stroked with

Chinese mariner's south-pointing compass graduated to 24 points.

lodestone always points in the same direction came, as far as is known, much later.[4] Attribution of the magnetic compass to the Chinese in antiquity is now questioned. However, the English word *lodestone* refers to its directional properties; the *lode* in old English is the *way*, and Chaucer called the navigator the lodesman. The first known specific reference in Chinese to the use of the south-pointing needle at sea is around AD 1100. There is a strong tradition in Italy that the magnetic compass was also invented in Amalfi in the early twelfth century. Unequivocal Arabic references[5] to the magnetic compass on a ship are somewhat later. Magnetic courses to steer first appear in both Chinese and Italian pilot books in the thirteenth century. The fact that the Chinese thought of their compasses as south-seeking and the Italian mariners thought of theirs as north-seeking suggests independent invention. In the late twelfth century an English monk, Alexander Neckham, described an item of equipment of a ship trading the English channel which is certainly a magnetic compass, although Latinists still argue whether the words mean that the needle floated on water or was pivoted.[6] The earliest extant unequivocal description of a pivoted needle compass is a document of 1269 (the *Epistola* of Peregrinus mentioned below).

In the earliest compasses an iron needle which had been stroked with lodestone to magnetize it was floated on a bowl of water by piercing it through a straw or a sliver of wood. Later, the needle was pivoted. When a compass card was fixed to the bowl, rough directions could be read by turning the bowl until the direction of the needle coincided with that of north on the card. In another early type, a piece of lodestone of undefined magnetic axis was fixed in a box on the lid of which was a pointer. The compass was calibrated on land by floating the box in a bowl of water over which a thread was drawn in the direction of north. The pointer on the lid was then so adjusted that it lay parallel with the thread. Thus, if the local direction of north was determined astronomically, magnetic variation at the place of calibration was compensated—which was perhaps not a good idea as charts and pilot books based on magnetic north became general.

There is a reference in 1380 to the floating card compass, in which the compass card itself is pivoted, with the magnetized needle fixed to it in the direction of north. In the era of Columbus some compass-makers offset the magnetic needle from the card direction of north by the amount of magnetic variation, so that it read true north at the place of manufacture, compounding the problems of navigation during the age of exploration. At least on his second voyage Columbus had both types of compass. This type almost died out, but not quite. One type of aircraft compass during the 1914–18 war was offset by the amount of magnetic variation on the western front.

Ship's heading

Lubber line

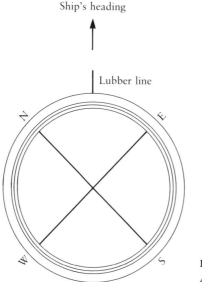

FIGURE 2.3
A fixed ship's compass.

At the next stage of the floating card compass, a marker or lubber line was fixed to the bowl and the bowl fixed to the ship so that the lubber line was in the direction of the ship's heading, which could then be read off the compass card (Fig. 2.3). As helmsmen could rarely read, the points of the compass were indicated by a system of diamonds and lozenges of various colours and lengths. North was marked with an elaborate fleur-de-lis. Sometimes east was marked by a devout cross.

Before the compass, direction was described by the name of the wind blowing from that direction. When neither landmarks nor the sky were visible, the wind was the only means of orientation. From the fourth century BC the Greeks used a twelve-wind system which continued into the Middle Ages side by side with an eight-wind system. As the compass improved and passed from being a device of last recourse to a standard steering instrument, the eight winds became based on magnetic north (north, north-east, east, etc.). The eight points of a quadrantal system became 16 points, then 32 points. Each point of a 32-point system was known as a *quarter* (a quarter, that is to say, of the basic quadrantal system). The nomenclature *north, north by east*, etc., as adopted by Spanish and Portuguese navigators, is illustrated in Fig. 2.4(a); but in Italy combinations of the old names of the eight quadrantal winds illustrated in Fig. 2.4(b) were adapted to create a 32-point compass rose.[7] In the age of exploration, Spanish and Portuguese compass cards had evolved to resemble the cards of some early twentieth-century English compasses.

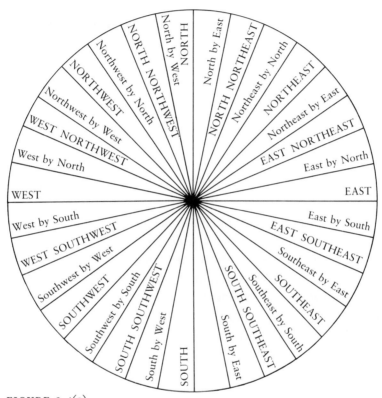

FIGURE 2.4(a)
Eight-point system divided into halves and quarters.

Eventually the 32 points became 64, a system which continued well into the twentieth century. It is now 4000 years since Babylonian mathematicians divided the circle into 360°, the system still in almost universal use despite sporadic attempts at decimalization (see Chapters 3 and 5) and the one used in astronomical navigation from the beginning. It is astounding how long the old binary system of compass direction endured and how deep-rooted it is. In modern Italian a northerly wind is still *tramontana* (from the mountain) whether there happen to be mountains to the north or not; the English words used well into the twentieth century are almost a literal translation of the orders Columbus gave in Spanish to the helmsman in 1492; and in French the compass rose is still *la rose des vents*. The move to the 360° compass was led by the aeroplane; but even during the Second World War, RAF compasses had the eight points of the thirteenth-century compass superimposed on the 360° grid.

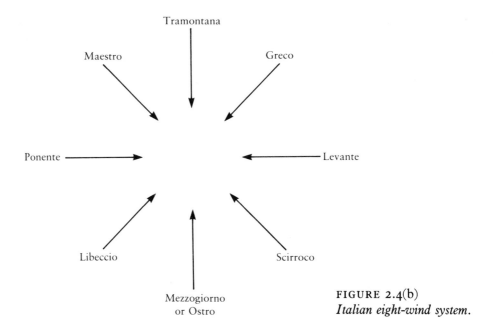

FIGURE 2.4(b)
Italian eight-wind system.

In the earlier centuries seamen were content to believe that *stella maris*, the pole star, was fixed in the heavens, and that the magnetic needle pointed to it, a view shared by some scholars. Jacques de Vitry, a bishop, wrote in 1218 'an iron needle touched by the lodestone always turns to the North Star, which stands motionless while the rest of the heavens revolves around it'. Even at that date a man of scientific temper could have demonstrated that both assertions were wrong; but the scientific temper did not exist, at least in Christendom. Petrus Peregrinus (Pelerin de Maricourt), who wrote his *Epistola de magnete* in 1269, was quite clear that the pole star revolved diurnally in a small circle around the true celestial pole; but he thought that the compass needle pointed to the true pole. So apparently did Roger Bacon, who wrote 'it is not the star but the part of the heavens which is effective.' These misconceptions are barely relevant. At that date navigators and scholars, with few exceptions, inhabited separate universes so remote that the compass illustrated in the *Epistola de magnete* is graduated in degrees, six centuries before this was standard practice with marine compasses.

Long before 1492 some scholars were aware of magnetic variation, the angle between true and magnetic north, now conventionally described in degrees east or west of true north. Magnetic variation began appearing on charts in about 1504. It is clear from the Journal of his first voyage that Columbus had not troubled to consider such matters before sailing west. In 1492 the distance of the pole star from the true celestial pole was about 3½°, so that at the latitudes he sailed its azimuth swung about 8° backwards and forwards diurnally. Columbus first noted it in his log[8] at the end of the first week (13 September 1492): 'At the beginning of the night the needles turned north-west, and in the morning they declined north-east somewhat.' Four days later he has second thoughts: 'The needles declined north-west a full point. In the morning the needles were true. The star appears to change its position, not the needles.' By 30 September he has quite made up his mind: 'Moreover, at nightfall the needles decline a point and at daybreak they are right on the star, from which it appears that the star moved as the other stars, and that the needles always point truly.'

As usual, the physical world was more complicated than Columbus thought; but he eventually came to realize that the needles do not 'always point truly'. His light-hearted approach to magnetic variation and the rotation of the pole star in the heavens before undertaking his voyage seems unprofessional. He relied almost entirely on his DR, which is greatly admired by some Columban specialists.[9]

Italian mariner's compass c. 1650.

As one sails westwards across the North Atlantic today there is a large increase in westerly magnetic variation. There is a story that this phenomenon terrified the crew of Columbus. Well it might! Given that the compass should point to the star of the Virgin Mary herself, it was clearly being pulled from its duty by some monstrous black hole ahead. The beginnings of the idea that longitude might be found by measuring magnetic variation (Chapter 6) have been traced to these observations; but it now seems likely that, on the route followed by Columbus on his first voyage from the Canaries to landfall in the Bahamas, magnetic variation changed little in 1492. The instrument of last resort had become, in the Atlantic, essential. Every captain jealously guarded his lodestones and his needles. We are told that Magellan carried 35 spare needles—a long way from the days of Alexander Neckham.

As far as the other two conditions precedent to DR are concerned, one can discern in the thirteenth century a coming together of various strands with the motivation to develop DR which the compass provided. The beginnings of the mathematization of navigation seem to have been an Italian initiative. This is not to say that parallel development of DR did not also take place in the age of the magnetic compass independently among the Chinese, the Arabs, the Vikings, and perhaps others; but those developments were not, as it will transpire, in the mainstream of navigational science.

One strand was the consolidation of local charts into relatively accurate charts covering a

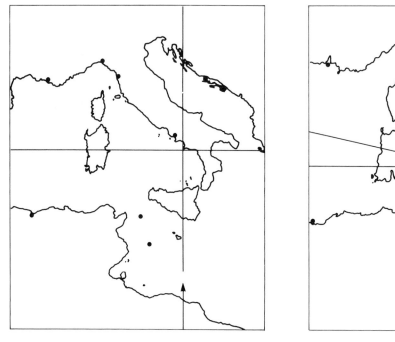
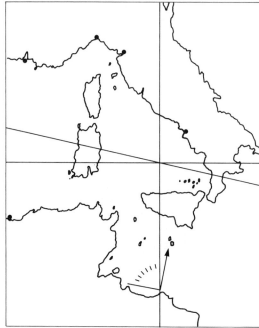

Central Mediterranean   Carta Pisana slewed

FIGURE 2.5
The Central Mediterranean as shown in the Carta Pisana *slewed.*

large area. The oldest surviving marine chart, the *Carta Pisana*, drawn on a sheepskin, is dated about 1275 (see the illustration on the opposite page). It extends from southern England to the Black Sea. As it is an Italian chart, the English Coast is unsurprisingly inaccurate; but the Mediterranean is very well represented. Figure 2.5 shows that the central and Mediterranean area, naturally the most accurately portrayed, looks right when it is slewed anticlockwise 10°–15°—an adjustment which may approximate to the magnetic variation in the area at that date.[10] There is no complete history of magnetic variation; but it has changed a great deal.[11] The conclusion that the *Carta Pisana* was based on surveys by magnetic compass and intended for use with a magnetic compass is inviting. From 16 points equally spaced on the circumference of each of two circles, straight lines called *rhumbs*[12] radiate, eight to the quadrant, all over the chart (Fig. 2.6). To find the required course the navigator lays his ruler on the chart in the required direction and adopts whichever rhumb lies parallel to it.[13] There is no suggestion of latitude or longitude; but scales are provided both horizontally and vertically, perhaps to allow for shrinkage. The construction of the chart required some geometrical skill. The cartographer must have known how to construct a right angle and to bisect any angle. Indeed, the great advantage of the binary system of dividing the circle as opposed to twelve-wind or 360° systems is the ease with which a binary system can be constructed with straight edge and dividers.

The pilot books complemented the charts. There is a Latin translation dated January

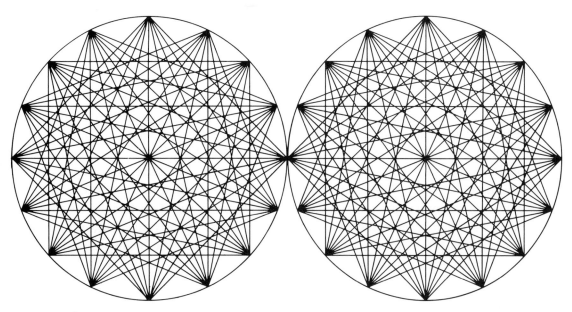

FIGURE 2.6
Delineation of rhumbs on the Carta Pisana.

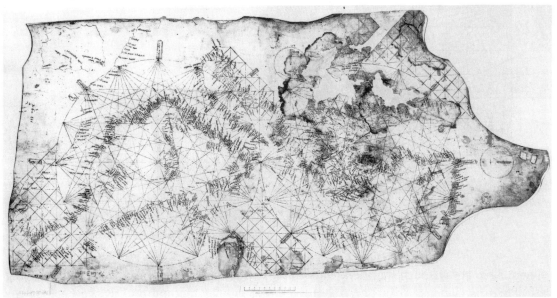

The Carta Pisana c. 1275. The oldest surviving European marine chart.

1296 in the copyist's hand of the *Compasso da navegare*, probably written half a century earlier in an Italian vernacular[14]. It is roughly contemporaneous with the earliest Chinese pilot books giving compass courses. The *Compasso* covers the whole of the Mediterranean clockwise from Spain, ending in Morocco. It gives rhumbs and distances from port to port, hazards to navigation, leading marks and landmarks, and depths of shallow waters, much as a modern yachtsman's pilot book does. That it was compiled from many sources is clear from the use of local names for wind directions. The quality of the data on which the *Carta Pisana* and the *Compasso* are based implies that some medieval navigators of the Mediterranean were numerate, skilful, and systematic.

Dead reckoning would be a simple matter if one merely read the required rhumb from the chart or pilot book and steered it as one does in a motor boat. Sailing ships must tack with the wind; the wind changes; and ships of those days could not sail within 90° of it. The obvious way to conduct the DR is on the chart itself; but the chart was too precious to be worn out. If one cannot draw on the chart, one may draw on something else. The 'circle and square' diagram illustrated in Fig. 2.7, which follows a manuscript of 1436, can be used with a pair of dividers to resolve distance run on any quarter into a pair of rectangular coordinates, which could be either a 'northing' and an 'easting', or an 'along-track' (advance) and an 'across-track' (departure). An alternative to the graph is the traverse board—a pegboard on which the distance run on each rhumb is pegged out.

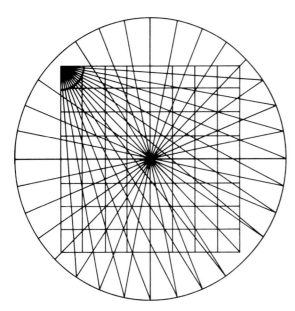

FIGURE 2.7
A fifteenth-century solution of the plane triangle.

There have always been mariners who prefer extracting numbers from tables to drawing lines. There is evidence that Traverse Tables, the tabular method of DR, go back to the thirteenth century; but the oldest extant tables, the *Toleta di Marteloio*, are in a Venetian manuscript of 1428. The table is entered with A, the number of quarter-winds by which the rhumb actually sailed differs from the required track to destination, in order to extract the advance along track and the departure from it for every 100 miles sailed. At point X in Fig. 2.8 the wind has changed, and it is practical to close on the desired track at an angle B. The second part of the table is entered with B (in quarter-winds) in order to extract the distance to run to closure and the advance during closure for every 10 miles of departure. In

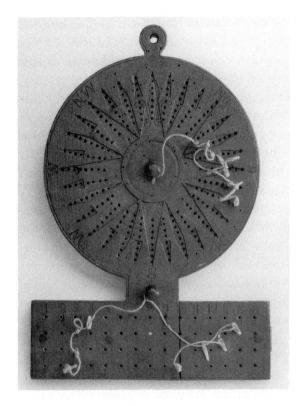

Traverse board c. 1800, German or Scandinavian.

effect, 100 cos A, 100 sin A, 10 cosec B and 10 cot B are tabulated. The values tabulated can be found with a pair of dividers from a careful construction of Fig. 2.7 which, thanks to the binary system of direction, can itself be constructed using only straight edge and dividers.

The timing of these developments relates to a revival of numeracy in Europe from the twelfth century. The introduction of what we now erroneously call arabic numerals was the key event. Arithmetic, particularly multiplication and division, is tedious by any of the ancient numerical systems. The key to our own perfected positional decimal system is the use and correct placement of a symbol for zero.[15] The invention of this symbol is attributed to the Hindus not earlier than about AD 500, which seems surprisingly late. For the abacus goes back at least to the days of Herodotus, and the abacus operator who has occasion to record his result, say 4 pebbles, zero pebbles, 7 pebbles, is almost obliged to write something like 407, 4–7, or whatever, but certainly not 47.

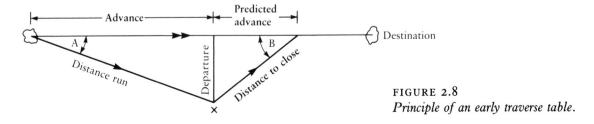

FIGURE 2.8
Principle of an early traverse table.

The positional notation was adopted by the Arabs,[16] learned from them by Leonardo of Pisa (Leonardo Fibonacci) in Algeria, and published to Christendom in his *Liber abaci* in 1202. It was adopted by people having a practical use for arithmetic, although Roman numerals survived in accountancy[17] in some parts of Europe until the eighteenth century, and in the volume numbers of the *Journal of Navigation* until 1962. The graphs and tables described above used the new system; but the claim that navigators were the first to apply mathematics to ordinary mundane occupations goes too far. Leonardo's geometric work was applicable to surveying rather than navigation. The mathematicization of navigation in Italy was contemporaneous with the Italian invention of double-entry bookkeeping. It was all part of a major cultural change precedent to the Renaissance.

From the fourteenth century on, the Portuguese had kept abreast of Mediterranean developments by engaging skilled Italian navigators; but their problem was different. In the nature of exploration, a coordinate system based on the known rhumb to destination is inapplicable. Northing (or southing) and easting (or westing) replaced distance run along track and across it. Northing became change of latitude at 17½ Portuguese leagues to the degree, and easting/westing became *departure*—from the meridian, that is, the sense in which the word is used in modern English. Departure was not yet related to change in longitude. Traverse tables such as the first part of the *Toleta di Marteloio*, traverse boards, and graphical alternatives were easily adapted. Traverse tables remained little changed in the early twentieth century, except that they could be entered with rhumbs in degrees.

The errors of DR are cumulative, and distances in the Portuguese explorations vastly exceeded those run between landmarks in the Mediterranean. There was also a need to identify the position of places discovered, especially those which were colonized. Two coordinates are required to express the position of islands; but only one ordinate is necessary along the African coast, because the coastline itself provided the other. Fortunately, the coast of Africa runs roughly north–south except in the Gulf of Guinea. It was time to re-discover the means of finding the latitude which Pytheas had used eighteen centuries earlier.

Prince Henry the Navigator, who probably never navigated a ship in his life, was the third son of King John I of Portugal and his English Queen, Philippa of Lancaster. Henry's great contribution to navigation was to found at Sagres a centre where Arabic mathematics and astronomy, learned mainly from Jewish fellow-travellers, could be applied to Portuguese navigation and cartography. It was a modest acquisition. The Muslims had become the custodians of as much Greek astronomy and mathematics as they understood. They added a more accurate figure of the earth, the system of enumeration they had learned from the Hindus, and some elementary trigonometry (Chapter 3). The astronomy and mathematics required to find the latitude is primitive. What a hocus pocus was made of it!

The pole star is the easiest. Figure 2.9 shows that the altitude of the true celestial pole, if it is indefinitely far away, equals the latitude. In 1492 the pole star was 3½° away from the pole; but, as Fig. 2.10 shows, it is a simple matter to devise rules to correct the observed altitude by the general orientation of the constellations in the heavens.[18]

Latitude from the altitude of the sun at local noon is more difficult. The first requirement

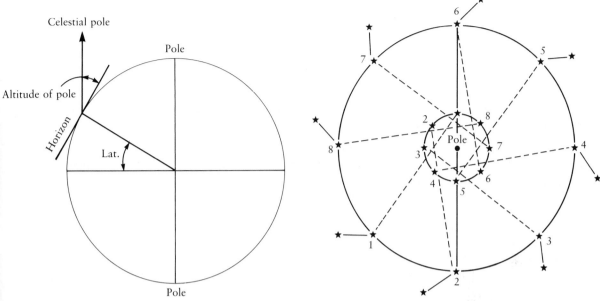

FIGURE 2.9
Latitude equals altitude of celestial pole.

FIGURE 2.10
The rotation of the Pole Star and the Guards about the celestial pole.

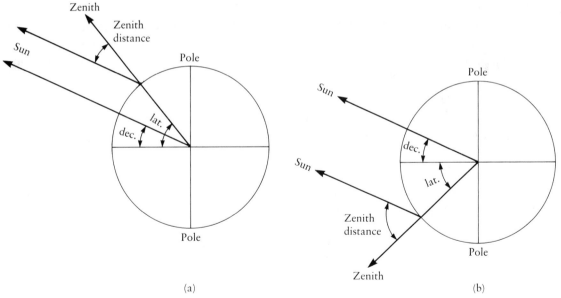

(a)

(b)

FIGURE 2.11
Latitude by noon sight. (a) Summer in northern hemisphere: (b) winter in Southern hemisphere.

is an almanac giving the declination of the sun, which varies from 23½°S to 23½°N over the year. The second requirement is to observe the sun at local noon, that is to say when the altitude is highest, since the local time is unknown. As Fig. 2.11 shows, the sun's distance in arc from the observer's zenith (zenith distance) is the difference between the latitude and declination if the observer and the sun are in the same hemisphere (summer); and the sum of the latitude and declination if they are in different hemispheres (winter). For seamen who were scarcely numerate the different rules were made more formidable by the hexagesimal system of expressing angle and the adoption of altitude instead of zenith distance, which, for much of the history of astronomical navigation, would have been more convenient. Perhaps altitude was adopted because the pole star came first. To the Portuguese mind in the late fifteenth century, *altura* was both the altitude of the pole and the latitude.

Having found the altitude of the sun at noon there are only the three cases below; but somehow the Portuguese made six rules of them.

Case 1. Summer, sun towards the equator:
Lat. = Dec. + 90° − alt.

Case 2. Summer, sun towards the pole:
Lat. = Dec. + alt. − 90°.

Case 3. Winter:
Lat. = 90° − alt. − dec.

These rules would be unwillingly learned by rote by seamen who would not be expected to understand them. Obviously the pole star was easiest until one sailed too far south to see it. There is no star close to the south celestial pole, and in the southern hemisphere navigators use the sun perforce.[19] A reason for preferring the sun, despite its complex regimen, throughout most of the history of astronomical navigation, is the motion of the ship. There are only two references against which the altitude of a body can be measured. One is a gravity sensor such as a pendulum; the other is the sea horizon. On land gravity is best; but at sea the sensor is grossly deflected by pitch and roll. Unfortunately the sea horizon and the pole star were not usually visible at the same time.

There is a copy of the *Regimento do astrolabio e do quadrante* printed in Lisbon about 1510; but the essence of the work is believed to have been established thirty years earlier. First there is 'the rule of the north' for correcting the observed altitude of the pole star. The rule is a human male figure with outstretched arms. Lines are drawn midway between his arms and his head and between his arms and his feet. Imagining the pole star to be at the navel, the position of the guards of the pole star (α and β Ursa Minor) with respect to the figure gives the correction to apply. The error of the correction would commonly be ½°. The figure was also used to tell the (local) time. The midnight position of the guards for each fortnight of the year was memorized (Taylor 1956).

The second part of the *Regimento* is a variant on a Traverse Table. It starts 'know that the degree of north–south is 17½ leagues, and sixty minutes make a degree'. How much easier if one minute had made a nautical mile; but this simplification did not occur to anyone at the time. The nautical mile seems to have evolved not from a desire for the simplest of units, but from a coincidence. William Bourne, writing in 1571, warned against using foreign charts because of the difference in length of leagues. The degree of latitude, he asserted, is 20 of our English leagues, 60 of our English miles. To Bourne, it appears, a nautical mile just happened to be an English mile. He was 17 per cent in error. Bourne, incidentally, thought that the pursuit of the longitude was a waste of time. For each degree of change of latitude the *Regimento* gives the departure (17½ tan rhumb) and distance run (17½ sec rhumb) on each of seven quarters. The author found it necessary to add that on the eighth quarter, east, the latitude (*altura*) is unchanged. The seamen were left to work out for themselves that when sailing, say, SW, the twentieth quarter, they were sailing the fourth quarter in reverse, and to apply the table accordingly. The third part is a table of declination of the sun. Recent sources available at the time included the *Liber directionum* of Regiomontanus and the *Almanach perpetuum* of Zacuto.

The first altitude-measuring instrument extensively used by seamen was the quadrant, re-introduced to Europe by Leonardo of Pisa in the thirteenth century. The quadrant of the sixteenth-century seaman bore a sighting device (two pinholes) along one edge, and the arc was graduated 0–90. From the centre of the arc a plumb line was suspended and read against the arc (Fig. 2.12). The observer sighted the pole star or the sun through the pinholes while his assistant read the alignment of the plumb line. Some quadrants were marked with the *altura* of harbours in Portugal and West Africa instead of degrees; but such instruments of course could only be used with the pole star. Its first recorded use at sea is by Diego Gomes in 1461.

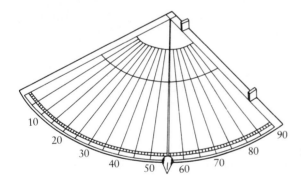

FIGURE 2.12
The mariner's quadrant.

Some forms of the astrolabe go back to ancient Greece. In the fifteenth century the astronomer's astrolabe was an elaborate instrument, involving mathematics, including stereographic projection, far in advance of that applied to navigation. The mariner's astrolabe, dating from about 1480, was a much simpler device, scarcely meriting the name. It consisted of a heavy disc or ring suspended from a thumb ring. The outer circumference of the disc was graduated in degrees, and the sighting device was a concentric alidade with pointers to read against the scale.

Thus both the quadrant and the astrolabe relied on apparent gravity to define the vertical, and so were deflected by the motion of the ship. They were of little use in any other than

Medieval Arabic astrolabe.

calm seas. There are surviving narratives recording landing parties going ashore to take the *altura*, and a poetic reference to Vasco da Gama hanging his astrolabe from a tree to find the *altura*. This is surveying rather than navigation. As a practical matter it worked while exploring the coast of Africa; but the astrolabe and the quadrant can have been of little use on transatlantic work. Columbus carried both. By the evidence of his *Journal* he did not understand how to interpret his readings, and his results with these instruments were greatly in error. Columbus was a DR man. His quadrant and astrolabe perhaps gave magic to his authority.

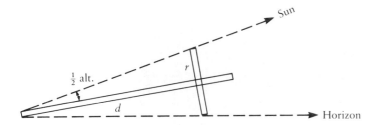

FIGURE 2.13
The cross-staff. The altitude
(= 2 tan^{-1}r/d) is read on a scale on the
rod d at the transom r.

The deflection of the apparent vertical by the ship's motion can be avoided by using an instrument which measures the angle of elevation of the body above the horizon, as the marine sextant has done since the eighteenth century. The cross-staff (Fig. 2.13) was known in Europe in the fourteenth century, but does not seem to have been used in navigation before the sixteenth century. It was perhaps inspired by the *Kamal* used by Arab navigators much earlier, and known to the Portuguese as the *Balestilha of the Moors*. Just as the Portuguese engraved the *altura* of places on their quadrants, the *Kamal* had a cord with knots corresponding to ports which the navigator took in his teeth while observing the sight. Tim Severin wrote in 1987 that a *Kamal* which he made gave him latitude at sea within 15′. The many defects of both instruments included ocular parallax, the difficulty in looking at both arms of the cross-staff at the same time, and the discomfort of squinting at the sun.

These disadvantages were largely overcome by the invention by John Davis of the backstaff[20] in 1595. The reason for the tardiness in the adoption of instruments using the horizon as reference may be that, as the horizon and the pole star are not usually visible at the same time, one is confined to the sun, with its more complex regimen. Two versions of the backstaff were described by Davis in his *Seamens' secrets*; and there were many subsequent variations. The essential principle of the backstaff, which was only superseded in the eighteenth century by the reflecting instruments described in Chapter 6, is that the observer stands with his back to the sun holding the instrument vertically. He views the horizon through a slit and slides a cross-member until the edge of its shadow coincides with the slit.

Navigation of the kind described in this chapter was beyond the ability of many seamen. On important voyages astrologers/astronomers of ambiguous function were carried. Petrus Nonius,[21] the great Portuguese Astronomer Royal, wrote in 1537 'These pilots! They do not know the Sun, Moon, or Stars, neither their courses, movements, nor declinations.' One would like to have asked the learned doctor what contribution he thought the science and

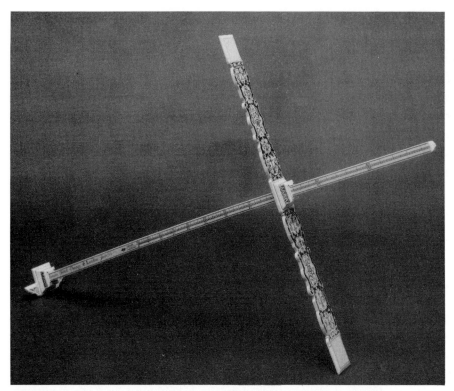

Ivory cross-staff c. 1700.

Ivory back-staff c. 1700. The diagonal scale is to 1'.

mathematics which he ornamented had contributed to navigation at that juncture. The only mathematics required are simple arithmetic, the concepts of angle, time, and distance, and a faith that similar triangles really are similar. Such mathematics had existed in Babylon 4000 years earlier. Science had not provided an instrument to measure the altitude of the pole star with usable accuracy in any other than a calm sea. The astronomy required to find the latitude is primitive. After all, the sum of the altitudes of any circumpolar star at upper and lower transits (which equals twice the latitude) can be used as a north–south ordinate of position[22] without even knowing the name of the star, still less its declination, or caring whether the earth is round or flat.

Notes to Chapter 2

1. By William Borough, Chief Pilot of the Muscovy Company (see Taylor 1950). The belief that the term was originally *Deduced reckoning* lacks evidence.
2. Early navigation off the north-west coasts of Europe relied heavily on soundings. Taylor and Richey (1962) tell of rutters which advised rounding the Breton coast not by visible landmarks but, in effect, by sounding the way along the edge of the continental shelf.
3. Magellan seems to have used a type of log in the early sixteenth century; but the first full description of streaming the log, and the method of timing by log glasses, is given in William Bourne's *A regiment for the sea* of 1574. Writing in 1599 Edward Wright called the DR position 'the point of imagination' because, although the compass defined the rhumb, the distance run was according to the mariner's imagination. Early seventeenth-century English logs were knotted at 42 feet intervals and used with a 30-second glass, implying a nautical mile of 5040 English feet. After many variations knots spaced at 47¼ feet were used with a 28-second glass, corresponding to a nautical mile of 6075 feet, very close to the actual average length of 1′ of latitude. In 1667 Louis XIV of France gave a German a fortune of 60 000 *livres* for a description of a sort of water-mill odometer of a type which was first proposed in Bourne's *Inventions and devices* (see Chapter 5). In 1865 Thomas Walker perfected the towing log (a rotor on a line with a register attached) which, according to Francis Hughes, in an Address to the Honourable Company of Master Mariners, was virtually unchanged in 1937. In recent decades Doppler logs have become common place (Chapter 12).
4. Knowledge of the directional properties of lodestone has been speciously attributed to the Sumerians and the Chinese in the third millenium BC, the Mexicans in the second millenium BC, and the Greeks of Homeric times. Some of these claims might even be true. For further references see May (1981).
5. One would expect a Chinese invention of a marine compass to be learned by the Arabs who traded with them. Some writers have suggested that it was the other way around, and it has also been pointed out that the early Arabic word for compass may imply a derivation from Italian.
6. May (1955).
7. As noted later in the chapter the *Compasso da navegare* shows that there were many local variations in the Italian names of winds in the thirteenth century; but in the sixteenth century there was a recognized Italian rose.
8. Vigneras (1960).

9. Notably Morison (1942). There is some doubt as to where Columbus learned his navigation. He seems to have grown up in Genoa, then a great maritime power. According to his son Ferdinand, he claimed to have been, in his early twenties, a captain in the service of René d'Anjou, a claimant to the throne of Naples; but there is no independent evidence that he was more than a common seaman before he arrived shipwrecked in Portugal. By Portuguese standards at the time he was never a master navigator.

10. Fig. 2.5 is based on Taylor (1960).

11. The magnetic pole oscillates slowly around the geographic pole. Secular change was confirmed by Gellibrand in 1635. In London, magnetic variation was 11°E in 1596, zero in 1652, and 24°W in 1815.

12. In modern English, *rhumb* has a mathematically precise meaning (Chapter 3); but in modern Spanish the course to steer is still *rumbo*.

13. Parallel rules were only invented in 1723 (by Bion).

14. Motzo (1947).

15. Decimals were extended to fractions by the Flemish polymath Simon Stevin at the end of the sixteenth century, but it is claimed that decimal fractions were used in China in antiquity. The decimal point did not become universal until the eighteenth century.

16. The Persian mathematician Muhammad ibn Musa al-Khwarizmi, to whom we owe the word *algorithm*, used the positional notation in about AD 810. It is said that the Mayan civilization had a symbol for zero, and that the ancient Chinese left a blank space on their counting boards to denote zero.

17. Bookkeeping is mainly concerned with addition, which is easy in the Roman system; but long division is tedious in it.

18. In the twentieth century experienced flight navigators estimated the *azimuth* of the pole star, with an accuracy of half a degree or so, by a glance at the lie of the Lesser Bear, and so checked their compass course without computation.

19. However, in the southern hemisphere, both the Portuguese and contemporary Arabs navigating down the east coast of Africa made what use they could of Canopus (the bright southerly star used by Posidonius) and the Southern Cross.

20. For interesting speculations on the accuracy of these instruments see Forty (1983, 1986). Taylor and Sadler (1953) suggested that the idea of the backstaff, conventionally attributed to Davis, may have originated with Hariot.

21. The latinized version of his name is used in this book. A Portuguese Jew who was known in Portuguese as Pedro Nunes, he is often called Pedro Nuñez in English texts, following Castilian usage.

22. Admittedly this would only be a winter regimen. In summer one cannot see both the upper and lower transit of any star.

CHAPTER THREE

Three Necessary Mathematical Inventions

✠

THE unwillingness or inability of navigators to adopt mathematical solutions to their problems and the unwillingness or inability of mathematicians to identify the mathematical nature of navigators' problems are recurring themes throughout the history of navigational science. For some centuries the navigators had an excuse. Mathematics was a black art. Mathematicians applied their skills to astrology. When savants were assigned to important voyages the master would not distinguish whether their advice on the navigation derived from astronomy or astrology in the modern sense of these words. As late as the sixteenth century many educated men were contemptuous of mathematicians. Roger Ascham, the brilliant tutor of the great Queen Elizabeth of England, wrote of them, 'how solitary they be themselves, how unfit to live with, how unapt to serve the world'.[1] More than a century later, just ten years before Newton's *Principia* was published, his namesake Dr John Newton could write 'I never heard of any grammar school in England in which mathematics is taught.'

The three mathematical inventions described in this chapter were all essential to navigation at some stage. Meridional Parts, the first to be described, was the only one specifically invented to meet a perceived navigational requirement. The others, spherical trigonometry and logarithms, were available—off-the-shelf and pre-packaged—when navigators began to need them in the eighteenth century.

Meridional Parts

As the Portuguese explorers were the first to suspect, the trouble with the DR navigation described in Chapter 2 is that the eastings do not add up, because the earth is round, not flat. If one sails from position Z in Fig. 3.1 an easting x followed by a northing y, one arrives

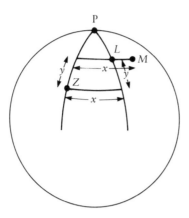

FIGURE 3.1
The uncertainty of easting.

at L; but if one sails the northing first followed by the easting, one arrives at M, because of the convergency of the meridians towards the pole. If northing and easting are the sum of different elements on a number of different tacks, all we can say without further and better particulars is that the DR position is not a point but the arc LM. As Martino Cortes wrote in 1551, in his *Breve compendio de la sfera y de la arte de navegar*, 'If two points on the equator are 60 leagues apart, two points on the same meridians at latitude 60° are only 30 leagues apart, but the chart, *being plane*, shows them still to be 60 leagues apart.'[2]

Petrus Nonius, the leading navigation theorist of the period, understood the true nature of the rhumb, or *loxodrome*, as a spiral around the earth cutting all meridians at the same angle, as in Fig. 3.2; but a solution was beyond him.

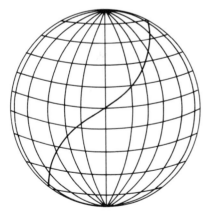

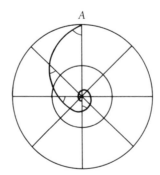

In equatorial and temperate latitudes   In polar latitudes   FIGURE 3.2
The rhumb line.

Today one would address the problem on a spherical earth in these terms. Since the radius of the parallel of latitude ϕ is the radius of the earth $\times \cos \phi$, if we take the unit of length to be a nautical mile equalling 1' of latitude, 1' of longitude is $\cos \phi$ nautical miles. Denote longitude λ, the direction of the rhumb α, and the length of the rhumb s.

$d\phi = \cos \alpha.ds.$

$d\lambda = \sec \phi.\sin \alpha.ds = \sec \phi.\tan \alpha.d\phi.$

Between points on the rhumb $\phi_1\lambda_1,\phi_2\lambda_2$

$\phi_2 - \phi_1 = s.\cos \alpha$ and $\lambda_2 - \lambda_1 = \tan \alpha \int \sec \phi.d\phi.$

The integral of $\sec \phi$ is $\log_e \tan [\pi/4 + \phi/2]$ (see also Note 3). If we call this function *meridional parts* (MP), diff. long. $= \tan \alpha.$diff. MP, and distance $=$ diff. lat. $\sec \alpha$.

One can work such problems with a table of meridional parts; or there is the graphical solution, in which the parallels of latitude are spaced in proportion to their meridional parts. The mathematical invention came back to front in that Edward Wright published tables of meridional parts in 1599 before logarithms or the calculus were invented, and upside down in that Mercator (Gerhard Kremer) invented the graphical solution (the Mercator projection) thirty years before that. It was not until about 1645 that Henry Bond noticed that a table of meridional parts was, in fact, a table of log tangents; but it made no sense to him. Near that date both Newton and Leibniz were born. Their independent invention of the calculus made the reasoning of the previous paragraph possible.

Mercator's mind may have worked on the following lines. If it is possible to project the globe on a chart in such a way that all rhumbs appear as straight lines cutting the meridians at the correct angle, all meridians and parallels of latitude must be straight lines cutting at right angles, because they are rhumb lines which cut at that angle. To ensure that all other rhumbs cut all meridians at the correct angle, we resort to that consequential notion of Archimedes. Consider any segment of a rhumb—AB in Fig. 3.3—short enough for the earth to be considered flat along its length—it can be as short as we please. The sufficient and necessary condition that the angle α is true is that the ratio AB:BC must be the same on the earth and the chart. By definition of the loxodrome, α is constant, and a straight line cuts all parallel straight lines at the same angle. As we would now say, *at the limit* scale at a point must be the same in all directions—although that scale will vary over the chart in some

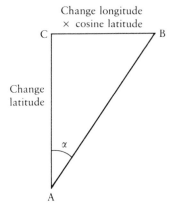

FIGURE 3.3
Element of a rhumb line.

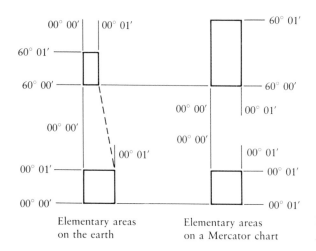

Elementary areas
on the earth

Elementary areas
on a Mercator chart

FIGURE 3.4
Mercator's waxing of the latitude.

systematic way. This is the property of *conformality* sometimes called *orthomorphism* by geographers because it necessarily implies that the *shape* of sufficiently small areas is preserved. Mercator achieved conformality by 'waxing' the latitudes, that is to say by increasing the scale towards the pole in proportion to the secant of the latitude (Fig. 3.4).

Mercator, born in Flanders, a pupil of Gemma Frisius (the first notable Dutch contributor[4] to navigational science), is generally considered to be the greatest of sixteenth-century geographers. He might have achieved some merit as a mathematician if the University of Louvain had been more sympathetic to his views on theology (he was briefly arrested for heresy in 1544). As it was, he earned his living as a maker of globes and maps. He achieved eminence as a cartographer in 1554 with a map of Europe. For centuries cartographers had followed Ptolemy with reverent lethargy and assigned to the Mediterranean a longitudinal extent of 62°. Mercator's studies of pilot books and other sources led him to reduce it to 52°—still about 10° too much. The lethargic reverence of cartographers was transferred from Ptolemy to Mercator. Until the work of the Académie des Sciences (described in Chapter 6) more than a century later, map-makers were still showing the extension in longitude of the Mediterranean as 52°. In an interesting note to his map Mercator dismissed the determination of longitude by eclipses as unpractical nearly two thousand years after Hipparchus proposed it.

Mercator first used his 'waxing' latitudes on his world map (included in the atlas *Theatrum* of Ortelius of 1569). It consisted of 24 sheets extending in full to 131 × 208 cm. With more valour than discretion the map shows the meridian of demarcation (Chapter 5). There are instructions for measuring distance and an *Organum directorium*, apparently for the construction of secants. The map is specifically entitled *For use in navigation*. By that criterion it was a failure. Seamen do not sail rhumbs on world maps—the continents get in the way. The explanation is in Latin; and a poor explanation it is. If the scale is to be proportional to the secant of the latitude, the chart distance of a parallel from the equator is a scale factor × the sum of inferior secants. Trigonometrical tables of the required accuracy were available at the time. It is therefore surprising that Mercator's meridional parts were so inaccurate. Perhaps he used a crude graphical construction. In fairness to Mercator, there is evidence that in 1569 many English navigators still regarded even the plane chart as black magic.[5]

The first correct explanation was Edward Wright's *Certaine errors in navigation*, published in 1599, which was still being sold a century later. It included an accurate table of meridional parts, which Wright computed by adding secants. The tables were circulated privately long before publication and were used by Jodocus Hondius, the Dutch cartographer, to produce charts on Mercator's projection more accurately projected than Mercator's own. Wright was a Cambridge mathematician, a friend of Briggs and Napier (see the section of this chapter on logarithms, pp. 50–2). His ideas seem to have developed from Petrus Nonius rather than Mercator.

The most curious part of this odd story is the meridional parts formula of Thomas Hariot,[6] the mathematical practitioner to Walter Ralegh. Hariot never published; but his formula for computing meridional parts was far in advance of the general state of mathematics at the time, and is now thought to have preceded Wright's work. Like Napier's logarithms, Hariot's formula for meridional parts presaged the calculus.

Despite the wide availability of Wright's clear exposition in the English language, many English navigators continued through the seventeenth century to use DR in the plane form which had evolved in the Mediterranean so long before. As Sir John Narborough put it:[7] 'I could wish all seamen would give over sailing by the false plain charts and sail by the Mercator's chart . . . but it is a hard matter to convince any of the old navigators.' If Edmond Halley is to be believed, John Wood, who apparently accompanied Narborough on his survey of the Magellan Straits in 1669 and should therefore have known better, used a plane chart while attempting the North-east Passage in 1676. Unsurprisingly he lost his ship, but survived to become a Fellow of the Royal Society.

Users of Traverse Tables simply used the mean latitude to convert departure to difference of longitude. Since Wright, it has been obvious that, in this method, the correct latitude to use is not the mean latitude but the latitude at which the secant is the mean. The matter was put right in 1805 in Workman's 'Mid-latitude Correction' table. As mid-lat $= \cos^{-1}$ (diff lat/diff MP), Wright and Hariot are inescapable after all.

The earth's shape more closely resembles an oblate spheroid, such that all its meridians are identical ellipses and all parallels of latitude circles, than it does a sphere (see Chapter 6). As the polar diameter of the earth is only about a third of 1 per cent shorter than the equatorial radius, errors in meridional parts so arising were not consequential to practical navigation; but late in the nineteenth century Atherton's meridional parts for Clarke's (1880) figure of the earth were published for cartographers by Her Majesty's Stationery Office. In the twentieth century these found their way into the nautical tables. The use of spheroidal meridional parts gives track angle to an accuracy which could not conceivably have been applied to navigation, but further distorts the accuracy of distance calculations. During the Second World War such textbooks and tables generally available to British seamen and airmen as treated of the rhumb line on the spheroid were wrong. The correct theory of the rhumb on the spheroid[8] was not generally available to navigators until 1950. To the practical navigator it does not matter; but to the historian it illuminates the quality of the mathematical practitioners concerned with navigation in the early twentieth century. From about 1940 the quality improved dramatically in less than one generation.

When the Wright principles were fully accepted, and charts showing magnetic variation became available, seamen (and later airmen) steered by the magnetic compass, as we still do in smaller ships and aircraft, adjusting the magnetic course to steer for local magnetic variation as they went along. After the Second World War, air navigation over northern Canada became important to the military because it was the airspace between the USA and the USSR, and to the airlines because it was the route between the West Coast of the USA and Europe. There was no merit in flying a spiral; and, before inertial navigation systems, no practical means of doing so. Even at latitude 60° over Hudson Bay, at jet speeds magnetic variation could change 40° in an hour. To the north-west, the magnetic compass failed completely as the direction of the earth's magnetic field approached the vertical. Clearly, true north is only the best reference if the pole is far away and there is available a heading reference which approximates to it. There was a fresh look at the fundamentals.

Early in the nineteenth century Gauss had given the general theory of conformal projection. In navigation the important corollaries of conformality are that all lines on the chart cut each other at the same angles as the corresponding curves on the earth, and that distances may be measured along those lines at the mean scale. On every conformal projection of a sphere there is a circle [the limiting cases being a great circle (Mercator) and a point (stereographic[9])]; where any great circle is straight, scale variation is zero and scale is a minimum. Everywhere else the scale increases, and the greater the scale increase, the greater the curvature of great circles.

The Mercator projection was perceived as a special case of two groups of conformal projection. The first group is those in which meridians appear as straight lines converging generally at angles less than their difference of longitude (conformal conic). The limiting cases are the Mercator (chart convergency zero) and the polar stereographic (chart convergency = difference of longitude). In the general case of the conformal conic scale is a minimum (and nearly constant), and great circles are straight, at the latitude at which chart convergency is true. The Mercator is also a member of that group of conformal projections on which the scale is a minimum along a great circle, the equator in the case of the Mercator. The general case became known as the oblique Mercator, and the other special case, with the great circle a meridian, is called the transverse Mercator.

Increasingly air navigators asked the question, 'what is so special about true north, the loxodrome, and the Mercator chart?' In high latitudes there was no good answer. Figure 3.5 shows that in 1955 the magnetic rhumb between Shannon (Eire) and Gander (Canada), which was the shortest direct North Atlantic crossing, was closer to the great circle than it was to the loxodrome, the convergency of the meridians approximating to the change in magnetic variation. Back to the *Carta Pisana*! On conformal projections other than the Mercator the direction of some meridian *on the chart*, often the Greenwich meridian, became *Grid North*, magnetic variation relative to grid north was *Grivation*, and lines printed on the chart joining

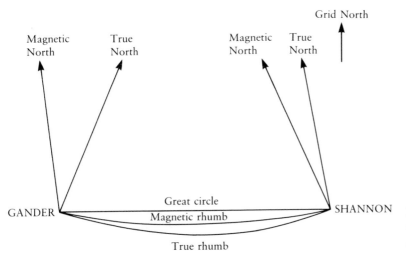

FIGURE 3.5
*Gander–Shannon on a
conformal conic.*

points having the same grivation were *Isogrivs*. While a conformal conic illustrated in Fig. 3.5 might be most suitable for a route such as Gander–Shannon, on a route such as Vancouver–Amsterdam, where the minimum time-path may pass through very high latitudes, an oblique Mercator based on the great circle route may be preferred, using the great circle itself as grid north. Over the entire area a straight line may be taken to be a great circle. Along the direct great circle route, scale is constant, three hundred miles from it the scale increase is only 0.3 per cent. For the purposes of practical navigation at the time, the chart was a 'true' representation of the earth. Thus did airmen outgrow the spiralling straight line.

The PZX Triangle

Trigonometry has ancient and diverse roots in surveying, architecture, astronomy, astrology, and the Greek passion for mathematics. We know almost nothing about Babylonian and Egyptian trigonometry. We can only surmise how Pytheas treated the tangent function when he found latitude and thus declination by measuring the length of the shadow of the gnomon (Chapter 1). Perhaps he used something like the *Geometrical Square* (Fig. 3.6) of Gemma Frisius nearly two thousand years later. The tangent and cotangent of any angle can be read. It is significant that the sides are labelled *umbra* ('shadow'), and curious that Gemma Frisius should, at that late stage, use a duodecimal system. Thus, if the ratio of the height of the gnomon to the length of the shadow is 7:12, the altitude is angle A; if the ratio is 12:7, the altitude is angle B.

The work of Hipparchus on chords is only known from later Greek writers. The oldest trigonometric tables we have (second century AD) are contained in Ptolemy's *Almagest*. It is revealing that in England, where classical Greek was taught in public and grammar schools for 400 years, we call an important Greek mathematical treatise (*Syntaxis mathematica*) by its Arabic name, which means 'The Greatest'. Hindu tables of sines were translated into Arabic in the eighth century AD. The cosine formula for oblique spherical triangles, basic to astro-

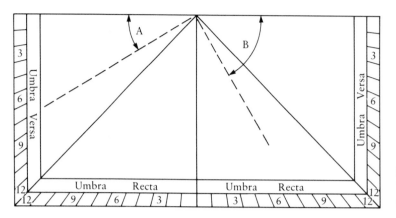

FIGURE 3.6
The geometrical square of Gemma Frisius.

nomical navigation, was given late in the ninth century AD by al-Baltani. Oddly, the cosine formula for plane triangles, which seems so much easier, is not found in extant European works until Vieta, the sixteenth-century French mathematician.

The special properties of right-angled and right-sided spherical triangles, which became important to navigation with the proliferation of 'short' methods of sight reduction from the late nineteenth century (Chapter 7), were explored by Ptolemy and Menelaus among the Greeks, systematized in Persia in the thirteenth century and in Western Europe in the fifteenth century by Regiomontanus (Johann Müller of Konigsberg). In 1619 Napier published his rules, which state in a compact mnemonic form all the relationships inherent in right spherical triangles.

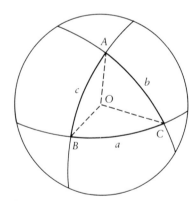

FIGURE 3.7
The spherical triangle.

The cosine formula is $\cos a = \cos b.\cos c + \sin b.\sin c.\cos A$, using the lettering of Fig. 3.7. The PZX triangle in Fig. 3.8 is conceived to be on the celestial sphere, concentric with the earth and of indefinitely large radius (Chapter 1). P is the celestial pole, Z the observer's zenith, and X the observed celestial body. The side PZ is 90° − latitude, the side PX is 90° ± declination, the side ZX is 90° − observed altitude, and the angle P is hour angle. If latitude is determined by the means described in Chapter 2, altitude is observed, and declination is taken from an almanac, hour angle can be found from the cosine formula as

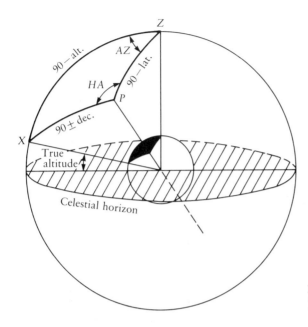

FIGURE 3.8
The PZX triangle.

cos HA = [sin alt. − sin lat.sin dec.] sec lat.sec dec.

If the time at some reference meridian, say Greenwich, is known, the Greenwich hour angle of the body (GHA) can be found from the almanacs. The longitude, east or west of Greenwich, is simply the difference between the GHA and the local Hour Angle (LHA), calculated from the formula given above.

In historical fact, the cosine formula has rarely been used in this way by navigators. When the chronometer was still a novelty, Maskelyne offered his 'Requisite Tables' which gave the simpler formula:

vers LHA = [sin *m* − sin *a*] sec lat.sec dec,

where *m*, *a* are respectively the meridional altitude and the altitude of the body, and the versine is (1−cos). The formula ignores the change in declination of the sun during the period between the two observations. More generally, the cosine formula has rarely been used in the form stated, because the calculation is simpler if the formula is written in the form

hav *a* = hav (*b* ~ *c*) + sin *a*.sin *b*.hav *A*,

where the haversine (hav) is half the versine.

Haversine tables have been available to seamen at least since 1805. With or without logarithms the haversine formula is always simpler than the cosine formula, and haversines are always positive. Until trigonometrical pocket calculators made trigonometrical tables irrelevant many efforts were made to simplify the solution of the PZX triangle; but these are part of the history of astronomical navigation (Chapter 7) rather than mathematics.

Logarithms

If logarithms had not been available, navigators would have made heavy weather of spherical trigonometry, and thus of astronomical navigation. With tables of log. trig. functions Maskelyne's formula becomes

$$\log \text{ vers } \text{LHA} = \log (\sin m - \sin a) + \log \sec \text{ lat.} + \log \sec \text{ dec.},$$

surely not too laborious a calculation once a day after all those centuries of weary sweat to find the longitude. Astronomical methods were based on log. trig. functions in the Royal Navy from the eighteenth century until 1953, when inspection methods (see Chapter 7) were adopted, scarcely twenty years before pocket calculators made the whole matter irrelevant.

The slide rule, a logarithmic analogue, was devised by Oughtred only eight years after Napier published the first logarithmic tables. Three centuries later, the circular slide-rule became the airman's primary navigational aid. Merely to find his true air speed, a pilot had to divide his indicated air speed by the square root of the ratio of the actual density of the atmosphere to the density assumed in the calibration of the instrument. Atmospheric density

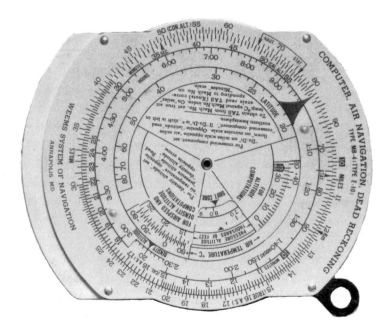

Dead reckoning computer (c. 1950) showing circular slide rule

was not measured directly, but calculated from atmospheric temperature and indicated altitude, itself a logarithmic function of pressure. The pilot merely set with his thumb the pressure altitude against temperature in a window on an appropriately calibrated circular slide-rule and read true air speed on the outer circular scale against indicated air speed on the inner scale. Without logarithms, astronomical navigation at sea would have been a dreary chore for two centuries; but without logarithmic analogues air navigation, during its first fifty years, borders on the unthinkable.

For centuries x^2 and x^3 were called (in Latin or the vernacular) 'x squared' and 'x cubed', which leads no further than whimsical speculation on what might be the product of a square and a cube. Immediately the notation x^2, x^3, and so on is adopted we see that $x^p . x^q = x^{p+q}$. The rule can be extended to fractions if we write $x^{1/2}$ for the squared root of x, $x^{1/4}$ for the fourth root of x, and so on. The rule is also true for negative powers if we follow the convention that $1/x^p$ is x^{-p}. It seems that for all positive numbers x, y there should exist a number p (which may be positive or negative) such that $y = x^p$. Let p be log y, then log $(y_1 \times y_2) = \log y_1 + \log y_2$. We have invented logarithms. With logarithmic tables we can add and subtract instead of multiplying and dividing. The problem is that we have no method as yet of calculating logarithms unless they are whole numbers or roots we know how to extract.

Logarithms, like meridional parts, seem to have come back-to-front. The notation x^2 and so on did not appear in print until 1637 in the *Géométrie* of Descartes. Working from about 1595, Napier finally published his completed logarithmic tables[10] in 1614. However, both Stevin and Hariot in the late sixteenth century had notations which invited the reasoning of the previous paragraph.

Among Napier's early papers is the pregnant table

	I	II	III	IIII	V	VI	VII
I	2	4	8	16	32	64	128

To an ancient Greek this is simply a table of related arithmetic and geometric progressions; but Napier saw, as no Greek did, the numbers in the tables as points in *continuous progressions*, like points on a line. He visualized two points moving along parallel straight lines, one (the number) moving at a constant velocity, the other (the logarithm) slowing down in proportion to its distance from some remote point on the line. Napier's formal definition of a logarithm is a statement in the differential calculus which was invented decades later. This statement, and the geometrical concept from which it derives, lead to an awkward base. In modern notation, the Napierian logarithm of x is $10^7[\log_e 10^7 - \log_e x]$. Napier envisaged his invention being applied to astronomy, the only activity at the time requiring masses of multiplications of numbers with many digits. These were usually the sines (or cosines) of angles. His table[11] is in fact a table of natural sines and log sines to seven decimal places for every minute of the quadrant. Thus log sine appeared before log! As usual, back-to-front.

Mathematicians come from every background. The peerless Gauss was of poor German peasant stock. Honoured to be mentioned in the same breath, Russell (whose mathematics was so pure that he defined his subject as that in which we do not know what we are talking about or care whether what we say about it is true) grew up an orphan in the home of his grandfather, a British prime minister whose earldom Russell inherited. John Napier came from the most unlikely source of them all. The eighth laird of Merchiston, he was born in 1550 into the murderous Scottish aristocracy, which seemed little changed since the days of Macbeth. The notorious Earl of Boswell was a relation. There was a little culture in the family. Napier's uncle, a bishop who officiated at the marriage of Boswell to Mary, Queen of Scots, recognized the boy's talents and encouraged his intellectual pursuits. Napier grew up to be a prominent and unbridled anti-papist in the Scotland of James VI; but except in matters of religion, he was a quiet and peaceable man, loved and admired by other mathematicians. There were none of the squabbles which disfigure the memory of Newton, nor the controversies among which Galileo delighted to live dangerously. Kepler was so captivated by Napier's logarithms that he inscribed *Harmonice mundi*, the work in which he announced his third law (Chapter 4), to Napier.

Henry Briggs, the Public Professor of Geometry in London, and a friend of Edward Wright, was so excited by Napier's invention that he went to Edinburgh to meet the great man. There is an eye-witness account of the meeting.[12]

> *Mr Briggs up into My Lord's chamber where almost one quarter of an hour was spent, each beholding the other with admiration before one word was spoken: at last Mr Briggs began. 'My Lord, I have undertaken this long journey purposely to see your person, and to know by what engine of wit or ingenuity you came first to think of this most excellent help unto Astronomy, viz. the Logarithms: but my Lord, being by you found out, I wonder nobody else found it out before, when now being known it appears so easy.'*

What an exquisite compliment to pay to a genius!

It was Briggs who realized the advantage of making the logarithmic base 10. Navigators would have found the logarithms of Napier difficult. It is the logarithms of Mr Henry Briggs which they have always used.

Tables through the Ages

All the Ancients were hampered by the lack of a good system of enumeration. The Egyptians and some of the Greeks imposed on themselves the impediment of expressing fractions with a numerator of one.[13] Even Archimedes wrote ¾ as ½, ¼. It is therefore unsurprising that the earliest mathematical table is one giving fractions of the form $2/2n+1$ as a series of fractions with the numerator 1, for example $2/9$ as $1/6 + 1/18$. This table is included in the *Rhind papyrus*,[14] indited about 1700 BC by Ahmose the scribe, who notes that he copied it from an earlier document. In this fascinating work Ahmose poses the problems and gives the answers; but he is a cryptic fellow. 'Loaves 60 for men 5, $1/7$ of men 3 above to 2 below.' The answer

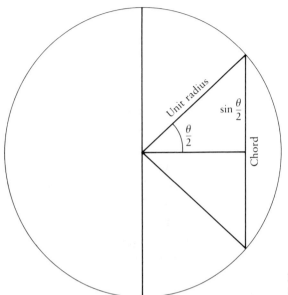

FIGURE 3.9
Chords and sines.

is 23, 17½, 12, 6½, 1. The total is 60, the numbers are in arithmetic progression, and the last two are a seventh of the first three; but how Ahmose did it is still his secret.

The oldest trigonometrical table we have is a canon of the *Almagest*, mentioned earlier in this chapter, which gives chords at intervals of ½°. Figure 3.9 shows that chord $\theta = 2\sin(\theta/2.)$, so the table is equivalent to a table of sines at intervals of a quarter of a degree. Ptolemy used the hexagesimal system of fractions, in which the only denominators are powers of 60; but any numerator less than 60 is permitted. Against 23° we read in the canon 23 55 27 meaning $23/60 + 55/60^2 + 27/60^3$, which to five decimal places is 0.39874. Thus sin 11½° = 0.19937, which is correct to the accuracy normally supplied by nautical tables. Ptolemy seems to have used a method of inequalities, calculating the limits by the extraction of square roots. Hindu sines and Napier's logarithms were also calculated by methods involving the repeated extraction of square roots. Before Ptolemy, Hero knew of a powerful rule: if x_1 is an approximation to $\sqrt{n}$, x_2 is a closer approximation, where $x_2 = \frac{1}{2}[x_1 + n/x_1]$. The series converges quickly; if 1.4 is taken as the first approximation (x_1) to $\sqrt{2}$, x_3 is correct to eight decimal places.

In the fifteenth century Regiomontanus computed a table of sines for every 1′ to six decimal places. In the sixteenth century Rheticus (a pupil of Copernicus) and his successors computed trigonometrical functions to fifteen decimal places, a formidable task which stands for ever. Briggs logarithms to base 10 were published in 1624 to 14 decimal places. In 1633 logarithmic trigonometrical tables by both Briggs and Vlacq were published. Briggs tabulated against decimal parts of a degree, but Vlacq tabulated in units of minutes of arc, the practice later followed in nautical tables.

It seems sad that the power series which would have reduced this prodigious labour vastly did not come earlier; but it is inevitable that the logarithms should have been invented first. Power series for e^x and sin x were sufficiently well-known in 1685 to appear in Wallis'

Algebra. Newton may have had them twenty years earlier. In 1668 Nicolaus Mercator gave the power series for $\log_e(1+x)$, convergent when $|x| < 1$. Some power series converge very rapidly. In the series

$$\sin x = x - x^3/3! + x^5/5! - x^7/7! + \ldots, \ x \text{ in radians}$$

the value of the fourth term is less than 0.000037 when $x=45°$.

The enthusiasm for metricization associated with the French Revolution led to 100 grades to the right angle, 100 minutes to the grade, and 100 seconds to the minute. The metric *Tables du cadastre* gave sine and tangent to 22 decimal places, and log sin. and log tan. to 14 decimal places. Although interest in the metric right angle has revived from time to time, this admirable proposal, which, together with a decimal time system, would have saved generations of navigators so much labour, has never been adopted.[15] Thousands of years ago the Babylonians decided that there were 360° in a circle; and that, to this day, is that—the most enduring edict in the history of our species.

Astronomical navigation is obsolete, and the pocket calculator is ubiquitous. At last the 360° circle is no burden to navigators. Belatedly, there are moves within the the International Maritime Organization and the International Civil Aviation Organization to decimalize the circle. As it is not within their power to decimalize the day, one wonders why they bother.

Freedom from manual computation is not the least of the benefits which modern technology confers on us. Gauss, gifted with one of the finest of brains, wasted years of his life on mindless astronomical calculations. Such calculations were the essence of Kepler's great work. Napier renounced important work on algebra to compute his logarithms; and we can only guess at the labour which went into the *Almagest*.

Notes to Chapter 3

1. Taylor (1967).
2. The author's free translation. Cortes knew that $\cos 60° = \frac{1}{2}$.
3. It follows from these equations that every loxodrome (except east-west) reaches the pole in a finite distance, but (with the exception of north-south) after infinite gyrations around the pole —a geometric analogy of convergent series. Many works on navigation and cartography, and even Webster's *Dictionary*, say that the rhumb *never* reaches the pole, a quaint solecism appropriately arising from the use of a temporal term to describe a concept without a time-dimension.
4. Gemma Frisius, as his name implies, came from Friesland, and so, like Mercator and Huygens, was Dutch in the modern sense. Some scientists of the Low Countries, notably Simon Stevin of Bruges, would today be Flemish Belgians.
5. Waters (1956).
6. George (1956); Taylor and Sadler (1953). As is illustrated in Chapter 4, Hariot would have been recognized as one of the great mathematical scientists of his time if his work had been publicized.

7. Crone (1966).
8. Williams (1950).
9. The stereographic projection was the only conformal projection known to the Greeks, and the only one which is a true geometric projection.
10. Like the meridional parts of Wright, the logarithms of Napier were circulated privately years before they were published. As so often happens in mathematics and physics, the idea was in the air. Just Bürgi, a Swiss, independently published a limited table of antilogarithms in Prague in 1620; but Napier's precedence is as unarguable as his stature.
11. Contained in *Mirifici logarithmorum canonis descriptio*, published in 1614. It also describes the evolution of his idea. The actual method of computation is described in *Mirifici logarithmorum canonis constructio*, published posthumously.
12. Quoted in Turnbull (1951).
13. The Egyptians made an exception of ⅔.
14. The papyrus is headed 'Directions for Knowing all dark things'. A brief and entertaining commentary is to be found in Newman (1956).
15. On a laudable French initiative the International Meridian Conference of 1884 (Chapter 5) resolved that 'The conference expresses the hope that the technical studies designed to regulate and extend the application of the decimal system to the division of angular space and time shall be resumed, so as to permit the extension of this application to all cases in which it presents real advantages.'

Naturally, nothing was done. The obvious reason for the long supremacy of 12 and 60 is that the factors of 12 are 2,3,4, and 6 and those of 60 are 2,3,4,5, and 6, so that the most common fractions of the foot, the dozen, the day, the hour, and the circle are whole numbers of the subsidiary units. Ten is an awkward base, but the decimal system is based on finger-counting, and ten is the number of fingers we have. Unfortunately French rationalism in the late eighteenth century did not take the great leap to a duodecimal system in which we would write twelve as 10 and a hundred and forty-four as 100, and so have the best of both worlds.

CHAPTER FOUR

A New Way of Thought

☩

Wнen Columbus sailed west the only major inventions in the preceding thousand years had been the Hindu system of numerical notation, printing, gunpowder, and the magnetic compass. Europe had advanced little beyond the civilizations of other eras. It has been remarked that in the year 1400 Europe knew less than Archimedes, who died in the year 212 BC. In Christendom, 1800 years after their times, Aristotle was still the basis of science and logic; Plato of humanist philosophy. In general, artefacts owed little to science or engineering (the astrolabe was a rare exception). Around AD 1600 something began in Europe which was to become the most important event in history; a new way of thought, uniquely European and Christian in origin and development, which led in only twelve generations to radio, the aeroplane, and machines of all kinds.

Modern science is not primarily an evolution of artefacts. Figure 4.1 is a picture of an unusual kite. There is a man sitting in it. Most kites acquire the airspeed necessary to generate lift by being tethered in a breeze. This man creates his own wind by driving a windmill by a treadmill. The kite, the windmill, and the treadmill were all used in the Dark Ages; but the man-powered aeroplane could never develop from them. So advanced is the science[1] required to produce the aeroplane illustrated that men walked on the moon before a man achieved the dream of the millennia and sustained flight by the power of his own muscles.[2]

All the artefacts peculiar to our civilization, such as television and space vehicles, have evolved, like earlier successful artefacts, from primitive models; but, unlike artefacts before the seventeenth century, the first model is now a direct consequence of advances in physics, chemistry, or both. To invent physics, one's mind should be cleansed of the accumulated wisdom of the ages, eschewing in particular the aprioristic physics of Aristotle and the idealism of Plato. One arbitrarily defines precise mathematical concepts such as *force* or *momentum*; one observes nature; one makes valid quantitative statements about what one sees

FIGURE 4.1
The Albatross man-powered aircraft.

in terms of the concepts one has invented. Then, and only then, does physics evolve: an evolution not of things, but of strange new ideas.

According to one medieval neo-Aristotelian, a thrown stone continues to move when the thrower releases it because the thrower has given to the thrown the quality of *virtus derelicta*. This notion seems to be related colloquially to our own notions of *momentum* and *impetus*, but giving names to notions does not help us to understand phenomena. The neo-Aristotelian ends where he begins. True physics only starts when we break the tautological circle. We define momentum as mass × velocity. We discover how it is acquired, conserved, and dissipated by measurement, observation, and experiment. If the concept of momentum had led nowhere, we would have invented another concept which did. The vital shift is from the question *why* the stone moves, which is ultimately unanswerable, to the question of *how* it moves, which is immediately observable.

A. N. Whitehead, a distinguished mathematician and a popular philosopher of science between the two World Wars, put it differently:[3] 'It is this union of passionate interest in detailed facts with equal devotion to abstract generalization which forms the novelty in our present society.' True as far as it goes; but that does not explain why physics already had relativity and quantum theory when biology, less amenable to mathematical analysis, was relatively primitive. In the memorable words of one modern physicist,[4] 'This *unreasonable* effectiveness (of mathematics in the physical sciences) is a wonderful gift which we neither understand nor deserve.'

Some of this was discerned in the seventeenth century by Edmond Halley, the only great scientist in history to be a navigator of professional quality (if we except the near-legendary Pytheas). In a note[5] originally intended for the edification of King James II, he wrote:

Truth being uniform and always the same, it is admirable to observe how easily we are enabled to make out very abstruse and difficult matters when once true and genuine Principles are obtained: And on the other hand it might be wondred, that, not withstanding the great facility of truth, and the perplexity and nonconsequences that always attend erroneous Suppositions, these great Discoveries should have escaped the acute Disquisitions of the best Philosophical Heads of all past Ages, and be reserved to these our Times. But that wonder will soon cease, if it is considered how great Improvements Geometry has received in our Memory . . .

It is clear in context that the improvement in geometry which Halley principally had in mind was the calculus.

Physics was not invented by three men; but three extraordinary men illuminate the historical process, which cannot be understood if any of the three is ignored. These men are Kepler, Galileo, and Newton.

Johann Kepler is famed chiefly for his three laws of planetary motion, which are:

1. The planetary orbits are ellipses with the sun at one focus.

2. The line joining a planet to the sun sweeps out equal areas in equal times.

3. The squares of the periods of the planets are proportional to the cubes of their mean distance from the sun.

The first two laws were published in 1609, and the third law in 1619. Among many other contributions to science Kepler also enunciated the first of the inverse square laws of action at a distance, that the brightness of light varies inversely as the square of the distance of the source. The others are gravitational, magnetic, and electrostatic. Kepler speculated that the sun attracted the planets; but if the idea that an inverse square law of attraction would explain his laws crossed his mind, its proof was beyond the mathematics of the time.

We see Kepler the man as a very ordinary, rather comic fellow in most respects: perpetually worrying about his health and about money; marrying the uncomely daughter of a miller for money; casting horoscopes for money; resenting his position as a paid assistant to Tycho Brahe, his inferior in intellect and his superior in wealth and rank. Kepler even managed to fall between the stools of Rome, Luther, and Calvin in those dangerous, disputatious times. He had neither the insight of Galileo and Einstein, nor the superhuman intellect of Newton and Gauss. He dreamed the wrong dreams. His mind was befuddled with neo-Pythagorean mysticism. He sought to show that the planetary orbits followed inscribed and circumscribed spheres of the regular polyhedra. He reached his unsought conclusions expressed in the three laws by painful devotion to the odd notion that a true theory must fit all the facts, and by unremitting labour in an unthankful cause.

Kepler exemplifies perfectly those qualities which Whitehead described as the *novelty* of our society. For ages, men had thought that as God, the circle, and the sphere were all perfect, the heavenly bodies must move in perfect circles in the heavenly spheres. Since they observably do nothing of the sort, wherever one tries to put the centre of the system, most astronomers, from Eudoxus through Ptolemy to Copernicus, added more circles, wheels within wheels, as if God were a clockwork maniac. Kepler too was imbued with such non-sense; but he was also the man who discarded 900 folio pages of long multiplication and division because observation disagreed with theory by 8′ of arc. It is on this quality and two others that his unique eminence stands. The others are: first, the accuracy and large volume of the facts at his disposal, built up over many years in the observatories of the prodigious Dane, Tycho Brahe; and secondly, the fact that in the end, despite the medieval mysticism with which he started, he began to perceive that physics and astronomy were one. Since ancient times, physics had dealt with the corrupt earthly world, astronomy with the sub-lime music of the celestial spheres. The idea that they were one was new, terrible—and essential.

Galileo Galilei, seven years older than Kepler, was born in Pisa, a few miles from Vinci, the birthplace of Leonardo a century earlier. His larger-than-life figure is famed for many things; but surely his greatest contribution to human thought was his insistent faith that the secrets of nature are written in the language of mathematics. The legend that he proved, despite the Aristotelians, that the acceleration due to gravity is the same for all masses by dropping weights of different sizes from the leaning tower of Pisa is now discredited; but it should be true.[6] The story illustrates perfectly Galileo's showmanship and his insistence that the only sources of valid statement about the physical world are experiment and observation. By common consent he is the founder of mechanics, the science at the heart of physics. Such essential notions as *force*, *momentum*, and *inertia* are implicit in his work, but he did not give them precise mathematical formulation. In fact, the Professor of Mathematics at Padua, the 'First Philosopher and Mathematician' to the Grand Duke of Tuscany, was not a mathe-matician of the calibre of such contemporaries as the Imperial Mathematician (Kepler), Napier, or Hariot—to say nothing of Descartes, who was a generation younger than the others.

Exposition, insight, and lateral thinking were Galileo's great gifts. It was not enough to discover the isochronism of the pendulum.[7] He went on to invent the pendulum clock and a kind of metronome to measure pulse-rates. It was not enough to discover that Jupiter had moons. He realized that they furnished a natural celestial clock which could solve the problem of the longitude. Within three years he was able to predict with some accuracy the times of immersion (eclipse) and emersion of the satellites from the shadow of the great planet.

The early history of the telescope shows how Galileo's arrogance and showmanship served the dissemination of scientific ideas. The telescope was invented in Holland[8] not later than 1608. In England, in mid-1609, Hariot was using the telescope to survey the heavens system-atically and to map the lunar surface. In 1611 Kepler published *Dioptrice*, which provided a theory of the telescope and suggested a convex eyepiece instead of the concave lens of the Dutch invention. Galileo made the Dutch version so much his own that it is sometimes still called the Galilean telescope. He demonstrated his much improved version to the Venetian Senate with such *élan* that they extended his tenure of the chair of mathematics at Padua (then under Venetian dominion) to life and doubled his salary. In 1610, with journalistic promptitude, Galileo published *Sidereus nuncius*, describing what he saw: thousands of new stars, four new 'planets' (the satellites of Jupiter), and the mountains and valleys of our own moon. The pamphlet of 24 octavo leaves was a sensation. God had created man in his own image, but denied man the vision to see the rest of his creation! A perfect celestial body turns out to be a rock as rough and irregular as the world alloted to sinful man. Hariot, as usual, published nothing.

Galileo's readability was another of his great contributions to science. He wrote in a clear and simple style, sometimes in Latin, sometimes in the Tuscan language stylized by Dante, Boccaccio, and Petrarch in the fourteenth century and eventually adopted as the Italian language in the nineteenth century, after the *Risorgimento*. A contemporary said it took a lifetime to understand Kepler, but Galileo could be understood in a few hours. Galileo is still readable. Hariot of course understood Kepler at once; but, to this day, there cannot be many who have worked through and comprehended Kepler's florid, verbose Latin. Kepler's work implied that the earth, like the other planets, revolves around the sun, contrary to the Christian belief at the time (following the system of Ptolemy and supported by Old Testament allusions[9]) that the earth is fixed and immovable, with the heavens rotating around it. The old idea of Aristarchus that the earth is a planet revolving around the sun had been revived by Copernicus two generations earlier. It is tritely said that the *De revolutionibus* of Copernicus was a turning-point in man's vision of the universe; but the first edition was very limited, and the world waited more than 400 years for a complete English translation, with less than breathless impatience.[10]

Anyone who reviled other scientists[11] and ignored or ridiculed their work, and even put the views of the Pope who had befriended him into the mouth of a simpleton[12] was bound to get his comeuppance. It came to Galileo in 1633. Liberal intellectual fashion has presented, in literature, theatre, and cinema, Galileo's trial by the Inquisition as a battle between enlightenment (Galileo) and dark reactionary superstition (the Inquisition), on the over-simplistic grounds that Galileo's belief that the earth revolves around the sun was heretical and punishable. In this bizarre and fascinating affair one's sympathies are with the Inquisition, although they convicted Galileo on forged evidence[13] not of his beliefs but of his disobedience.

The theological position on science in Rome was reasonable. If a scientific theory which appears to be contrary to scripture can be *proved* to be true, scripture must be re-interpreted. The proposition: *the earth is round* had been a case in point. If a scientific theory which appears to be contrary to scripture is consistent with observation but cannot be proven, it may be described as a working hypothesis which *saves the phenomenon*; but it may not be taught as a truth. The work of Copernicus was encouraged during his own lifetime by the Vatican through the reigns of three popes. As Oisander's Preface to *De revolutionibus* stressed, it was a working hypothesis which did not challenge religion.

Eppur si muove ('. . . and yet it does move') was said to have been muttered by Galileo at his recantation, in which he swore to abandon the false notion that the sun is the centre of the universe and immovable, while the earth is not the centre of the universe, and moves.

Whether Galileo said it or not, he believed that the earth *really* moves, but he could not prove it; and neither can we—there are no fixed points in space. Ironically, the relativity of velocity is implicit in Galilean dynamics, as Newton realized. Galileo had been the first to realize that a velocity may be resolved into different components which may have different causes (as in the case of a thrown stone); but to the question of the relativity of velocity, his mind was closed. The earth *really* moves. *Reality* is the province of science. The secrets of nature are written in the language of mathematics. The cogent words of friendly warning given by Pope Urban VIII, 'You must not necessitate God,' went unheeded. Urban's simple phrase elegantly encapsulates a profound religious difficulty with Galilean thinking.

Galileo did a disservice to science by seeking to extend its province too far. To a much lesser extent, so did Kepler when he wrote 'It is a most absurd fiction that natural phenomena can be explained by false causes.' Newton put it right. He did not believe in the *reality* of gravity; 'that one body may act upon another through a vacuum . . . is, to me, so great an absurdity'; and again, in a letter to Bentley, 'You sometimes speak of gravity as essential and inherent to matter. Pray do not ascribe that notion to me.' The following words of Newton in the first book of *Principia* sound like Oisander's *Preface* to the work of Copernicus a century earlier, 'I nowhere take it upon me to define the kind or the manner of any action, the causes or the physical reason thereof.' Galileo's greatest offence was that for thirty years he ignored or denied the validity of Kepler's Laws. To the end of his life he maintained that the planets moved in perfect circles. Perhaps he never mastered Kepler's work. Perhaps Kepler's Laws were wrong because Galileo did not invent them.[14] Perhaps, after all, Galileo's mind was imperfectly cleansed of the old ideas he ridiculed so.

Isaac Newton, born the year that Galileo died (1642), triumphantly vindicated Galileo's unreasonable faith in mathematics. His three laws of motion are deceptively simple. They are, in effect:

1. If no force is exerted on a particle, its state is unchanged; that is to say that it remains at rest or continues to move in a straight line at a constant velocity.

2. The action of a force on a particle is to accelerate the particle in the direction of the force, according to the rule: force = mass × acceleration.

3. The action of two particles on each other is equal and opposite.

The Law of Gravity is that any two particles of mass m_1, m_2, at a distance d apart exert equal attractive forces on each other of Gm_1m_2/d^2, where G is a universal constant of a value depending on the units of mass and distance chosen. Newton showed how Kepler's Laws follow from these principles. He also showed that the Third Law was incomplete. The square of the period of the orbit is also inversely proportional to the sum of the masses of the Sun and the planet. He estimated the mass of the earth from its size and likely specific gravity, and thus calculated the mass of the Sun and of Jupiter. He deduced the spheroidal form of the earth under centrifrugal and gravitational forces, and calculated what the ellipticity of the meridians should be. He showed how the gravitational pull of the moon and the sun acts on such a spheroid, and how this explained the precession of the equinoxes and tides. All this and much more from those simple little laws.

The effect of the publication of Newton's *Philosophiae naturalis principia mathematica* (*Principia* for short) in 1687 was as sensational as *Sidereus nuncius* 75 years earlier. Newton gave mankind a wonderful vision of a universe governed by precise mathematical laws, as applicable to a whole planet as to a grain of sand. This vision really was a turning-point in human thought. It inspired men to seek unity and symmetry in nature—it demonstrated the unreasonable effectiveness of the mathematical method, the fertility of asking *how* rather than *why*.

Much of Newton's work in dynamics, his invention of the binomial theorem, and of the differential and integral calculus (which he called 'fluxions' and 'inverse fluxions'), was done before he became Lucasian Professor of Mathematics at Cambridge at the age of twenty-six. He did not publish *Principia* until he was forty-five. It was Robert Hooke who first stated unequivocally that the motion of the heavenly bodies was a problem in dynamics; and Hooke had indeed approached the concept of universal gravitation. As so often, the idea was in the air. The story goes that Hooke, Halley, and Sir Christopher Wren (an astronomer as well as an architect) were speculating one day on the orbit of a body under an inverse square law. Halley mentioned the inconclusive conversation to Newton, who replied that he had proved that it was an ellipse years before. Newton could not find the proof, so he did it again. Halley encouraged Newton to write *Principia*, and financed its publication out of his own pocket. Although most of the ideas had been in young Newton's head twenty years earlier, one essential link had been missing. To show that laws about particles apply to massive planets, it is necessary to show that a homogeneous sphere acts on external bodies under an inverse square law of gravity as if its mass were concentrated at the centre. This is not as easy as it looks. The problem defeated the young Newton. When the solution did occur to him he was interested in other things. Without Halley there might have been no *Principia*.

Newton's other great contribution to physics was in the field of optics, in which he was as offhand as he was in dynamics. As telescopes had become more powerful the image became blurred and coloured,[15] because, as Newton knew, the refraction of light varies as its colour, i.e. with its frequency. Newton's solution was the reflector telescope, in which the light-collecting element is a mirror (or at that time a speculum) instead of a lens. The Royal Society heard of it, and Newton sent an example. A week later, apparently as an afterthought, he added an explanation, with descriptions of illustrative experiments. He explained how white light is a mixture of all the colours of the rainbow, and how they may be separated by prisms and white light may be reconstituted again from them; but that if light of any colour passes through a prism its nature is unchanged. He also studied interference phenomena, and the coloured rings on soap bubbles.

Stephen Hawking concluded *A brief history of time* with personal sketches of great physicists. Einstein is a hero, Galileo is a 'goodie', and Newton is a 'baddie'. With all the deference which is due to the man acclaimed as the greatest mathematical physicist to occupy the Lucasian Chair since Newton himself, this view seems naïve. Certainly Newton was a secretive, eccentric loner. He regretted ever sending his note on *Optics* and wrote 'I was so per-secuted with discussions arising out of my theory of light that I blamed my own imprudence for parting with so substantial a blessing as my quiet to run after a shadow.' He was then only thirty-three. In his middle age, with most of his great achievements in the past, his fame blossomed. He became a forgettable member of Parliament for the University. Newton first became involved in politics when he sought to prevent James II of England from admitting a Benedictine monk as a Master of Arts of the University. The Stuarts seem to have been plagued by the anti-papist sentiments of great mathematicians. The king's grandfather, when James VI of Scotland, had been vigorously exhorted by Napier (Chapter 3) to cleanse his family, household, and court of Catholic sympathies.

For the last 24 years of his long life Newton was re-elected annually President of the Royal Society. During these years he engaged in acrimonious argument over who invented what. In the case of Hooke, one might have some sympathy with Newton; but his treatment of Leibniz was disgraceful. The German philosopher invented the calculus[16] quite indepen-dently of Newton. It was not his fault if Newton failed to publish promptly; but at this stage Newton was mentally ill. There were no psychiatrists in the seventeenth century; but even by the standards of the time, Newton's 'phrenitis' at one stage of his middle age was such that (according to Huygens) his friends were keeping him shut up. A little later Newton became first Warden, then Master, of the Mint. He was knighted by Queen Anne and buried in Westminster Abbey.

Newton devoted much of his time to secret experiments in alchemy; but it was not apparent at the time that the transmutation of base metals is not a viable object of chemistry; nor is it astounding that in later life Newton valued his studies in theology and mysticism more than his scientific work. The modest confines he ascribed to the empire of physics have already been noted. About a million words of private papers survived; but for more than a century they were suppressed to protect Newton's name. He was a closet heretic of the Arian persuasion.[17] He was also fascinated by pre-Christian mysticism and apocalyptic literature. By such means the man who publicly declared 'hypotheses non fingo' ('I do not speculate') sought to pry into the mind of God.

Lord (John Maynard) Keynes, who studied many of these papers, called Newton 'the last of the magicians, the last of the Babylonians and the Sumerians'. In an essay in praise of the balance of ordinariness, Aldous Huxley wrote of Newton 'As a man he was a failure, as a monster superb.' The Westminster Abbey inscription reads 'Let mortals rejoice that such and so great an ornament of the human race has existed.' Gauss was less loquacious. To the 'Prince of Mathematicians' Newton alone was simply *Summus*, the top.

The three towering figures sketched herein were not alone. New ideas blossomed like flowers in the desert after rain throughout the seventeenth century. Mathematics without Descartes would be a structure missing a main spar. Some of the work of the men associated with *L'Académie des Sciences* is the subject of other chapters. Eleven years before *Principia* the Danish astronomer Roemer proved that light has a finite velocity by relating the difference between the observed and the computed times of immersion of Jupiter's moons to the earth's distance from Jupiter. His value for the speed of light was only 25 per cent in error—an astonishing achievement considering the state of dynamics at the time, the accuracy of measurement, and the quality of contemporary ephemerides. All these achievements reflect a major cultural change in the seventeenth century—the beginning of the Age of Reason. That is why Galileo the publicist is so important and the silent Hariot is not. Scientists did not proliferate until the scientific idea soaked into European culture.

The emergence of dynamics led, in subsequent centuries, directly to the perfection of astronomical navigation and tidal prediction; to inertial navigation systems; to thermo-dynamics and thus to steam, internal combustion, and jet engines; to meteorology; to aerody-namics and the aeroplane. Less obviously it led to electromagnetism, and thus to radio and electronics generally. Only two hundred years after Newton died, aeroplanes were navigated by radio.

Magnetism and electricity were late developers compared with dynamics. Nature does not provide electricity in a form suitable for study of its properties; but magnetic force has been palpable for millennia. Speculation on its nature was wild. To Gilbert[18] it was an *effluvium*, to Descartes *vortices*, to Coulomb a *fluid*. H. T. Pledge thoughtfully observed:[19]

> *In these subjects, theories exact enough for mathematical development only came a hundred years later than in the case of gravity, a sound reflection of the relative complexities of the cases. To understand early difficulties, we must remember the lack of the vital distinction of charge (or in magnetism, pole) and field, a distinction which exists already drawn in the case of gravitation.*

One must add that the great achievements of the seventeenth century in dynamics and astronomy were based on observations using simple measuring instruments, whereas observa-tions of magnetic and electrical phenomena require more advanced apparatus. Even the elementary fact that magnetic and electrical forces vary, like gravity, as the inverse square of the distance had to wait for the delicate torsion balance[20] in the eighteenth century.

Nevertheless electricity did not escape the explosion of science in the seventeenth century. In 1663 Otto von Guericke produced the first continuous electrical generator by holding his hand against a rotating ball of sulphur. The fact that certain materials could be charged by rubbing one against the other had been known at the beginning of Greek science. Significantly it was only in the age of Newton that anyone made a machine to do it. Such simple toys led Stephen Gray to the observation in 1729 that materials which would not take an electric charge themselves, notably metals, could conduct it large distances, apparently in an instant, which suggested to the mind of Charles du Fay the notions of *conductor*, *insulator*, and *current*. Charged objects either repel or attract each other. Were there two kinds of current? Franklin suggested that there was only one kind of current, and that the two kinds of charge arose from either an excess or a deficiency of whatever it was that flowed.

As early as 1752 Leonhard Euler had envisaged light, electricity, magnetism, and gravity as disturbances in a ubiquitous ether, all propagated at the same velocity. Such philosophizing was prerequisite to radio and the future of navigation; but the experiments necessary to develop the notions of that great mathematician were impossible without a supply of electric current. In 1786 a physiologist named Luigi Galvani noticed that some muscle and nerve tissue from frogs' legs impaled on a copper hook twitched when the hook was hung on an iron rod. A unique contribution of physiology to physics. While Galvani worked on the physiological implications, a physicist friend, Alessandro Volta, concentrated on what was happening between the metals. His researches led to the first electric battery, the voltaic pile, described in the Transactions of the Royal Society in 1800. The electromotive force (EMF) and the capacity were both tiny; but development was so fast that in 1812 Sir Humphrey Davy had a battery with two hundred porcelain cells, a total plate area of nearly 1000 square feet, immersed in a very dilute solution of sulphuric and nitric acid. It has been calculated that the EMF was about 200 volts, and the reports of Davy's demonstrations leave no doubt that it was capable of delivering large currents, at least for a short period. The dyke had been breached, and nineteenth century physics flowed in.

In 1819 Oersted in Copenhagen showed that an electric current flowing through a straight wire deflected a magnetic needle. It made no apparent difference if glass were interposed. Maximum deflection occurred when the needle and the wire lay parallel. Two years later young Michael Faraday showed that the magnetic field (as we would now say) around a straight wire conductor is cylindrical with the wire as axis. These discoveries were formalized in 1823, when Ampère showed that identical magnetic fields are produced by a magnetic shell of any size and shape and an electric current flowing through a circuit of the same size and shape.

Faraday has been described [21] as 'possibly the greatest experimental genius the world has known'. The son of a blacksmith, he was apprenticed to a bookseller at the age of fourteen, and read his master's wares to such effect that Davy engaged him as an assistant. Sadly, that moderately great scientist seems to have become jealous of his hired help. As President of the Royal Society he unsuccessfully sought to prevent the election of Faraday to Fellowship. In 1825 Faraday became Director of the laboratory of the Royal Institution, where he had earlier worked as Davy's assistant. In 1831 he showed that when a current flowing through a circuit changes, a current is momentarily induced across empty space in a secondary circuit —a sensational result. He even used it to magnetize a needle by placing the needle in a solenoid in the secondary. In subsequent experiments he showed that, more generally, an EMF is induced in a circuit when the magnetic flux linked through it changes. He produced continuous current in a copper disc by rotating it in a magnetic field—the first dynamo.

In 1845 Faraday showed that a magnetic field may rotate the plane of polarization of light, demonstrating, in his own words, that 'all natural forces are tied together and have one common origin'. There were other portents. In 1822 Fresnel pointed out that physical quali- ties have dimensions which can be reduced to powers of mass (m), distance (s), and time (t) —the basis of our cgs (centimetre gram second) system. Thus the dimensions of velocity are st^{-1}, of force mst^{-2}, and so on. Extending the notion to units of electricity and magnetism, there are two possible systems. We can arrive at our unit of electricity in cgs units in terms of unit electrostatic force at unit distance, or in terms of the current required to produce unit magnetic force at unit distance. The ratio of the two systems has the dimensions of velocity. In 1848 Kirchoff noticed that its value was the speed of light, within the limits of experimental error at the time.

It had been Robert Hooke, that fount of brilliant ideas not followed through, who had first proposed a wave theory of light, and Christiaan Huygens who had developed the idea. Huygens explained refraction by a construction of wavelets at the surface, a device which was later used to find the minimum time-path of trans-Atlantic aeroplanes. Newton demurred, among other reasons because seventeenth-century wave theory did not explain why light cannot travel around corners like sound. There is a more formidable difficulty. A wave of what in what? Particles can travel through empty space but a wave of nothing is nothing. Newton's distaste for action at a distance has already been noted. Neither man made a clear distinction between longitudinal and transverse waves; and Huygens did not make the distinction between pulses and continuous waves. A corpuscular theory evolved, based on Newton's reservations and claiming his authority. In the eighteenth century little progress was made, and new discoveries such as aberration (Chapter 6) seemed to favour a corpuscular theory.

So often in the history of science there is a happy contemporaneity of events. While Faraday, Ampère, and others were making such discoveries in magnetism and electricity, there was a renaissance of the wave theory of light in the hands of Thomas Young, Augustin Fresnel, and others. Young explained Newton's interference rings in terms of continuous waves instead of Huygens pulses. In a classic experiment he showed that if light from a remote source passed through two very small pinholes in a screen, a pattern of coloured bands was projected on to a parallel screen if the light was white, and a pattern of light and shade if the light was monochromatic. He showed how wave theory explained the phenomenon, and estimated the wavelength to be in the region of half a millionth of a metre. Malus, Brewster, and others explored the polarization of light. Fresnel, developing mathematical theory, explained diffraction, aberration, and double refraction. At this stage the wave was still longitudinal. Then Fresnel discovered that light beams polarized in different planes could not be made to interfere with each other. Young realized the implication that the waves must be transverse, not longitudinal. The wave-theory explanation of refraction required that the velocity of light in water should be less than in air. Corpuscular theory required the opposite. Foucault showed that in fact the velocity is less in water. The stage was being set for the greatest synthesis since *Principia*. The mathematicians from Euler onwards, notably Lagrange, had already provided the basic tools for the job.

Faraday had conceived the idea of lines (or rather tubes) of force in magnetic and electric fields as lines of elastic strain in the ether. The more difficult perception that the magnetic field consists of moving lines of electric force, of changes of electric strain in the ether, is suggested by the notion that the magnetic field caused by current in a wire is due to the *motion* of the electric particles which are the cause of electrostatic phenomena. The self-taught Faraday was not a mathematician. James Clerk Maxwell was a brilliant one. Like Kepler, he was the first of something and the last of something else. It might be said that his work was a most elegant product of the old classical physics which Galileo envisaged and Newton forged; it might be described as the beginning of the new mathematical physics, the abstract reasoning of which cannot be expressed in any non-mathematical language and the conclusions of which cannot be described in images which we can visualize.

Maxwell's system is formulated in two famous symmetrical equations, one of which describes the nature of electric and magnetic fields, the other their relationship. In physical terms they imply a pervasive ether, filling all space, vibrating with transverse waves of electric and magnetic force. Maxwell certainly did not discover radio; but it is clear to us that he implied it, and he himself believed that light was only a small part of the spectrum. If Maxwell's field equations are valid statements about nature, radio is out there somewhere. This was not the issue at the time. The field equations were consistent with everything which was known about electric and magnetic fields and light; but they were silent on some electrical phenomena such as electrolysis.

The great issue was whether light is electromagnetic radiation. The fact that a magnetic field rotated the plane of polarization of light suggested that it was; but light had no detectable magnetic field or pressure. Maxwell's theory was consistent with the wave theory of light as it had evolved. Maxwell's compelling argument was that his theory required the velocity of wave propagation in empty space to equal 'the number of electrostatic units in one electromagnetic unit' (his phrase). This had been determined experimentally by Weber and Kohlrausch as 310 740 km/sec, compared with:

speed of light in air according to Fizeau	314 858 km/sec.
speed of light in air according to Foucault	298 000 km/sec.
speed of light deduced from aberration[22]	308 000 km/sec.

Maxwell had no doubt. As he put it in 1864: 'The agreement of the results seems to show that light and magnetism are affections of the same substance and that light is an electromagnetic disturbance propagated through the field according to electromagnetic laws.'

Although Maxwell's theory was communicated through papers published by the Royal Society in 1864, the final elaborated structure appeared in 1873 in his *Treatise on electricity and magnetism*, which James Newman described as 'one of the most splendid monuments ever raised by the genius of a single individual'. Maxwell seems to have made no attempt to verify his theory by experiment; but any impression of Maxwell the mathematician perfectly complementing the experimental genius of Faraday is not consistent either with the fact that when *Treatise* appeared Maxwell was Professor of *Experimental* Physics at Cambridge, or with Maxwell's previous record as an experimenter.

There was no frenetic rush in the laboratories to be the first to create a radio wave; in fact the ideas of Maxwell were only slowly assimilated on the Continent. Many able experimental physicists of the period would have had difficulty with the mathematics. No known material vibrated with transverse waves. The palpitating ether does not appeal to the fastidious; and

Newton would have been among them. There are no fixed points in Newtonian space. It is a funny old universe in which radiation has a fixed frame of reference and matter does not. Besides, as with Einstein in the twentieth century, many phenomena which confirmed Maxwell's theory were not discovered until later. The value of the pressure of light on matter which the theory predicted was not confirmed experimentally until 1899.

Hermann von Helmholtz, professor of physics at Berlin, was one who understood Maxwell without endorsing his theory. He suggested a line of research to his former pupil Heinrich Hertz, professor of physics at the Karlsruhe Polytechnic. The experiments of Hertz in 1886–8, realized with the simple device illustrated in Fig. 4.2, led to the greatest transformation of navigation in its history. The oscillator was electrically resonant at about 75 megacycles per second, corresponding to a wavelength of 4 metres, in the region of 10 000 000 times the wavelength of visible light. The receiver was simply a loop of wire with a spark gap. These experiments convinced the scientific world of the reality of electromagnetic radiation predicted by Maxwell. Radio began—but this is to anticipate other chapters.

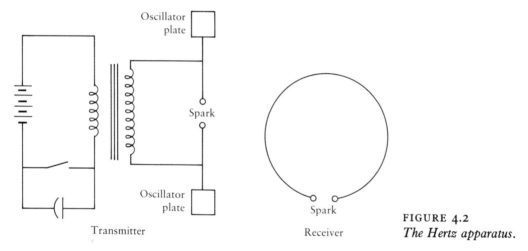

FIGURE 4.2

The Hertz apparatus.

Yet it seems Hertz was not the first to produce radio waves. David E. Hughes was a curiously premature figure in the transition from theoretical physics to radio engineering. Hughes was born in London in 1831, the year that Faraday discovered induction in that city. At the age of twenty-four he invented a type-printing telegraph instrument which was immediately successful and continued in use in some telegraphic circuits until the 1930s. Hughes was also acclaimed for his many other contributions to telephony and telegraphy. In 1879 (a decade before the famous Hertz experiments) he demonstrated to scientists that it was possible to transmit signals through solid walls without the use of a connecting wire. He walked about Great Portland Street London W1 with a telephone ear-piece hearing signals from a transmitter hundreds of metres away. Apparently he accepted the verdict of distinguished Fellows of the Royal Society that it was just a case of Faraday induction. There is some justification for the comment in the *Globe* newspaper twenty years later:[23] 'Hughes' experiments of 1879 were virtually a discovery of Hertzian waves before Hertz, of the coherer before Branley and of wireless telegraphy before Marconi.' The key word is *virtually*. It is most unlikely that Hughes himself could follow Maxwell's abstruse and highly mathematical theory of electromagnetic radiation which his own experiments verified, or see their profound significance. Sadly, as Maxwell died in 1879, he was unable to seize on the strange results of Hughes himself.

There was a rhyme which went, with apologies to its unknown author,

> *Nature and Nature's laws lay hid in night:*
> *God said 'Let Newton be', and all was light.*
> *It did not last. The Devil's cry of 'Ho,*
> *Let Einstein be' restored the status quo.*

Nothing could be further from the truth. The villain, if villain there be, was an American physicist, Albert Michelson. While Hertz was inventing radio, he and a colleague, Edward Morley, were comparing the velocity of light from different directions in space. The experiment was conducted many times, and there could be no doubt. The velocity of light relative to the observer is always the same. The Inquisition would have expected this result—naturally the ether is stationary relative to the earth; but, if Galileo was right, we are hurtling towards some star in the plane of the ecliptic at a thousand miles a minute. Six months ago we were hurtling away from it at the same speed. How can light from the star have the same speed relative to us on both occasions? The work of Christian Doppler and Armand Fizeau in the 1840s had explained the perceived shift of the spectrum of starlight in terms of the star's relative velocity in the line of sight (the Doppler effect of Chapter 12). Every star has a definite velocity through the ether; but the observer's is always zero. Even if we discard the ether and Maxwell and all his work, the Doppler effect and the Michelson–Morley result seem incompatible.

Imagine Bob and Tom to be flying in opposite directions each at 500 knots. By agreement, when they are 100 n.m. apart Tom flashes a signal to Bob. The signal travels at the speed of light relative to Bob, according to Bob, and to Tom, according to Tom. How long does it take to get there? Tom will calculate a later time of arrival than Bob. Bob's watch will show his calculations are right. If the arrival of the signal triggers an immediate response, Tom will find that the response arrives precisely in accord with his own calculation. Just when Hertz vindicated Maxwell's theory, Michelson made the physical model associated with it seem untenable.

The Dutch scientist Lorentz came to the rescue, writing equations which were consistent with both Maxwellian theory and the Michelson–Morley result. One feature was that the length of anything moving in the ether contracted in the direction of motion, including our yardsticks on which any measurement of velocity must depend.[24] This was sufficient to explain the Michelson–Morley result.

Throughout the story which this book relates there is a time for things to happen and a confluence of events which brings them about: global navigation in the context of the Renaissance of western Europe; in the seventeenth century the dynamics of Galileo, the astronomy of Kepler, and the calculus converging in Newton's great synthesis; in the early nineteenth century developments in optics, contemporary with experiments in electromagnetism which the invention of the electric battery made possible, leading to the great synthesis of Maxwell; in the early twentieth century the simultaneous appearance of the aeroplane and of radio, which provided the means of navigating it. So, in its turn, relativity was heralded by nineteenth-century developments in pure mathematics. Previously, geometry had been both mathematics and physics, a (faulted) exercise in logic and a statement of fact about the universe we inhabit. During the nineteenth century, in the hands of Georg Riemann and others, geometry became an exercise in pure reason in which space could have any number of dimensions and there could be different kinds of space-time.[25]

One of the others was William Clifford. Forty years before Einstein propounded the *General* Theory of Relativity in 1916, young Clifford (he was only thirty-four when he died) presaged it in a short contribution to the Cambridge Philosophical Society. Clifford was not, like Einstein, a scientist seeking to understand evidence or save phenomena—there was nothing to understand or to save at the time. He was an abstract reasoner speculating on possible reality. Then there was Georg Cantor's work on the Theory of Sets in the early 1870s which seemed to imply that some infinities are more infinite than others. There was a critical reappraisal of the logical foundations of mathematics and of logic itself. In the apt phrase of the Viennese mathematician Hans Hahn 'the crisis in intuition' was in the air. The clear implication was that our most fundamental perceptions of the world outside our own minds, including our perception of space and time, may be invalid. It was a matter for science, not mathematics, to determine what kind of space-time we in fact live in. At the same time mathematicians were crafting the tools for the job—not least the tensor calculus.

Albert Einstein, a German Jew working as a patent clerk in Zurich, saw that our intuitive perception of space (formalized in Euclidean geometry) and of time (implicit in the dynamics of Galileo and Newton) may be at the root of the paradox of the Michelson–Morley result. This was the question which Einstein addressed in his *Special* Theory of Relativity (1905). As Minkowski, the great exegete of relativity, put it 'Space in itself, and Time in itself sink into shadows and only a kind of union of the two exists.' What we perceive as reality is merely a three-dimensional perspective of a reality of more dimensions. The aeroplane pilots Tom and Bob had necessarily different perspectives; and it all depends on your point of view. Mankind was given a new vision of the universe, and the phenomena were saved.

Meanwhile another crack appeared in the structure of what we may now call classical physics. In 1900 Planck announced that some aspects of black-body radiation could only be explained on the basis that radiation is emitted in tiny but discrete lumps equal in size to the frequency of the radiation times a universal constant. Frequency is characteristic of a wave, quantum of a particle. Can radiation be both after all? This time the phenomena were saved by Quantum Theory. As we approach the first centenary of these saviours of the phenomena, some phenomena are considered to be saved by Relativity Theory, and some by Quantum Theory: but there is no sense in which they can both be true in their present form. So much for Kepler's belief that phenomena cannot be saved by false causes! One modern writer[26] on the philosophical implications of Quantum Theory roundly declares 'We are now certain that the world is not a deterministic mechanism, but what it is we cannot say.' The word *certain* jars; but for the moment the Inquisition is winning the great but unspoken debate of 1633.

Old ideas continue to serve navigation long after pure science has left them behind. In astronomical navigation the celestial sphere still rotates around the immutable earth. The dynamics of Newton still serve to calculate the ephemerides. Clark Maxwell's theory is adequate for the most refined radio engineering at normal radio frequencies. It is the ring laser gyro (Chapter 9) and other applications of higher frequencies to navigation that have brought it within the realm of quantum theory. Relativity entered navigation with high-precision fixing by satellite (Chapter 12).

In recent decades the digital computer has come from nothing to become the heart of any sophisticated navigation system. The ability to perform in seconds the calculations on which Kepler spent a lifetime is more than mere labour-saving; together with the ability to process and store (with ready access) vast quantities of data in a small space, it has led to a totally new approach to the solution of practical problems by complex algorithms instead of by the heuristic process we call judgement. This new way of thought about navigation is the subject of Chapter 14.

Although the computer revolution is a late-twentieth-century phenomenon, the essential idea that large arrays of simple yes/no (or $+/-$ or 1/0) devices can control complex processes and perform complex calculations goes back to the beginning of the nineteenth century. In the Jacquard loom, exhibited in 1801 by Joseph-Marie Jacquard, the needles move through holes in a block of wood. A perforated card is inserted which only allows through those needles in a position corresponding to a perforation on the card. Thus each pattern of perforations corresponds to a quite different pattern of finished cloth. At the time, this was perceived only as another step in the mechanization of the textile industry. In retrospect the Jacquard loom is only a special case of the punched card, which was successfully applied so much later to mechanical data-processing.

An intermediate step was the 'analytical engine' of Charles Babbage, in which the amount to be operated upon and the nature of the operation were to be entered by perforated cards, a principle he invented in 1834 but never realized as a working machine. Earlier, Babbage had a machine which would tabulate to eight decimals any function of which the second order difference was constant. He embarked on much more ambitious machines with promises of government funds which were not renewed. Babbage was an honoured English mathematician of his day, Lucasian professor of mathematics at Cambridge. His designs required a precision of manufacture which may have been beyond the engineering of his time.

Babbage has been described as the father of computers; that title might equally be applied to George Boole, a younger contemporary whose concern was not with calculating machinery. His work on symbolic logic[27] in the mid-nineteenth century led to the notion that logic is mathematics limited to the numbers 0 and 1. Boole developed a powerful algebra of logic with rules different to those of ordinary algebra. We can check, for example, that $(A+B)\times(A+C) = A+(B\times C)$, where A,B,C, are proposition, $A+B$ means either A or B but not both, and '×' means 'and', by considering the sentence: the statements 'a parent is male or female' and 'a parent is male or mother' are equivalent to the statement a parent is male or (female and mother)'. In 1938 C. E. Shannon pointed out in the *Transactions* of the American Institute of Electrical Engineers the application of Boole's calculus to the design of telephone switching circuits, which were becoming very complicated by the standards of the time. The rules of Boolean algebra apply if '+' means in parallel, '×' means in series, and A,B,C, etc. mean the actuation of relays. The application of the rule $(A+B)\times(A+C) = A+(B\times C)$ is illustrated in Fig. 4.3. The '=' sign in this application conveys the meaning that actuation of any combination of relays has the same effect in both circuits. Complex circuits could be stated algebraically without being drawn, and a large number of circuits to perform a desired function could be derived quickly. However, Boole's calculus is not a calculus of variations (Chapter 13), and provides no direct means of finding the circuit of least components.

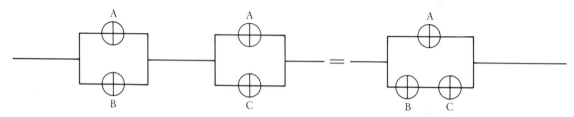

FIGURE 4.3
Current flows in both circuits only if either relay A or both relays B and C are activated.

The binary system of counting in yes/no terms, as if we had only two fingers—0,1,10,11,100,101,110, etc., had long been known. Boole had shown how arithmetic could be described in terms of logic, and how his calculus could be applied to arithmetical operations. In 1938 it was a short step from the perception of the analogy between logic and telephone circuits (accompanied by the misappropriation of the word *logic* by electrical engineers) to the realization that relay circuits could be digital computers were they not so slow. The software of the digital computer as we know it derives from Boolean algebra. The hardware derives from electronic components originally developed to meet the needs of radio, and to that extent is discussed briefly at the end of Chapter 10.

Notes to Chapter 4

1. Principally low-speed aerodynamics and very light-weight synthetic materials with the required properties.
2. In 1959 Henry Kremer offered a prize for the first man-powered flight over a one-mile figure-of-eight course. It was won in 1977. The first moon walk was in 1969.
3. Whitehead (1925).
4. E. P. Wigner, Nobel prizewinner.

5. Published many years later in the Royal Society of London's *Philosophical Transactions*, **19**, 445–57 (March 1697).
6. Simon Stevin of Bruges demonstrated the point in 1590.
7. In fact the simple pendulum is only isochronous for small swings (Chapter 6).
8. The telescope has been attributed to spectacle-makers Lippershey and Jannsen of Middelburg, and also to James Metius (brother of the mathematician of that name) of Alkmaar. It has been suggested that the reflector telescope, usually attributed to Newton, was invented by Leonard and Thomas Digges (father and son) a century earlier, and thirty years before the invention of the Dutch instrument. Publication of the device could have been suppressed for military reasons. Both the Digges were noted theorists of navigation in Elizabethan England.
9. The foundations of Christian geocentric dogma at the time relied on such fragments of Holy Scripture as Joshua 10:13 ('and the sun stood still . . . and hasted not to go down about a whole day') and Psalm 104:5 ('who laid the foundation of the earth, that it should not be removed for ever'). The authority of Ptolemy at the time (Chapter 1) gave some intellectual weight.
10. *De revolutionibus orbium coelestium* was published in 1543, shortly before its author's death. The first complete English translation was published in Chicago in 1952. Koestler (1959) slyly lists some distinguished historians of astronomy, including the author of a Copernicus Memorial Address to the Royal Astronomical Society, who were apparently unaware of the true contents of *De revolutionibus*.
11. Balthasar Capra had the misfortune to point out mathematical errors in Galileo's explanation of a device called a 'compasso geometrico e militare'. Galileo responded with a pamphlet describing poor Capra as 'a greedy vulture swooping at the young to tear their tender limbs to pieces', 'a malevolent enemy of mankind', etc., etc. (Koestler 1959).
12. In *Il dialogo* (1632).
13. The issue at the trial was not the validity of world systems or their relation with Christian doctrine. It was not even whether *Il dialogo* defended the Copernican system. It was whether or not Galileo personally had been forbidden from teaching the system *in any way whatsoever* seventeen years earlier. The evidence that he had, which is still in the Vatican files, is considered to be a forgery. In fact Cardinal Bellarmine, the leading Roman theologian of his day, had written to Galileo on 26 May 1616 that the opinion that the earth moves around the sun is contrary to Holy Scripture and could be neither held nor defended; but it could be discussed as a hypothesis. Perhaps the object was merely the public humiliation of a man who was manifestly too big for his boots. He was sentenced to recite penitential psalms once a week for three years but allowed to pass this dreadful duty to his daughter. His 'imprisonment' was as the honoured guest of his patron and supporter, the Grand Duke of Tuscany.
14. 'It was granted to me alone to discover all the new phenomena in the sky and nothing to anyone else.' The words are Galileo's (Koestler 1959).
15. The achromatic lens came later.
16. It is to Leibniz that we owe the notation dy/dx. Newton wrote $\dot{x}$ for dx/dt and Fermat $f'(x)$ for dy/dx. After three centuries we still use all these notations.
17. Newton's successor in the Lucasian Chair, William Whiston, was hounded from the University because of his Arian (Unitarian) professions in 1710. Apparently unabashed, Whiston played an important part in the activity leading to the Longitude Act of 1714 (Chapter 5).
18. William Gilbert, physician to Elizabeth I of England, published *De magnete* in 1600. He made a globe of lodestone and used it to demonstrate his theory that the behaviour of the compass needle and the phenomenon of dip (noticed by Robert Norman, navigator, in 1576) were caused by the magnetism of the earth itself, an idea familiar to Mercator much earlier (see Chapter 8).
19. Pledge (1939).

20. Coulomb's Law, enunciated in 1785, states that force varies as the product of the charges and inversely as the square of their distance apart. He invented the torsion balance in 1777. Coulomb was preceded in the matter of the balance by Michell; in the law he was anticipated by Cavendish.
21. By Professor E. N. da Costa Andrade.
22. Aberration is explained in Chapter 6. As maximum aberration is so slight, the accuracy is impressive. Maxwell presumably quoted it because it was the only indication of the speed of light in empty space—the other results were in the atmosphere. The modern value, determined from measurements of both light and radio waves, is 299 792 km/sec.
23. Quoted in Clarricoats (1967).
24. Suggested independently by Fitzgerald, hence 'The Fitzgerald contraction'.
25. A vivid if incomplete analogy which was in the air concerned the citizens of flatland, whose two-dimensional universe included north–south and east–west but not up–down. Their perception of the universe would be a Euclidean plane in which straight lines went on for ever. Their Riemann might develop equations which describe a sphere perfectly; but he could not imagine what one looked like. Their Einstein might show that in fact the equations which describe their space correspond to the equations of the surface of a sphere, a space unbounded but limited so that straight lines were really great circles. Continuous contraction or expansion of their sphere would not be measurable, because the measuring rods would contract or expand too. The radius of their sphere, the third dimension of a two-dimensional space, would be time.
26. Herbert (1985).
27. *Mathematical analysis of logic* (1847) and *An investigation of the laws of thought on which are founded the mathematical theories of logic and probabilities* (1854).

CHAPTER FIVE

A Political History of the Longitude

✠

OSCAR Wilde once argued that nature imitates art. Certainly history occasionally emulates a romantic novelette. In 1469, when Prince Ferdinand of the minor kingdom of Aragon, eighteen years old, eloped with his cousin Isabella, the beautiful nineteen-year-old sister of the king of Castile, all the elements of romance were there: the impecunious youth galloping in disguise through hostile country, his life in constant danger, and even borrowing money to pay for the wedding.

There is a different view of the episode. It was Ferdinand's first step in the elimination of Islamic governance in western Europe, the unification of Spain under Ferdinand and Isabella, the creation of an important new European state, the discovery of America, the creation of a great empire there, and the first major impetus to navigational science. When Ferdinand died, nearly half a century after his elopement with Isabella, he was king of all modern Spain, Sardinia, Sicily, and southern Italy, and of the beginnings of a rich empire across the ocean. As Machiavelli put it, 'he has risen, by fame and glory, from being an insignificant king to be the foremost king in Christendom; and if you will consider his deeds you will find them all great and some of them extraordinary.' Ferdinand was a Machiavellian archetype.

There were obstacles. At two critical moments an unlikely gentleman of Aragonese origin saved the day for Ferdinand. Rodrigo Borgia became archbishop of Valencia and a cardinal by nepotism in the strict sense. He became Pope Alexander VI by his own courage and skill. Francesco Guicciardini, the great sixteenth-century historian (a Florentine as usual) thundered against Rodrigo 'As his accession to the papacy was foul and shameful—for he bought with gold so high an office—so similarly his government was in agreement with its vile foundations.' These words are still re-echoed in the twentieth century. It is not fair. Simony was normal management technique in the fifteenth-century church, and the cardinals who took his gold were Italians.[1] Alexander's use of murder as an instrument of ecclesiastical politics has been greatly exaggerated by his enemies, and his incest with his daughter Lucrezia has never been proven. A pope who forbids his mistress to make love to her husband on pain of excommunication is undeniably eccentric; but his great and conscious influence on the course of history has been largely ignored. He was the man who started the Great Pursuit of the Longitude. He was also great-grandfather to a saint,[2] an unusual distinction for a pope.

Ferdinand's first problem was that his marriage to Isabella was no marriage because the necessary papal dispensation he had shown to Isabella and the officiating priest was a forgery. His second problem was that the heiress to the kingdom of Castile was not the King's sister but Joan, the daughter of the king. Any claim on behalf of Isabella could only be based on the veracity of the king's sad appellation, 'Henry the Impotent'. Such a claim would be (and was) energetically denied by all the might of Portugal whose king, Afonso V, was Joan's husband.

In Rome in 1473 Pope Sixtus IV and his vice-chancellor, Rodrigo Borgia, understood the Iberian situation perfectly. Rodrigo Borgia went to Spain with a secret dispensation valid retroactively and with powers to give it to Ferdinand or silently to destroy it as he judged fit. Rodrigo decided for Ferdinand and gave him the dispensation. By skilful diplomacy and advocacy, Rodrigo achieved a brilliant reconciliation of the king of Castile with his sister and an acceptance of her by the Castilian court.[3] Henry died shortly afterwards. When Ferdinand's father died, Ferdinand and Isabella ruled jointly as the 'Catholic Sovereigns' of Castile and Aragon, despite Portugal. Muslim Granada was conquered in 1492, and Navarre south of the Pyrenees was absorbed in 1512.

Although the existence of Atlantic islands to the west of north Africa had long been known,[4] European powers did not seek to claim dominion over them before the fifteenth century. The Azores were settled by the Portuguese from about 1432. In 1479 it was agreed that the Canaries were Castilian and Madeira was Portuguese. Only the Portuguese explored the Atlantic coast of Africa south of the Spanish Canaries and the Moorish Sultanate of present day Morocco (Chapter 1). In 1481 Pope Sixtus IV published a bull of demarcation *Aeterni regis* which gave Portugal dominion 'over whatever lands are discovered or gained from *beyond* [south of] the Canaries'. This was a concession to the only bidders, and a practical one because latitude could be measured. It was a matter of ascertainable fact whether a place was south of the Canaries.

On his first voyage Columbus set course due west from one of the most southerly harbours in the Canaries and subsequently tended south of west. In fact, all the Caribbean islands he cruised were south of the Canaries and—in any sense of the word—*beyond* the Canaries. As was mentioned in Chapter 2, Columbus did not know how to determine the latitude properly, and it appears from his *Journal* that all his latitude determinations were much too high; but it is clear from the *Journal* that he thought the demarcation only applied to Africa. On his return he was forced by bad weather to seek shelter with the Portuguese, first in the Azores and then in the Tagus. On 4 March 1493, when he anchored off Lisbon, he noted in his diary that he wrote at once to the king of Portugal so that the king might know he did not come from Guinea but from the Indies. He boasted freely of his voyage. On 9 March

Columbus was received in audience by King John II, and noted in his diary 'The king said that according to the capitulation which had been made between the sovereigns that conquest belonged to him. To this the Admiral replied that he knew nothing of these things save that the Catholic Sovereigns had commanded that he should not go to La Mina (a Portuguese colony in Africa) or any part of the Guinea.'[5]

By international law in the Christian world King John was right. Providentially, Rodrigo Borgia had become Pope Alexander VI the previous August. The news of Columbus can scarcely have reached Rome before April. On 3 May Alexander (as we must now call him) dashed off a new bull of demarcation, *Inter caetera*, giving the Sovereigns of Castile and their successors title to all the lands *towards the Indies* discovered or to be discovered by their servants provided such lands had never been in the possession of a Christian prince. Ferdinand and Isabella presumably understood the provisions of *Aeterni regis*; but on 4 March they were far away in Barcelona. Their envoys did not reach Rome until 25 May. The result was a new version of *Inter caetera*. The story is that Alexander called for a map of the world and, with his finger, drew a north–south line from pole to pole through a point which was one hundred leagues west of the Azores. All to the west of it was Spanish, all to the east of it Portuguese, excepting of course all lands already under the dominion of another Christian prince. Alexander was exquisitely Delphic. There was no way anyone could say where the meridian was. The anti-meridian, the other half of the boundary, was a matter beyond the wildest speculation.

The Portuguese accepted that the demarcation line should be a meridian but, having the stronger navy, negotiated in 1494 a shift of the meridian to that which is 370 leagues west of the Cape Verde Islands (The Treaty of Tordesillas). There were hilarious provisions for the determination of the meridian by joint teams of savants and seamen; but it was recognized by an exchange of notes in 1495 that it could not be done. His Most Catholic Majesty Henry VII of England saw no difficulty in giving his patent to John Cabot, who planted the English flag in what is now Canada in 1497. As a practical matter, the Portuguese took Brazil, the Spaniards the rest of South and Central America; but, in North America, the English, and later the French and the Dutch, ignored *Inter caetera*.

When Magellan crossed the South Pacific in 1521 (Chapter one), he must have crossed the anti-meridian somewhere; but no one could say where to the nearest thousand miles.[6] In particular the kings of Spain and Portugal had no means of ascertaining which of them, under the terms of the treaty their predecessors had made in 1494, had title to the Spice Islands, the attainment of which had been the original motive for exploration. Portugal had reached the Spice Islands going east in 1511. Magellan had sailed north of the islands going west in 1521.

The king of Spain had originally sent Magellan west to the Spice Islands on the advice that under the terms of the Treaty of Tordesillas the islands were in the Spanish hemisphere. After the *Victoria* circumnavigated the globe (Chapter one), the king initiated an inquiry in which Fernando Columbus, Sebastian Cabot, and Amerigo Vespucci participated. It was concluded that the Spice Islands were 50° within the Spanish hemisphere, an error of a little more than 50°. The more the Portuguese had tried to push the Tordesillas line west to get Brazil, the closer they pushed the boundary on the other side of the world towards the Spice Islands (the Moluccas), which lie just within the Portuguese hemisphere. It did not matter: long before the technology to settle such matters existed, the Dutch had driven the rest of the Europeans out of the islands.

The first problem in finding the longitude astronomically is time measurement. Even if one has the astronomical data, the skills, and the instruments, to determine where one's meridian lies in the firmament at some moment, one cannot relate it to one's meridian on the rotating earth unless one knows where some standard meridian has rotated to in the firmament. The meridians are rotating faster than the speed of sound at the latitudes Columbus sailed. In 1500 the likely error of the best clocks on land was about 10 minutes a day. After a few weeks at sea, clock error could correspond to a longitude error as wide as the ocean.

The longitude lost its significance as a confine of empire; but a hundred years later, the commercial, economic, and military consequences of transatlantic navigation without knowing the longitude—of not knowing where exactly places were in the New World—seemed intolerable. In 1598 Philip III of Spain offered lavish prizes for the discovery of the longitude. During the next fifty years further prizes were offered by Portugal, Venice, and Holland. The Great Pursuit of the Longitude gained momentum.

These incentives did not advance science. One might as well have offered large rewards in 1939 for the invention of the atomic bomb. In both cases the correct course for the politician was to apply the disposable money to the organization of systematic research. That was the way of Jean Baptiste Colbert, the power behind the throne of Louis XIV of France who in 1666 founded the Académie des Sciences with the principal object of improving maps and charts.

Scientific academies were to play an important part in the dissemination of scientific ideas from the seventeenth century, although earlier Italian academies had not endured. The *Academia secretorum naturae*, formed in Naples in 1560, was short-lived. Galileo was a member of the *Accademia dei Lincei* formed in Rome in 1603, but that too was impermanent. From about 1645 a group calling themselves the *Philosophical or Invisible College* started meeting in London. In 1662 the group was chartered by Charles II as *The Royal Society of London for improving Natural Knowledge*, and the Royal Society has played its unique part ever since.[7] The Académie was different. Colbert wanted not a market-place of ideas but a factory of ideas. No one, not Prince Henry the Navigator two centuries earlier, had sought to organize science in the service of navigation on the scale that Colbert did. He sent personal invitations to the principal scientists of Europe. Newton and Leibniz declined; but Huygens, Roemer, and others accepted.

Coincidentally, Giovanni Domenico Cassini, the professor of astronomy at Bologna (an important centre of ephemeris calculation in the seventeenth century), published for 1668 ephemerides giving the times of immersion (eclipse) and emersion of each of Jupiter's principal satellites in hours, minutes, and seconds, with illustrations on each opposing page of the

78

appearance of the planet and the grouping of the satellites around it. The observation any-where of the immersion or emersion of the satellite gives the time at the observatory for which the ephemerides were prepared. This was precisely the method of determining the time at some standard meridian (and hence the observer's difference of longitude from it) which Galileo had envisaged more than half a century earlier, and had worked so hard to perfect. Cassini was just the man the Académie needed; but there was a difficulty. Since his appointment eighteen years earlier at the age of twenty-five to the Chair of Astronomy at Bologna, which was part of the Papal States, Cassini had established a formidable reputation as a scientist and engineer, and had made himself very useful to Pope Clement IX. The pope and the senate of Bologna were suitably persuaded to the temporary loan of Cassini. He himself was offered 9000 livres a year (Huygens had settled for 6000), and arrived in Paris in 1669. The French took a broad view of 'temporary'. Giovanni Domenico Cassini became Jean Domenique, a French citizen, in 1673, and founded a unique scientific dynasty which ended only with the French revolution. He, his son, and his grandson and great-grandson were successive Directors of the Paris Observatory.

It was the French Académie, under the leadership of the Italian Giovanni Cassini and the Dutchman Christiaan Huygens, which pioneered the determination of the longitude on land. By 1700 the longitude of many places in the world was known relative to the meridian of the Paris Observatory. The methodology, relying on pendulum clocks and telescopic observations of the moons of Jupiter, was quite unpractical at sea. One possibility was the lunar distance, an extension of the idea of Hipparchus two thousand years earlier (Chapter One). As the moon appears to revolve in the firmament in about 27 days or so relative to the stars, the angle between the moon and a suitable star, or the sun, defines the date and time, assuming one knows the month. There are many formidable difficulties, which are discussed in detail in the next chapter. One is inherent: we can do nothing about it. As the moon appears to revolve in the celestial sphere (as defined by the fixed stars) only once a month, and the celestial sphere appears to rotate in a little less than a day, all errors of measurement, calculation, and prediction of place of the moon are multiplied by a factor of about 30 when used to determine the time.

The political acts which eventually led to the finding of the longitude at sea were English. A Frenchman, Le Sieur de St Pierre, who had some influence with Louise de Kéroualle, a mistress of Charles II of England, sought reward from the king for his own worthless version of the lunar distance. His importunity had far-reaching consequences. A Royal Commission was appointed in 1674, and a young English astronomer, John Flamsteed, assisted. Flamsteed reported to the Commission that his observations showed that the best lunar tables available were sometimes in error by 12' in arc, and that, with the passage of time, Tycho Brahe's catalogue of the bright stars, although still the best available, was in error by as much as 6'. These errors alone could cause errors in the longitude of more than five hundred miles in equatorial latitudes. His report led directly to the foundation of the Greenwich Observatory and the appointment of Flamsteed as the first Astronomer Royal, only a few months after St Pierre's proposal was first introduced to the king.

The Royal Warrant of 4 March 1675 directed 'our Astronomic Observator', John Flamsteed,

> *forthwith to apply himself with the most exact care and diligence to rectifying the tables of motions of the heavens, and the places of the fixed stars, so as to find out the so-much desired longitude of places for the perfecting the art of navigation.*

The Observatory itself was established by a warrant dated 22 June,

> *in order to the finding out of the longitude of places and for perfecting navigation and astronomy, we have resolved to build a small observatory within our park at Greenwich . . . according to such plot and design as shall be given you by our trusty and well-beloved Sir Christopher Wren . . .*

The original text of these warrants is quoted because it is rare that government directives in science have been followed so scrupulously for so long. Only in modern times did the main thrust of the work of the Observatory go outside the remit of the first warrant, and the lovely building Wren built for it cease to be used 'for perfecting the art of navigation'.

The state of navigation became perceived as a public scandal, especially in England from 1707. In that year Admiral Sir Clowdisley Shovel and two thousand of his men died when his fleet ran aground on rocks off the Scilly Isles, west of Cornwall.[8] At the time, all the navigators in the fleet except one agreed that they lay to the west of Ushant in Brittany. In 1714 'several Captains of Her Majesty's Ships, Merchants of London, and Commanders of Merchantmen' petitioned the House of Commons in these terms:

> *That the Discovery of the Longitude is of such Consequence to Great Britain, for Safety of the Navy, and Merchant Ships, as well as Improvement of Trade, that for want thereof, many ships had been retarded in their Voyages, and many lost, but if due Encouragement were proposed by the Publick for such as shall discover the same, some Persons would offer themselves to prove the same, before the most proper Judges . . .*

The House referred the matter to a committee, which consulted Newton, Halley, and others. Newton's gloomy views were included in the committee's report considered by the House of Commons on 11 June. He quite rightly said that observation of eclipses of Jupiter's satellites was unpractical by reason of the length of the telescopes required and motion of the ship. Despite Newton's own theoretical work, and nearly forty years of observations by Flamsteed at Greenwich, Newton was obliged to report that the moon's theory was not yet exact enough for the lunar distance method. For that matter neither were the instruments. Another possibility Newton contemplated was an accurate seaworthy clock. He was equally pessimistic: 'by reason of the Motion of a Ship, the Variation of Heat and Cold, Wet and Dry, and the Difference of Gravity in different Latitudes, such a Watch has not yet been made'. The fact that the impediments to accurate clocks could be defined so specifically—

although he should have included friction and wear—suggests, at least to the late-twentieth-century mind, that they could be overcome.

Apparently Parliament hoped so. The last Act signed by Queen Anne before her death provided for large prizes of up to £20 000 for finding the longitude. To illustrate the magnitude of the sum, Flamsteed started as Astronomer Royal with £100 p.a., and was required to provide the Observatory instruments out of this stipend.

The Board of Longitude appointed under the terms of the Act to consider claims was inundated by proposals as absurd or, at best, as impractical, as those which had fatigued Philip III of Spain so long before. The proposal of Isaac Hawkins, who thought he understood Newton's global tidal theory, is particularly to be savoured. All one needs is world-wide tide tables and a barometer. The height of the barometer gives the height of the tide above mean sea-level, and thus the longitude.[9] The standards set by the Act seemed impossible of achievement. The whole thing became a joke, and for half a century no prizes were awarded.

This time however there was a difference. The prospect of great wealth wonderfully concentrates the minds of some men. The incentive of the prize-money motivated the devotion of a lifetime to the painstaking care and exquisitely refined manufacture which were required in the state of eighteenth-century engineering to make a seagoing clock accurate. Earning such wealth and getting it are different things, as John Harrison was to discover. His No. 4 chronometer was triumphant beyond the dreams of astronomers. After sea trials on a voyage in 1761 from Plymouth to Madeira and Jamaica, No. 4 was only 5 seconds in error, corresponding to an error in longitude of a mile or so. The most stringent requirement of the Board of Longitude expressed in time was two minutes. The whole of the £20 000 was Harrison's—or so he thought. The Board procrastinated, and called belatedly for fresh trials. Perhaps there was a suggestion of irony in an editorial note in the *Connoissance des Temps* of 1765 'Il est juste que Harrison jouisse en la France de la gloire dont on ne le juge digne dans sa patrie.' One modern writer[10] has gone so far as to describe Harrison as 'the victim of a series of unsurpassed chicaneries perpetrated by scientists and politicians in concert'. Chapter 6 of this book gives a more equivocal judgement.

The temptation to give prizes to the prize-givers is irresistible. To Philip III of Spain the prize for missing golden opportunities. For sixteen years he brushed aside Galileo, the only man then alive who had a clue. The prize for coyness goes to the States-General of Holland, who flirted with Galileo for years and even gave him a gold chain, but could not bring themselves to act before he died. To Louis XIV of France, the great sun-king himself, the prize for credulity of bucolic degree. Without consulting Colbert, he gave a German in 1667, as a cash advance, sight unseen, on the invention of an Englishman made many years earlier (outlined in Note 3 of Chapter 2) which did not even address the problem, the sum of 60 000 livres—ten times the annual salary he paid Huygens.

Finally, the prize for getting it right must go to King George III of England. Eleven years after the triumph of No. 4, Harrison, then in his eightieth year, went in desperation to his king. George III is not the most admired of English monarchs; but he heard Harrison out, and personally observed Harrison's No. 5 almost daily in the royal observatory at Kew. The total error over ten weeks was 4½ seconds. 'By God Harrison', roared the king, 'I'll see you righted.' He did too! Disregarding the example of his unfortunate predecessor Charles I, the king threatened to appear in person at the House of Commons if Harrison did not get justice. Fortunately this was not necessary. For once king and parliament were agreed, and the Board of Longitude was overruled. Harrison received before he died his full reward. So, despite the scientists, the bulk of the English prize-money went to John Harrison, Yorkshire carpenter turned clockmaker, and the first man to find the longitude accurately at sea.

The final risible episode in the political history of the longitude was the Washington Conference of 1884, The International Prime Meridian Conference,[11] the main result of which was to establish Greenwich as the prime meridian and Greenwich Mean Time as the standard from which all other zone times should be derived.

The Prime Meridian.

Under the first four Astronomers Royal the Greenwich Observatory had attained such pre-eminence that the distinguished French mathematician and astronomer, J. J. Delambre, could write (in an elegy to Maskelyne) 'if by any great revolution the work of all other astronomers were lost, and this collection were preserved, it would contain sufficient materials to raise again, nearly entire, the edifice of modern astronomy; which cannot be said of any other collection . . .'. In 1884 British marine cartography led the world. It was claimed at the Conference that 72 percent of all world shipping used Greenwich, and the remainder used ten different meridians widely distributed. The USA had been divided into time zones, all differing from GMT by a whole number of hours. The American Nautical Almanac referred time and angle to Greenwich. Between 1871 and 1883, four international scientific conferences (three geographical, one geodetic) had recommended the adoption of the Greenwich meridian.

The Washington Conference met in eight sessions of no more than three hours each, which apparently were so fatiguing that they lasted the whole month of October. The conclusions of the conference would have been foregone if it had not been for the French. The Paris Observatory had once led the world in the finding of the longitude, and had been a *de facto* prime meridian; but in 1884 it was clearly a non-starter. The French avoided loss of face by not proposing it. Instead they proposed a meridian in the Pacific, but only gained the support of Brazil and the Dominican Republic. On the actual vote for Greenwich, the French contented themselves with a dignified abstention. The Dominican Republic delivered the only negative vote. The wording of the resolution defines the meridian as passing through the transit instrument (i.e. Sir George Airy's transit circle) at Greenwich. So the matter was settled—except in England and France. In England the entire survey system is based on a meridian 19 feet west of the transit circle.[12] In France GMT as such did not exist. Legal time was defined as Paris Observatory time less an interval of 9 min. 21 sec., which happened to coincide (to the nearest second) with the difference of longitude between the Paris Observatory and the transit circle at Greenwich.

Finally, Sir George Airy, the man so signally honoured, had written in 1879 'As to the need of a Prime Meridian, no practical man wants such a thing.'

Notes to Chapter 5

1. One Italian cardinal at the time of Rodrigo's accession who had no need of Borgia gold was Giovanni de' Medici, a scion of the most wealthy family of private citizens in Europe. He was then sixteen years old. In childhood he had been presented with about 25 profitable ecclesiastical offices, including the Abbey of Monte Cassino, once a great centre of Christian learning (Hibbert 1974). When the boy-cardinal became pope in his turn he said 'God has given us the papacy. Let us enjoy it'. God, it seems, helped those who helped themselves. Incidentally, Giovanni, as Pope Leo X, appointed his fellow Florentine, Guicciardini, Governor of Modena and Reggio and Commissioner General of the papal army: a nice demonstration of why history is written the way it is.
2. St Francis Borgia, a distinguished Jesuit.
3. Chamberlin (1974).
4. The Canaries appear on the Ptolemy map (Chapter 1). The Portuguese discovery of Madeira is dated 1418 or 1420, and of the Azores, about 1427. The Laurentian portolan, an Italian map which shows the correct position of Madeira, nine of the Canaries and eight of the Azores, was dated 1351, suggesting earlier discovery of the islands by the Genoese; but it is now thought to be early fifteenth-century.
5. Vigneras (1960).

6. The log of Francisco Albo, Elcano's navigator on the return voyage of the *Victoria* (Chapter 1) has survived. Elcano took a direct route from Timor to the Cape of Good Hope, presumably to avoid the Portuguese. On 1 May 1522 Albo thought they had rounded the Cape and lay 57 leagues (about 200 n.m.) west of it. The next day they sighted land to the north-west, probably the East London area. They must have been about about 500 n.m. east of the Cape. In the Pacific his estimates of longitude seem to have been as much as 30° in error. Like the hero of *Around the world in eighty days* they discovered when they arrived home that their calendars were one day in error.

7. Another important seventeenth-century development in the dissemination of scientific ideas was the introduction of scientific journals. Both the *Journal des Savants* and the *Philosophical Transactions of the Royal Society* appeared from 1665.

8. Apparently the Admiral himself scrambled ashore and was murdered by local women for his rings (May 1960). May analysed 44 log books of the fleet which have survived. The impression gained of the state of navigation in the Royal Navy in 1707 is appalling. There is no reason now to believe that the lack of a means of measuring the longitude was an important factor in the incident (see also Chapter 8).

9. Newton's tidal theory is explained in Chapter 8.

10. J. R. Newman.

11. Malin (1985).

12. The Re-triangulation of Great Britain (1935–62) was fitted as closely as possible to the nineteenth century Principal Triangulation. The Re-triangulation gave the longitude of the Airy instrument as 00° 00′ 00″.418 E. Subsequent investigation showed that the prime meridian of the Principal Triangulation had been through the centre of the Pond transit instrument, which was removed after the Airy instrument came into use in 1851. As far as could be determined a century later the (unmarked) site of the Pond instrument was 00.″30 west of the Airy instrument (Ordnance Survey 1967).

CHAPTER SIX

The Great Pursuit of the Longitude

✠

THE direct relationship between time measurement and longitude determination by astronomical means has long been understood. In essence, the position in space of the observer's zenith is found by the measurement of the zenith distance (or its complement, altitude) of heavenly bodies. Because the earth rotates on its axis once a day this information cannot be translated into position on the earth unless the time is known. The latitude is known but the longitude is not (see Fig. 6.1). As has already been remarked in Chapter 5, because the moon appears to revolve in the firmament in about 27 days or so relative to the stars, the angle

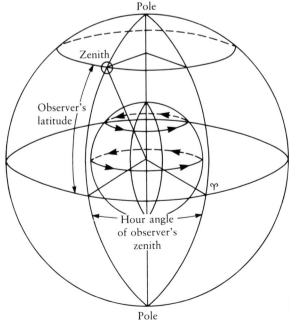

FIGURE 6.1
Without the time longitude is indeterminate.

between the moon and a suitable star or the sun (the lunar distance) defines the date and time—assuming one knows the month, and that sufficiently accurate ephemerides and instruments are available. It is said that Regiomontanus proposed to find the time by the method of lunar distance in the fifteenth century; but only a charlatan would have recommended using his ephemerides for the purpose, even if the requisite instrument for measuring angles precisely had been invented.

The matter is much more difficult than Hipparchus could have realized. There are five formidable obstacles:

1. As the earth rotates once a day but the moon only revolves once a month, all errors of observation, prediction of the moon's place, and calculation are multiplied by a factor of about 30—hence the stringent requirement for system accuracy. Even aberration and nutation, which were not discovered until the eighteenth century, have their effect.

2. The moon is only 30 earth-diameters from us, so the place in which we see it depends on our own position on the earth's surface. We only see it in its predicted place when it is at our zenith. When the moon is on the horizon the parallax is about 1° (see Fig. 6.2). To the errors of parallax must be added the errors of atmospheric refraction, which vary, for any given atmospheric density, roughly as the cotangent of the altitude.

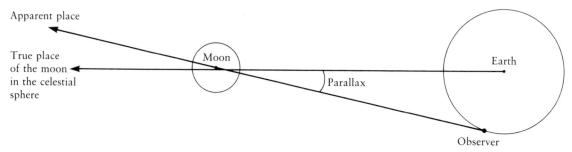

FIGURE 6.2
Lunar parallax.

3. The lunar orbit is very difficult to predict—hence the moon's long association with inconstancy. Because the pull of the sun on the moon is twice as great as the pull of the earth, the lunar motion can only roughly be described as a Keplerian orbit around the orbiting earth. The principal effects of *perturbations* are that the moon's orbit rotates in its own plane, so that the *anomalistic* month, the period between perigees, is five and a half hours longer than the sidereal month, and the axis of the orbit is rotating (precessing) with a period of 18.6 years, more than a thousand times faster than the rate of precession of the earth's own orbit (the precession of the equinoxes).

4. The calculations are extremely complicated and inherently unsuitable for seamen.

5. A very precise instrument for the measurement of angles is necessary.

All these obstacles, except the refraction problem and the need for the instrument, apply to any lunar method. In any case, eclipses are impractical at sea because of their infrequency. Even occultations (eclipses of stars by the moon) can only be used when an occultation occurs; furthermore, the leading edge of the moon is only dark for half the month.

On his second voyage Columbus sought to find the longitude of Santo Domingo by the method of Hipparchus, using ephemerides of Regiomontanus which predicted the time of an eclipse at Nuremberg. If the *Journal* of Columbus is any guide to his astronomical knowledge he would have required help even to attempt the task. The error was 23°—more than a thousand miles. An attempt in 1541 to find the difference in longitude between Toledo and Mexico by similar means was no more successful. Vespucci's method compared the predicted hour of the conjunction of a planet and the moon at a Spanish observatory with that observed in the New World. That was equally doomed for the reasons given. In the sixteenth century both Johan Werner and Peter Apian suggested lunar-distance methods using the cross-staff; so did Jean Rotz, a Frenchman who was Hydrographer to Henry VIII of England. His elucidation of his method is extant. It was hopelessly crude.

The lunar-distance method was frequently revived over the centuries. When Galileo was still alive, Morin proposed to find the longitude at sea by lunar distance. His spherical trigonometry was correct, and so was his theory of parallax; but the lunar tables then available were nowhere near predicting the place of the moon with usable accuracy, and the instruments then available would be wildly inaccurate. Like many other pursuers of the longitude he glossed over the obstacles to material achievement. Gemma Frisius is often quoted as suggesting in 1530 that the solution was a good clock—not very helpful in itself at a time when the error of a good clock was about ten minutes a day. After a few weeks at sea the error could be wider than the Atlantic. For many generations the determination of the longitude at sea by astronomical means seemed impossible to sensible men.

To fix position at sea one needs to measure some predictable quality of place. There may be some such quality other than the direction in space of the observer's vertical. The only one ever to be considered was the earth's magnetic field. In 1602 a group which included both Edward Wright and Henry Briggs considered finding the *latitude* by the dip of the magnetic needle; and even today dip is sometimes called magnetic latitude.

The notion of using magnetic *variation* as a measure of *longitude* is much older. In the days of Columbus some thought that magnetic variation was a direct measure of longitude. One had only to refine methods of measuring the angle in the horizontal plane between the needle and the pole star. So insidious was this idea that for centuries many charts showed the prime meridian through a point where the magnetic variation was thought to be zero, although João de Castro had shown in the 1530s that there was no obvious connection between longitude and magnetic variation.

A century after the discovery of America both Simon Stevin, the Flemish polymath, and Edward Wright were speculating on fixes by the intersection of the isogonal with the latitude found astronomically. In *Havenvinding* (published in Flemish in 1599 and translated into English by Wright) Stevin wrote: 'For some people hope to find it (the longitude) through the variation of the compass, ascribing a pole to the said variation, calling it a magnetic pole, but it is found on further experience that the variations do not obey a pole.' He goes on: 'People going to St Helena have arrived at the latitude but not known whether to go west or east.'

His solution was a table based on data by Petrus Plancius (first cartographer to the Dutch East India Company) showing the magnetic variation of places and whether it increased to the east or the west. Thus, arriving at the latitude of St Helena, say, measuring the magnetic variation, one knew from the table whether the island lay east or west. Stevin suggested that the direction of true north (and hence the magnetic variation) should be found by bisecting the angle between the direction of shadows when the sun was at equal altitudes forenoon and afternoon; a suggestion which had far-reaching applications in later times.

Earlier, Mercator, assuming that the needle points to some magnetic pole on the earth's surface, computed its position by spherical trigonometry from variation at two widely spaced points. Naturally he was wildly in error. Others who speculated on magnetic variation as a function of longitude included Bourne in the sixteenth century and Bond in the seventeenth century. Ralph Walker was still seeking to find the longitude from the variation in 1794 when the chronometer was already entering into general use, and the lunar distance was at its short-lived peak.[1]

Before the longitude could be found at sea, good practical navigators logged the latitude and the magnetic variation as a pair of quasi-x,y coordinates. By the mid-seventeenth century the true azimuth of the sun could be determined on long voyages more accurately than time, leading in 1665 to the publication of Andrew Wakeley's *The mariner's compass rectified containing tables showing the true hour of the day the sun being on any point of the compass*.

In 1674 Charles II sponsored a scheme to find the longitude by compass; but it was in 1694 that, on the initiative of Edmond Halley, the Royal Society invited the Admiralty 'to compass the globe to make observations of the magneticall needle'. The hope was entertained that data could be provided to enable seamen to find the longitude by the magnetic means canvassed for so long. The Admiralty agreed, and appointed Halley himself to command HMS *Paramore*.

Halley was one of the greatest British scientists of his day, and a navigator. We have the word of Flamsteed, then the Astronomer Royal, that on Halley's return he 'now talks, swears and drinks brandy like a sea captain'. Halley, of all men, cannot have believed that the longitude could be found at sea from the magnetic variation. At the time, the difference between the magnetic variation in English ports and those in the principal English colonies in North America was only a few degrees, and there was not the least prospect of measuring the magnetic variation at sea with an accuracy of one degree by practices normal to seamen. Besides, it is no good surveying a quality of place if one does not know where the place is; and *Paramore* had no means of determining the longitude not available to other ships excepting the unique quality of her captain. According to his log, Halley became on this voyage the first man to find the longitude at sea—after a fashion. With a 'five or six foot telescope' he observed appulses and occultations[2] of the fixed stars by the moon to find the time, giving him, he claimed, his longitude within about a degree, an improvement on his DR. Gellibrand had established the secular variation of the needle before Halley was born. The magnetic survey, at best, would be of ephemeral value.

Halley completed his magnetic survey of the Atlantic in 1700, and the following year published his chart of the Atlantic showing *isogonals*[3] or, in his own words, 'the curve lines which are drawn over the seas on the chart do show at one view all the places where the Variation of the Compass is the same'. Historically, this was a major development. For the first time true rhumbs could be steered by magnetic compass; but the Great Pursuit of the Longitude was not advanced in the least. Before radio, astronomy was the only way.

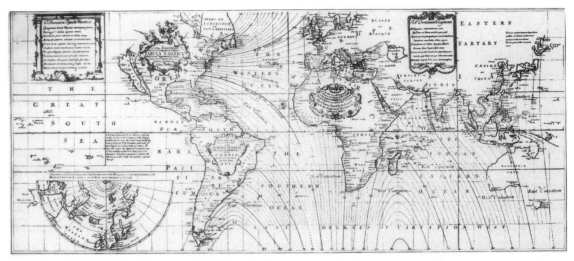

Edmond Halley's chart of world magnetic variation.

The object of the Académie des Sciences, according to Louis XIV himself, was to correct maps and charts.[4] There were two quite separate tasks: the determination of the size and shape of the earth, and the measurement of the latitude and longitude of places on it. As it is impractical to lay measuring rods over the oceans, the size and shape of the earth could only be inferred from direct measurements over relatively small areas of land. Direct measurement of distance in the horizontal plane presents formidable difficulties over hills or even over wooded terrain. The key invention of triangulation was suggested by Gemma Frisius and applied by Tycho Brahe. In this system only the length of one baseline is strictly essential: others may be calculated by the sine formula from the relative azimuths of their extremities (see Fig. 6.3).

Seventeenth-century geodesy by triangulation begins in 1617 with Snell's facetiously entitled *Eratosthenes Batavus*,[5] which gave the length of a degree of latitude in Holland with an error of about 3½ per cent—no better than the Baghdad determination so many centuries earlier. Richard Norwood did better in 1635. He measured the difference of latitude between two points near the Tower of London and York Minster respectively with a five-foot quadrant, and measured the distance with chains. His error was less than 1 per cent.

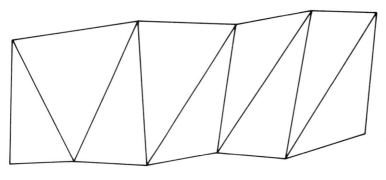

FIGURE 6.3
A single triangulation chain.

In Chapter 4 the nascence of modern science was described in terms of the evolution of new ways of thought and their dissemination in European culture. Another aspect, signally exemplified by the Académie, was the development of measurement and better instruments, and insistence on care, accuracy, and the perfection of observational skills. It was a new approach, and led to a new technology. Jean Picard showed how things had changed in fifty years. In 1669 the Académie assigned Picard, in effect, to measure the curvature of the earth north of Paris. One terminal point was near Paris, the other near Amiens. Thirteen great triangles were used. It is believed to have been the first survey to employ logarithms and telescopic sights with cross-hairs. Picard claimed that his checks showed that none of his azimuths were in error by more than 1'. He found by stellar transits that the arc between his terminal points was 1° 11' 57". His triangulation gave the distance as 133.371 km,[6] so that the length of the degree of latitude north of Paris was 111.219 km, which Picard later reduced by 9 metres after reconstruction of the triangulation calculations. This result is correct within the limits of error of the factor used here to convert from Picard's unit of length, the *toise*, to metres. It is an improvement on Snell of two orders.

The size of the earth known, the next thing was its shape. As has already been noted, the theoretical work of Newton and Huygens implied that under gravitational and centripetal forces a liquid homogeneous world would take the form of an oblate spheroid described by the rotation of elliptical meridians about their (minor) polar axis. As most of the earth's surface is water it seemed reasonable to assume that the earth's shape, as defined by mean sea level, would approximate to this.[7] If the meridians are not perfect circles the latitude found by astronomical means is not the *geocentric* latitude but the *geographic* latitude, defined as the angle the vertical makes with the equatorial plane. The rate of change of distance along the meridian with respect to geographic latitude equals the radius of curvature of the meridian. The radius of curvature of an ellipse is a maximum when its radius is a minimum and vice versa[8] (see Fig. 6.4). Thus, reasoned the savants of the Académie, the shape of the earth was to be found by measuring the variation with latitude of the length of a degree of latitude. Cassini and his son[9] extended the triangulation of Picard north to Dunkirk and south to the Pyrenees. They concluded that the length of a degree of latitude increased towards the equator, so that, if the earth is spheroidal, it is prolate, with its polar axis longer than its equatorial diameter.

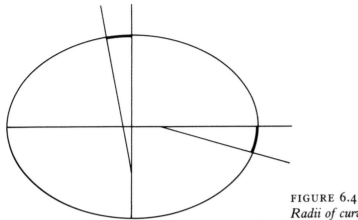

FIGURE 6.4
Radii of curvature of an ellipse.

A dispute, which dragged on for many years between the English 'earth-flatteners', who followed Newtonian theory, and the French 'prolatarians', who followed the measurements of the Cassinis, was finally resolved by the French in favour of the English. In 1735 the Académie sent Bouguer and De la Condamine to measure the length of a degree of latitude in what is now Ecuador, and Maupertuis was sent on a similar mission to Lapland. The results, together with the figure of Picard for Paris, showed that the length of a degree of latitude does indeed increase from the equator to the poles in a manner broadly consistent with Newtonian theory. Voltaire wrote a rhyme to De la Condamine congratulating him on finding by such tedious labour what the dead Newton had known without leaving home; he also congratulated Maupertuis on flattening both the earth and the Cassinis. The result might have been anticipated in Paris. For sixty years the odd behaviour of Académie pendula in equatorial regions had been a signal that, in this matter, the Cassinis had been wrong and Newton had been right.

From those days through the nineteenth century progressively more refined figures for the ellipsoid of reference were found; but the earth is neither homogeneous nor liquid. In the twentieth century, geodesy progressed beyond the stage of trying to fit the earth to an ellipsoid, to the definition of that shape (the geoid) which most closely resembles the form of the earth. However, at the end of the Second World War there were large tracts of the earth, the Matto Grosso of South America for example, still to be surveyed. Even at the birthplace of modern geodesy there was, at that late date, a difference of coordinates of the same control point between British and French survey systems of 191 metres, despite the obvious importance of the precise difference of longitude between the reference meridians of the Paris and Greenwich observatories. It is only because of recent work in these fields that the precision of which satellite navigation systems are capable can be realized cartographically.[10] Also, anomalies in the shape of the earth and in the direction of the apparent vertical are significant at the level of potential accuracy of such systems. There is little merit in knowing the geocentric position of an aircraft accurately if the chart coordinates of the runway do not agree.

Back in 1668, the Académie had pondered for two years on the various means of finding the longitude which had been proposed from Hipparchus onwards. They rightly reduced their options to those seminal ideas of Galileo, the pendulum clock and the moons of Jupiter. Jupiter is so far away from us that parallax is negligible. Because of its great mass and great distance from the sun the orbits of its satellites, unlike that of our moon, are nearly Keplerian.

For pendulum clocks they already had the man. Christiaan Huygens, who came to the Académie from Holland in 1666, had demonstrated his first pendulum clock in 1657 with an error of about 10 seconds a day—this at a time when the error of a good clock might be 400 seconds a day.[11] His *Horologium*, published in the following year, explained the principles and mechanism of pendulum clocks driven by weights or springs like other mechanical clocks, but regulated by the pendulum, which is isochronous (of constant period) for small swings, provided that its mass and form, and the force of gravity, are unchanged.

Cassini, the great expert on Jupiter's moons, arrived in Paris in 1669 under circumstances described in the last chapter. He exemplifies perfectly the practical aspect of seventeenth-century science, and quickly became the *de facto* leader of the Académie, a status which was formalized when he was appointed Director of the Paris Observatory.

By 1676 Cassini's earlier ephemerides had been revised and extended by teams of scientists whose telescopes were continuously improving, and Cassini was ready to start determining the longitude of places using the moons of Jupiter as a clock. The enthusiasm of the Académie was infectious: data poured in from volunteer collaborators, including Halley. For the first time, the longitude of hundreds of places (relative to the Paris Observatory) was determined. French hydrographers and cartographers used the data and the methods pioneered by Picard to produce charts and sailing directions which led the world for a century.

It is a matter of everyday observation that light is refracted when it moves from one medium to another. The Greeks speculated on the phenomenon, and both Tycho Brahe and Kepler worried about the effect of possible atmospheric refraction on their observations. The Académie were working to an accuracy where such things matter. The first scientific statement about refraction came from Snell (already mentioned as *Eratosthenes Batavus*). His law states that the ratio of the sines of the angles of incidence and refraction is constant for any pair of media. Cassini applied this law to the atmosphere, assuming that the atmosphere is homogeneous and finite, that is to say that the light from a star is bent just once as it enters the atmosphere. The refraction in such a model depends on the radius assigned to the atmosphere, but Cassini's expression may be made to give good results at altitudes greater than 10°. Picard's tables were published in *Connoissance des Temps*, and served for a period. In the eighteenth century it was recognized that refraction by the atmosphere depends on air density, and is therefore a continuous process. Refraction tables were produced with corrections for atmospheric temperature and density.

The 'finding out of the longitude of places' in the New World was a more formidable task, which required many expeditions over a more extended period. Two are of particular interest. In 1672 Jean Richer was sent to Cayenne (5°N), and found that his pendulum clock which had been so carefully regulated in Paris inexplicably lost about 2½ minutes a day.[12] Earlier experiences in transporting pendulum clocks about Europe had shown that they beat the same time everywhere. Cassini concluded there had been some error. A year later Huygens produced his second masterpiece on the subject, *Horologium oscillatorium*, which materially advanced the theory of centrifugal force and showed how the period of the pendulum varies as the square root of its length. Fourteen years later, Newton showed (in the third book of *Principia*) that the period also varies inversely as the square root of gravity.[13] This was the true explanation of Richer's result, and, had the Académie realized it, important evidence of the shape of the meridians. Hooke had suggested using pendula to study gravity.

Political events and the religious intolerance of the times cannot have helped free co-operation between Dutch, French, and British scientists during the period. In the two decades before the *Principia* England was intermittently at war with Holland. A year after they were published William, Prince of Orange, became King of England, and promptly declared war on his old enemy Louis XIV. Anglo-French hostilities of one kind or another recurred until the final defeat of Napoleon and the end of the French imperialist dream in 1815. At that date the Great Pursuit of the Longitude was quite over.

The expedition of Varin, des Hayes, and de Glos to the Cape Verde Islands and Guadeloupe and Martinique (1681–3) is of particular interest because Cassini's instructions show the thoughtful and careful attention to the techniques of observation and experiment which is one of Cassini's great contributions to practical science. Pendulum clocks were carried rated to both mean solar time and sidereal time. Before shipping they had been carefully calibrated for temperature correction. A variety of redundant methods were used in a well-thought-out system of checks once the clocks were set going at some arbitrary setting. One method was the solar equal altitude. An altitude of the sun is taken some hours before noon, the time is noted and, the direction of the shadow is marked. The time at which the sun declines to the same altitude in the afternoon is noted, and the direction of the shadow is marked. The average of the two times is local apparent noon; and the bisector of the angle between the two shadows is true north. The experiment was repeated over several days, and the clocks were rated and adjusted to read local time. The sidereal clock was similarly rated by several transits of a convenient star, and set to read local sidereal time.

In retrospect one wonders why they bothered with the sun, given the complications introduced by changes in declination and the equation of time over the duration of the observations. Latitude was found by transits of the sun and the stars. When all was done, the local times of the eclipses of the moons of Jupiter by the planet were noted. The drill was elaborate. Night after night, times of immersion were calculated from the observed clock time when the first satellite's distance from the planet equalled its own diameter, when it touched the planet, and when it disappeared completely behind it; and conversely on emersion. The longitude was simply the difference between the local time and the Paris time of these phenomena (extracted from the ephemerides), converted to units of angle. By such means the Paris Observatory under Cassini led the world in the finding out of the longitude of places, and indeed in the charting of the world. Its direct contribution to the finding out of the longitude at sea was modest.

Huygens had built pendulum clocks for use at sea from 1660, long before he went to

France. Two of his spring-driven pendulum clocks were tested on an English ship in 1664. Reports were mixed. Later, in Huygens' Académie days, his weight-driven cycloidal pendula went on sea trials in French ships; and in 1669 Huygens wrote careful instructions for the operation and care of pendulum clocks at sea. Regardless of the reports, it follows from the theoretical work of Newton and Huygens himself that no pendulum clock, however gimballed and protected from the motion of a ship of those days, could perform properly in rough seas. There was no way of insulating the pendulum from the centripetal forces caused by the motion of the ship, and the pendulum is inherently incapable of distinguishing between them and gravity. It is the old problem of the astrolabe and the quadrant at sea, revived in the twentieth century by aircraft bubble sextants.

In France, hopes for the pendulous marine chronometer dragged on for far too long. In 1720 the set subject for a *Prix Rouillé* was the regulation of the pendulum at sea. It was won by a Dutchman; but his device cannot have been practical. In 1725 the Académie was looking in desperation at water-clocks and hour-glasses. Attempts to use the celestial clock of Jupiter at sea convinced both the Académie and English scientists of its impracticality. Even when the observer's chair and the telescope were gimballed, the object could not be kept in the narrow field of vision of a telescope of sufficient magnifying power. Back to the proposals of John Werner and Gemma Frisius two centuries earlier.

The scene now shifts to England. Scientific horology there began with Robert Hooke, who seems to have been the first to realize that a successful marine chronometer cannot be pendulum-regulated. Contemporaneously with the first Huygens pendulum clock, Hooke studied spring-driven non-pendulous marine chronometers, and catalogued their sources of error more specifically than Newton's famous report many years later mentioned in the preceding chapter. Hooke understood that the force exerted by a spring is directly proportional to the extent to which it is tensioned; he demonstrated twenty different ways of applying a spring to a balance to improve the constancy of its period of oscillation. Ironically, Hooke saw little advantage in finding the longitude at sea, and illustrated a gift for being totally wrong at times when he wrote 'no king or state would pay a farthing for it'.

Newton's statement to the Committee in 1714 (Chapter 5) viewed the practicality of both the moon and the non-pendulous clock as means of time-measurement at sea with well-founded pessimism. The prize payable under the terms of the 1714 Act (Chapter 5) was £10 000 for the longitude within one degree, £15 000 within 45', and £20 000 within 30'. These terms required a system accuracy of a clock of 4 minutes, 3 minutes, and 2 minutes of time. The corresponding system accuracy for a lunar distance method was 2', 1½', and 1' respectively. A modern analysis[14] indicates that, despite all the work of the Académie, the lunar longitude tabulated in *Connoissance des Temps* for the years 1695–1701 was frequently 10' in error, giving a 5° error in terrestrial longitude.

'Our astronomical observator', John Flamsteed, was Astronomer Royal for 44 years. *Historia coelestis Britannica*, published after his death by his assistants, catalogued nearly 3000 stars. It was a monumental achievement, but not really a happy one. Flamsteed was a perfectionist, never content to publish data which could be improved, and continually pestered by Newton, then long past his prime, for lunar data to perfect a theory of the lunar orbit, a task which has only been completed in modern times by powerful computers. Newton of course made great strides; but he did not approach the standards demanded by the prize-money.

Halley, who became the second Astronomer Royal, told the Royal Society that he could predict the place of the moon within 2′—not quite good enough to claim the prize-money. The maximum permissible system error could not be absorbed by the ephemerides. The astronomer's problem was not limited to the lunar theory. Flamsteed's massive accumulation of stellar data suggested that the stars themselves were moving in a way which could not be explained by the precession of the equinoxes. The differences were slight; but given the exigent requirement of the lunar-distance method, even an error of the order of 0.1′ in stellar data was not insignificant.

James Bradley (who became the third Astronomer Royal in 1742 on the death of Halley) announced *aberration*[15] in 1729. As noted in Chapter four, Roemer had shown that the velocity of light is finite in 1676. The ratio of the speed of light to the speed of the earth in its orbit is roughly 10 000:1, so that when the direction of the source of light is at right angles to the direction of the earth's trajectory, the apparent direction of the source is deflected by 1/10 000 radians, which is 0.3′. Bradley went on to announce (in 1748) *nutation*,[16] which causes the coordinates of all heavenly bodies to oscillate with an amplitude of another 0.3′ and a period of 19 years. To perfect a lunar theory of the required standard, all the observations of the past seventy years had to be reviewed for aberration and nutation.

In the same year as Bradley announced nutation, Leonhard Euler, a Swiss who was one of the greatest of eighteenth-century mathematicians, published a paper on irregularities in the motions of Saturn and Jupiter employing novel methods of analysis. Tobias Mayer of the University of Göttingen[17] applied Euler's methods to the prediction of lunar motion, with results which were submitted to the Admiralty in London in 1754. Bradley found Mayer's predictions accurate within 75″. Mayer was one of the few prize-seekers who fully understood that *system* error was the only criterion. He proposed his own instrument, the repeating circle, which was capable on land of an accuracy of 0.2′. Things were looking up for the lunar distance!

Mayer's tables and repeating circle were tried at sea by a distinguished navigator, Captain John Campbell, in 1757–9; but no conclusions were reached. In 1761 Nevil Maskelyne, a young astronomer, gave more extensive trials on a voyage to St Helena and back. It seems that the results, much as one might have expected, gave the longitude within a degree or so; but the calculation took Maskelyne and the ship's officers assisting him four hours—that was just to find the time!

The calculation problem was reduced to more manageable proportions by Maskelyne himself. When he was appointed Astronomer Royal he introduced the *Nautical Almanac*, a step of great historical importance even if it was a century later than *Connoissance des Temps*. In his almanac Maskelyne included, at three-hour intervals, precomputed distances of the moon from one or more bodies selected from the sun and bright stars. After correction for parallax and refraction, Greenwich apparent time (GMT from 1834) could be found by interpolation. Local apparent time could be found from observations of the sun in the morning or the evening, given the latitude found at noon. The difference, converted to units of angle, is the longitude. A case, not a good case perhaps, could be made, fifty years after the Act of Longitude was passed, and some 170 years after Philip of Spain offered his prize, that the longitude could at last be found within one degree by a 'generally useful and practical method'.

The *Nautical Almanac* became a cottage industry in itself, with a growing number of calculators and comparers working from their homes to calculate, check, and edit the data. The Board of Longitude was reconstituted[18] in 1818 with a salaried secretary, with the function of the superintendence of the *Nautical Almanac*. Table 6.1, taken from the first secretary's report,[19] shows how accuracy improved over the years. The marked improvement in longitude in 1809 is indirectly due to the theoretical work of the French mathematician Laplace (see also Chapter 8). The table may not be correct; but it is presumably indicative of general progress.

YEAR	CELESTIAL MEAN	LATITUDE MAX.	CELESTIAL MEAN	LONGITUDE MAX.
1783	14″	114″	30″	90″
1789	13″	80″	27″	87″
1805	8″	36″	31″	68″
1809	8″	43″	8″	29″
1813	7″	31″	6″	34″
1817	5″	25″	5″	22″

Table 6.1. The error of the lunar distance tables

The practicality of the lunar distance depended equally on the development of instruments to measure angle at sea within the permissible limits of system error. The requirement for greater precision in such instruments was not limited to the lunar distance. The greater the uncertainty as to the longitude, the more important it is to sail precisely along a known parallel of latitude to an island destination or a rendezvous at sea. The deflection of the vertical by centripetal accelerations in the motion of the ship precluded any development of the quadrant and the astrolabe. Even in the twentieth century, aircraft bubble sextants with automatic averaging devices gave poor results at sea; and, in any case, did not answer the lunar-distance problem. The limitations of the cross-staff and backstaff have been described in Chapter 2. The trick is a reflecting device in which the image of the body is brought into coincidence with the sea horizon for altitude measurement and with the circumference of the moon for lunar distance.

It is believed that Robert Hooke made (in 1666) the first instrument to bring two objects together by observing one body directly and the other through a mirror. The principles of

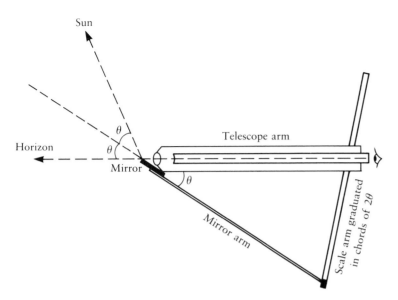

FIGURE 6.5
Principles of Hooke's reflecting quadrant.

his *reflecting quadrant* are illustrated in Fig. 6.5. At that date the lunar distance was impractical, and the instrument was intended for altitude measurement. The arm containing the axis of the telescope and that carrying the mirror form a plane perpendicular to that of the mirror and are of equal length, so that the scale arm can be graduated in chords of θ. The instrument is held vertically with the horizon just visible at the tip of the mirror. The telescope arm is slid until the image of the observed body is also at the tip of the mirror. The angle θ is found from a table of chords, and doubled to find the altitude. Alternatively, the scale could be graduated directly in units of 2θ as in Fig. 6.5.

Newton's reflecting octant, probably built about 1677, is illustrated in Fig. 6.6. The frame is a brass plate in the form of a sector of arc of 45° graduated 0–90° (in all reflecting instruments employing two mirrors the angle between the two objects sighted is *twice* the angle between the planes of the mirrors). A telescope is fixed to one radius of the plate. Two specula (metal mirrors) have their planes at right angles to the plane of the plate. One is fixed with its lower edge in line with the axis of the telescope. The other is mounted on a radius arm. The plate is held vertically so that the horizon is sighted at the edge of the fixed speculum, and the radius arm is adjusted so that the image of the observed body, seen through the two specula, coincides with the horizon. An obvious advantage over the Hooke instrument is that alignment is easier because one sees the sea below the horizon. Although said to have long been displayed in the shop-window of Thomas Heath, a famous instrument-maker, it appears to have been largely forgotten, and was first shown to the Royal Society on the occasion marking the first centenary of Newton's birth.

In 1692 Halley had (in his own words) 'a sea quadrant wherein both the horizon and the Object shall be seen distinctly and enlarged at one view in the common focus of the Telescope'. He went on presciently 'when the longitude shall be found out by the motion of the Moon this, or such an instrument, must be the tool to observe with'.

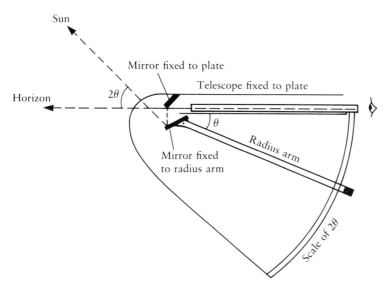

FIGURE 6.6
Principles of Newton's reflecting quadrant.

In 1731 John Hadley demonstrated to the Royal Society two reflecting quadrants. The first was inconsequential. The second, illustrated in Fig. 6.7, is the modern marine sextant in embryonic form. The great advantage over earlier reflecting quadrants is that the horizon glass is only half silvered, the half furthest from the frame being clear. The index arm is turned until the image of the object is seen beside the horizon anywhere in the field of vision. The difficulty in a moving ship of bringing both to the edge of the mirror is eliminated. When the index arm is correctly set, and the instrument is rocked gently in the vertical at right angles to its plane, the object just touches the horizon at the vertical boundary between the silvered and clear section of the horizon glass. In Hadley's own prolix words to the Royal Society 'though the Ship rolls ever so much, provided the Instrument be kept in, or near, an upright Posture, though it be leaned forward or backward therein, yet the Image of any Object, when once brought to the edge of the sea, will remain there absolutely immovable'. This 'quadrant' might have been called an 'octant', because the index glass need only rotate through 45° to measure altitudes up to 90°; but this term came into use later.

The same Campbell who conducted the first sea trials of the Mayer system suggested in 1757 extending the arc to 60°, so that lunar distances up to 120° could be measured. The result was the *sextant*, which was to become, together with the chronometer, the most essential instrument of navigation after the compass until the advent of reliable radio-navigation systems. At first Hadley employed a diagonal dividing scale; but he subsequently turned to vernier scales,[20] which permit reading to the nearest 1'. Many improvements to the marine sextant were introduced over the years, including prisms to eliminate horizon glare, electric lighting, and so on; but perhaps the most important improvements to Hadley's instrument were the tangent screw for fine adjustment of the index arm and the introduction of glass mirrors. Specula, which quickly tarnished at sea, were replaced by silvered glass mirrors when technology in that field was sufficiently advanced. The great accuracy required of such mirrors and of sun-shades, was an important motivation for precision engineering. In the

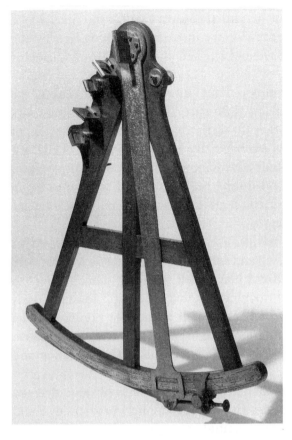

A Hadley quadrant by J. Bird (1750).

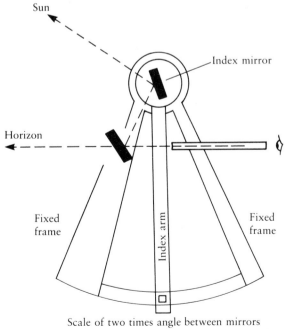

Scale of two times angle between mirrors

FIGURE 6.7
Principles of Hadley's reflecting quadrant.

seventeenth century great scientists made instruments with their own hands—men like Hooke were skilled fashioners of metal. In the eighteenth century instrument-making, led by the chronometer and the sextant, became a separate technology, and an industry ready-made for the needs of the industrial revolution.

Meyer's reflecting circle mentioned earlier employed the same optical principles as the quadrants of Newton and Hadley, with the major difference that the index mirror was mounted at the centre of a graduated circle, so that the angle could be read at either end of the diametric limb on which the index glass was mounted. By taking an average of the two readings, index error was eliminated—a significant advantage in the early days of precision fabrication. Campbell had rejected the instrument during the sea trials of 1757–9 as being too cumbersome; but it was improved. For a period, some enthusiasts carried a sextant for altitude and a reflecting circle for lunar distance.

Then there was the problem of getting the navigators to use the lunar distance. As in Portugal and Spain two centuries earlier, as in England in Edward Wright's day, navigators did not take kindly to new-fangled ideas. The Royal Navy used sea-going schoolmasters to introduce the lunar distance into the Lieutenant examination, and sent ship's masters (navigators) to school ashore. The older masters proved to be such intractable pupils that the course was soon confined to newly appointed masters. Perhaps, in the end, the greatest contribution of the lunar distance to navigation was that it forced its mathematization and gave the impulse to a new breed of navigators.

To the twentieth-century mind reviewing the matter in retrospect, it is obvious that the lunar distance was doomed from its very beginning. Even if astronomical predictions could be made perfect, it is unconscionable to us that the longitude error would be for ever thirty times greater than the latitude error. It is obvious to us, if not perhaps to Newton, Halley, or their contemporaries, that a clock can always be improved.

It was mentioned earlier that scientific horology began in England with Hooke; but, as usual, his brilliant work was inconclusive. Horology advanced in England in the hands of George Graham, the inventor of the deadbeat escapement, and others. John Harrison was the son of a Yorkshire carpenter, and learned his father's trade. In his first pendulum clock, built when he was only twenty-two, all the wheels were made of oak except the escape wheel. His first major contribution was the gridiron pendulum, which took advantage of the different coefficients of expansion of steel and brass to pin them together in such a way that the effective length of the pendulum was invariant with temperature. A Huygens pendulum, built of a steel rod with a lead bob, went faster in winter than in summer. Harrison's second great invention was the grasshopper escapement. A pendulum clock he built in 1726 had a random error of about a second a month—an improvement over Huygens comparable with that of Huygens himself over the mechanical clocks of his day.

In 1728 Harrison went to London in pursuit of the prize-money. Halley prudently steered him away from the Board of Longitude and towards Graham, then recognized as the leading English horologist. With the guidance (and probably the financial help) of Graham, Harrison developed his No. 1 marine chronometer, and obtained a certificate from the Royal Society, signed by Halley, Bradley, Graham, and others, that the *principles* of the instrument promised to meet the requirements of the Act. The trials (in 1736) were inconclusive. Harrison got a certificate signed by the master that, on sighting the English coast on return from Lisbon, Harrison's position by chronometer (a word invented by Jeremy Thatcher in 1714) was correct, and the DR was 'above 1 degree 26 miles' in error. He also got £500 from the Board to develop No. 2. This instrument never went to sea. By the time Harrison was ready, England was at war with Spain, and the clock was too valuable for its capture to be risked. It weighed 165 pounds with its case and gimbals. No. 3 weighed only 101 pounds with case and gimbals; but Harrison himself was not satisfied with it. Throughout, he was encouraged by some leading members of the Royal Society, and received modest cash advances from the Board.

The most famous of all chronometers: Harrison's No. 4 (1759).

No. 4, the most famous of all chronometers, was ready in 1759. After more than 30 years of refinement of many ingenious devices fabricated with exquisite precision, Harrison was satisfied. He wrote 'I think that there is neither any Mechanical or Mathematical thing in the world that is more beautiful or curious in texture than this my watch or Time-Keeper for the longitude.' No. 4 took the form of a huge watch, 13 cm in diameter, which was not gimballed but lay on a soft cushion, always in the same attitude, in a box.

No. 4 went to sea in 1761, but without its creator. John Harrison was then sixty-eight years old, and his son William was the acolyte of the precious device. Nine days out of Plymouth on the first leg to Madeira, William's longitude differed from the DR by 1° 29'. The Captain agreed for trial purposes to assume William's longitude. At dawn the next morning the look-out sighted Porto Santo ahead. After the ocean crossing to Jamaica, No. 4 was 5 seconds in error, corresponding to about a nautical mile in longitude, after correcting for the rating agreed at Portsmouth. William and the instrument were shipped home in a sloop which encountered stormy weather, and the rigorous rules about attitude were abandoned. Nevertheless, when the watch was independently checked at Portsmouth, its total error over the whole five-month period (after allowing for the agreed rating) was only one minute 53 seconds, corresponding to 28' of longitude, despite the rude treatment on the sloop.

The dramatic circumstances under which Harrison got his money twelve years later have already been described in Chapter 5. At the same time Mayer's widow was voted £3 000, which was much diluted on the way to the old lady in Hanover, and Euler received £300. The Harrison case is curiously controversial to this day, although the facts are voluminously recorded and unarguable. The populist view that Harrison was a simple uneducated rustic genius repeatedly betrayed and nearly defeated by powerful scientific gentry who wanted the money for themselves is, at best, simplistic. As already mentioned, he was helped and encouraged in the early years by Halley and others. In 1749 the Royal Society gave Harrison the Copley Medal, its highest award, an extraordinary homage to an uneducated man by the leading scientists of the day.

The scientists who pursued the lunar distance would not have been human if they had not hankered after the prize-money—Bradley is alleged to have told Harrison to his face that he (Bradley) would have shared the prize-money with Mayer if it had not been for Harrison's blasted clock. The scientists who devoted so much of their lives to the lunar distance were not lightly to abandon it. In later years the arch-villain (in Harrison's view) was Nevil Maskelyne, fifth Astronomer Royal, father of the *Nautical Almanac*, fanatical arch-priest of the lunar distance, and arch-enemy of all mechanics and Harrison in particular; but there is no evidence that he schemed for his own personal enrichment.

Besides, in the twenty-five years between No. 1 and No. 4, the delays (except for the consequences of the Spanish war) were all of Harrison's own making. Like many later inventors, he deferred too long putting his material to the test in the pursuit of perfection. The real case against giving the full award to Harrison after the triumph of No. 4 in 1761/2 was clearly stated by the Commissioners at the meeting of the Board of Longitude in February 1765. The prize was for 'a generally useful and practical method'. Harrison had demonstrated the *feasibility* of chronometric fixing with an accuracy to which the lunar distance could never pretend; but his method was not available for general employment. Harrison demonstrated no principle which could be generally useful and practical. He had spent two years just on the fine adjustment and rating of his instrument. He was secretive and offered no plans or drawing. There was not the remotest possibility that a copy of No. 4 could be put aboard every ship. The Board had to pay the enormous sum of £450 to Larcum Kendall to make an exact copy[21] of No. 4. Perhaps the greatest importance of Harrison is that he introduced navigation to two things which were later to dominate it—economics and machinery. The objections to No. 4 as the solution to the Great Pursuit were to be re-echoed by those to many inventions in the future.

No. 4 was the first but, as is so often the case with firsts, it was not in the mainstream of the history of its kind. Harrison was secretive, and horology was developing quite independently of him, notably in France. The instruments of Pierre Le Roy, which were so widely famed that a century later Jules Verne would write that the hero of *Around the world in eighty days* 'was as exactly regulated as a Le Roy chronometer', were performing on sea trials with an accuracy of the same order as No. 4 only a few years after William Harrison's historic voyage to Jamaica. If the chronometer, by bringing engineering into navigation, is a turning-point, it also represents a turning-point in this book, since engineering technicalities are beyond its province. Two quotations from an authority[22] must suffice:

> *There can be no doubt at all that the inventor of the modern (writing in 1923) chronometer is Pierre Le Roy. Nothing can rob Harrison of the glory of having been the first man to make a satisfactory marine timekeeper, one, too, which was of permanent usefulness, and which could be duplicated as often as necessary. But No. 4, in spite of its fine performance and beautiful mechanism, cannot be compared, for efficiency and design, with Le Roy's wonderful machine.*
>
> *If we contrast this marvellous machine with No. 4, which, in its own way, is equally remarkable, Le Roy's superiority as a horologist is evident. Harrison took the escapement, balance, and general arrangement of the ordinary watch of his day, and by fitting a remontoire and maintainer, an automatic regulator, and diamond pallets, aided by high-numbered wheels and pinions and lavish jewelling, he compelled it to be an efficient timekeeper. Le Roy attacked the matter from an entirely different standpoint, and obtained his results not by nullifying defects, but by eliminating them. The difference is fundamental—Harrison built a wonderful house on sand; but Le Roy dug down to the rock.*

Skills in chronometer manufacture quickly spread. By 1785, Thomas Earnshaw had produced several chronometers scarcely distinguishable from some early-twentieth-century models. Indeed, some of his designs were still in use in the twentieth century. Mass production and quality control followed more slowly. Before the age of steam, the Admiralty do not appear to have valued knowledge of the longitude as highly as Parliament had done. It seems that chronometers were issued neither to the fleets blockading the Bay of Biscay from 1794 to 1813, nor to Nelson's fleet of 1805, although doubtless some officers carried their own. We have the authority of Admiral of the Fleet Lord Fisher that 'It is a historical fact that the British Navy stubbornly resists change.' It was only in the late 1850s that three chronometers were issued to all HM ships.[23] Three chronometers were a minimum for confidence, because if only two were carried and they differed, there was no indication which was wrong—a consideration which later led to triplicated automatic aircraft landing-systems (Chapter 10).

In the early decades of the nineteenth century price was still an obstacle in smaller merchantmen. In ships which traded between ports without time signals the accumulative nature of chronometric error was a serious disadvantage of the instrument, especially in the early years when the longitude of some lesser ports was not known with adequate precision to set the chronometer by calculating hour angle. In such circumstances there was nothing but the lunar distance, except on those voyages of exploration equipped to observe Jupiter's moons when ashore. The problem was slowly resolved by the spread of accurate surveys, by the electric telegraph, and finally by radio time signals.[24] When radio time signals became universally available, the chronometer was obsolete—a wrist-watch with a sweep second hand met the requirement. Before astronomical navigation itself became obsolete, digital quartz watches more accurate than marine chronometers were to be found on many a schoolboy's wrist.

The lunar-distance tables dragged on in the *Almanac* until 1906; but it is unclear to what extent they were used at sea.[25] The lunar distance was the great tribulation of young officers seeking to pass examinations, and the sustenance of a growing army of mediocre mathematicians, many of them divines, who, in a world offering little comfortable employment for men of their talents, became the pedagogues of navigation. The worst chore for the seaman was 'clearing the distance', the correction for parallax and refraction. By 1797 Mendoza y Rios was able to describe forty methods of doing it. Throughout the nineteenth century they kept coming. Presumably the last was that of the Reverend William Hall, a conspicuous naval instructor known also for 'Mr Hall's devil stick', a slide-rule of his own devising. In 1903 the Admiralty deleted the 'lunar' from the syllabus while Mr Hall's method was at the printers. Perhaps the 'lunar' was kept alive over 130 years by the likes of the Reverend Maskelyne and the Reverend Hall. Captain Lecky, whose sagacity in matters marine was revered, wrote in his famous *Wrinkles*[26] 'The writer of these pages, during long experience at sea (i.e. since 1855) . . . has not fallen in with a dozen men who had themselves taken Lunars or had even seen them taken . . . They are in fact as dead as Julius Caesar.'

Notes to Chapter 6

1. If the needle everywhere were to point to some fixed place on the earth's surface, the position of an observer who knows his latitude and variation is trigonometrically determinate. In fact, the isogonal would be what came to be known in the age of radio bearings as 'the line of constant bearing' (Chapter 10). Unfortunately terrestrial magnetism is not like that. Walker's ingenious instrument combined a sun compass and a magnetic compass (see also Chapter 8 and Hutchins and May 1952).

2. Waters (1989). The extension of the idea of Hipparchus to occultations and appulses has been attributed to Vespucci. An appulse occurs when the moon passes through its closest point to a star. How Halley acquired the lunar ephemerides to achieve the accuracy he claimed remains a mystery. As mentioned elsewhere in the text, the lunar longitude tabulated in *Connoissance des temps* at that period was often 10′ in error, corresponding to an error in terrestrial longitude of 5°. Halley never applied for the prize for finding the longitude within 1°, although he had every opportunity to do so from 1714 on.

3. Some sources refer to the use of isogonals by the Jesuit Christopher Borrus a century earlier. After Halley, isogonic world charts were largely left to private enterprise. The first Admiralty chart showing world-wide magnetic variation is dated 1858.

4. Either the king changed his mind or Colbert had different ideas. Members of the Académie included the king's own physician, chemists, anatomists, and a botanist. Perhaps Colbert was an early believer in inter-disciplinary synergy.

5. Willebrod Snell, chiefly remembered today for his law of refraction, was professor of mathematics at Leiden, the latinized name of which is *Lugdunum Batavorum*.

6. The metre was not adopted in France until 1799. The unit of length used by the Académie (and also by Snell) was the *toise*, six French feet, which were rather longer than English feet. The *toise* is converted here at 1 *toise* = 1.949 m. On 15 April 1903, a letter was published in *The Times* suggesting that the *Almanach Hachette* was inaccurate in attributing a length of 325 mm to the old French foot, of which there were six in a toise. On 2 May 1903 Hachette et Cie indignantly replied 'L'ancienne toise de France était de 6 pieds et mesure *exactement* 1 mètre 949 millimètres . . .'. This seems to be the last word.

7. Newton's prediction was that the ratio of the equatorial diameter to the difference between equatorial and polar diameters should be 230. Geodesists were not more accurate for another hundred years. The figure adopted for the International Ellipsoid of Reference is 297.

8. With the geometry of Descartes and the calculus of Newton it was easy to show that, for an oblate spheroid, the radius of curvature at geographic latitude ϕ is $a[1 - \frac{1}{4}e^2(1 + 3\cos2\phi)]$, where a is the equatorial radius and e the eccentricity of the meridians, and higher powers of e are ignored.

9. Jacques Cassini succeeded his father as Director of the Paris Observatory in 1712 and published *De la grandeur et de la figure de la terre* in 1720.

10. Analysis of the orbits of artificial satellites was used for geodetic purposes decades before satellites specifically intended for navigation were operational. The results suggest that the earth is slightly pear-shaped, with an elevation at the north pole of 15 metres and a depression of the south pole of 20 metres. Sir Richard Phillips (1767–1840) would have been pleased. He is quoted by King-Hele (1964) as saying 'The world is shaped like a pear, not like an apple as those fools of Oxford say.' Presumably he meant Cambridge.

11. The precision of Huygens pendulum clocks was crucially important to the accuracy of Picard's survey mentioned earlier. The accuracy of time-measurement on land over the centuries is graphically illustrated by Pledge (1939). There was a curious consequence of the accuracy of pendulum clocks on land. It had long been known to astronomers that the apparent solar day, the interval between two successive noons, is not constant, and Kepler's laws tell us why this is so; but it was the pendulum clock which brought the fact to general cognizance, and demonstrated what a bad timekeeper the sun really is. Tables were inserted in clock cases giving the difference between mean and apparent time, in effect the *Equation of time* used by seamen to find the hour angle of the true sun from a chronometer reading mean time.

12. This expedition was also of importance because its observations were used to determine the parallax of Mars, indicating the scale of the solar system.

13. In Newtonian terms, the equation of motion of a simple pendulum with a small weighty bob and a weightless rod of length l is $l\ddot{\theta} + g\sin\theta = 0$, where θ is the displacement from the vertical in radians. If θ is small this may be written $l\ddot{\theta} + g\theta = 0$. On integration the period is given as $2\pi \sqrt{l/g}$. The period is therefore a function of gravity and the length of the rod, itself a function of temperature and the coefficient of expansion of the rod. If the rod is of steel, it will lose one second a day for each 2.2° rise in temperature. If the deflection of the pendulum is large, the pendulum is not isochronous. A second-order approximation is period = $2\pi\sqrt{l/g} \times 1.000019\alpha^2$, α being the half swing in degrees. The clock-maker must therefore make α small and nearly constant.

14. Gingerich and Wether (1983).

15. Fifty years earlier Robert Hooke had speculated on *annual parallax*, the change in a star's position during the year because of its finite distance. If it could be measured, the distance of the star could be determined in terms of the diameter of the earth's orbit around the sun; but any such parallax would be small in relation to possible errors due to refraction in those days. Hooke's solution was to observe a star in the constellation *Draco* which was almost overhead in London at its transit, thus virtually eliminating refraction. The star's position did seem to shift, but in a way more consistent with errors of instrument or observation than with annual parallax. Bradley repeated the observations with more refined instruments than had been available to Hooke, and measured the fluctuations. If annual parallax was the explanation, the maximum fluctuation would be between December and June. In fact it was between September and March. Bradley hit on the explanation which fitted, and used it to improve on Roemer's estimation of the speed of light. Robert Hooke's name frequently appears in these chapters. Professor of Geometry at Gresham College, he combined superb mechanical skills with an original and creative intellect in the best seventeenth-century tradition; but his work (as can be seen in context) was often inconclusive. Overshadowed by Newton, his name is perpetuated in Hooke's law of elasticity.

16. The rotation, of radius $9''$ and period 18.6 years, of the earth's polar axis.

17. Göttingen was in the electorate of Hanover; and the Elector of Hanover was King of England. The 'personal union' may have helped Mayer.

18. It was dissolved in 1828, 114 years after its institution.

19. Forbes (1965). Celestial latitude and longitude differ from declination and hour angle in that the reference plane is the ecliptic rather than the equator. The reference point for the prime meridian is the same in both cases, the first point of Aries (Υ), where the sun crosses the equator northbound.

20. The use of dividing scales goes back to a quadrant of Petrus Nonius in 1522. The vernier scale, essentially in its present form, was invented by Pierre Vernier in 1638.

21. This was the instrument which gave Captain James Cook such excellent results. On the conclusion of his second voyage of exploration, Cook wrote in the log that on making land about Plymouth on 29 July 1775, the error in longitude by Kendal's watch was only $7'45''$. How Cook took sights to such accuracy he does not say; but there is the entry in his own hand. While commanding *Endeavour* five years earlier Cook had remarked 'an observation (of longitude) to within $30'$ is a degree of accuracy sufficient for all nautical purposes'.

22. Gould (1923).

23. D. W. Waters (personal communication)

24. In 1905 the US Naval Department initiated regular time signals; but they were not available world-wide until several decades later.

25. Officers of the East India Company seem to have been regular users of the lunar-distance method even when equipped with a chronometer. Captain George Vancouver may be among the few to have checked his chronometers by lunar distance; but, like Vasco da Gama finding the latitude (Chapter 2), he went ashore to do it.

26. Lecky (1881).

CHAPTER SEVEN

Astronomical Navigation with Sextant and Chronometer

✣

THE 'mechanicks' had solved the problem which had defeated the scientists for generations, and had added injury to insult by acquiring wealth in the process. Until the advent of radio and the perception of the military value of the aeroplane, navigation, which had so long been the muse of science, became its peripatetic camp-follower. In particular, no mathematician of genius addressed the systematization of astronomical navigation with chronometers.

In 1796 Gauss was nineteen years old. He had already proved the law of quadratic reciprocity where others had failed. If he had chosen to concentrate on the navigator's problem then or, better still, some years later, when his interest had turned to conformal projection, he might have reasoned along such lines as these:

> *As the use of the marine sextant requires the horizon to be visible, seamen prefer to observe the sun. They determine the latitude at noon. After the sun has been observed again in the afternoon or the morning the three sides of the PZX triangle are known; seamen calculate the hour angle of the sun, and hence find their longitude (Fig. 7.1). The navigator should be able to fix his position when he needs to, and when he can; the sky may be obscured at noon and for much of the day. The noon observation, or any observation of culmination, is messy, since it involves not merely measuring the altitude, but also determining its maximum value.*
>
> *The information provided by any observation of the sun's altitude at a known time is that the observer lies on a circle, radius the zenith distance, centred on the subsolar point (Fig. 7.2). I shall call this the position circle. The fix provided by two observations on different azimuths is ambiguous, because two circles intersect at two points; but usually there is no doubt which is correct, because the two points are thousands of miles apart (Fig. 7.3). Each position circle is defined by an equation.*

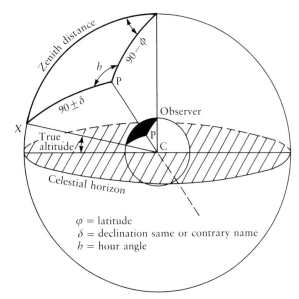

FIGURE 7.1
The sides of the triangle are known.

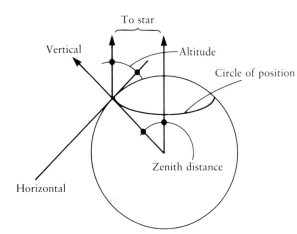

FIGURE 7.2
The astronomical position circle.

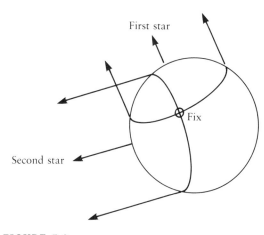

FIGURE 7.3
The astronomical fix.

We compensate for the ship's movement between the two observations by displacing the subsolar point of the first observation accordingly.[1] The problem is to solve two simultaneous equations with two solutions, one of which is impossible.

A solution by computation is tedious for seamen;[2] a combination of graphics and computation is easier. Unless the altitude of the sun is very high, the position circle appears as a straight line (which I shall call the position line*) on a suitable conformal projection in the vicinity of the position. When the altitude is 45°, the departure of the position circle from the great circle over 100 n.m. is only 1.2 n.m. One could assume a latitude. The three sides of the PZX triangle being known, it can be solved for hour angle (giving assumed longitude) and azimuth. The position line could then be drawn*

modified that the result of the three equations which must be solved is always a tangent and therefore read on the inner scale. This instrument was favoured by such noted astro practitioners of the 1930s as Francis Chichester and Donald Bennett.

One esoteric device, the *Astronomisches Richengerat* (originally proposed by Professor A. J. Bastien for Air France but taken up by Zeiss about 1940) uses rotation of an equatorial stereographic grid in the plane of the observer's meridian; thus P and Z are on the outer circle. If P is the pole, the grid is of declination and hour angle; if Z is the pole, the grid is curves of equal altitude and azimuth. The grid is engraved on a glass disc which can be rotated in a metal frame to which are attached a fixed microscope focused on the rim, and a second microscope which can be focused on any point on the plate. The fixed microscope is used to set the grid in the polar mode and the mobile microscope is set at the point on the grid corresponding to the declination and hour angle of the body observed. The fixed microscope is then used to rotate the grid in an angle equal to the assumed colatitude. The azimuth and computed altitude are then read through the mobile microscope. The device was successfully used by the Luftwaffe and in U-boats; it later gave satisfaction to a single-handed sailor on an Atlantic voyage.

There was some interest in the days of airships in analogue devices which reconstructed the PZX triangle by a system of arcs and circles. The *Spherotrigonometer* was employed on the *Graf Zeppelin*. Generally, such devices were too large and heavy for contemporary aeroplanes, and interest in them was only sustained for use as a compass. The Bumstead Sun Compass was used by Byrd and Floyd Bennett on their flight to the north pole in 1926. The hour circle, inclined by the amount of the colatitude, was driven by clockwork. When the azimuth circle was turned until the sun was aligned, the true heading could be read against a lubber line. The need for frequent resetting of latitude and longitude and the absence in most aeroplanes of a suitable site discouraged their use. The *astrocompass*, on similar lines but without the clockwork (being intended not as a steering compass but as a means of checking the magnetic compass), was produced in tens of thousands. It was widely used in astrodomes during the Second World War, and later in airlines, until an astrodome, complete with sextant and navigator, was sucked out of an early pressurized airliner, spelling the demise of the astrodome, and with it the astrocompass. The periscopic aircraft sextant became universal. Every time a sight was taken true heading could be checked by setting the calculated azimuth on a grid ring and reading the aircraft heading directly against a lubber line on the mounting.

The fact that the airman had no need to see the horizon when taking a sight led to a great revival of the use of the pole star for latitude determination (see Chapters 1 and 2). Before HO 249 (see below), the pole star was probably the airman's preferred celestial body because of the simplicity of the calculation. The correction to the altitude of Polaris to find the latitude can be expressed as a series. The first term depends only on the declination and hour angle of the star, the second also on its altitude. From 1834 three tables were provided in the *Nautical Almanac*, the first two corrected for the first two terms in the series and the third for the effect of the precession of the equinoxes on the position of the star. The British *Air*

Almanac tabulated a Q correction against LHA♈ assuming an altitude of 45° and a secondary correction, which was only necessary in arctic latitudes, for altitude.

Except for the revival of the use of the pole star to find latitude, astro, in the end, was based on inspection tables and the intercept method. Of the inspection methods intended exclusively for airmen, two are of particular historical importance. *Astronomical Navigation Tables* (ANTs) were prepared in 1938 to meet an RAF requirement, were republished in the USA by its Hydrographic Office (as HO 218), were translated into French and Spanish, and were the principal Allied means of sight reduction in the air during the Second World War. Bound in volumes covering only 5° of latitude are two quite different tables. In the first, against argument latitude, LHA, and declination in whole degrees, computed altitude is tabulated to the nearest minute, azimuth to the nearest degree, and an interpolation factor is tabulated to correct altitude for minutes of declination. The declination range is only 0°–28° to cover sun, moon, and planets. The second table was calculated for the exact declinations of 22 selected stars. They are entered with the *name* of the star, latitude, and the star's assumed local hour angle to read altitude and azimuth.

After the war, the final step was the star section of *HO 249 Computed altitude and true azimuth for all latitudes*. A large double page in a single volume is devoted to each whole degree of latitude. Entered with LHA♈ at intervals of 1° (2° for latitudes greater than 69°), altitude and azimuth are tabulated (to the same degree of accuracy as ANTs) for six preferred stars, which are reselected at intervals of 15° of LHA♈. Thirty-eight stars are used in all. All the navigator has to do is extract GHA♈ from the almanac for the time of the intended fix (even that would be unnecessary if he had a *sidéromètre*)), assume a latitude and longitude, apply the latter to GHA♈ to obtain LHA♈, open HO 249 to the page of the assumed latitude, and read the altitude and azimuth of the six selected stars all on the same line of LHA♈ (see Fig. 7.12). The improvement over ANTs, in terms of arithmetic and turning over of pages is obvious. As importantly, such tables, which became the final solution, led naturally to scheduled fixing and the habit of precomputation.

Two companion volumes provided tables of computed altitude and azimuth for use with sun, moon, and planets, on identical principles to ANTs (already described) but with a

Lat. 21° N

LHA ♈	Alkaid		ARCTURUS		SPICA		REGULUS		POLLUX		Dubhe	
	Hc	Zn	Hc	Zn	Hc	Zn	Hc	Zn	Hc	Zn	Hc	Zn
180	54–37	030	58–46	087	52–14	146	61–17	257	31–37	291	47–43	350
181	55–05	029	59–42	087	52–45	147	60–22	257	30–45	291	47–33	349
182	55–32	028	60–38	087	53–15	148	59–27	258	29–52	291	47–22	348
183	55–58	027	61–34	088	53–44	150	58–33	259	29–00	291	47–10	348
184	56–23	026	62–30	088	54–11	151	57–38	260	28–08	292	46–58	347
185	56–48	026	63–26	088	54–37	153	56–42	260	27–16	292	46–45	347
186	57–11	025	64–22	089	55–02	154	55–47	261	26–24	292	46–32	346
187	57–34	024	65–17	089	55–26	156	54–52	261	25–32	292	46–18	346
188	57–56	023	66–13	089	55–48	158	53–57	262	24–41	292	46–04	345
189	58–17	022	67–10	090	56–09	159	53–01	262	23–49	293	45–49	344
190	58–38	021	68–06	090	56–28	161	52–06	263	22–57	293	45–33	344
191	58–57	019	69–02	090	56–45	163	51–10	263	22–06	293	45–17	343
192	59–15	018	69–58	091	57–01	164	50–14	264	21–14	293	45–01	343
193	59–32	017	70–53	091	57–15	166	49–19	264	20–23	293	44–44	342
194	59–48	016	71–49	092	57–28	168	48–23	265	19–31	294	44–26	342

FIGURE 7.12
15° of HO 249 actual size.

totally different layout and arrangement more appropriate to the faster, longer-range aircraft of the period. The three volumes (published in Britain as AP 3270) became standard for astro navigators throughout the Western world, and quietly crept into marine use.

A defect shared by all tables calculated for specific stars and astrographic methods is the need, after a time, to correct for the precession of the equinoxes. At first this was done as a correction to the tables or curves, or as a correction to observed altitude. It was belatedly realized that it is much simpler to correct the observer's zenith, that is to say, the fix itself.

In arctic regions the pole as an assumed position is beguilingly simple. The computed altitude is the declination, and the direction of the azimuth is that meridian along which hour angle is zero. This led to the use of abnormally long intercepts in astro in polar regions, and a close scrutiny of the curvature of position circles on the polar stereographic projection. Special tables prepared for the Ellsworth and Hollick–Kenyon trans-Antarctic flight of 1935 permitted plotting position lines up to 700 n.m. from the intercept, using the pole as an assumed position. From about 1950 there was intensified interest in polar air navigation, as the north polar regions became the airspace intermediate between the USA and the USSR, and the air route between Northern Europe and the west coast of North America. More sophisticated astro techniques particular to very high latitudes were evolved.

There were difficulties in obtaining heading information, especially near the north magnetic pole, when the sun was just below the horizon for extended periods, providing too much light to see the stars. The solution was the most revolutionary development in the observing instruments of astronomical navigation since Hooke's reflecting quadrant three centuries earlier. The Pfund *Sky Compass* sensed the direction of the sun by analysis of the polarization of light in the sky. Direct sunlight is not polarized, but light scattered in the atmosphere (mainly in the blue part of the spectrum, as we can all see) is plane-polarized, and the polarization is perceived to be a maximum at points 90° from the sun. The sky compass became as superfluous as the rest of astro on the introduction of inertial systems (see Chapter 9). One problem of polar astro for which there was no satisfactory solution was the refraction correction for sun sights taken at negative altitudes. The refraction depended on the (unknowable) air density on the long path of the light through the lower atmosphere.

During the Second World War the Japanese Hydrographic Office produced an *Altitude and azimuth almanac* tabulating altitude and azimuth directly at such places of interest as Okinawa. This must surely be the ultimate in sight reduction, and the ultimate service of astronomers to navigators; but the multitude of possible assumed positions make such almanacs impossible in general usage. Altitude and azimuth almanacs may be regarded as an extreme case of precomputation, part of the realm of flight planning. An elegant example of precomputation is the altitude–time graph used by an RAF aircraft *Aries III* to home by astro on to the north pole in 1952. The altitudes of the sun and moon at the pole, and at the aircraft, are plotted against time. The azimuths of both bodies (relative to a Greenwich grid) are written in at ten-minute intervals. As can be seen in Fig. 7.13, the aircraft tracks parallel to the sun line through the pole, about 30′ down-sun, gradually converging on the moon line through the pole, which the aircraft reaches at 18.30. Course is then altered to track the

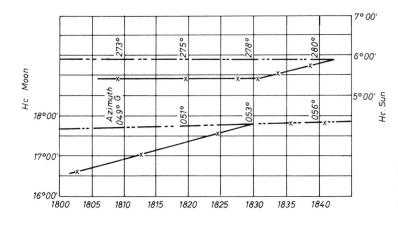

FIGURE 7.13

Aries III *astrohoming graph for 90°N in 1952.*

moon line through the pole, converging on the sun line, which it intersects over the pole at 18.42.

Sir Francis Chichester once remarked that the advantage of astronomical navigation is that the system is controlled by an authority which is not political. He should have added that the same authority degraded the reliability of the system by providing us with cloudy skies. Indeed, it is the sporadic unavailability of the system when it is most needed that led to the great contributions of Sumner and de Magnac. Ironically, when a vehicle for which astro would generally be available arrived, in the form of the high-flying jet, the inertial systems which would make astro obsolete were on the horizon. Astro's demise was mourned by its practitioners. Astronomical navigation was a satisfying craft. More than forty years ago, at the end of a long flight from Brazil to West Africa, the writer was obliged by radio failure, for the first time in his young life, to descend from a four-star fix through cloud over the sea on to a marine light. When we broke cloud and there was the light, exactly where it should have been, the sensation was more of harmony with the universe than satisfaction with oneself. A computer display is not the same thing.

Notes to Chapter 7

1. Gauss presumably would have realized that one cannot transfer a small circle along a spiralling rhumb without distorting it. As the distortion is entirely negligible over the distances involved in navigable latitudes one hopes he would not have allowed himself to digress.

2. Nevertheless, astro-fix by computation was always implicit in the double altitude method, and has been revived from time to time ever since in many forms, latterly for the use of yachtsmen with programmed or programmable trigonometrical pocket calculators.

3. César François Cassini, Director of the Paris Observatory and grandson of Giovanni, produced such tables in 1770.

4. Master mariners used to have to buy their own charts. There is a story that they resisted position-line navigation because they did not wish their charts to be worn out by junior officers drawing lines on them.

5. Raper was one of the most influential exegetes of nineteenth-century navigation. His book

Practice of navigation and nautical astronomy earned him the Gold Medal of the Royal Geographical Society. First published in 1840, the book was issued in the Royal Navy as ship's stores. The last edition appeared in 1920.

6. Quoted in Cotter (1968).

7. Lecky (1881).

8. In the *Proceedings of the Royal Society* in 1871 (Vol. 19) Thomson published a paper entitled 'On the determination of a ship's place from observations of altitude'. He proposed a 'short' method of dealing with the Sumner line which was complex and tedious. Later the same year he published an 'Amended Rule' which was a considerable improvement. Its particular historical interest is that his ideas subsumed the intercept method four years before St Hilaire's famous paper appeared.

9. *New altitude and azimuth tables between latitude 65N and 65S for the determination of the position line at sea*, Japanese Hydrographic Dept., 1920, English-language text 1924.

10. The US Navy Science and Research Laboratory at Langley Field undertook a systematic study of the problem in 1918. They tried cloud and haze horizons and experimented with a dipmeter which measures the angle between the forward and back horizons. They constructed the artificial horizon mentioned in the text and extensively evaluated results in the air with this instrument and Willson's bubble sextant, obtaining significantly better results with the latter. The conclusion of their report, entitled *The navigation of aircraft by sextant observations*, and dated 20 January 1919, is breathtaking: 'It will be seen from the foregoing that the problem of navigating an aeroplane by astronomical means may be regarded as solved, with all the accuracy which is requisite in aerial navigation.'

    In the meantime Captain T. Y. Baker RN (two other contributions of this ingenious man are mentioned in the text) had modified a marine sextant with prisms so that it gave a view of both the forward and back horizons. The instrument was entrusted to Lt. Cdr. K. Mackenzie Grieve RN who, with Hawker, would have been first across the Atlantic in May 1919, had radiator problems, after more than a thousand miles, not made them the first survivors of a mid-ocean aeroplane ditching. Unfortunately the instrument was damaged in transit, and Mackenzie Grieve used an ordinary marine sextant. He is quoted as saying: 'I preferred to navigate chiefly by celestial observations and my position by the stars when picked up was practically correct. I used a cloud horizon instead of a sea horizon because the sea was hardly visible at any part of the time we were in the air.'

    As this seems to have been the first operational use of astronomical navigation in aeroplanes we must suspend disbelief in the viability of cloud horizons.

11. Not everyone understood the difficulties of gyro-stabilized aircraft sextants so well at the time. H. E. Wimperis, the Director of Research at the British Air Ministry, said to the Royal Aeronautical Society in 1919 'gyrostatic methods of preserving the level are more attractive in theory, and thanks to the energy and ingenuity of inventors, there is good prospect of practical success being achieved.' It never was. However, Artificial Horizon Periscopic Sextants employing advanced gyroscopic technology, described in Chapter 9, were successful in submarines.

12. In Britain the bubble sextant is often attributed to L. P. Booth of the Royal Aircraft Establishment, Farnborough, whose work was known early in 1919 to Lt. (later admiral) R. E. Byrd USN, who had been entrusted with planning the navigation of the US Navy's crossing of the Atlantic via the Azores by flying boat in May 1919. Byrd seems to have been unaware of Willson's instrument. Captain G. Coutinho of the Portuguese Navy also devised a bubble sextant in 1919, which he conceived to be a kind of astrolabe.

13. Lt. Cdr. (later Captain) P. V. H. Weems retired from the US Navy to found his own navigation company. He was influential in the development of astro from the mid-1920s to the late 1940s.

CHAPTER EIGHT

Victoriana

☩

IN 1890 Commander Thomas Hull was preparing a new edition of Raper's *Practice of navigation and nautical astronomy*, first published in 1840 (see Note 5 to Chapter 7, p. 126). In fifty years science had transformed civilization, with railways, electric telegraphs, and machines of all kinds. In 1840 the Navy's capital ships were wooden sailing vessels which Drake would have recognized. In 1890 they were steam-powered ironclads which we would recognize as battleships; but so little had navigation changed that Hull could write 'Little could be done to improve this, the best of practical works on Navigation at Sea.' Hull could not know that in another century navigation would be largely based on electronics and inertial systems, which have their roots in developments during those fifty crucial years in the history of science and engineering. These are matters for subsequent chapters; but Hull could see with his own eyes developments affecting navigation in his own times, and it is with those that this chapter deals. They have their roots many centuries earlier and go on into the twentieth century; but they all still have a Victorian flavour, because it was during that period that their present shape was formed.

The Magnetic Compass in Iron Ships and Aeroplanes

So great was the problem in Hull's day that at some compass positions in the new battleships the directive force on the needle was only a quarter of the horizontal component of the earth's magnetic field. From 1876 compasses could be affected by dynamos which had been installed for electric searchlights. The effect of the large currents used in early radio circuits was yet to come.[1] Hull did what he could. The principal feature of his edition of Raper was a new chapter on the magnetic compass and its deviation by Captain W. Mayes, the Superintendent of the Admiralty Compass Department.

The problem of deviation of the compass by ferrous material in the ship was, in fact, much older than the ironclads. There was iron in ships before there were compasses. The earliest known reference to the deviation of the compass by iron is by João de Castro, a famous sixteenth-century navigator and viceroy of Portuguese India; but it is scarcely credible that no one noticed earlier the effect on the compass of shifting cannons, chains, and anchors.

In the eighteenth century iron was increasingly used for many purposes, not least the growing armament of warships; but even the most respected of navigators were unaware of the problem. We are told that Captain Cook kept his iron keys next to the compass, and that Captain Bligh kept his pistols in the binnacle. William Wales, who accompanied Cook on his second and third voyages as a scientific observer, kept detailed records of his many observations of magnetic variation, and concluded that it varied with both the ship's heading and the position of the compass itself in the ship; but he did not state the obvious explanation that the compass was deviated by the ship's magnetism. Mention was made in Chapter 6 of Walker's variation-measuring device (a combined sun and magnetic compass) which, Walker hoped, would enable the longitude to be found from the variation. Murdo Downie, who was instructed by the Admiralty to test the device, found that the indicated variation depended on the position of the instrument, and correctly concluded in his report in 1794 that 'the vicinity of iron in most ships has an effect in attracting the needle'. No one paid the least attention.

Walker's meridional compass.

Quite apart from the matter of deviation, the compass, for two centuries and more, did not receive the attention of princes, scientists, and instrument-makers which, in the same period, had been devoted to the longitude and astronomical instruments. It was mentioned in Chapter 5 that the loss of Admiral Sir Clowdisley Shovel and his thousands on the rocks of the Scillies in 1707 led indirectly to the Act of Longitude and the eventual 'finding out of the longitude' at sea. The incident may have had nothing to do with the longitude. An investigation of the 145 compasses carried by the squadron revealed that only three of them were serviceable. A modern study[2] of the surviving 44 logs showed no evidence that on any of the ships had any allowance been made for variation on the entire voyage from Gibraltar. When one recalls that some Portuguese rutters of the fifteenth century showed the magnetic variation of places in Africa, this seems peculiarly disgraceful. Something might have been done about both these matters for much less than £20 000.

A century later, in 1820 to be precise, Professor Peter Barlow of the Royal Military Academy was asked to inspect the compasses in the naval store at Woolwich. Barlow reported that the 150 instruments he saw were 'wretchedly defective' and 'would have disgraced the arts as they stood at the beginning of the eighteenth century'.[3] He castigated designers, manufacturers, and storekeepers alike. In the early part of the Crimean War, the first war in which screw-driven, steam-powered ships were used, the Hydrographer of the Navy reported to their Lordships that the Admiralty Compass Department was in the respectable hands of Mr James Brunton, whose qualification was 'the rank and education of a Sergeant of Artillery'. This was in Faraday's England! The previous year (1853) the total annual expenses of this department, charged with repairing all Naval Standard Compasses and supervising the adjustment of naval compasses generally, was £373—a far cry from £20 000 for Harrison's No. 4. in the previous century.

The scandalous neglect of the most important instrument of navigation should be viewed in the context of almost total ignorance about magnetism itself until the eighteenth century, although knowledge of terrestrial magnetism had been greatly extended in the course of the Great Pursuit (Chapter 6). The absence of any theory of magnetism (Chapter 4) had three important practical consequences in compass design, manufacture, and use. First, it was not known how to make strong permanent magnets—the magnetism of the compass needle had to be refreshed frequently by stroking with lodestone. Secondly, the dynamics of the pivoted needle were not understood. On a firm land base, a pivoted needle which is constrained to rotate only in the horizontal plane moves, if its motion is not damped, under the influence of the horizontal component of the earth's magnetic field exactly as does the simple pendulum under the influence of gravity, although not even that was understood. Forces generated by the motion of the ship enter into the equation of motion of the needle, and also bring the vertical component of the earth's magnetic field into it. In modern times the vertical component (Z) has typically been double the horizontal component (H) in English waters. Thirdly, in the absence of a useful theory of magnetism, the deviation of the compass could not be approached analytically.

Dr Gowin Knight, a London medical practitioner, came to the fore when he demonstrated to the Royal Society in 1745 his ability to make magnets much more powerful than any others. This led to his being consulted on ships' compasses from about 1749. Unsurprisingly, he was appalled at what he saw, and had little difficulty in making better compasses than the others then in general use. In particular, he employed flat bar (quasi-permanent) steel magnets instead of the conventional iron needles, which, after so many centuries, then gradually died out.

Knight was unaware of the dynamic problem. He employed a single magnet, fixed above the card to avoid piercing it, and balanced by a ring below the card. As a result, the moment of inertia of the rotating assembly was much greater in a north–south direction than in an east–west direction, causing a torque on the needle towards a direction at right angles to the axis of roll of the ship. The dynamic problem was analysed in the mid-nineteenth century by Archibald Smith. The moment of inertia about east–west and north–south axes can be made equal by employing two equal magnets fixed symmetrically on either side of the north–south line of the card, so that both their lengths subtend 30° at the pivot. The same effect is achieved with four magnets if the outer magnets subtend 45° and the inner magnets 15°.

One can understand that the humble compass did not arouse the intellectual curiosity of scientists in the way that astronomy and even terrestrial magnetism did, but the indifference of navigators, indeed their disrespect for the compass—which must have cost so many of them their lives—is another matter. It may relate to a lack of confidence in DR arising in part from uncertainty as to leeway, which, at the extreme, could be 30°. The distinction between leeway, drift, magnetic variation, and compass error, the four different causes of the difference between the compass course steered and the true track made good, was not addressed. Fanning writes[3]

> experienced masters and pilots of the period used sometimes to make an allowance when shaping a course on regular passages, although they were generally unaware of why it should be necessary to do so and could not have explained why it might be required when sailing in one direction but not in another. This allowance was often referred to as 'in draft' and we are told that in HMS Victory it sometimes amounted to one and a half points (17°). Of the many factors which contributed to inaccurate and often disastrous navigation, the error of the compass was fast becoming the most potent, but it was still the least understood.

The analysis of the deviation of the compass by the ship's magnetism, as it evolved in the nineteenth century, predicates that the ship's magnetism is of two kinds, induced and permanent. Hysteresis is ignored. Magnetism is induced instantaneously in the soft iron of the vessel by the earth's magnetic field. The magnetism so induced changes when the ship alters course or moves to a part of the world where the earth's field is different. The permanent magnetism of a ship is assumed to have been induced in its steel by the earth's field during construction, the vibration caused by the hammering and riveting allowing the molecules of the steel to align themselves permanently in a way that is determined by the lie of the ship during construction. The model is crude, but it has worked surprisingly well. In wooden sailing ships induced magnetism predominated; as steel became increasingly used, permanent magnetism acquired a corresponding importance. In aircraft there is usually no soft iron.[4]

The effects of induced magnetism may be illustrated by horizontal and vertical soft iron bars. One (parameter a) lies horizontally in the direction of the bow, as in Fig. 8.1. It will

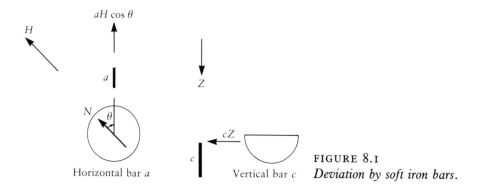

FIGURE 8.1
Horizontal bar a Vertical bar c *Deviation by soft iron bars.*

have the greatest intensity of magnetization when it lies in the direction of the horizontal component of the earth's field (H), that is to say when the ship is heading north or south; but it will not deflect the compass needle, but merely change the directive force on it. When the bar is at right angles to H (ship heading east or west) no magnetism will be induced in the bar, and there will be no deviation. Deviation is a maximum on the quadrantal headings, and the value of the deviation is the same for all values of H, because the deviating force varies as the directive force. Magnetism is induced in the vertical bar represented by parameter f by the vertical component (Z) of the earth's field and, so long as Z does not change, the effect of the bar on the compass is indistinguishable from that of a horizontal permanent magnet of the same value in the same position. However, when the ship moves to the magnetic equator ($Z=0$), the magnetism of the bar diminishes to zero, and in the opposite hemisphere polarity is reversed, whereas the field due to a permanent magnet would have remained unchanged.

Perhaps the first man to see a glimmering of all this was Captain Matthew Flinders, who, in the course of his survey work, became aware that his compass bearings of a landmark changed with every alteration of course. In 1801 Flinders was sent in command of a vessel to Australia. On his way to the Cape he determined that the deviation of the compass was greatest on east and west headings and least on north and south headings. Furthermore, he noticed that the deviation decreased in equatorial latitudes, where magnetic dip approached zero, and increased again in the opposite direction in the southern hemisphere. Flinders suggested a 'counter attractor' to compensate: 'Take a strong bar of old iron, of such a length that when one end is let into the deck, the other will be nearly upon a level with the compass card.'[5] The 'Flinders Bar' was not introduced for another fifty years.

In a series of papers published in Paris from 1824, Simeon Denis Poisson, who made many mathematical contributions to electromagnetism, analysed the deviation of the compass by induced ship's magnetism in terms of the nine parameters illustrated in Fig. 8.2. Although these dimensionless parameters are an abstract concept, the iron bars of Flinders are a close analogy. When the ship is level, the last three parameters only affect the vertical component of the field at the compass, and thus cause no deviation; but when a sailing ship is heeled, which it normally is in a wind, they have a component in the horizontal. It is not difficult to

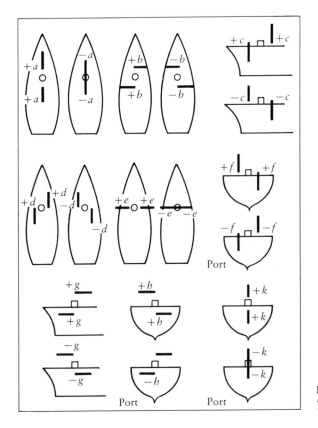

FIGURE 8.2
The nine rods equivalent to Poisson's parameters.

show that, provided *a* to *f* are small numbers in absolute terms and the ship is upright, the deviation in radians is

$$\tfrac{1}{2}(d-b) + c\tan D.\sin\theta + f\tan D.\cos\theta + \tfrac{1}{2}(a-e).\sin 2\theta + \tfrac{1}{2}(b+d)\cos 2\theta$$

where θ is the course and D is the angle of dip ($\tan^{-1} Z/H$). These deviations can be corrected, as Flinders saw, by iron bars having an equal and opposite effect. Poisson was, of course, perfectly aware of the potential deviation of the compass by permanent magnets; but he rightly believed that, in the wooden sailing ships of the period, with their anchors, chains, shot, cannon-balls, and so on, induced magnetism would predominate. The perfected theory of compass deviation in such ships thus finally became available just as they were becoming obsolete.

In the course of what was probably the first comprehensive magnetic survey of a ship, Commander E. J. Johnson showed in 1835 that the iron paddle-steamer *Garryowen* was a very different matter. The ship was tightly moored and warped around all points of the compass. A theodolite was used to take bearings relative to the ship's heading of landmarks of known magnetic bearing, and so to measure the deviation of the compass in fifteen positions aboard ship. From a historical point of view, perhaps Johnson's most significant observation was the effect of warping the ship on compasses ashore. The proximity of the bow and the stern deflected compasses on the quay in opposite directions. Johnson rightly concluded that the ship itself was a permanent magnet.

In 1837 Professor (later Sir) George Airy, the Astronomer Royal, began to interest himself in the matter. To a mathematician of his calibre it was apparent at that date that if (as we would now say) the permanent field at the compass position is resolved into components P, Q, R respectively in the directions of the ship's longitudinal axis, the starboard beam and the vertical, the deviation of the compass in radians when the ship is upright, provided P and Q are small in comparison with H, is $(P/H) \sin \theta + (Q/H) \cos \theta$. This takes no account of the effect of permanent magnetism on induced magnetism nor of heeling error. Airy conducted observations on two iron ships, and published his conclusions in the *Transactions of the Royal Society* in 1839. His conclusions may be summarized as follows.

1. Induced and permanent magnetism were present in both ships, but the permanent magnetism was by far the more effective.

2. That (as we would now say) 'swinging the ship' to find deviation around the compass enables the constants in an approximate formula of his own devising to be determined.

3. These constants known, the ship's permanent magnetism may be countered by a suitably situated permanent magnet, and its induced magnetism by a suitably situated 'scroll' of soft iron. By such means 'the compass may be made to point exactly as if it were free of disturbance'.

4. Vertical permanent magnetism is too slight to produce material heeling error ['It appears . . . therefore that there is no fear of great disturbance of the compass by the heeling of the ship.']

5. [It will be apparent to the reader of the above discussion that P and cZ have identical effects at any one magnetic latitude, as do Q and fZ. Airy recognized this, despite his broad assertion quoted in 3. above.] One of the constants consists of two parts which cannot be separated by experiment at one place. They can be separated by analysis of the constant in two different magnetic latitudes.

6. The 'uniformity' of induced magnetism may be presumed; but the invariability of permanent magnetism over a period of years is by no means certain.

Airy laid the foundations of compass compensation in ships and aircraft; but his system was flawed in two respects. Heeling error was a much more serious matter than Airy imagined. Furthermore, in many vessels of the period, vertical soft iron parameters (c and f) were much larger than Airy had supposed. His method, which was to compensate them (being indistinguishable from P and Q) by permanent magnets had the effect of increasing the deviation when the ship moved from one hemisphere to the other. In consequence, compass compensation fell into disrepute for some years, particularly among the many who did not understand it. If one swings a ship and determines the deviation of a compass on all headings, one may either correct it, as Airy proposed (and Flinders before him), or prepare a deviation card. It was not generally realized until later in the century that the real case for compensation is not to save the navigator or helmsman the trouble of reading a correction card, but to ensure that, as far as possible, the directive force on the needle is close to H on all headings. The matter became more important as more iron and steel were used.

The name of Archibald Smith has already been mentioned in the context of his analysis of the dynamic problem (in 1841). In the previous century a London physician had made notable contributions to the subject; now it was the turn of a London barrister, which Smith was—he was also a competent mathematician. As Fanning[3] puts it:

> Smith had presented a series of papers to the Royal Society (in 1841, 1844 and 1845) in which he derived, from Poisson's original fundamental equations, a series of elegant and precise formulae which were both practical and easy to apply, enabling the various portions of a ship's magnetism to be analyzed numerically. He thus succeeded for the first time in reducing a very complex problem to a set of rules and coefficients which could readily be understood by the intelligent non-mathematician and which, in their essentials, are still in use today'.

In the simple case, with all parameters and components of the ship's magnetism small and the ship upright, Smith's formula for deviation is $A + B\sin\theta + C\cos\theta + D\sin 2\theta + E\cos 2\theta$, a result which we might anticipate from the discussion above. The coefficients A, B, C, D, E are still so called, and they can all be found by simple arithmetical operations on deviations found on the cardinal and quadrantal points. In a full analysis higher terms of $\sin\theta$ and $\cos\theta$ occur, as we might expect from Fourier's theorem (mentioned below in the section on Tides, p. 147). Smith went on to perfect the theory, including such matters as the induction of magnetism in surrounding soft iron by the compass needle itself.

In the last chapter mention was made of the contributions to astronomical navigation of (Sir) William Thomson (later Lord Kelvin). He himself claimed that his close attention was first attracted to compasses by the necessity to write an obituary on Archibald Smith for the Royal Society. Be that as it may, his work on compasses was of much greater importance to seamen than his work on astronomical navigation—and of pecuniary advantage to himself.

Thomson started in 1874 with a paper containing a mathematical analysis of the perturbation of the compass by roll as opposed to heeling. He showed that the perturbation could be very large if the period of oscillation of the needle was small in relation to the period of roll. He saw that it was necessary to make compasses of longer period, and knew that the period of a freely pivoted undamped magnetic needle was $2\pi\sqrt{(K/MH)}$ where K is the moment of inertia and M the magnetic moment. K cannot be made large by making the card massive (on considerations of pivot friction), but only by concentrating the mass of a light

Thomson's 10 inch card compass

system in the periphery. M can be made small by using short but powerful magnets. Liquid damping makes the period longer. In 1876 Thomson patented his first compass. It had a very light paper card with an aluminium rim. The weight of the 9-inch card was only 7 per cent of the weight of the 7½-inch card of the Admiralty Standard Compass. The compass gimbals were supported on knife edges, and, although the card itself was dry, some liquid damping was provided. The magnets were short and as powerful as could then be.

The same patent included a binnacle which was the ancestor of all well-designed binnacles since. To correct Smith's coefficients B and C, two pairs of small scissor magnets were carried. The resultant field of a pair of small scissor magnets varies as the cosine of half the angle between the plates, and so is susceptible of simple screw adjustment. Such scissor magnets are still used to compensate simple magnetic compasses for permanent magnetism. Coefficients D and E were compensated by soft iron spheres. Heeling error due to permanent magnetism was corrected by a vertical blade magnet the position of which was adjusted by a clamp. Coefficient A of course was corrected simply by realigning the lubber line. Like Airy a generation earlier, Thomson understood that like should be compensated with like, permanent magnetism by permanent magnets, induced magnetism by soft iron; but it was inescapable[6] that if a ship were swung in only one place, the effects of parameters c and f cannot be separated from P and Q, nor can the parameters of heeling error (g, h, k) be separated from component R. Thomson visualized that his compass would be compensated whenever necessary by the ship's officers so that no corrections for deviation would be required. He had an advantage over Airy in that the increased use of steel had brought acceptance of the Airy principle of correction.

At the end of the nineteenth century dry card compasses were still favoured, although it had long been known that floating the system in liquid reduced pivot friction, and the damping which the liquid provided could be used to extend the period; back in 1813 Crow had patented a liquid compass in which the card was used as a float and the swirl effects which were an important objection to liquid compasses were reduced by making the card small in relation to the diameter of the bowl. The other perceived disadvantages of liquid-filled compasses included leakage of liquid, expansion of the liquid in high temperatures, paint discoloration, and complexity of maintenance. At its height of popularity, spare parts for Thomson's dry card compass could be found at many a chandler, and the compass could easily be repaired at sea—considerations which were to be reflected in the attitude of users of other navigation systems in the earlier part of the twentieth century. Besides, masters liked to see a lively compass—it showed that it was working.

The great apparent defect of the dry card was its response to engine vibration, the firing of broadsides, and even rough weather. The dry card was almost useless in high-speed buffeted vehicles such as the new torpedo boats, to say nothing of aeroplanes. Although dry card compasses continued to be used in merchant ships well into the middle of the twentieth century, the key step in the eventual victory of the liquid compass was Chetwynd's patent liquid compass[7] of 1906, which rediscovered one of Crow's principles nearly a century earlier. The ratio of the card diameter to the bowl diameter was so reduced that the card was virtually free of the influence of liquid swirl around the perimeter of the bowl.

Crow's patent liquid compass (1813).

At the beginning of the twentieth century two novel vehicles, the submarine[8] and the aeroplane, were introduced, each with its own unique navigational problems. The submarine, when submerged, is a sealed enclosed steel vessel within which no magnetic compass can

137

operate properly. The first solution was a sealed non-ferrous binnacle fixed outside the submarine which could be read inside it by a telescopic device. As early as 1908 these were being replaced by external projector binnacles, which displayed the heading on a ground glass screen before the helmsman.

The year 1908 also saw the first sea trials of the gyrocompass, an instrument, discussed in detail in the next chapter, which has no magnetic sensor. It relies on the force of gravity, the rotation of the earth, and the properties of the gyroscope to seek true north. In historical fact it was the needs of the submarine which first led Anschütz-Kaemphe to develop this instrument. In later years, at least in larger naval vessels, the gyrocompass virtually superseded the magnetic compass, which became, in such ships, a stand-by. Indeed, the battleship HMS *Vanguard* had a triplicated gyrocompass system with over 200 repeaters but no magnetic compasses. In 1947 it was steered for a few hours by the stars during a complete power failure. For reasons explained in the next chapter the gyrocompass could not be applied to the aeroplane, which thus became, after its military potential was understood, the principal challenge to science in the field of *magnetic* compasses. The technology described below which responded to that challenge also found marine application, notably in small high-speed naval surface vessels.

The earliest compasses to be tried in aircraft were designed for other purposes and were generally useless. The problems immediately perceived were vibration and buffeting, and large angles of bank, including complete inversion. Obviously, only liquid compasses would serve; but, despite extra provisions for absorbing vibration, the earliest compasses designed specifically for aircraft would sometimes spin—the vibrating pivot of the compass reproducing the juggler's trick of spinning a plate on the tip of a billiard cue. This difficulty was solved in 1915 by the inverted pivot, the first development in compass technology inspired by the aeroplane. In this arrangement, the pivot is fixed to the magnetic assembly and bears

FIGURE 8.3
A vertical card compass. The RAF P3.

on a jewelled cap fixed on a stem arising from the bowl. Another early innovation was the vertical card illustrated in Fig. 8.3, which enabled the pilot to look at the compass horizontally instead of looking down to read it; an early example of what came to be called, later in the century, 'a *head-up* display'.

Despite such measures the aircraft compass was useless in anything other than straight and level flight. The correct explanation was published by Keith Lucas of the Royal Aircraft Factory in 1917. When the aircraft is correctly banked in a turn, the compass needle or card rotates in the plane defined by the aircraft's lateral and longitudinal axes, that is to say at right angles to the *apparent* vertical. The magnetic assembly is as incapable as the bubble in the airman's sextant of distinguishing between gravity and other forces. Figure 8.4 is in the vertical plane through magnetic north, the aircraft are flying due east or west, and the dip of the Earth's magnetic field is 65° (in the direction T in the figure), typical of southern England at the time. In 4(a) the aircraft is straight and level; the compass needle points north. In 4(b) the aircraft is correctly banked at 25°, and there is no directive force on the needle. In 4(c) the aircraft is correctly banked at 45°, and the direction of the directive force is reversed. North has become south. On all other headings there is some deviation at all angles of bank and, provided that the angle of bank is less than the complement of dip, the deviation is at its maximum on north—hence the inapposite name *northerly turning error*. Heading north, the turning error in correctly banked turns over England is very roughly 30° with 15° of bank and 60° with 45° of bank. The effect can be that the swing of the compass (say towards west), is greater than the rate of turn (in this case towards the west), giving the impression that one is turning east. If a pilot attempts to fly in cloud by magnetic compass alone, the slightest turn quickly tightens until the 'g' forces on the pilot's body signal the tightness of the turn but not its direction.

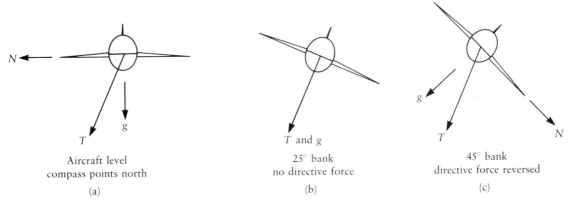

Aircraft level compass points north	25° bank no directive force	45° bank directive force reversed
(a)	(b)	(c)

FIGURE 8.4
Turning error.

The immediate reaction was two opposite opinions. One school held that the period of the compass should be very long to damp the deviation during the turn, the other that the compass was useless in turns, and the period should be as short as possible, so that the compass would quickly return to normal when the aeroplane levelled. In Britain the argument was resolved by the invention in 1918 of the aperiodic compass, with the characteristic illustrated in Fig. 8.5. The inventors, G. R. C. Campbell and G. T. Bennett, achieved aperiodicity using six very small magnetic needles mounted on a light frame carrying four damping filaments but no card, only a north–south pointer. There was a rotatable verge ring carrying parallel wires aligned north–south with respect to the markings on the verge ring. One such compass, widely used by the Royal Air Force during the Second World War, is illustrated in Fig. 8.6. To determine the course, the pilot had to rotate the verge ring until the grid wires were parallel with the needle. To steer a course, it was set on the verge ring and the aeroplane was flown so that the needle lay parallel with the grid wires.

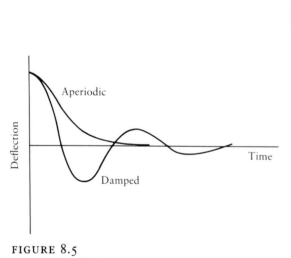

FIGURE 8.5
Compass oscillations.

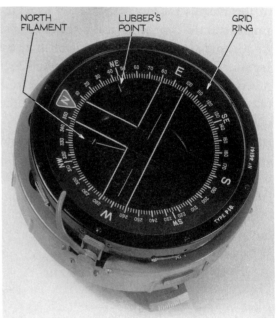

FIGURE 8.6
The P 10. RAF aperiodic grid steering compass. World War II.

Although the principles of the Campbell–Bennett compass dominated RAF steering compasses for thirty years, it had two manifest disadvantages compared with the vertical card compass. A manual operation was required to determine what the actual course was whenever the pilot was not flying a pre-set course; and a compass the pilot had to look down on was likely to be subject to stronger deviating fields than a compass at eye level. For these reasons the vertical card compass won the day in the world as a whole, despite the near-perfect aperiodicity of the British grid steering compass.

From about 1920 it was recognized that the defects of the simple magnetic compass in aeroplanes were irremediable. Northerly turning error was inescapable. There could be no binnacle remote from the engine and its magneto, guns, electrical circuits, and radio apparatus; the compass had to be positioned where the pilot could read it when he could spare a moment from more pressing activities. There was still no prospect of adapting the gyro-compass to aircraft. Three tangled threads may be distinguished. One was the development of means to present to the pilot the output of a magnetic sensor in the tail or the wing-tip, far from the deviating fields in the cockpit;[9] another the development of magnetic sensors other than the pivoted needle; a third was the various ways of using the short-term stability of a gyroscope to smooth the output of the magnetic compass during turns and accelerations.

The remote-reading pivoted needle compass was invented before the first aeroplane flew. Von Peichl's[10] *Electric Patent Compass* of 1892 may have been the first. The idea was that when at rest and aligned, the needle lay between two contacts fixed to the bowl. Any change of heading caused a contact one way or the other, and a follow-up motor turned both the bowl and the remote indicator until the contact was broken.

An instrument invented by Karl Bamberg in 1920, claimed to be the first remote-reading aircraft compass, had a metal disc, cut to act as a shutter, which was attached to the compass float. Electric lamps below the float were focused on selenium cells above the float, each of which formed an arm of a Wheatstone bridge.[11] When the shutter was so aligned with respect to the selenium cells that equal light fell on them, the aircraft was on the pre-set heading and there was no current in the zero-centre galvanometer across the bridge. Remote-reading instruments such as this and the *Pioneer* instrument used by Lindbergh (see below), which relied on a galvanometer to indicate whether the pilot was left or right of a pre-set course, were known at the time as *telecompasses*.

Albert Patin's compass of 1935 was perhaps the first successful self-synchronous remote-reading magnetic compass displaying the heading on 360° dials. The magnetic element trailed delicate brushes at intervals of 120° over a toroidal potentiometer which was energized (d.c.) in parallel with a similar potentiometer at the repeater. The three brushes were connected through slip rings and moving coils to similar brushes on the repeater potentiometer, the coils and brushes being fixed to the spindle carrying the repeater card. The coils were in the field of a permanent magnet. When the orientation of the brushes on the potentiometer at the repeater did not agree with that at the compass, the d.c. current flowing through the coils at the repeater produced a magnetic field which, in reaction to the permanent field, turned the repeater card until there was balance. An improved version of this compass, combined with a gyroscope, was successfully used by the Luftwaffe during the Second World War.

The main RAF distant-reading compass during that war, known simply as the DRC, was under development at the Royal Aircraft Establishment from 1925 to 1940, and reminds one of von Peichl's device. At the master unit a gyro was fixed to the inner frame. For 2.5 seconds in every 7-second cycle (the period of the compass was 14 seconds) the magnetic element was clamped. If the inner frame was not aligned with the compass, a contact was made, precessing the gyro electrically in the desired direction, and so turning the inner frame. The transmission system was not self-synchronous, but it developed a very large torque, enabling it to drive mechanical analogue navigation and bombing instruments.[12]

An alternative to the pivoted needle is a device which produces electrical currents proportional to the component of the earth's magnetic field in various directions relative to the aircraft's axes. In 1924 the Pioneer Instrument Company produced an earth inductor compass which was later successfully used by Lindbergh on his solo New York–Paris flight. The instrument consisted of an electrical generator (driven at very high r.p.m. by a windmill in the slipstream) in which the only magnet was the earth's magnetic field, and a zero-centre galvanometer. The pilot set the required heading by a 'controller'. This action, through a flexible shaft, oriented in azimuth adjustable brushes which collected the current and conducted it to the galvanometer. As electromotive force induced in a coil is proportional to the rate of change of magnetic flux linked with it, the meter read zero when the axis of the coil through the brushes was perpendicular to the magnetic meridian. Although many ingenious remote-reading pivoted needle compasses were invented, mainly between the two World Wars, it was inevitable that earth inductor compasses would win the day, if only because a remote pivoted needle requires some ancillary device to convert the orientation of the needle into electrical signals to the indicator before the pilot.

The key to inductor compasses was the development during the 1930s of metal alloys, variously known as mu-metal and permalloy, having the magnetic qualities of idealized soft iron. There is virtually no hysteresis, so that if a strip of permalloy is placed in the centre axis of a coil the magnetism of the strip will alternate with any alternating current flowing through the coil. The intensity of magnetization will vary almost linearly with the current up to its saturation point; beyond that value no increase in the field will produce any increase in the intensity of magnetization of the strip.

Figure 8.7 illustrates the basic principle of a saturable inductor variously known by the trade names 'fluxgate' (Pioneer, later Pioneer Bendix) or 'fluxvalve' (Sperry). The primary coil is wound in series in opposite directions around two identical parallel permalloy strips. The secondary coil is wound around the whole assembly. The primary a.c. excitation is sufficient to saturate the strips. In the absence of any other magnetic source, the total flux linked with the secondary will be zero. If however there is a component of the earth's magnetic field parallel to the strips, it will have no effect on the strip momentarily saturated in the same direction, but it will reduce the magnetization in the opposite direction of the other. The net result is that an electromotive force (EMF) is induced in the secondary at

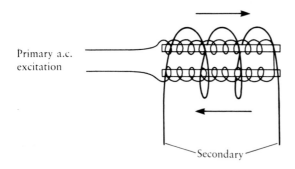

Primary a.c. excitation

Secondary

FIGURE 8.7
A fluxvalve element.

twice the frequency of the primary excitation, and of a magnitude that varies with the component of the earth's field parallel to the strips. Three such devices arranged as the sides of an equilateral triangle, or equidistant spokes, constitute a sensor of the earth's magnetic field. As an illustration of principle only (real instruments are more complicated), Fig. 8.8 shows how the EMF induced in the three secondaries could be used, after amplification and rectification, to reproduce at the indicator an amplified analogue of H which can be displayed on the instrument panel by a magnet on a spindle. Apart from the indicating needle itself, there are no moving parts. The invention of the saturable inductor is attributed to H. Antranikian in 1936; but Ettore Caretta, working in Italy at about the same time, may have had the first inductor compass with no moving parts other than the indicator itself.

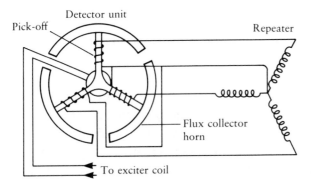

FIGURE 8.8
Basic principle of a simple fluxvalve compass.
Primary, amplifier and rectifier not shown.

Stable heading references were obtained by combining gyros with magnetic compasses in one of three ways:

1. *The gyro direction indicator.* A simple gyro, which need not be highly precise, and with no north-seeking capability, mounted so that the rotor spin axis is normally horizontal, can be used as a heading reference provided that it is frequently reset to the magnetic compass when the aircraft is in straight, level, unaccelerated flight. It is odd that such an instrument was not generally known until the late 1920s (see Chapter 9). The French navy had first tried such instruments on a ship forty years earlier. Simple directional gyros are still used on light aircraft. The demand for accurate aircraft heading references in high magnetic latitudes led in 1950 to the Kearfoot N1 compass, incorporating a gyro with a random error of less than 1° per hour.

2. *Gyrostabilized compass platforms.* An inductor sensor, but not a pivoted needle, may be maintained in the horizontal plane by a gyro precessed by a gravity sensor such as a pendulum.[13] The gravity sensor is, of course, incapable of distinguishing between gravity and other forces, but the precessing force is arranged to be so weak that erroneous signals during a turn are insufficient to produce significant turning error unless the aircraft is continuously turning, over an extended period, in the same direction. This was the principle of the Pioneer Fluxgate Compass developed in the USA during the Second World War, and widely used in airlines in the early years after that war.

3. *Gyromagnetic compasses.* The precession of the directional gyro may be controlled by a

magnetic sensor. As in the gyrostabilized compass, the precessing force is chosen to be so weak that the erroneous signals received for the duration of a 180° turn do not produce significant turning error. As turning error is equal and opposite on northerly and southerly headings, it does not matter if the aircraft is continuously turning—it cannot turn steeply for long in one direction in one sector. The first gyromagnetic compasses (already described) employed pivoted needle magnetic sensors; but in the 1940s realization that the sensor should be a saturable inductor became general. The Pioneer Fluxgate was replaced by the Sperry Gyrosyn. The sensor, a fluxvalve installed in the wing-tip, weighed less than ½ kg and required no maintenance, whereas instruments such as the DRC required the care of skilful mechanics. Its output controlled the precession of a gyro, which replaced the directional gyro on the pilot's instrument panel. In effect the resetting of the directional gyro had become automated. Any aircraft permanent magnetism in the wing-tip was compensated by an electrically induced, remotely controlled field—the first major innovation in compass compensation since Thomson's binnacle.

Both this Part and that on astronomical navigation have stressed the response of science to the peculiar needs of the aeroplane. This reflects the explosion in technology in the aviation era, of which indeed the aeroplane itself is a part, and the growing importance of the aeroplane in war and peace. Also, the aeroplane (like the submarine) posed novel navigational problems. In the case of astro it was the need for a real-time system with immediate application of frequent observations to navigation and the difficulties of determining the vertical accurately without a horizon. In the case of heading reference systems it was northerly turning error, the fact that the pilot sits where the aircraft's magnetic field is strong, and the impracticality of the gyrocompass, which provided the mariner and the submariner with an alternative to the magnetic compass.

Tides

Early navigators of the coastal waters of north-western Europe were concerned with the tide for several reasons. No one wishes to be stranded at low tide; in the English Channel, for example, and near most estuaries, there are very shallow waters and sometimes shifting sandbanks. Even after the compass was in common use, DR could not be relied upon because of the currents and tidal streams. In the prevalent cloudy skies and limited visibility, seamen relied heavily on soundings, which had to be interpreted according to the state of the tide. Finally, sailing with the tide was as important as sailing with the wind. The use of the tidal stream to achieve his objective was an important part of the navigator's art in such waters.

As the Mediterranean tides are so small, the subject was scarcely addressed in ancient Greece.[14] The tide is one natural phenomenon on which the imperialist Romans were better informed. It embarrassed them during the invasion of Britain. Pliny the Elder was aware in the first century AD of the twice monthly spring and neap tides. He knew that at a particular place there was a roughly constant interval (the lunitidal interval) between the moon's crossing the meridian and high tide; but he associated the tide only with the moon, and not with the sun.

All this and more must have been known to sailors in coastal tidal waters in prehistoric times. It is a matter of common observation that the amplitude of the tide is a maximum near new moon and full moon; that in most places the interval between two high tides is about 12½ hours; that high tide occurs when the moon is in a certain part of the sky; that as one goes along an ocean coast the lunitidal interval may increase or decrease, but as one goes up a tidal estuary the tide always becomes progressively later; that the mean level of high and low tide is roughly the same at neap and spring tides; and so on.[15] From such pragmatic knowledge, tidal records, and lunar almanacs, tables of tidal prediction were made in the Middle Ages; but the cause of the tide was an unfathomable mystery. Before Newton, even such later luminaries of reason as Galileo and Descartes were fanciful; but both Galileo and Kepler surmised that the tide was causally related to the rotation of the earth and the apparent motion of the moon and sun.

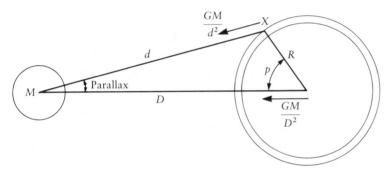

FIGURE 8.9
The attraction of the moon.

Newton asked himself what would happen to water constrained in a canal encircling the globe. Fig. 8.9 is a section of such a canal making a great circle coplanar with the moon. By the law of gravity, every particle in the universe is accelerated towards every other. The acceleration of the earth as a whole towards the moon as a whole is GM/D^2, where M is the mass of the moon and D the distance between the centres of the two bodies. The acceleration of the particle of water X in the canal towards the moon is GM/d^2, where d is the distance of X from the centre of the moon. When the zenith distance (p) is less than 90° (approximately), $d<D$, and, relative to the earth as a whole, the particle is accelerated towards the moon. Conversely, if $p>90°$, the particle is accelerated away from the moon.

Since the angle at M (parallax) is always less than 1°, and R/D is less than 0.02, $1/d^2 - 1/D^2 = 2R.\cos p/D^3$ approximately. The reader is subjected to this elementary mathematics in order to show that as gravitation is an inverse square law, tidal attraction is an inverse cube law (approximately). That is why, although the gravitational attraction of the sun is two orders higher than that of the moon, the tidal attraction of sun is slightly less than half[16] that of the moon. Newton realized that, in consequence, the form of a liquid non-rotating earth would be the combination of two prolate spheroids. As the moon rotates around the

FIGURE 8.10
Combination of sun and moon effects at spring tide.

firmament once a month, spring tides occur fortnightly when the push–pull of the moon and the sun are most nearly colinear, that is at full moon and new moon (Fig. 8.10). At any new or full moon the amplitude of the spring tide will depend on how far the moon is from the earth and from the plane of the earth's orbit, being greatest when the moon is at its closest to the earth and also in the plane of the earth's orbit; in fact at an eclipse which happens to coincide with the moon being at its perigee. The colinear condition for a maximum spring tide is called *syzygy*—surely the most improbable word in the English language.

A curious feature of this incident in the history of science is that although Newton, in one little step, took us from total ignorance of the cause of tides to a complete understanding of the primary cause, his work did not lead directly to any improvement in tidal prediction. Apart from extraneous influences, of which wind is the most important, there are two formidable difficulties. The continents get in the way. The earth does rotate, and that rotation affects the dynamics of a particle moving over it in a way which was not understood at the time. The oceans are swirling about in a fantastically configured bowl which rotates once a day, and its waters are subjected to the varying tidal forces of the sun and moon.

The Newtonian theory of tide did not, in itself, 'save the phenomena'. On the hypothesis that water can instantaneously take up an equilibrium position, ignoring the tidal attraction of the sun, taking the moon's declination as zero (which it is on average), the amplitude of the 'equilibrium' tide is, in centimetres, only $25\cos^2$ latitude. Along the North Atlantic coasts of the continents the amplitude of the tide is commonly 10 times that and more. In the Bay of Fundy the tide may exceed 15 metres, compared with an equilibrium-form tide of 13 centimetres. At the oceanic islands the magnification of the equilibrium-form tide is commonly in the range 2–4.

It was known that tide amplitudes along continental coasts are larger in the North Atlantic than in most parts of other oceans, and tidal amplitudes are small at mid-ocean islands, implying that in the deep ocean the tides are small—a fact that there was no way of confirming. One may imagine the North Atlantic as a vast bay confined within the promontories of West Africa and South America, suggesting two speculations. One is that the bay is perpetually pounded by the great southern ocean which encircles the earth virtually unimpeded, and is as one with the Indian Ocean and the great Pacific. This idea does not explain why tidal amplitudes at Atlantic islands are commonly so much smaller than along the continental coasts. The other speculation is that the North Atlantic does it nearly all by itself. One might think of the high amplitude of Atlantic tides as a swirl affect, or perhaps, by analogy with acoustics, one might imagine the Atlantic to be resonant, the Bay of Fundy particularly so. It is this speculation which proved fruitful.

The history of this difficult science becomes highly technical from the late eighteenth century. Once again, there are three tangled skeins, but they are more tangled. One is the evolution of fluid mechanics, a science in itself. Another is the massive accumulation of data —long-term tidal records at specific places, and the correlation of the records of one place with those of another. The third is the development of harmonic analysis, statistical analysis, and mathematical modelling generally.

Newton's ideas were further developed by Colin Maclaurin, Daniello Bernoulli, and Leonhard Euler in essays they submitted for an Académie prize of 1740. They all showed that under the combined influence of the sun and the moon, an ocean-covered non-rotating earth would take the form of a prolate spheroid with its axis approximately aligned with the direction of the moon. Maclaurin considered the effect of the earth's rotation; Bernoulli computed the variation of tidal force with the lunar distance of the sun; and Euler showed that it is the horizontal component of the tidal force which causes the tides, and that this is greatest where the altitude of the moon is 45°.

The greatest single step, after Newton himself, was taken by the French applied mathematician Pierre Simon de Laplace[17] from about 1773. His work on the equations of motion of large rotating liquid masses under gravitation led to the now famous 'Laplace Tide Equations', the solution of which would, in the words of the distinguished twentieth-century tidal theorist Joseph Proudman 'determine completely, at least in theory, the tidal currents and elevation over the entire oceans and for all times, given a complete description of the tide-generating forces and the boundaries of the ocean basins'.

At least the mechanical question is settled now, but it is scarcely thinkable that a description of the (3D) boundaries of the ocean basins sufficiently comprehensive to predict accurately tidal stream and elevation at all places and times on purely dynamical considerations will ever be possible.

In the early nineteenth century the Ecole Polytechnique of Paris was peculiarly rich in applied mathematicians whose work happened to be relevant to navigational science. Poisson has been already mentioned in this chapter. His predecessor in the Chair of Mathematics at the Ecole was Jean Fourier. The idea of Harmonic Analysis has its roots in 'the music of the celestial spheres' of Pythagoras, which inspired Kepler so (Chapter 4). In 1822 Fourier gave it precise mathematical form.[18] Provided that certain conditions are met, if y is a function of x,

$$y = A + \Sigma B_n \sin nx + \Sigma C_n \cos nx.$$

over the range $-\pi \leqslant x \leqslant \pi$. The coefficients $(A, B, C,)$ can be determined if sufficient values are known. The harmonic analysis of complex cyclical functions is a powerful tool in science—Fourier's own special interest was the theory of heat. To take a simple example: Smith's coefficients of compass deviation were derived from Poisson's analysis of the cause of deviation. Without knowing or caring why the compass deviates we could reach the same result by swinging a ship and treating the heading as x and the deviation as y in a Fourier series. The significant difference between compass theory and tidal theory is that we can know everything that needs to be known about ship's magnetism to predict deviation but we can never know sufficient about the 3D geometry of the ocean basins to predict tides on those data alone. If compass deviation is small, we can predict it accurately ignoring all B, C terms except B_1, B_2, C_1, C_2. In the harmonic analysis of tides, many more coefficients are needed.

In 1835 an assistant professor at the Ecole Polytechnique, Gaspard de Coriolis, published in its *Journal* a modest paper entitled *Sur les équations du mouvement relatif des systèmes de corps*, with significant results. Coriolis simply applied the Newtonian laws of motion to a particle moving in a way defined relative to a rotating frame of reference. If a particle moves over the surface of the rotating earth at a constant speed V in a straight line, i.e. in a great circle, there is an acceleration at right angles to track in the amount of $2\omega V\sin$ lat, where ω is the angular velocity of the earth. It is known as the *Coriolis* or geostrophic acceleration. If the particle follows a different curve, such as a rhumb line, there are additional terms, now known in meteorology as cyclostrophic effects. A formal proof would be inappropriate here; but a brief informal demonstration is given in Note 19.

Coriolis effects are important in such disparate applications as ballistics and the airman's bubble sextant. In meteorology they are paramount. Outside equatorial regions air generally moves so that the pressure gradient and the Coriolis force are equal and opposite. In oceanography, the Coriolis effect, if not as paramount as in meteorology, is essential to the understanding of the dynamics of the oceans. To give an example, if latitude is 40° and V 1 knot, a particle acted upon only by geostrophic force will move in a circle of radius 3 n.m. It can be found by observation that in temperate latitudes in a typical semidiurnal tidal regime, an object just submerged (to keep it out of the wind) typically moves in a circle a few miles across semidiurnally.

Decades before Coriolis described the effect named after him Laplace had included it in his tidal equations. Neither did he wait for Fourier's work. He stated that it must be possible to predict future tides by relating historical tidal records to the position of the sun and the moon. He was right. Harmonic analysis is practical because tide at a place does bear a linear relationship with tide-generating forces. Laplace did not limit himself to theory, but instituted systematic tidal observations at Brest.

In England in the earlier part of the nineteenth century the attention of John Lubbock, William Whewell, and others was directed at discovering what the sea really does. From about 1832 self-registering tide gauges, providing a continuous record of the height of the tide, began to spread, the first being at Sheerness.

Whewell organized simultaneous observations of tides at different places on the European and American coasts of the Atlantic in 1835. He produced the first cotidal charts, showing lines joining places where the high tide occurred at the same time. As far as the Atlantic as a whole was concerned this activity was a little like a palaeontologist's reconstructing a complete animal from a few fossilized bits of bone and tooth without knowing whether they came from the same animal. Typically, there were only two known points on a cotidal line, one on either side of the ocean. The rest was inference—unsound inference as it happens.

Furthermore, the dynamical studies suggested that shallow-water tides were atypical; clear of the continental shelf the tides could be very different to those measured on a gauge a few miles way. Until modern times it has not been possible to measure deep-water tides.

Whewell had more luck with the shallow waters of the North Sea. Tidal observation at a growing number of places on the Continent and in the British Isles enabled him to produce a cotidal chart of the North Sea of some significance. A comparison of tides on the English and continental coasts led him to think that there were two rotating tidal systems, in which there would be points of zero tide (amphidromic points). In 1840 Captain William Hewett confirmed by measurement one such point in the Southern Bight of the North Sea in about 20 fathoms. Amphidromic points enabled Whewell to return to the old speculation that Atlantic tides are largely a reaction to external pressures, by explaining away the small amplitude of tide at the islands as an amphidromic phenomenon. Airy and others opposed. It seems that Whewell himself came to see that the idea was far-fetched. Since those days, a major line of development of the science has been to combine the approach of Whewell with that of Laplace, gaining progressively more insight from dynamical studies of oceans in model basins to make progressively more valid inferences from the ever-improving data; but a synoptic approach to tides is always difficult.

Harmonic analysis prospered on the basis of the linearity of the relationship between actual tides and the equilibrium-form tide. Laplace's conviction that a given astronomical configuration always produces the same tide at a specified place had been demonstrated beyond doubt. In 1882 Sir George Darwin (a son of Charles) proposed a system of tidal constituents which gained widespread international acceptance. The ten largest constituents, which may be regarded as the ten principal components of the total equilibrium-form tide, are listed in Table 8.1. The coefficients relate to the relative amplitude of the constituents. The nineteen-year term corresponds to the effect of the rotation of the lunar orbit relative to the ecliptic, with a period of 18.6 years, which of course is also the period of nutation. One can see why tides were so long regarded as part of the empire of astronomy.

Name	Speed °/hr	Coefficient
Lunar fortnightly	1.098	0.078
Solar semi-annual	0.082	0.036
Nineteen yearly	0.002	0.033
Lunisolar declinational	15.041	0.265
Larger lunar	13.943	0.189
Larger solar	14.959	0.088
Principal lunar	28.984	0.454
Principal solar	30.000	0.211
Larger lunar elliptic	28.440	0.088
Lunisolar declinational	30.082	0.058

Table 8.1. Ten of Darwin's leading tidal harmonic constituents

The scheme instigated by Darwin was originally proposed by William Thomson (Lord Kelvin), who turned his versatile and prolific mind to the matter of computation. He invented the mechanical harmonic analyzer, a true analogue computer which, by a system of cords, pulleys, and cranks, could generate the sum of a number of trigonometrical functions of different amplitudes and frequencies, in effect $\Sigma a_r\sin(b_r t + c_r)$, where a_r, b_r, c_r are characteristic constants of the rth constituent and t is the time from a known epoch. Using Darwin's 10 constituents, a tidal curve at a port for a year could be drawn in four hours. Tidal prediction was a major incentive to the development of analogue computers. By 1910 there was a machine capable of handling all the 37 constituents which Darwin had shown to be necessary.

A Thomson Tide-Predicting Machine made by A. Légé.

The development of the digital computer stimulated interest in methods of analysis of complex records generally, which had hitherto been impractical. From the 1960s W. H. Munk, D. E. Cartwright, and others pioneered spectrum analysis of tidal data in ways which do not rely on the Victorian perception of the Pythagorean music of the celestial spheres. In 1990 inexpensive software for portable personal computers which enabled tidal prediction in seconds was widely available at low prices.

Lights

From the beginning, lights have been used to guide navigators, and sometimes to mislead them. The Pharos[20] of Alexandria, built about 280 BC and one of the wonders of the ancient world, consisted of a tower 120 metres high on which a fire of wood burned. Subject to visibility and the brightness of the fire, it could be seen from a ship 40 km away.[21] The ancient Romans built lighthouses on the coasts of their empire, including one at Dover. Lighthouses continued to be maintained in the Middle Ages, sometimes by religious houses as a Christian duty. Typically, a fire of wood (or coal where available) was maintained in a brazier atop a stone or brick structure, although candles and oils were also used. Such lights had to be readily accessible, and required constant attendance. There was no way of identifying them, so two or more lights in the same area could be misleading. Luminosity was variable and uncertain. Most of it was wasted, because it could not be concentrated seaward. Some lights were potentially dangerous, because homing towards them on certain bearings could lead through shoals. The navigator required previous knowledge of which were the sectors in which it was safe to lie off the light. The surge in maritime traffic from the sixteenth century to the present has been paralleled by the growth in the number of lights. There were no dedicated marine lights in America until 1716; in 1820 there were more than 50 in the USA alone, where their numbers had reached about 10 000 in 1960.

The first major improvements on the technology of the Pharos came in the eighteenth century. From 1763 crude reflectors were fitted to oil-burning lights on Merseyside, concentrating the light in the estuary. In 1784 Aimé Argand invented an oil-burning lamp suitable for maintaining the steady bright light required. These developments led to parabolic mirror reflectors to concentrate the light into a beam. From this point, several avenues open if the beam is made to rotate. The periodicity of the beam (later, beams) can be made a means of positive identification, so that several lights may be installed in the same area without confusion, enabling the navigator to fix his position by cross-bearings. The light may also be obscured or coloured red on dangerous bearings.

Two things in particular justify the placement of *Lighthouses* in this chapter: the inventions of dioptric and catadioptric lens systems, and of electric light. Between them, they revolutionized lighthouses in Victorian times. Catoptric optical systems (those employing the simple laws of reflection) are limited in their application because of practical problems caused by the size of the mirrors which would be required in major lighthouses. We owe the optical system of modern lighthouses to Augustin Fresnel, a French physicist who, unlike his contemporary Laplace, was neglected in his own time. Among many achievements, he invented the dioptric lens, which employs only the refractive property of glass to make the equivalent of a large lens by concentric rings of small prisms, and catadioptric systems, which employ both reflective and refractive elements. The practical consequence was that sharp horizontal pencil beams of light could be produced by optical systems large enough for a powerful lighthouse and rugged enough for the heat which such lights generated. With such optical systems lights could be made fixed, flashing, group flashing, isophase (equal periods of light and darkness), occulting, and group occulting. It became standard practice to print the characteristics of lights on the charts.

Electric carbon arc light was installed at the Dungeness lighthouse in 1862, the large current required being provided by generators driven by steam engines. Such systems had their problems, and electricity was not generally used world-wide until high-powered filament lamps of sufficient reliability became available in the 1920s. Later developments included the use of electric arcs in mercury and inert gases. At sites at which electricity is not available, dissolved acetylene contained in cylinders was the major development. A flashing apparatus which made unmanned lighthouses practical without electricity was invented by N. G. Dalén in 1906.

Finally, an idea originated with lighthouses—a very simple idea, that was to reverberate throughout the age of radio. Suppose a light flash is visible in all seaward directions, followed by a slowly rotating thin beam. Given the characteristics of the light, the time interval between the flash and the beam defines the 'radial', the bearing of the ship from the light.

Notes to Chapter 8

1. Trials in the British Navy in 1901 showed that operation of the large inductor coils then in use perceptibly deflected the compass at a distance of 30 feet.
2. May (1960).
3. Quoted from Fanning (1986), a source on which the writer has relied heavily in these paragraphs.
4. In some types of military aircraft during the Second World War fitted with armour-plating, very large deviations were caused by firing the cannons. The effect could last for several days—a type of magnetism which can neither be described as permanent nor as instantaneously induced.
5. In 1803 Flinders, unaware that his country was once again at war with France, sailed into harbour in Mauritius, where he remained a prisoner of war until 1810. His hosts courteously allowed him to remit the report from which this quotation comes to the Royal Society, where it was read in 1805.
6. Theoretically the parameters of induced magnetism can be completely separated from the components of permanent magnetism by an analysis of the results of swinging in different attitudes in one magnetic latitude. This experiment has been tried with aircraft; but it could scarcely be done to a ship.
7. Commander (later Captain) L. W. P. Chetwynd was the superintendent of the Admiralty Compass Department from 1904 to 1912.
8. Cornelius van Drebel is usually credited with building the first true (oar-powered) submarine in 1620. During the American Civil War steam-powered submersibles were used, but the funnel and the hatch were necessarily above the surface. The submarine as we know it had to await the means of generation and storage on the surface of sufficient electrical energy to power the vessel when submerged. The first order for the construction of submarines for the British Navy was given in October 1900.
9. Aircraft structures are generally non-ferrous. Unlike a steel or iron ship, there are places within the aircraft almost free of deviation by structure, notably the wing-tips.

10. Joseph von Peichl, an officer of the Austro-Hungarian Navy, had also invented an ingenious and successful compass compensating device in 1875 which became standard in the navy he served. It was subjected to strangely inconclusive trials in the British Navy over twelve years. Perhaps one defect was that it was not invented by William Thomson.

11. Photoelectric systems were also developed for special-purpose marine compasses, notably in Italy and Germany. In the 1930s there were some hopes of a cathode-ray compass. A beam of electrons is deflected by a magnetic field. By Fleming's rule, if the cathode-ray tube is vertical, with the display uppermost, the beam is deflected to the east. The principle has been employed (by the Minneapolis–Honeywell Regulator Company, as it was then called) in a marine compass; but early hopes were never realized.

12. Hine (1968) is a convenient reference for these systems.

13. Problems with gyro-stabilized vertical sensors discussed in the context of aircraft sextants are negligible in the aircraft compass application.

14. Posidonius is said to have studied tides near Cadiz. He knew that spring tides were fortnightly, and associated them with full and new moon, but erroneously believed that there are semi-annual peak spring tides at the solstices. Strabo quotes Seleucus of Babylon (fl. 150 BC) as believing that equinoctial tides are regular and solstitial tides irregular.

15. Bede, who lived beside the river Tyne in the eighth century, knew all this, and suggested a nineteen-year cycle, corresponding to the period of rotation of the lunar orbit about the ecliptic, and anticipating Darwin's third constituent (Table 8.1) by some eleven centuries.

16. Unit of mass: the sun. Unit of distance: 1,000 km.

	SUN	MOON
Gravitational attraction	$4.5G \times 10^{-11}$	$2.5G \times 10^{-13}$
Tidal attraction	$3.8G\cos p \times 10^{-15}$	$8.3G\cos p \times 10^{-15}$

17. Laplace, like Newton, was one of those rare great mathematicians who was honoured in his own country in his own time. Napoleon made him a Senator and a Count of the Empire; after the Restoration he was made a Marquis.

18. In *Théorie analytique de la chaleur*, described by one British historian of science as one of the most important books of the nineteenth century. A more formal proof was given in 1829 by Dirichlet, who also added a further condition. The idea goes back a century to Daniello Bernoulli.

19. As an informal demonstration of the geostrophic equation, take a particle moving at a velocity V in a straight line relative to a disc rotating anti-clockwise at angular velocity $\dot\theta$. V is resolved into components $\dot x$, $\dot y$ relative to axes x, y on the disc. The velocities relative to fixed axes x', y' are shown in Fig. 8.11(a) and the corresponding accelerations in Fig. 8.11(b). The accelerations $-x\dot\theta^2$, $-y\dot\theta^2$ correspond to those of a particle fixed to the disc. In the spherical case they are directed towards the centre of the parallel of latitude and subsumed within the perception of gravity of a stationary observer. The resultant of the remaining accelerations is $2V\dot\theta$. If the y and x axes respectively represent north and east in the horizontal plane, $\dot\theta = \omega \sin$ lat. (Chapters 3 and 9). The Coriolis effect is implicit in the earlier work of both Euler and Laplace.

20. Perpetuated as the generic name for lighthouse in several modern languages, such as *phare* (French) and *faro* (Spanish, Portuguese, and Italian). The Libyans and the Cushites had erected lighthouses three centuries before Pharos was built.

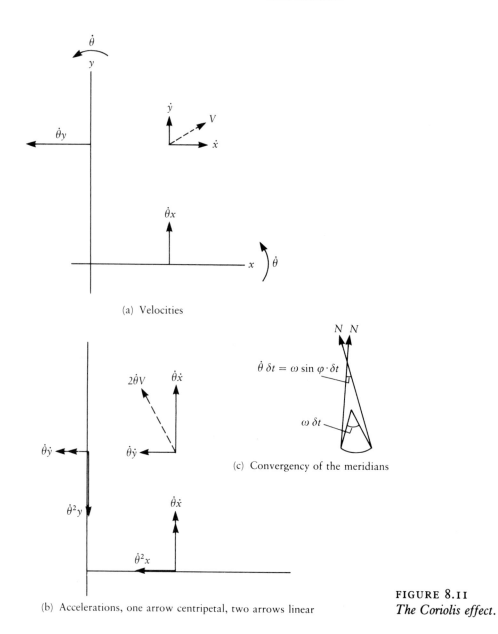

(a) Velocities

(c) Convergency of the meridians

$$\dot\theta \, \delta t = \omega \sin \varphi \cdot \delta t$$

$$\omega \, \delta t$$

FIGURE 8.11
The Coriolis effect.

(b) Accelerations, one arrow centripetal, two arrows linear

21. As a convenient but very rough rule, the maximum visual range of an object in nautical miles is the sum of the square roots of the heights above the sea surface of observer and observed in feet.

CHAPTER NINE

Self-Containment

✠

A NAVIGATION system which requires no data from outside the vehicle is to be preferred, especially by military users. The visibility of the heavens or the earth cannot be relied upon. Some radio systems transmit, and the transmission may be detected by an enemy. No radio signals can reach deeply submerged submarines. All radio systems receive signals with which an enemy may interfere. Even to civilian users in peacetime, it is not entirely satisfactory to be completely dependent on the correct functioning of radio equipment on the ground or in space managed by miscellaneous authorities not under the user's control.

Given the starting position and velocity of a vehicle, and a complete history of acceleration from the start, its present speed, direction, and position are determinate. It follows from Newton's laws of motion that a system of gyroscopes and pendula can provide a measure of the direction in space of acceleration and its quantum. If DR navigation is the integration of velocity vectors with respect to time, inertial navigation is the double integration with respect to time of acceleration vectors. The calculation is complicated by the accelerations due to the earth's gravity, the rotation of the earth, and the curved motion of vehicles which are constrained to be at or near the surface of the earth. The acceleration due to the gravity of the rest of the universe is of course equal and opposite to the accelerations in the earth's orbit, apart from the slight tidal effect. The engineering required to implement such a system is as exquisitely refined and complex as the principle is exquisitely simple.

Position and motion data are not enough. Navigation also implies orientation and control. The gyroscope is a powerful tool of both. Historically, orientation applications came first. The story has three parts: developments of the gyroscope in the nineteenth century leading to the gyrocompass; the working gyrocompass and other applications of the gyroscope to orientation and control, mainly in the first part of the twentieth century; and finally, in the latter part of the twentieth century, the refinement of engineering to manufacture gyros and accelerometers of the precision requisite to a full inertial navigation system, in parallel with the development of computers of the power and speed needed to manipulate their output.

A gyroscope is a rotor so mounted that its axis of rotation is free to rotate about orthogonal axes, as in Fig. 9.1. The axis may take any direction in space, however the instrument is placed. Subject to external torques, the stability of a gyroscope's axis in space is determined by its angular momentum (or *moment of momentum*), that is to say the product of its moment of inertia and its rate of spin. Hutchins and May (1952) give a graphic example of this stability. A certain external torque applied to the axis of a particular gyroscope rotates the axis through 90° in 1½ seconds when the rotor is not turning. When the rotor is spinning at 8600 r.p.m., the same torque takes 21 minutes to turn the axis through 90°, and this time the turn is in a direction at 90° to the direction of the torque. The gyro *precesses*. In Fig. 9.2 two small opposite segments of the rotor are moving about the axis AB in necessarily opposite directions at a velocity *r*. The torque *T* is applied at B, causing the velocity vector *t* at X and Y in the direction shown. The resultant velocity at X and Y is *p*. The corresponding motion of the axis is a precession in the direction P, which is at right angles to the torque and the axis itself.

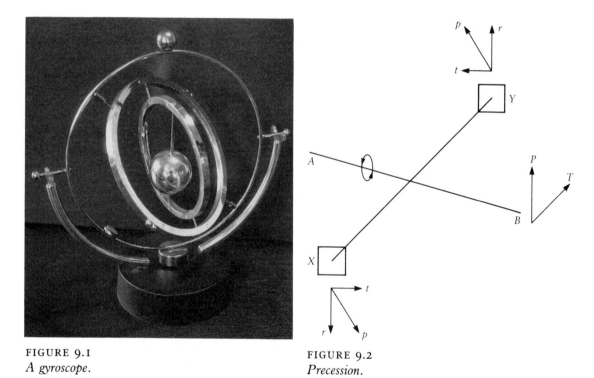

FIGURE 9.1
A gyroscope.

FIGURE 9.2
Precession.

The earth is a gyroscope,[1] and its gyroscopic qualities became relevant to celestial dynamics from Newton onwards. Newton explained the precession of the equinoxes, a mystery for at least two thousand years, along the following lines. The main forces acting on all particles on the earth's surface are the earth's gravity and the centrifugal force caused by the earth's rotation. In consequence, the form of the earth is roughly an oblate spheroid described by the rotation of the minor (polar) axis (Chapter 6). As a result of tidal acceleration (Chapter 8) there are torques tending to bring the earth's equatorial plane in line with the ecliptic and the moon's orbit. The torque caused by the moon is twice as great as that caused by the sun, because the tidal acceleration is twice as great; but, on average over a long period, the earth's axis precesses in a direction at right angles to itself and the sun. The angular momentum of the earth is so great that the period of the precession of the equinoxes is 26 000 years. The pole of the moon's orbit describes a small circle around the pole of the ecliptic every 18.6 years. The corresponding precession of the earth's axis is nutation (Chapter 7). It also gives rise to the 'nineteen year' tidal constituent (Chapter 8). From Newton until the early nineteenth century, the study of the gyroscope, like the early study of tides, was the province of astronomers; but there were no man-made gyroscopes.

In the mid-eighteenth century Serson studied spinning bodies, and had an artificial horizon stabilized by a spinning top. One of the earliest references to a true gyroscope is the description in Gilbert's *Annalen* for 1818 of a device made by G. C. Bohnenberger some years earlier, consisting of a metal spheroid mounted on three rings rotatable about axes mutually at right angles so that the axis of the spheroid could take any direction. The difficulties of manufacturing a gyroscope to the required precision, and of providing continuous drive to the rotor, are the explanation of its slow development. In the twentieth century small aircraft gyroscopic instruments have been successfully driven pneumatically, and rotation on the windmill (turbine) principle could have been sustained by bellows; but the writer is unaware of any such devices of an early date. A hand-generated marine gyroscope was demonstrated in Brest harbour by Edmond-Paulin Dubois; but serious development of marine gyroscopic instruments in the late nineteenth century had to wait for electrically driven rotors, generally attributed to G. M. Hopkins in 1878, although Trouvé experimented with one in 1865.

The idea of rotation must have been in the air when Coriolis published his famous paper (Chapter 8), because in the following year (1836) Edward Sang, addressing the Royal Scottish Society of Arts, said

> *Conceive a large flat wheel poised on several axes all passing directly through its centre of gravity and whose axis of motion is coincident with its principal axis of rotation. The direction of its axis would then be unchanged but, on account of the motion of the earth, it would appear to move slowly.*

Since Newton, so much had been obvious, but no one is recorded as having said it so explicitly before. Foucault demonstrated the principle in 1852, and gave the gyroscope its name.

Sang and Foucault were only saying that the axis of a gyro with two degrees of freedom tends to point to a fixed direction in space. If it were trained on a star it would track it. The gyro shows the rotation of the earth in exactly the same way as a star does. If the axis points to the celestial pole its apparent direction is not changed by the rotation of the earth. Until modern times[2] it was not possible to use that property of the gyro as a compass, because imperfections in the manufacture of the instrument, wear, and changes of temperature cause imbalances and torques which precess the instrument. This precession is usually called *wander*, which itself has two elements, one which is characteristic of the permanent imbalance of the instrument (which may be compensated or calibrated), and another more serious element, which is random and unpredictable. It was not until 1950 that an aircraft gyro direction indicator with a random wander of only 1° per hour was available.[3] This standard of accuracy was invaluable in aircraft flying for a few hours in very high magnetic latitudes; but it would have been of little value as a ship's compass, and at the beginning of the century wander of the best instruments was an order of magnitude higher.

The solution lay in a beautiful idea which led to the gyrocompass in the early twentieth century. If a gyro is aligned so that its axis points at a star rising on the north-eastern horizon, say, three things will happen. The axis of the gyro, in the course of tracking the star, will tilt and rotate; it will also wander in some random fashion from the star because of imperfections in the instrument. If the gyro is now enclosed in a casing which is made bottom-heavy, the gyro, as it tracks the star, tilts upwards, and the torque caused by the pendulosity precesses the gyro towards the west. Similarly, when the axis is pointing to the north–west the precession is towards the east. Thus the combined effect of the earth's rotation and horizontal precession proportionate to tilt (when the instrument is stationary on earth) is that the direction of the axis appears to describe an ellipse centred on north. Wander, random or not, merely modifies the shape of the ellipse. The centre is still true north. Finally, all motion of the axis relative to the earth may be damped, causing the ellipse to degenerate into a spiral

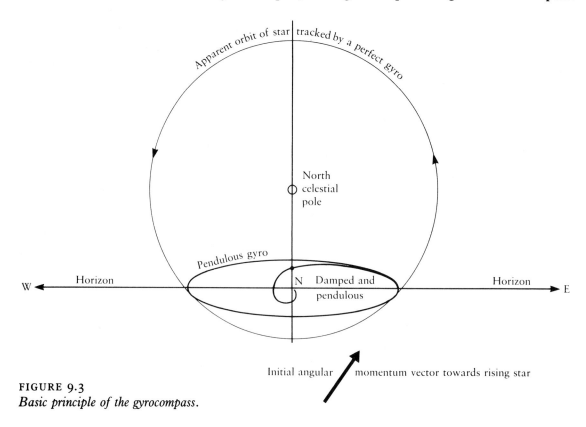

FIGURE 9.3
Basic principle of the gyrocompass.

centred on north (Fig. 9.3). Damping precession may be a torque proportional to tilt applied to the vertical axis of the system, just as the pendulosity applies a torque proportional to tilt about the east–west axis. The gyrocompass is thus a gyro tied by gravity and the earth's rotation into pointing true north, just as the gyromagnetic compass described in the preceding chapter was tied into pointing to magnetic north by the earth's magnetic field.

The behaviour of the gyrocompass is modified by the ship's motion. As the ship moves over the earth's surface its horizontal plane both rotates and tilts. Also the ship rolls and pitches, and turns on occasion; these motions cause centripetal accelerations which deflect the apparent gravity, and so affect the torques on the system.

In essence, the gyrocompass is an instrument in which the only stable position of the axis of the rotor is along the horizontal component of rotation of the gravity vector, which, for an observer stationary on the earth's surface, is of axis north–south at a rate of 15.04°/hr x cos lat. (15.04°/hr corresponds to 360° per sidereal day). The gyrocompass is inherently incapable of distinguishing between rotation of the earth and rotation due to motion of the instrument over the earth. If a supersonic aircraft were flying north-west at a speed such that the resultant of that speed and that due to the earth's rotation were due north, the gyro-compass would point due west. *Speed error* is one reason why gyrocompasses were never considered for aircraft. The east–west component of the speed of a ship has a negligible effect on the rate of rotation of the gravity vector; but the north–south component deflects the gyro axis (towards the west if northerly) by about 1° per 10 knots in latitude 50°. The deflection varies as the secant of the latitude. The simplest way of correcting speed error is to offset the lubber line by a correction depending on the north–south component of speed and the latitude. The effect of roll is reminiscent of soft iron parameters a and e (Chapter 8). It is called *intercardinal error*, because if the axis of the ship's oscillation is in a cardinal direction the effect is either zero or cancels itself in a complete period. It is a maximum when the axis of oscillation of the ship is quadrantal.

The primitive notion that a gyro might be precessed by gravity to become north-seeking goes back to Foucault; but he neither developed the idea nor had any means of maintaining rotation. Elmer Sperry, whose name was later to become synonymous with gyroscopic instruments, credited Van den Bos of Leiden as being the first to disclose the basic principles of the gyrocompass in a patent application of 1884. Professor O. Martienssen is sometimes credited with the first complete mathematical analysis of the gyrocompass in about 1905.[4] He was sceptical about the practicality of the device, because he understood the errors caused by the motion of the ship.

Hermann Anschütz-Kaempfe's interest in polar exploration and submarines led to his work on gyroscopic direction-indicators. No magnetic compass can be satisfactory within the enclosed steel hull of a submerged submarine.[5] His first instrument, which was not a true gyrocompass, was tried on the German cruiser *Udine* in 1904, and was demonstrated to foreign navies in 1905 at a price equivalent to £600. Commander Chetwynd of the British Navy was unimpressed. The trials showed that although the instrument was not deflected by broadsides (which greatly affected dry card magnetic compasses of the time) it reacted badly to roll. The instrument consisted of a horizontal directional gyro stabilized by two smaller gyros with vertical axes to resist roll; but, as will be apparent from the foregoing, this was not the way to do it.

The first true gyrocompass was made by Anschütz-Kaempfe, and received its sea trials on board the battleship *Deutschland* in 1908. It was, by subsequent standards, a simple device. A single pendulous gyro floated in a bath of mercury, eliminating gimballing. Damping was by a jet of air which exerted neutral pressure when the gyro was horizontal, but otherwise exerted a torque about the vertical axis proportional to the angle of tilt. Inevitably, the device was beset with many problems. The greatest design defect was the absence of any correction for intercardinal error. In 1906 Anschütz-Kaempfe had been joined by his cousin Max Schuler, a mathematician. The Anschütz/Schuler solution was a three-gyro system arranged in the form of an isosceles triangle, which was normally approximately equilateral. The angular momentum of the two smaller gyros, so linked that the angles which they made with the main (north-seeking) gyro were equal, in theory at least negated the effects of pitch and roll. One of Max Schuler's greatest contributions to the gyrocompass was the realization that, if the period of oscillation of the gyro-pendulosity loop is 84 minutes,[6] the correct torque is provided during a turn to precess the compass during the turn to its new stable position (ballistic deflection). By modern criteria the gyrocompass was still in an early stage of development.[7]

Rather earlier, according to a story attributed[8] to Schuler, an American inventor, Elmer A. Sperry, was given a conducted tour of the Anschütz works in Kiel and somehow gave the impression that he did not understand all the technicalities. He went back to New York and formed the Sperry Gyroscope Company. The first Sperry gyrocompass appeared in 1911. To be fair to Sperry, he had been active in the gyrostabilization[9] of ships and aircraft since 1907. All gyrocompasses rely on the same fundamental principles; but the ways in which the required torques may be generated and applied are multifarious. Sperry's instrument was simpler than the latest Anschütz, and conceptually different. Sperry achieved both pendulosity and damping by a 'bail' weight attached eccentrically so that a small part of the torque was about the vertical axis of the system. A wire suspension provided a frictionless vertical axis. A new invention, the 'floating ballistic gyro'[10] was designed to provide equal and opposite torques to those caused by roll and pitch.

Sperry and, after his death, his company achieved a dominance in the field of gyroscopic instruments sustained over many more decades than is usual at the pace of twentieth-century technology. Inventiveness, creativity, and engineering excellence were prerequisite. Marketing skills helped; and history was on the side of Sperry. In 1914 Anschütz was excluded from some of its best markets by war. The United States won both World Wars, and Germany lost them. From the beginning, Sperry related himself as closely as possible to the Royal Navy, which could then claim to have the most powerful surface fleet in the the world. In 1913 the Sperry company opened its European office in Victoria Street, London, a few metres from the office of the Admiralty Compass Department. A year later, Sperry formed an English company.

Indigenous competition by British companies was stifled by an incident which, if not savoury, does not discredit Sperry himself. In 1916, an English company, S. G. Brown, sought to patent a novel gyrocompass, but was precluded by wartime security from a public patent. The Brown gyrocompass was given extensive sea trials in 1917 by Admiralty officials *and a Sperry executive*. At this stage both the Anschütz and the Sperry instruments had many problems. The floating ballistic gyro, in particular, was not proving a satisfactory solution to intercardinal error. Two battleships reported errors of 40° in heavy seas. The performance of Brown's instrument on the trials was superior to the Sperry installation, especially in such weather; but at that stage of the war, the Admiralty officials were more concerned with improving the Sperry installations at sea on hundreds of ships than in starting a production line for a completely new instrument. The 'mercury control' developed at the Admiralty Compass Observatory, in the words of Sperry's own New York patent attorney[11]

> *has proved one of the greatest steps forward since the gyrocompass was invented, firstly since it eliminates at one stroke the causes of serious deviations due to rolling and pitching of the ship, especially when on an intercardinal course, and secondly since no extraneous damping means need be employed, the very element which imparts meridian-seeking properties being employed also to damp the compass.*

The patent was sold to Sperry. Brown accused Admiralty officials of stealing his ideas and giving them to Sperry. The quarrel between Admiralty officials and the Brown company dragged on for more than a decade. The Royal Navy became part of Sperry's domestic market.[12]

No self-educated man since John Harrison so profoundly influenced navigational science as Elmer Sperry. He exemplified perfectly in his persona and work the inventiveness and ruthless, creative entrepreneurial energy spawned by the American culture in the late nineteenth century. A Baptist of puritan stock, he loudly advocated the total prohibition of alcohol, and embodied the Protestant work ethic of his time and country.[13] Sperry grew up and received a high-school education in a rural community. At the age of twenty he filed his first patent application, entitled 'Dynamo-electric machine'. At the age of twenty-three he formed the Sperry Electric Light, Motor, and Car-Brake company, capitalized at $ 1 000 000. The principal assets offered to subscribers were the patent applications of its founder, his creativity, inventiveness, and energy. The issue was fully subscribed.

Sperry's early work was mainly related to the use of electric carbon arcs for illumination —an old invention going back to Humphrey Davy in 1808, but made a practical system of illumination by men such as Sperry. Significantly, Sperry's early inventions involved *automatic feedback*, the means by which machines control themselves by measuring their own state. The concept is ancient. In the first century AD there was a water-clock in Alexandria in which the water-level was controlled by a valve on the same principle as that employed in a twentieth-century WC. A more elegant example is the 'fantail', invented by Edmund Lee in 1745, by which a windmill is made to head into wind *automatically*. The fantail is fixed with its axle at right angles to the main axle and drives the track wheels which turn the main axle into wind. If the main axle is not pointing directly into wind there is a component of wind in the direction of the fantail axle which turns the sails of the fantail and thus turns the main axle into wind. A little later, the centrifugal governor of James Watt's steam engine was an important step at the beginning of the industrial revolution. Gyroscopic instruments and controls rely heavily on automatic feedback.

The gyrocompass led naturally to the ship's autopilot, which Sperry addressed from about 1912. His 'Metal Mike' was a classic servomechanism, nascent cybernetics.[14] If a novice takes the helm of a big ship his recognition that the ship is drifting off course (as opposed to oscillating about the mean) is belated. As the response to control is slow, the novice then over-corrects and the ship's head passes through the desired heading with high angular momentum. The novice then over-corrects in the opposite direction and the ship swings back and forth. Sperry analysed in mechanical terms the intuitive 'feel' of the skilled helmsman which enables him to dampen yaw. He 'eases off', lessening the rudder angle as the rudder responds, and 'meets the helm', putting the rudder over to the other side to reduce angular momentum to zero as the desired heading is reached. Anticipation is the name of the game. In 'Metal Mike' an error signal triggered power to the rudder-turning engine for a period proportional to the error. As the sensed error reduced, feedback reduced the rudder angle, which was eventually reversed by a 'throwback' mechanism to reduce angular momentum to zero at zero error.

It is doubly ironical that the first application of gyros to aeroplanes was, as far as the writer is aware—of all things—an automatic pilot. In 1914 Elmer's son, Lawrence Sperry, dramatically demonstrated the *airplane stabilizer* by flying low near Paris with both his hands in the air, while his mechanic walked about a wing and the ailerons could be seen responding to maintain straight and level flight. Fortunately for the mechanic, it was a biplane. Apart from being the first to sustain powered aeroplane flight, the Wright brothers' great conceptual contribution was, contrary to all received wisdom at the time, to design their aeroplane for negative stability. The philosophy of the Wrights was that in the man–machine system it was the man who provided stability by operating movable surfaces; and here, only eleven years later, was young Lawrence taking the man out of the system!

Sperry's airplane stabilizer unsurprisingly found little application to the aeroplanes of the First World War. As far as civil application was concerned, there was a popular misconception that the stabilizer made aeroplanes safer, expressed in a *New York Times* headline on 20 June 1914 in the terms 'The Sperrys have made airplanes safe'. The military application immediately perceived was the 'aerial torpedo'. Lawrence Sperry, whose company operated quite independently of his father's, hit a target at 90 miles in 1922 using radio signals to the stabilizer to navigate the unmanned aeroplane to the target; but the 'flying bomb', as it was later called, did not become an effective weapon until the last years of the next World War.

Apparently Lawrence Sperry found his own idiosyncratic application of the first aeroplane autopilot by becoming the founder member of what later came to be called 'The mile high club'. Unfortunately they did not remain a mile high. According to a well-publicized story, the aeroplane flopped into a pond and sank; but Lawrence and the young lady with whom he had chosen to consummate this eccentric aeronautical 'first' were recovered alive but unclothed.[15] Lawrence was lost over the sea in a solo flight at too early an age for his potential to be realized; but his flamboyant personality is as enduring a memory as his bold and imaginative engineering.

The Sperry 'airplane stabilizer' was a true autopilot. Until the 1940s autopilots required quite frequent slight manual adjustments to maintain heading and attitude. It was only with the advent of the gyromagnetic compasses described in the last chapter that autopilots were locked on to a required heading. Nevertheless, earlier generations of autopilots served two invaluable purposes. First, they flew more steadily than human pilots—a matter of some importance to the accuracy of astronomical navigation. Secondly, by relieving the pilot of a tedious task, the autopilot was the beginning of the change of function of the human element in the man–machine system from operator to monitor—a task, it seems, for which we are more suited. In modern times the autopilot has become a component of the flight-management system in some operations. If, some day, the human pilot is removed from the airline flight-deck, it will not be to economize on his salary, but for fear that he might touch something. There are already airliners with flying control systems which override the commands the pilot gives to the system by the forces he exercises on the controls when the machine thinks fit—a premonitory view of the monitor monitored.[16]

When Lawrence so dramatically demonstrated the Sperry airplane stabilizer in 1914, it was irrelevant. There were far more urgent requirements for gyroscopic instruments in aeroplanes. A ship may be steered by magnetic compass alone on the blackest night or in the thickest fog; but, for the reasons described in the last chapter, one cannot fly an aeroplane in cloud by magnetic compass. The slightest turn quickly tightens, and one cannot even sense in which way. When a spirit-level is fixed laterally before the pilot, the bubble is deflected by centripetal forces, and remains central if the turn is correctly banked. Some early pilots tied a thick cord to a strut to show the direction of airflow so that they could detect sideslip when the turn was not correctly banked (the principle is still employed by some glider pilots). Orientation about the lateral axis (attitude) was a little better. When early pilots could see enough of the ground to fly straight, but it was too hazy to see the horizon, they deduced attitude by reading the engine tachometer in conjunction with the air-speed indicator (which measured the difference between the dynamic and static atmospheric pressure). A little later, they were further assisted by barometric instruments which indicated altitude and rate of climb. Such instruments yield attitude information with significant delay; and they do not help the pilot to fly straight. Without gyroscopic instruments to display to the pilot instantaneous information on his orientation the aeroplane would have been of little practical use.

As early as 1916, the US Office of Naval Aeronautics outlined a requirement for indication to the pilot of the horizontal plane and of the direction of heading—in effect a requirement for a gyroscopic artificial horizon and a gyro direction indicator. Elmer and others addressed these problems at the time, but they were not resolved for another decade. Sperry did however produce a gyroscopic turn indicator and a pressure-differential side-slip indicator. These instruments, together with a spirit-level, enabled the pilot to control the aeroplane in azimuth without a visible horizon.

On a famous occasion in 1929 James Dolittle took off, climbed, cruised, descended, and landed a few hundred metres from the start, entirely by reference to an instrumental display. In addition to a specially designed radio homing device the instruments were: an altimeter, a magnetic compass, an air-speed indicator, a turn and bank indicator, a clock, a gyroscopic artificial horizon, and a gyroscopic horizontal direction-indicator. The last two, both then new Sperry products, gave the pilot an immediate perception of his orientation on all axes. From that date the automation of air pilotage and navigation developed in tandem with the display to the pilot of orientation, position, and speed. The successful solo flight of Wiley Post around the world in 1933, using a Sperry autopilot and a cockpit display not dissimilar to that of Dolittle nicely illustrated the marriage.

The design of a conventional gyrocompass system is all about sensing accelerations and applying the requisite torques to a rotary system made to be as perfectly balanced and as frictionless as possible. The subsequent development of such systems is partly a reflection of developments in related technologies—the refinement and mathematicization of servo-mechanisms and the cybernetic approach, the gradual change from mechanical devices to electrical sensors, the application of computers and precision torque motors, and—ultimately—the elimination of moving parts, including the rotor itself.

In another sense, the later development of the gyrocompass is an edifying illustration of how twentieth-century technology led to systems designed to serve the ultimate purpose of the vehicle, subsuming navigation *en passant*. From the beginning, one of the great advantages of the gyrocompass over the magnetic compass was the power available to drive an unlimited number of repeaters, a course recorder, and the auto pilot. One major application of gyro-scopes to warships is the stabilization of weapon platforms[17] and radar antennae. Conven-tionally, the gyrocompass employed a horizontal spin-axis gyro, while gyros employed in weapon and radar stabilization had vertical spin-axes. About 1950 it was realized that the gyrocompass of the period detected tilt about an east–west axis more accurately than the vertical gyros indicated the zenith. The next step was to combine the meridian-seeking gyro of the gyrocompass with another horizontal gyro with its axis at right angles. The Sperry Mark 19 stabilized gyrocompass thus provided in the early 1960s both a north reference and a vertical reference. Fanning (1986) tells us that when it was installed on the *Ark Royal* it was possible to remove 19 separate weapon and radar stabilizers.

An odd consequence of all this was the 'one-star fix', the most radical development in astronomical navigation since the chronometer. Astronomical navigation of submarines pre-sents obvious difficulties. The horizon is too close for accurate periscopic observations of it when submerged. The Artificial Horizon Periscopic Sextant Mk IV employed the submarine SINS (ship's inertial navigation system) to define the horizontal plane. Later versions of the Sperry Mark 19 defined both north and the vertical with such accuracy that in the 1960s the Submarine Celestial Altitude Recorder was able to measure both altitude and azimuth of a single star to provide a one-star fix with an accuracy of the order of 1 mile (Fig. 9.4).

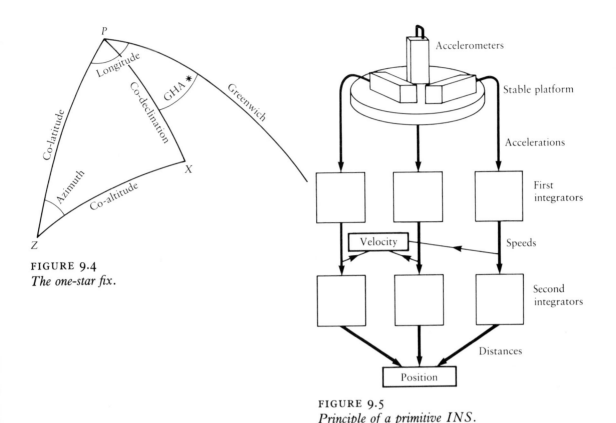

FIGURE 9.4
The one-star fix.

FIGURE 9.5
Principle of a primitive INS.

Primitive designs for true inertial navigation systems (INS) go back to the 1920s. The output of three accelerometers mounted orthogonally as in Fig. 9.5 on a platform stabilized in space by gyroscopes gives, on integration, speed and distance run (the reading of the odometer of a car is equivalent to an integration of the speedometer reading). Any device, such as the spring balance used in kitchen weighing-scales, which can measure force on a proof mass, may perform as an accelerometer. So much had been obvious from the beginning of the century; but the building of a useful device presented formidable difficulties. One is the way errors build up with time due to the integration process. Suppose an accelerometer to have a constant error of 0.000001 g (one millionth of the acceleration due to gravity at the earth's surface), equivalent to 0.068 knots per hour. The error in distance run may be negligible for the brief period of powered flight of a ballistic missile; but for a submarine it builds up to thousands of miles in weeks under the polar icecap. Another is the precision requirement in absolute terms. We have admired the accuracy of the Sperry Mk 19 gyro-compass, which defined the vertical with an accuracy of 1'. If a platform, supposed to be horizontal, is in fact tilted at 1', the component of g in its plane is 19 knots per hour.

The fact that accelerations due to gravity and the rotation of the earth are of the same nature as (and therefore indistinguishable from) accelerations in the motion of the vehicle over the earth has been seen in previous chapters as a problem in navigation instrumentation in various contexts. Suppose an observer in a sealed sound-proofed capsule has only one instrument, a spring balance calibrated in kilograms, with a 1 kg weight suspended from it —in effect an accelerometer calibrated in units of g. If the instrument does not read unity, he can conclude that he is not stationary on the surface of the earth. If it reads zero, he may be in free fall or in orbit with the engine off. Time will tell. If it reads unity, he may be stationary on the surface of the earth; he may be in powered orbit with a thrust equivalent to g in an 'upwards' (for want of a better word) direction; or he may be in free orbit with the engine off in a vehicle spinning about an axis 'above' the balance.

The accuracy of which a spring balance is capable is far too low to serve as an INS accelerometer. Besides, as has already been seen in other contexts, the twentieth-century requirement has been increasingly for sensors with an electrical, electromagnetic, or latterly, electro-optical output. A common type of accelerometer employed in INS in the 1980s was the 'force-feedback' device illustrated[18] in Fig. 9.6. A non-ferrous pendulum is fixed on a nearly frictionless hinge so that it can swing in one plane only. A coil is fixed to the pendulum in the field of magnets fixed to the case. When the vehicle accelerates, the pendulum tends to lag. Any deflection of the pendulum from its null position is sensed by a pick-up, the output of which is amplified and conducted through the coil, providing a restoring force on the pendulum to eliminate the deflection. The current in the coil is proportional to the magnetic force on the pendulum which balances the specific force due to acceleration. Therefore the current required is proportional to the acceleration.

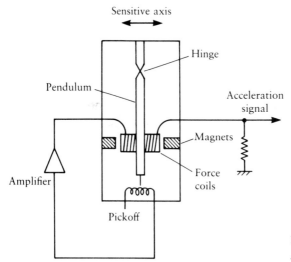

FIGURE 9.6
Pendulous, force-feedback accelerometer

Three such accelerometers mounted on a platform on mutually orthogonal axes sense the total acceleration vector. For terrestrial vehicles the horizontal velocity is of major interest, and gravity is large compared with accelerations in the motion of most such vehicles relative to the earth. It was therefore logical to seek to make the platform horizontal for terrestrial vehicles. There is a way to do this. In Fig. 9.7 the platform is stabilized in the horizontal

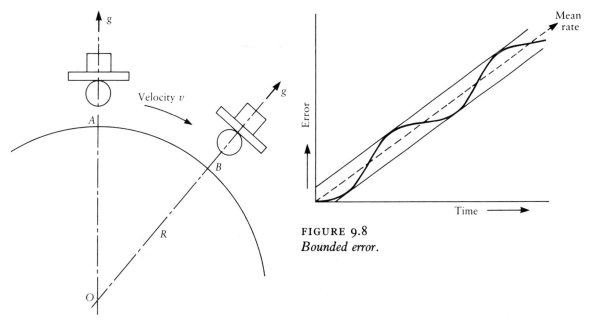

FIGURE 9.8
Bounded error.

FIGURE 9.7
Movement of a horizontal platform.

plane when the vehicle is stationary at the starting-point. At any subsequent moment at which the recorded speed is v in direction x, the gyro is precessed by a torque motor at an angular rate equal to v/R, R being the radius of the earth. Thus the platform remains horizontal subject to error. The beauty of the arrangement is that the system bounds its own errors. Suppose the system over-estimates v or the torque motor over-reacts so that the platform is tilted too much. A component of g is now in the plane of the platform in the opposite direction to v, so that it is perceived by the system as a retarding acceleration, slowing down the forward tilting of the platform, which consequently oscillates about the horizontal. Suppose the vehicle is stationary but the platform is tilted 1′ towards south. Subject to errors in other components the system will sense this as an acceleration of 19 knots per hour towards north, and restore equilibrium. Gravity works to keep itself out of the system; but while it is doing so an oscillating erroneous velocity (and therefore an erroneous integration of distance run) is recorded, as in Fig. 9.8.

The technique applied is called 'Schuler tuning', because the idea appeared in a paper[19] published by Schuler in 1923. Schuler thought the idea was trivial: its application was not then apparent. Figure 9.9 shows a compound pendulum pointing vertically downwards. It is suspended at P with its centre of mass at G. The distance PG is a and the length of the dumbbell is d. An elementary dynamic analysis shows that such a device has an extraordinary quality if $a = d^2/4R$. If the earth were perfectly spherical the pendulum would continue to point to the centre of the earth as it was transported about the surface, even if there were no gravity. If the pendulum is disturbed, it oscillates under gravity with a period of $2\pi\sqrt{(R/g)}$,

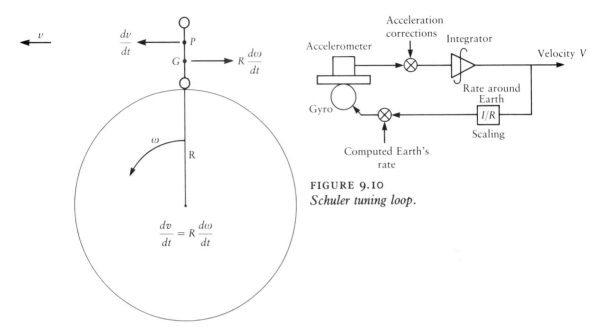

FIGURE 9.10
Schuler tuning loop.

FIGURE 9.9
Transport of a Schuler pendulum over a gravity-free sphere.

the period of a simple pendulum of length R, with the bob at the earth's surface. It is the mysterious 84.4 minutes period used by Schuler to eliminate ballistic error in the Anschütz gyrocompass. For a homogeneous sphere R/g is a function only of density, so the period would be the same on a spherical planet of any size having the same density as the earth.

A mechanical Schuler pendulum is impossible of construction. As Schuler pointed out, if d is 4 metres, a = 0.6 microns; but the servosystem described above behaves just like one. The oscillation period of 84 minutes (which is seen in Fig. 9.8) is a characteristic of the earth, being a function only of R and g. To compound matters, the earth is not spherical, the direction of g is not towards the geometric centre of the earth, and neither R nor g are everywhere the same. Since the platform is turning in space, velocity components are not simple integrals of historic acceleration relative to the platform. The effects of the rotation of the earth and Coriolis accelerations (Chapter 8) must be included by separate loops, as illustrated in Fig. 9.10.

Walter Wrigley, a distinguished worker in the field, has remarked that every history of inertial navigation has a different perspective on the story. There is one obvious reason. When Elmer Sperry was a young man, the first action of an aspiring inventor was to patent his ideas—only then did he try to make them work. The German navy in 1904 saw no obstacle to inviting the British navy to attend trials of the first Anschütz instrument aboard a German cruiser. There has probably never been a time when workers in the field of navigational science enjoyed better international communication. In contrast, for the last sixty years, the development of navigation has largely been directed by perceived military requirements and financed by military budgets in secret. It is claimed for example that Siegfried Reisch was the first (in 1945) to use what came to be called 'Schulerian tuning' in the USA from 1950 on; but when American workers first heard of Reisch their own work was much more advanced. After the end of the Second World War the development of INS for weapon systems proceeded in the USA and its allies in total isolation from parallel work in the USSR and its allies. One hopes that the Russians will tell their own story.

There can be no agreement on who 'started' INS—the candidates range from Galileo to Schuler. One of the more entertaining, advanced by Claud Powell, is an Irishman who wrote a letter to *Nature* in 1873 suggesting that if a ball were suspended from the roof of a railway carriage, a complete history of its 'shocks' would give velocity. He went on 'Further it is possible to conceive the apparatus as so *integrating* its results as to enable the distance and direction . . . to be read off.'

It was the development in Germany of missiles for the Second World War which led to the first successful if primitive INS. Missiles are the obvious field for INS to start, because the relatively short duration of the operation minimizes the accumulation of error. As there is no human pilot, navigation and control may be an integrated system. The V-1, the first successful long-range guided surface-to-surface air missile, was truly an 'aerial torpedo', using a unique pulse-jet engine and an accelerometer in the autopilot system. This was not INS; but the V-2, a much more advanced weapon developed by the Peenemunde team led by Wernher von Braun, was guided by basic inertial sensors during the thrust period. When the desired velocity was reached (after about one minute) an inertial system shut down the rocket motor. The payload was a one-ton conventional warhead. About 1000 were fired at London during the last months of the war. London was fortunate that the weapon was not developed earlier. In 1942 the prototype system used two gyros with two degrees of freedom for flight control, and an accelerometer for velocity. The model used against London had a platform stabilized by three gyros with one degree of freedom which later became the INS norm.

Von Braun and his team were taken to Texas at the end of the war, and formed the nucleus of post-war development of missiles in the USA. In the early post-war period the development of INS was principally concerned with missiles. The thermonuclear bomb and other developments, of which the refinement of INS was among the most important, led in 1954 to the Intercontinental Ballistic Missile capable of the delivery at a range of 5000 miles of a warhead of total destruction. A few years later the strategic shift to submarines as covert launching vehicles for such weapons was a major impetus toward the development of Ship's Inertial Navigation Systems. The British SINS Mk I showed that accelerometers are not strictly essential to an INS. It used gyros in null-acting servos to provide latitude (which is in effect a by-product of the gyrocompass itself); longitude was provided by a clock and a 'memory gyro'.

The most important sources of error in conventional gyroscopes are pivot friction and instability of the mass centre. In SINS, for example, the required mass centre stability was 10^{-8} cm. One solution is to mount the rotor in a closed can and float the resulting unit in liquid of the same mean density, so that there is no pivot friction. The known viscosity of the fluid modifies the behaviour of the instrument, making it a 'rate integrating' instrument. Precise temperature control is required to maintain the viscosity and density constant; inspection and maintenance of complex and delicate machinery submerged in fluid is also a problem. The rotor may also be supported on a gas-lubricated bearing. There is also the electrically supported vacuum gyro, in which the rotor consists of a sphere levitated either electrostatically or electromagnetically in a vacuum. The Dynamically Tuned Free Rotor Gyro has advantages in terms of relative ease of repair and ruggedness. The best of these refined mechanical gyros improved the accuracy of performance by several orders of magnitude.

The ring laser gyro must be one of the oddest developments in the history of navigation. A gyroscope with no moving parts! In 1913 Sagnac had demonstrated the shift of interference fringes when a system of mirrors reflecting two light beams travelling in opposite directions around a closed optical path is rotated. There is a light-source at A in the equilateral triangle ABC (Fig. 9.11), and mirrors at B and C pitched so that light goes around the circuits ABCA and ACBA. If the system is rotated, the path of the light which goes around the circuit in the same sense increases in length, because AB_1 is longer than AB, etc. Similarly the path of the light rotating in a contrary sense is diminished. Since the speed of light is 300 000 km/sec, the angle between AB and AB_1 is minute at any imaginable rate of rotation, and the increase/decrease in the length of the path may be taken to vary linearly as the rotation rate.

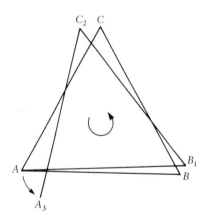

FIGURE 9.11
Path of light in a ring laser gyro.

Although rotation is *in principle* susceptible to optical detection, and the shift of the interference fringes may be observed, there was no practical application to gyroscopy, because ordinary light is not coherent. The beam of a laser (Light Amplification by Stimulated Emission of Radiation) does not diffuse. It is narrow, at a single frequency; it is coherent. The principle was expounded in 1958 by A. L. Schawlow and C. H. Townes. T. H. Maiman made one work, using a ruby crystal as an emitter, in 1960. The realization of the application to gyroscopy must have been nearly immediate. Triangular ring lasers were being publicly demonstrated within three years—probably earlier in secret.

The 'lock-in effect' was a fundamental difficulty. The output signal of a ring laser gyro is a beat between the two counter-rotating beams; the frequency of the beat varies linearly with rotation rate, except that (owing to interaction between the beams) when the rotation rate drops below the lock-in rate the output drops precipitately to zero. The lock-in rate may exceed 1°/min. The solution to the problem developed by Honeywell was to vibrate the instrument with an appropriately named dither spring, imposing an alternating rotation at a rate several orders of magnitude higher than the lock-in rate. Obviously, in any such oscillation there are two moments in every cycle when there is zero rotation and a little information is lost, leading to a random error which grows as the square root of time. A later solution employed piezo-electric techniques. Despite such difficulties, in 1986 ring laser gyros were available commercially with 'bias rates' of the order of a thousandth of a degree per hour, 'random error' of the order of a thousandth of a degree per square root hour, and scale factor error of the order of one in a million.[20]

The success of the ring laser gyro raised the wider question of how best to use light to sense rotation. One alternative to the ring laser is the fibre-optic gyro, and doubtless there are others. The nuclear magnetic resonance gyro is perhaps even more esoteric than optical gyros. This may be only the beginning of the application of the dynamics of atoms and sub-atomic particles to rotation-rate sensing. We do not know what else is under 'classified' development.

There is no single figure of merit for gyros, or for whole systems. In submarines which may remain submerged for weeks there is a rigorous requirement to minimize errors which grow with time; but the rotation rates will not be large. In an agile aircraft the ability to measure rotation rates over a wide range may be the greater challenge. Gyros working on quite different principles may be optimum in different applications.

Early INS used analogue computers. The rapid development of precision gyros, largely thanks to military budgets during the Cold War, has been paralleled by the development of powerful high-speed digital computers at low cost, weight, and volume—arguably the most remarkable technological development of our times. Computer power and gyros such as the ring laser, capable of measuring rotation rate precisely over a wide range of rates, led logically to the strapped-down INS[21] illustrated in Fig. 9.12. The platform or 'cluster' of gyros and accelerometers is fixed to the aircraft. There is no feedback to the gyros, which are purely and simply rotation-rate sensors. All the feedback is within the computer—which, when one thinks about it, is where it belongs.

At the beginning of this chapter the gyro was seen simply as a device which tends to point in a fixed direction in space, which it still is in the gyro direction-indicators used on smaller aircraft. In gyromagnetic compasses this property is used to smooth the output of a dynamically unstable sensor of a different source of direction data, terrestrial magnetism. The same property was used in primitive INS to provide a stable platform for accelerometers. The phenomena of precession and gravity were employed in the marine gyrocompass to provide orientation in the horizontal plane, and in the aircraft artificial horizon to define the zenith. Feedback, first used in gyrocompasses, becomes more complex in the Schuler tuning loop of

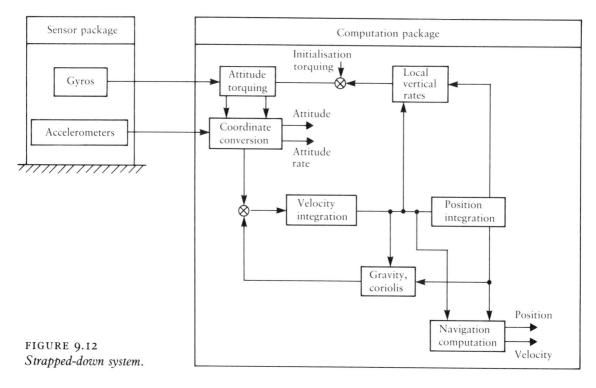

FIGURE 9.12
Strapped-down system.

some INS. Finally, the gyro becomes simply a sensor of rotation rate, part of a system with no moving parts.

Our changing perception of the application of INS to our needs is illustrated by its eventual impact on airline navigation, which of course was far from being an object of the original development of INS. It was perceived initially as an accurate system of DR navigation with the capability of making astronomical fixing unnecessary in areas, principally oceanic, where radio fixing was inadequate. INS trials on board airliners in regular service began in 1963 under the surveillance of the US Federal Aviation Agency. The Boeing 747 became the first airliner in which INS was fitted as standard equipment in 1968. The largest aircraft in the world was also the first airliner intended for transoceanic flight which had no provision for astronomical navigation and no navigator station—not even a chart table.

The INS was employed as an automatic DR system, with an error rate of about one nautical mile per hour. Typically, the flight plan was inserted in the computer, usually in the form of the latitude and longitude of 'way points'. There were essentially two outputs, one used in the normal autopilot mode to maintain the aircraft on the flight-planned track, the other in the display of position, motion, and orientation to the human pilots. They could have their latitude and longitude, distance/time to next way point, distance off flight-planned track, track and ground speed, and true or magnetic heading. As the equipment had no magnetic sensor, the computer carried a world-wide map of magnetic variation in memory. The need for it arose from a navigation practice which goes back to the *Compasso da Navegare* and the *Carta Pisana*. From the development of the radio range and the airways concept in the 1930s it was standard practice to express the direction of radio beams, airways, and even runways relative to magnetic north; and INS had to conform to this established practice.

Such a system may be perceived merely as the automation of the flight navigator function; and for some years INS was not fitted to short-range aircraft. In the 1980s the perception changed. Owing perhaps to its inherently continuous output, INS was seen as a central source of data and control to which radio navigational data were supplementary, and INS became standard on new short-range airliners, except for the smallest. Modern flight-management systems show clearly that this too is a misconception. It is not the INS which is at the heart of the matter, but the computer it brought with it. The sensors of acceleration and rotation rate are just two of many inputs to the flight-management computer. At sea, the evolving perception of the application of INS to navigation has been quite different. INS could never be a largely autonomous system at sea because of the longer 'mission times' involved. In the modern submarine, INS is an input, along with others, to the navigation subsystem of the overall weapon system of the ship. The navigator remains part of that subsystem. He even plots on a chart!

The automation of airline navigation led by INS is also illustrative of the problems which automation causes at the man–machine interface. Human navigators have always made mistakes; but experienced ones seem to have some kind of feedback system in their heads which often enables them to sense when something is wrong. Machines have no equivalent sense, and as men become more remote from the navigation they lose theirs. The magnitude of blunder at the interface is virtually unlimited. It is as easy to insert the longitude of a way-point 100° in error as 1' in error. At least one incident involving the loss of many human lives is known to have been caused by an erroneous way-point insertion, which is also the most probable explanation of the straying of a Boeing 747 shot down in Russian airspace. The pilot of a twin-engined airliner which lost one engine shut down the wrong engine, with fatal consequences. Preoccupation with his highly sophisticated navigation computer may have been a contributory factor.

This chapter is entitled 'Self-Containment'. Self-contained navigation is a military ideal, especially applicable to submarines covertly submerged for long periods because radio waves only penetrate a few metres of water; but in peaceful commerce complete self-containment is not the way to go. Both at sea and in the air navigation is increasingly about safe and efficient traffic-flow—as it has long been on the roads. In particular, the density of air traffic imposes a requirement for traffic control both to avoid collision in the air and to maximize runway utilization. In such circumstances navigation becomes a co-operative system involving the navigation of all the craft in the space.

There has been no reference in this chapter to the navigation of space vehicles, which are, of course, an important application of INS; but space vehicles have an enormous advantage over terrestrial vehicles. They have a far better definition of fixed directions in space than any gyroscope—stars which never set and never hide behind cloud. The main uses of inertial systems in space are for stabilization, smoothing of star-sensor information, and the measurement and control of velocity increments when rockets are fired. The difficulties of navigation in deep space include the very long periods of operation, and the complexity of the gravity field in which the craft is in free fall for most of the time.

Notes to Chapter 9

1. However, the term 'gyroscope' applied to the earth is not appropriate etymologically. Leon Foucault described his toy as a 'gyroscope' because it enabled him to view the gyration of the earth.

2. Naturally, when such an instrument could be engineered there were better ways of achieving the object.

3. The Kearfoot N1 compass was basically a refined and sophisticated gyro direction-indicator with the spin axis maintained in the horizontal as defined by its case, not by gravity.

4. Grant and Klinkert (1970).

5. Iron-ore carriers also have their own special problems with the magnetic compass. Such ships, trading the Great Lakes, were among early users of the Sperry gyrocompass.

6. Eighty-four minutes is the period of a simple pendulum of length the radius of the earth when the bob is at the surface of the earth. Schuler's name is associated with it. See also Note 19.

7. Einstein, who left Switzerland in 1913 to become the Director of the Kaiser Wilhelm Institute in Berlin, personally advised on some later improvements to Anschütz gyrocompasses.

8. Grant and Klinkert (1970).

9. Schlick in Germany and Brennan in Britain pioneered gyrostabilizers from about 1904.

10. A suggestion of Professor J. Henderson, adviser to the Admiralty, developed by Sperry.

11. Fanning (1986).

12. After an association of more than fifty years the Sperry UK company was selected by the Admiralty to manufacture the British SINS (Ships Inertial Navigation System). By that date Sperry in the US was not the leader in American inertial navigation.

13. Sperry wrote to Mussolini 'You are the outstanding advocate and example of the dignity and even sanctity of work which is the underlying national ideal in America.' Quoted in Hughes (1971).

14. A servomechanism is one in which the signal of an error is amplified or converted to a means of correcting the error. Since response to control is rarely instantaneous, arrangements to provide stability, to avoid 'hunting'—oscillation about the zero-error state—may be complex. The term *cybernetics* was introduced in 1948 (long after Sperry's death) by Norbert Weiner to describe the science of communication and control to achieve desired goals.

15. Davenport (1978) gives a detailed account of the incident.

16. Some professional pilots object in principle to the machine's having the last word; but there was no outcry when anti-skid brake units were introduced in the 1950s. The fuse on a household appliance may be regarded as a case of the machine's having the last word.

17. Not to be confused with the gyroscopic gunsight, which uses the torque caused by slewing a gun trained on a moving target to offset the sight by the required deflection.

18. Figures 9.6, 9.7, 9.10 and 9.12 follow S. G. Smith (1986).

19. 'Die Störung von Pendul-und Kreiselapparaten durch die Beschleunigung der Fahrzeuges', Schuler Max. 1923, *Physikalische Zeitschrift*, **B24**. There is a translation in *Navigation*, USA, **14**, 26. Let m be the mass of the dumbbell, v the velocity of its transportation along the earth's surface, I its moment of Inertia, ω its angular velocity of rotation relative to a fixed direction in space. There is no gravitational field. $ma. \, dv/dt = I.d\omega/dt$. Since $I = md^2/4$ and $a = d^2/4R$,

$dv/dt = R.d\omega/dt$, so ω is also the angular velocity of the whole system about the centre of the earth. If gravity is introduced and the pendulum is disturbed the period of a small oscillation is $2\pi\sqrt{I/mga} = 2\pi\sqrt{R/g}$. It has been pointed out that Schuler's demonstration is only valid for motion in great circles, and attention has been drawn to similar studies by D'Alembert in the eighteenth century. Perhaps too much significance has been ascribed to this paper; but it features heavily in all the literature.

20. S. G. Smith (1986).
21. Strapped-down systems had been used earlier for low-accuracy applications such as autopilots.

CHAPTER TEN

The Homing Quality of Radio

✠

A RADIO bearing is a position line like any other, and may be used like any other; but it has a quality of transcendent importance. The accuracy of the position line increases indefinitely as the distance decreases. It is this *homing* quality of radio which made air navigation in cloudy conditions practical, leading eventually to the routine of automatic landing of airliners with hundreds of passengers aboard when the visual range is no more than that required to navigate the taxiways after landing. It is through the aeroplane rather than the ship that the homing quality of radio has had its greatest impact on our civilization, and has stimulated the development of sciences undreamed of when the first radio bearing was taken.

From the beginning of radio its main application was to communications, especially after broadcast programmes began in the early 1920s. It was not until the preparation for the Second World War that significant funds were applied to research into radio navigation. Even then, the main thrust was towards radio *counter*-navigation, the use of radio to 'see' enemy vehicles, especially bomber aircraft, discussed in the next chapter. The homing quality of radio, invaluable in peacetime, is ambivalent in war. It cannot be applied to weapon delivery if the enemy declines to transmit. It is damaging if the enemy uses one's own transmissions to home on to his targets. The history of radio direction-finding in the first fifty years after Hertz's experiments described in Chapter 4 has therefore three aspects: the development of radio communication technology; its application to direction-finding (D/F); and the adaption of the state of the art to the multifarious needs of diverse navigators.

The early workers following Hertz were scientists pursuing an exciting new field of physics rather than inventors. The Victorians were not slow to find applications for discoveries in electricity, as telegraphs, dynamos, electric motors, and electro-plating show. Some eminent scientists of the period were entrepreneurial; but the application of radio to communication over the horizon seemed far-fetched. If radio waves (or Hertzian waves as they were then called) were of the same nature as light they should, like light, move in straight lines, subject to refraction; they should not curve around the earth's surface.

Nevertheless, some scientists were sanguine. In 1892 Sir William Crookes specified the requirements for wireless telegraphy: transmission energy concentrated on a narrow frequency band; receivers tuned to that frequency; the means to direct the beam from the transmitter to the receiver. Early experimenters naturally thought of the last as lenses, by analogy with light.[1] The directional properties of receivers had been a feature of Hertz's earliest successful experiments; when the loop was turned so that its plane was at right angles to the transmitter there was no spark. Throughout the period, point-to-point communication was a stronger motivation for improvement of the directional properties of antennas than the needs of navigation.

The first important improvement on a loop of wire with a spark gap as a receiver (the original Hertz receiver, see Chapter 4) was the coherer–decoherer, a by-product of telephony technology,[2] which relies on the decrease in the electrical resistance of loose iron filings in the presence of an electromagnetic field. Using a Hertzian oscillator as a transmitter, and a coherer–decoherer as a receiver, Sir Oliver Lodge in 1894 detected a signal at 100 metres which, despite Hughes (Chapter 4), has been claimed to be the first radio communication.

One should not seek too close an analogy between Guglielmo Marconi and Elmer Sperry (Chapter 9). Marconi studied physics at Bologna and at Livorno under notable researchers[3] in electromagnetism, and then retreated to his father's estate to pursue his research privately; later in life he was awarded the Nobel prize in physics. None of this was Sperry's style. Radio was too big a field for one man to dominate it for as long as Sperry dominated gyroscopes; but Marconi's early pre-eminence in radio was equally remarkable, considering the intellectual quality of other workers and their number. He shared with Sperry determination, vision, energy, inventiveness, creativity, precocity, and entrepreneurialism. They were both in businesses in which feedback proved abundantly fruitful; but, unlike Sperry, many of Marconi's major achievements did not depend on it.

Marconi's first important invention, at the age of twenty, was the earthed antenna.[4] He discovered that range could be extended to more than 2 km by connecting one side of the gap to earth and the other to a vertical wire with a plate on top. He also improved his coherer. He then discovered that range could be much extended by using a long horizontal antenna supported at some distance above the ground. It seemed that, despite the physicists, radio waves could be trapped into following the earth's surface. At the age of twenty-one he went to England,[5] formed his own company, took out patents, interested British government departments, and demonstrated radio communication with dazzling rapidity. In 1897 he communicated with ships up to 20 km away.[6] Two years later he bridged the English Channel. In 1901 he bridged the Atlantic, receiving in Newfoundland the letter S in Morse from his station in Poldhu, Cornwall. He was then twenty-seven. Soon he was selling so much marine radio equipment that by 1904 there was an international distress call for ships at sea.[7]

How could Marconi's results be possible? The earth's surface does conduct electromagnetic

The spark-gap transmitter used in Marconi's early experiments. (The type was invented by Righi.)

The self-restoring coherer used by Marconi to receive the first transatlantic signal in 1901.

radiation considerable distances at the lower frequencies, the sea being the best conductor and the ice-caps the worst; but this was not a sufficient explanation. The idea that the upper atmosphere may be electrically charged had been mooted in the 1880s in the context of systematic changes in geomagnetism.[8] O. Heaviside in England and A. E. Kennelly in the USA independently suggested that Marconi's results could only be explained on the hypothesis of wave reflection by electrically charged upper levels of the atmosphere.

The higher the frequency the greater the density of free electrons in the atmosphere required to produce reflection, and the less the absorption. From 1925 techniques of direct measurement were developed by E. V. Appleton and M. A. F. Barnett in England and by G.

Breit and M. A. Tuve in the USA. Appleton and Barnett originally used a wave-interference technique; but the pulse technique pioneered by Breit and Tuve became general. The refinement of techniques at ultra-high frequencies in several countries in the 1930s led to radar (Chapter 11). High-altitude rockets and satellites enabled the ionosphere to be probed from within and from above in the 1960s. Knowledge of the distribution of free electrons in the atmosphere, and its variation with time, place, and solar activity, became comprehensive.

Although it is now recognized that from 50 to 300 km the atmosphere is ionized throughout, the picture which had emerged about 1940 was of three, or rather four, layers. The lowest, the D layer, active in daylight, is lightly ionized and reflects only low frequency (LF) and very low frequency (VLF)[9] radiation. The E or Heaviside layer, of the order of 100 km above the earth, reflects medium frequencies (MF); it is thicker and denser at night. The F or Appleton layer, in the region of 300 km above the earth, reflects high frequencies (HF). Within the belt of the F layer there are two levels of concentrated ionization, F_1 (the lower) and F_2. The earth also reflects radio waves, which is why communication right around the world is possible in the mode illustrated in Fig. 10.1. The ionization of the atmosphere is not normally sufficient to reflect very high frequencies (VHF) or ultra-high frequencies (UHF).

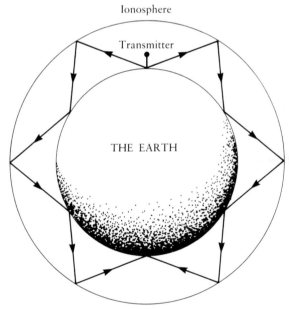

FIGURE 10.1
Radio communication around the globe.

Marconi encountered the consequences of an ionized atmosphere in 1902. Experimenting aboard a steamship, he found that he could receive Poldhu at 2000 miles at night, but only at about 700 miles by day. He obtained more consistent results at lower frequencies, leading to the era of pumping into the atmosphere vast quantities of energy at very long wavelengths. Wavelengths as long as 20 km were employed, and arc oscillator transmitters with an output of 1 megawatt[10] were in use before 1920. At very low frequencies and very high power the ground wave was effective over a considerable distance, especially over the sea, and extended by D- and E-layer reflection. The compelling reason for use of LF and VLF seems to have been the relative ease of obtaining high-power transmitter output. Like Hertz before him, Marconi's early experiments were in wavelengths of a few metres (VHF). As we now know, the ionosphere does not normally reflect at such frequencies; but the reason for switching to LF was the perceived need for power.

At the receiver, the coherer had been replaced by magnetic, electrolytic, and crystal[11] detectors of various kinds; but, except for crystals, these devices were not in the mainstream of history. During the 1880s several experimenters had noticed that electric currents will flow one way in an evacuated tube between a heated filament and a cold plate, but not the other way. Free electrons around the heated filament travel through space to the cold plate if it is at a higher potential. In 1904 Sir John Fleming invented the thermionic valve, which was to dominate radio until the transistor. His device, a simple diode, merely rectified the alternating current received from the antenna to operate a d.c. display device such as an ink trace or a galvanometer. In its original form it was insensitive to weak signals.

The potential of the thermionic valve began to be realized from 1906, when Lee De Forest invented the triode valve illustrated in Fig. 10.2. Whereas in Fleming's diode the signal was applied between cathode and anode, in the triode the signal was applied between cathode and grid. When the potential at the grid was positive the free electrons were accelerated towards it and shot through it; when the potential at the grid was negative, the electron flow was blocked. In consequence, if a small signal was applied to the grid, a larger signal was received at the anode. De Forest had converted Fleming's rectifier into an amplifier. It was soon found that the efficiency of the triode could be much increased by nearly perfect evacuation of air, and that amplification could be increased using cascades of triodes, the anode output of one triode being the grid input of the next. A major step, in 1913, was the application of the feedback principle (see Chapter 9). Positive feedback[12] improved sensitivity and selectivity; more importantly, it could make the system self-oscillating at a tuneable

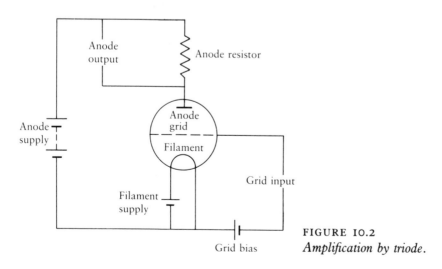

FIGURE 10.2

Amplification by triode.

frequency—to become a transmitter in fact. In the nature of the construction of a thermionic tube it was not capable of megawatt output; but it was capable of much higher frequencies and much higher frequency stability on a narrower band than the high-frequency alternators and arc oscillators that generated (and consumed) so much energy.

Such energy was unnecessary if one had a stable, narrow band-width HF transmitter, as Marconi discovered about the time that Appleton started his investigation.[13] Marconi found in 1923 that at a distance of 1400 miles he received a much stronger signal on a wavelength of 15 m from a 1 kw transmitter at Poldhu than from an LF transmitter at Caernarvon with an output in the region of 100 kw. By the mid-century most long-distance point-to-point communication was HF.

The first apparatus specifically designed to measure the direction of an incoming radio signal has been attributed to John Stone in 1904; but by 1907 a variety of systems had been patented, illustrating that the fashion of the time, of patenting an idea and making it work afterwards, was not limited to gyroscopic systems. Three means of providing a radio position line were recognized and developed. All are in use today. One is a ground station with a directional receiving antenna which provides bearings on demand, the D/F station. A chain of several intercommunicating D/F stations may provide a position. The equipment required on board the ship or aircraft is a transmitter and receiver; only one user may be served at a time; and there is a requirement for operators at the land station. Alternatively, the directional receiving apparatus may be installed on the ship or aircraft. The practical constraints of on-board installations, and the deviation of the apparent direction of the signal by reflections from the structure of the ship or aircraft (quadrantal error), coupled with the fact that such systems only give the bearing relative to the heading, so that the true bearing is subject to compass error, degrade the accuracy of the system. The advantages are that the equipment may be used with any identified broadcasting station or non-directional beacon[14] (NDB) of known position; users do not interfere with each other; and no co-operation is required from the transmitter, which may even be hostile. Finally, there is the directional beacon, a ground transmitter radiating a directionally differentiated signal so that receivers can identify the radial on which they lie by the signal they receive. Any number of users can be served simultaneously, and no operators are required on the ground. With some such systems, the receiver requires no special equipment.

The position line given by the bearing of a land station from a ship is a quite different curve to the position line given by a bearing of the ship from a station. The propagation path must be assumed to be a great circle. The information provided by a bearing from a shore station is that the vessel lies on the great circle passing through the station at an angle to its meridian reciprocal to the bearing. At different points on that great circle the bearing of the station from the vessel is different (see Fig. 10.3). The position line defined by a bearing of the station from the vessel is the line of constant bearing, the locus of a point having that bearing (see Fig. 10.4). As plotting was normally on a Mercator projection the practical problem was to reduce either curve to a rhumb line. Initially the matter was ignored,[15] later the standard practice was to apply the 'conversion angle' in the sense illustrated in Fig. 10.5.

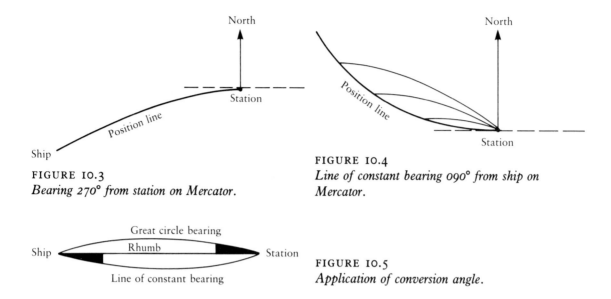

FIGURE 10.3
Bearing 270° from station on Mercator.

FIGURE 10.4
Line of constant bearing 090° from ship on Mercator.

FIGURE 10.5
Application of conversion angle.

Conversion angle, calculated as ½ diff. long. x sine mean lat. (half the convergency of the meridians), a coarse but adequate approximation, appeared in tables and in scales on some charts. In equatorial latitudes it could be ignored. In temperate latitudes it was used only when the difference of longitude exceeded 5°.

The 'small loop' invented by Captain J. H. Round of the Marconi company was an obvious sequel to Hertz's observation that the loop of wire with a spark gap which was his receiver gave no spark when its plane was at right angles to the transmitter. The direction-finding property of the loop derives from the phase difference of the signal received in the two vertical members of the loop because of their different distances from the transmitter. If the plane of the loop is perpendicular to the incoming signal the phase difference is zero and no signal is received across the loop. In any other position the signal across the loop is 90° out of phase with the incoming signal, and (if d/λ is small) reduced by a factor of $2\pi d/\lambda$, where d is the difference in the distance of the two vertical members from the transmitter and λ is the wavelength (Fig. 10.6). Round explored the figure-of-eight polar diagram[16] of the closed loop antenna illustrated in Fig. 10.7. The inherent 180° ambiguity may be resolved by connecting

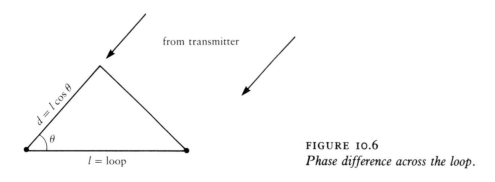

FIGURE 10.6
Phase difference across the loop.

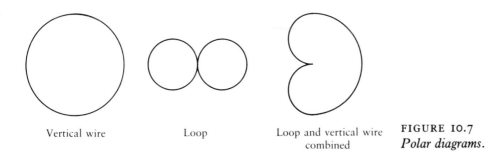

Vertical wire   Loop   Loop and vertical wire combined

FIGURE 10.7
Polar diagrams.

the loop to a simple vertical antenna giving the cardioid (heart-shaped) polar diagram seen in the figure. As the null of the cardioid is less sharp than that of the figure-of-eight, the bearing (or its reciprocal) may be found using the loop alone, and the cardioid used only to resolve ambiguity. Round's loop was long before its time. The basic problem, before the triode, was the lack of means of amplifying a signal which is necessarily weak.

The dilemma, caused by the practical difficulty of rotating a large loop, and the low signal obtained from a small loop, was resolved by E. Bellini and A. Tosi in 1907. They used two identical vertical loops fixed at right angles. Each was connected to a fixed coil of a radiogoniometer, and the search coil was rotated until a null was heard (Fig. 10.8). If the current flowing in one coil is proportional to $\cos \theta$ and the current flowing in the other is proportional to $\sin \theta$, the voltages induced by each in the search coil are equal and opposite when that coil is at right angles to the bearing. A Bellini–Tosi system was fitted to a British ship in 1912.

By 1917 receiver and D/F technology had improved sufficiently for Round to track the German fleet at the battle of Jutland by its radio communications.[17] At that period Germans perceived radio direction-finding mainly as an aid to navigation, the British as a source of intelligence on enemy movements. Both applications became highly developed by all concerned in the Second World War; but, after Jutland, combatants would never again think they could broadcast with impunity.

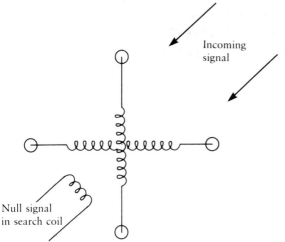

Incoming signal

Null signal in search coil

FIGURE 10.8
Bellini–Tosi system in plan section.

A Bellini–Tosi direction-finder of 1907. (The radiogoniometer is to the right.)

As the amplification problem disappeared (from the 1920s) more fundamental problems emerged. Elementary D/F theory assumes that the signal is a vertically polarized wave travelling horizontally. When it is reflected from the ionosphere it is neither vertically polarized nor travelling horizontally, so errors may ensue. These difficulties were partly overcome at land stations by the Adcock balanced pair vertical antennas with buried couplings. The idea, which produced a great improvement in accuracy, seems to have been suggested in about 1918; but it was not general practice until the late 1930s. Another problem was discovered; the simple derivation of the cosine (figure-of-eight) polar diagram relies on the assumption that d/λ is a small number. If it is not small (say less than 0.1) there is an 'octantal' error, analogous to the odd points of a 16-point compass. When it is 0.5 the peak error is about 7°.

In the 1920s D/F equipment on ships became general. From 1935 D/F equipment was mandatory on all large ships on the British register. In the next ten years its use became so widespread that in 1946 the US Coastguard ceased to provide ships at sea with bearings on request. To all the difficulties of D/F in the early years must be added the limitations of shipborne equipment and the errors already described. Early installations included Bellini–Tosi systems the size of the ship. As amplification at radio frequencies (RF) improved, as superior techniques such as the superheterodyne receiver developed, the size of the antennas diminished; but the Bellini–Tosi principle continued to be favoured. Quadrantal error, often amounting to 10°, was corrected; but, as the error varies with frequency, it was desirable that NDBs should be concentrated in a fairly narrow frequency band.

Each frequency band was found to have its own limitations in respect of accuracy, range, 'night effect' (ionospheric distortions), regularity, and diurnal variation. In the 1930s the preferred D/F frequencies were in the MF and HF range. In 1950 aeronautical NDBs operated mainly in the 315–405 kHz band, and marine NDBs in the 405–525 kHz band, except that 410 kHz was reserved for shore D/F stations. At that stage there were so many marine NDBs around the coast of the British Isles that interference became a problem, and there was a need to keep power output low. In general, ships used NDBs at much shorter ranges than aircraft, 100 n.m. being rarely exceeded. A survey[18] made in that period of the accuracy of bearings taken by ships from marine NDBs showed that 87 per cent were accurate to within 1°, and 95 per cent within 2° at the close ranges commonly used.

The fact that many aeroplanes of the earlier period were biplanes enabled large Bellini–Tosi loops to be rigged around the wings and the fuselage, which as yet did not have metal skins. In the early 1930s some RAF biplanes had a fixed loop enclosing the whole area between the wings. To take a bearing the aircraft had to be pointed towards the null—ideal for homing one might think; but, as a matter of practical pilotage, flying to a null is not easy, especially against the background of ignition interference in those days. The ingenious solution of Captain James Robinson was a smaller loop in the vertical plane of the fuselage (called the main coil) which received a maximum signal when the aircraft was pointing at the transmitter. Switching the wing coil on and off produced no change in the signal if the wing coil was at a null. When it was not at a null the direction to turn towards the null was found by a phase-reversal technique. The basic defect of such a homing system is that to home in a straight line (great circle) the heading must be offset from the direction of the station to correct for the drift due to crosswind. If the aircraft is pointed directly at the station it reaches it from a downwind direction, following the curve illustrated in Fig. 10.9.

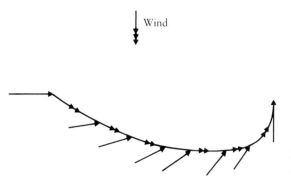

Wind

FIGURE 10.9
Homing without drift correction.

The pilot needs a display of relative bearing in order to offset drift. As receivers improved, the size of the aircraft loop was reduced. It became a manually operated small loop (often retractable during the earlier period, later enclosed in aerodynamic fairing) instead of a goniometer. Calibration for quadrantal error became general.

The automation of the direction-finding (ADF) was the next major step. The radio compass, when tuned to a station, displays on a 360° rose the bearing of the station relative to the heading. If the rose is driven by a gyromagnetic compass (the RMI), the magnetic bearing of the station is displayed. Twin ADFs with bearings displayed by two needles of different colours on a single RMI became standard in some operations. If the rose is a gyrocompass repeater, the true bearing is displayed. The ADF was obviously ideal for homing; but the continuous visual presentation of bearing also had a great advantage when used as a position line abeam. 'Night effect' is not a constant error; and careful observation of the way the bearing changed enabled the worst effects of ionospheric reflections at night to be filtered—a useful practice in the 1940s and 1950s. Usable range of a 2 Kw NDB in the 200–400 kHz band is up to 500 miles over the sea. The aircraft radio compasses of the 1940s had an external loop encased in an aerodynamic fairing which was turned by an electric motor governed by a servosystem (Chapter 9). The development of materials of high permeability (Chapter 8) and of miniature radiogoniometers led to the replacement of the rotating loop by a Bellini–Tosi system consisting of a cruciform core of ferrite slabs only 2 cm thick, which could be recessed into the aircraft skin.

In the late 1930s frequency multiplier technology permitted crystal-controlled push-button VHF operation.[19] The frequencies adopted were in the region of 120 MHz, wavelength 2.5 metres. The use of VHF is an illustration of the way in which the increasingly rich diversity of products which science was able to offer navigation found its diverse applications. VHF is not normally reflected by the ionosphere, so that range cannot be relied upon much beyond line-of-sight, say 200 miles at modern jet cruising altitudes, after allowing for atmospheric refraction. The advantage in war is that the enemy cannot eavesdrop if he is not within range. The advantage in peace is that shore or ground stations may use the same frequency without interference if they are suitably distanced. The channel is virtually free of static, and D/F bearings taken from a carefully sited station are sharp and accurate within about 2°; but reflections from the structure of the craft render conventional D/F by the craft impracticable except for homing (radar techniques for airborne D/F at VHF and UHF are described in Chapter 11).

As a dipole (half wavelength) antenna is only 1.2 metres long the D/F station may be mobile and the antenna array rotatable. A quarter-wavelength whip antenna only 60 cm long may be a permanent fixture on the smallest craft—a far cry from the long trailing antennas which formerly had to be wound in and out of aircraft, and the long wires festooned over ships. VHF became the usual channel for short-range communications of all kinds, short-range D/F from fixed stations, and short-range directional beacons. Initially, channels were widely separated; but increasing usage demanded, and improving technology permitted, successive reductions of the spacing.

A neat application of VHF, an early example of what it is now fashionable to call C³I (command, control, communication, information), was the navigation of RAF fighter aircraft during the Second World War.[20] Range could be made adequate by remote links. The ground controller needed to know where his aircraft was. The pilot needed to know the course to steer. Both needs were satisfied by chains of VHF D/F stations, in direct communication with the controller, obtaining their bearings when the pilot spoke to the controller.

Marconi had discovered very early that the inverted L with a very long horizontal member had highly directional properties. He arranged an array of 32 receiving antennas, each aligned with a point of the compass. The antenna receiving the loudest signal was the one aligned with the transmitter. Telefunken had the more fruitful idea of laying the 32-point array at the transmitter. A start signal was radiated on all antennas, followed by a one-second transmission on each antenna in sequence from north. There was even a stop-watch calibrated in the points of the compass. To get his bearing from the transmitter, the user started the watch on the start signal and stopped it when the sequentially radiated signal was at its loudest. This was the first practical directional radio beacon, a concept which had its origin in lighthouses (Chapter 8) and was to be re-echoed through the decades in more sophisticated devices. Telefunken installations were used to assist the navigation of aeroplanes and airships bombing London during the First World War,[21] but we are not required to believe the claim made in 1915 that the system accuracy was 5°.

This application illustrates the defect of the radio position line in war. As the accuracy diminished with distance from Germany, the system was more useful going home than when seeking the target which was the primary object of the exercise. In contrast, had the British used the equipment to bomb Germany, the system would have been most valuable *to them* when seeking the target. This was the last time such impunity was possible. The Sonne system (a brilliant German concept described in Chapter 12), intended in the Second World War to assist U-boat navigation, was used with great success by RAF anti-U-boat patrols.

The Telefunken approach was refined by Marconi, who installed at Inchkeith in 1921 the first 'wireless lighthouse'. This system eliminated the stop-watch. As the antenna array, consisting of two paraboloids, rotated one revolution in two minutes, a different letter of the morse code was signalled in each sector, each sector signal being separated from the next by the station identification signal. The user merely turned down the volume control until only one or two letters could be heard. The loudest letter identified the radial. This system operated on 50 MHz, an early example of the use of VHF to obtain a sharply defined beam. It was perhaps before its time. Subsequent installations of marine directional beacons in Britain (the best known was the Orfordness beacon, which operated until 1947) used lower frequencies and the stop-watch method. There is no reason why these beacons should not have been used by aircraft; but it appears that was not the practice.

The basic concept of the Lorenz system, the 'course-setter', patented by Otto Scheller in 1907, was to have far-reaching consequences in air navigation, although it does not seem to have worked well at the time. Two identical horizontal antennas aligned in different directions have identical outputs except that one transmits in Morse code the letter A (·—) and the other the letter N (—·). Each has maximum radiation in the direction in which it lies and a minimum at right angles to that direction. On the four radials which are the bisectors of the angles between the two antennas a continuous note is heard, Fig. 10.10). Elsewhere either the A or the N predominates. The navigator equipped with D/F may use the transmission

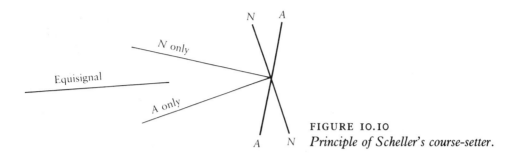

FIGURE 10.10
Principle of Scheller's course-setter.

as a NDB. The user equipped only with an ordinary receiver may use the continuous note as he passes through it as a position line, or he may use it to *home* on to the transmitter. This mode of use was later to influence the development of air navigation profoundly; but although further development was pursued during the First World War in the 500-metre band, the project was abandoned. Clear equi-signals were received on the ground but not in the air; perhaps because of the polarization effects of the long trailing antennas which were necessary at the time.[21]

Although directional beacons of various forms continue to serve mariners, they have never been, and never could be, more than a useful *aid* to navigation. In the air, systems which trace their roots to the ideas of Telefunken and Scheller in 1907 became a *means* of navigation. Without radio beams transmitted from the ground and interpreted in aircraft, air transport as we know it would have been impossible.

Scheller's principle was further developed in the US from about 1924. Initially the device transmitted A ($\cdot$—) from one of a pair of crossed-loop antennas, and N (—$\cdot$) from the other, producing four symmetrically arranged beams of equisignal. The next step was the invention of goniometric techniques to permit the beams to be laid askew in virtually any desired direction. Homing on a beam, arrival overhead was signalled by the 'cone of silence' where only the station identification signal was heard. In the 1930s the US was covered coast to coast with a network of radio ranges with their beams pointing to each other at such intervals that at least one was within aural range at nearly all times (Fig. 10.11). So long as the flight

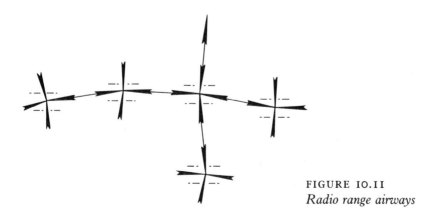

FIGURE 10.11
Radio range airways

was confined to the 'airways' defined by the beams, the only equipment required (other than the blind flying instruments described in Chapter 9) was a compass, an MF receiver of a type then to be found in nearly every American home, a chart depicting the radio range network, the safety altitude on each sector, and the location of airfields in relation to the network.

For the first time for centuries, navigators without visual reference to terrain required neither protractor nor dividers, and were indifferent to latitude and longitude. It was, arguably, the greatest revolution in navigation since the chronometer. Most of the navigator's routine became pre-flight planning. The flight plan, range by range, became the only navigation document. The log consisted of recording on it the 'actuals'—altitude, time overhead, fuel consumed and remaining. In the cone of silence the pilot set course following his flight plan to the next range, adjusting heading as he heard N or A. It became normal practice to report arrival over selected 'checkpoints' by radio. When the need for a federal air traffic control system was perceived, both the airways and the position-reporting procedure were already in place.

The system was efficacious but not perfectly efficient. Radio ranges were in the MF spectrum, which is subject to static and beam-bending. Some extra flying distance was involved, because the ranges rarely followed a great circle route from departure to destination. The concentration of traffic on airways artificially enhanced the risk of collision, and therefore stressed the need for traffic control. Nevertheless it was probably on the US continental airways network that optimum routeing of aircraft began. Greater aircraft range and increasing density of airways offered alternative routeings on the longer sectors, and the quality of the meteorological service and the communications facilities were, at the time, better than those available on any other sectors in the world of comparable length. By the end of the Second World War the US radio range coverage had been extended as far south as Brazil, and there were fragmentary chains in north–west Africa and some parts of Europe. Some 600 radio ranges were installed. Radio ranges were often installed in line with the main runway, with one beam laid along it. As Fig. 10.12 illustrates this extended navigation *by* radio to the approach phase, provided cloud base was not lower than safety altitude and visibility below cloud was adequate.

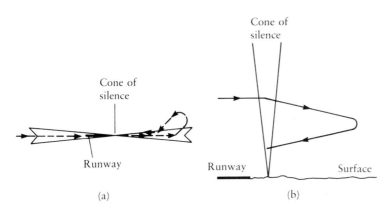

FIGURE 10.12
Radio range approach (to land to the west). (a) Horizontal; (b) vertical (vertical and horizontal scales do not agree).

If the concept that aircraft should be track-guided by direct presentation to the pilot and only provided with progress information at discrete intervals by the track guidance system itself was understood at all in Europe, it certainly was not accepted. There were some NDBs, not always strategically placed. From 1934 there was a European MF D/F fixing service which provided (in morse code) latitude and longitude by triangulation from the network of D/F stations. At some airports (London airport, Croydon from 1928) there were D/F stations offering QDM ('your magnetic course to reach me is . . .') service, also in morse code. One did not need a sextant to navigate over Europe in those days; but one did need protractor, dividers, a plotting chart, and a radio operator.

The plethora of imperfect electronic riches which was the Second World War's legacy to navigation offered a confusing choice to civil aviation. During the war the British in particular had developed short-range hyperbolic systems (Chapter 12) which were far more accurate than the radio range, and operated on frequencies less subject to static. The British argued vehemently that they could cover an area like Europe, or the US for that matter, more cheaply, reliably, and accurately than the VHF omnidirectional radio range (VOR) with which the US proposed to replace the radio range. The 1947 Conference of the International Civil Aviation Organization accepted the US proposal to make the VOR the international standard short-range navigation aid. US influence and interest at the time[22] were so overwhelming that no proposal opposed by the US was likely to succeed; but they were right. Hyperbolic position lines were no way to orchestrate air traffic before airborne computers. In 1959 the Decca Navigator Company were able to offer visual display to the pilot of track and distance to go to any selected waypoint from hyperbolic data by *Omnitrac*—but it was then too late. In civil aviation on routes over developed countries (but certainly not in marine applications or transoceanic air navigation) hyperbolic systems were before their time in relation to computer technology.

In 1936 thoughts had turned in the US Civil Aeronautics Administration to the eventual replacement of the radio range with a beacon having the omnidirectional quality of the Telefunken device thirty years earlier. After many vicissitudes the eventual result was the VOR. The VHF carrier wave in the 112–118 MHz band carried two modulations at 30 Hz.[23] The phase difference between the two modulations defines the radial. Initially the phase was rotated at the transmitter by a synchronous motor turning the free coil of a goniometer—a solution reminiscent of a Scheller patent of 1916. The receiver measures the phase difference (0–360°).

The pilot's controls were an on/off switch, a frequency selector, and a radial selector (the omni-bearing selector). There were traditionally two displays, still used on smaller aircraft. On one a vertical bar is deflected to the left or right of the centre line of the indicator (bar to the left, beam to the left) in a non-linear proportion to the displacement of the aircraft from the radial selected. The other used an RMI already mentioned in the context of ADF.

Over the first forty years there were many design improvements, some of them radical; but, from the user's point of view, the principle is unchanged. The introduction of Doppler VOR from the 1960s reduced the error of the transmitted signal to less than a degree on 95 per cent of occasions. Errors of airborne equipment are price-related. The price of a 'navcom' designed to provide a light aircraft with VOR reception and display, plus VHF communication, is more than an order less than that of equipment designed to perform the same functions on large airliners. By 1970 there were about 1000 VORs in the US alone.

ICAO later specified distance-measuring equipment (DME) to be sited contiguously with VORs. The VOR/DME station became a 'point source system' defining the position of any aircraft within range by its distance and bearing (rho–theta coordinates). Thus, in the US from the 1930s, in Europe from the 1950s, point-source systems were the means of navigating aircraft over land; but the arguments in favour of such systems which were so cogent when they were introduced have long since been made irrelevant by the computer. The 1959 Omnitrac computer which converted hyperbolic position lines into rho–theta coordinates with respect *to any desired checkpoint* (not merely those at which VOR/DME were installed) was mentioned earlier. In the 1970s computers were sold, at prices affordable to owners of light aircraft, which translated two VOR bearings into rho–theta coordinates with respect to any third point, so that the pilot could have a VOR/DME display of his bearing and distance from a grass field without any radio installation. In the 1990s, sophisticated flight-management systems on large modern airliners may track a radial nominally defined by a VOR, while actually relying on more accurate data sources than the VOR (Chapter 14). Today, the best arguments for the VOR system of navigation are that it is there, that everyone is equipped for it, and that everything is geared to it.

Lorenz in the 1930s was among the first to offer a track guidance system specifically for the approach to landing.[24] Track guidance was provided by vertically polarized radiation on 33 MHz. A dot signal indicated that the aircraft was to the left of the beam, a dash to the right. Three 'marker' beacons with beams pointing vertically upwards signalled the pilot his progress as he passed them, and some glide-slope indication was provided by a signal-strength meter. One of the nicer compliments paid by the RAF to Germany at the time was the adoption of the Lorenz system (further developed in Britain by the Standard Company) as the Standard Beam Approach (SBA), which was introduced in the RAF in 1939 and became standard equipment in larger RAF aircraft for much of the war. In one version there were two vertical markers: the inner, at 50 yards, signalled by high-pitched dots, and the outer, signalled by low-pitched dashes; the beam pattern was formed by interlocking A's and N's, as in a radio range. It was neither popular nor successful during the war for many reasons;[25] but its lack of positive glide-slope information was a fundamental defect.

In the late 1930s the US Army Signal Corps began work on the system later to be known as SCS51, which had two fundamental advantages over SBA. The glide path was positively defined by a beam; and the display to the pilot was visual. Track guidance was provided by the 'localizer' at the far end of the runway, radiating a beam along it on 100 MHz. The glide path, inclined at 3° to the horizontal and intersecting the horizontal plane of the runway in the touch-down area, was provided by a UHF (300 MHz) beam transmitted from the runway threshold. There were two or three coded 'fan' markers giving spot indication of distance to touch-down. The system is illustrated in Fig. 10.13, the display to the pilot in Fig. 10.14.

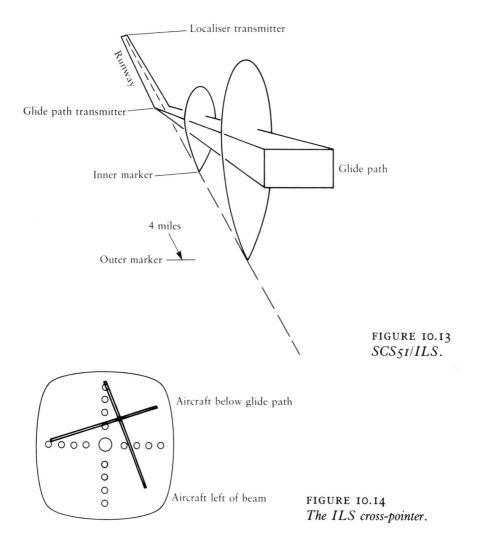

Localiser transmitter

Runway

Glide path transmitter

Inner marker

Glide path

4 miles

Outer marker

FIGURE 10.13
SCS51/ILS.

Aircraft below glide path

Aircraft left of beam

FIGURE 10.14
The ILS cross-pointer.

Consistent with the VOR display, the information displayed is not the action to take, but the location of the beams relative to the aircraft. In 1948 ICAO adopted a version of the SCS 51 as the standard approach aid under the name of *Instrument Landing System*, ILS.

It is thus a fact that, despite all the advances in technologies of all kinds during the past half-century, for most of the history of radio, for most of the history of the aeroplane, the standard air navigation system for flight over developed countries and the standard approach-to-land system have remained unchanged in principle since they were developed in the United States during the Second World War.[26] Of course, in both cases, the hardware, the means by which the defined objects of the equipment are met, has changed over the years in line with the state of the art, and with it the standards of accuracy, reliability, and serviceability.

The advantage of the very high frequencies employed for both localizer and glide path is a sharply defined beam; the correlated disadvantage is the susceptibility of the beam to unwanted reflections from structures or terrain in the vicinity. For these reasons it was concluded that the pilot of a passenger aeroplane should not rely on the glide path below 200 feet. There was another compelling reason: if the runway is first sighted below 200 feet there is little time for the pilot to orientate himself and take corrective action, and for the aircraft to respond to the controls before the flare must commence and the drift must be kicked off.[27]

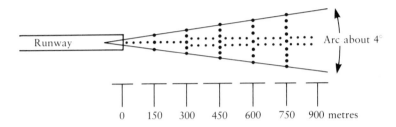

FIGURE 10.15
A high-intensity lighting pattern.

The partial solution was the high-intensity approach lighting pattern[28] illustrated in Fig. 10.15. By such means the visual range required to proceed to a landing by visual reference was reduced from about 2000 metres to 600 metres. Thus the minima for landing a passenger aircraft at a suitably equipped airport became a decision height[29] of 200 feet and a runway visual range of 600 metres, which later came to be called *Category 1 conditions*.

From the early days of aviation there were attempts at blind landing. One of the earliest such systems, in 1916, was a weight suspended from the aircraft on a line of 15 feet. When it hit the ground a red light went on in the cockpit, warning the pilot to commence his flare. In the 1930s there was interest in automatic landing systems for the recovery of pilotless aircraft. In the late 1930s Siemens attempted to develop a complete coupling of an automatic pilot to radio beams for azimuth, guidance, and distance-measurement, and to a radio altimeter for height. They were certainly on the right lines; but the system was only demonstrated on wide grass fields with slow aeroplanes.

The process which eventually led to the safe routine of automatic landings of large high-performance passenger aeroplanes on narrow runways started in 1944 when the USAAC demonstrated the SCS 51 in England to the British, culminating, in January 1945, in a landing of a Boeing 247D in the total darkness of a wartime 'black-out'. British interest in the potential of such systems led to the formation a few months later at the Royal Aircraft Establishment (Farnborough) of the Blind Landing Experimental Unit (BLEU). It was, over the next few decades, to pioneer automatic landing of passenger aircraft in conjunction with a British company, Smiths Industries. There was a good reason for British leadership in this field—British weather! Weather at London Airport was below Category 1 conditions nearly 5 per cent of the time, compared with less than 2 per cent at New York and Boston, and less than 1 per cent at Dallas and Chicago.

The story is edifying in two respects: it illustrates how the perceived homing quality of radio has drawn to navigation a range of diverse applied sciences such as information theory, the theory of servomechanisms and control, human physiology, and the properties of semiconductors, among many others; it shows how methodical scientific analysis with an iterative and pragmatic application of developing technologies can, with patience, convert the inherently dangerous into the almost perfectly safe. It also shows what a slow process it is, if safety is not to be compromised at any stage, and the idea is to be 'sold' to such diverse parties as airlines, passengers, pilots, and airworthiness authorities.

The programme did not start with the assumption that the object was fully automatic landing. The object was to land in conditions far inferior to Category 1; but, as remarked above, in such conditions there was insufficient time for the transition from pilotage by instruments to flare, drift kickoff, and touch-down relying on the belated evidence of the pilot's eyes. It had been clearly established that machines can be designed to fly more accurately[30] than people, and to react more quickly. To generalize the point, in the latter half of the twentieth century it is often easier to design an accurate and reliable system to perform a complex function if a human operator is not included in the control loop in the normal operating mode. The human pilot monitors the operation, and may resume command at will, knowing that he might be physiologically incapable of completing the landing procedure, and would have to get back to the safety of the air and think again. With many misgivings, not least among practising pilots, it became accepted internationally that the system should be fully automatic, at least until the aircraft had touched down.

In the 1950s the research programme at BLEU came under 11 main headings.[31] In the sequence in which they are listed here the first 8 relate to the system itself, and the remaining three to the crew's ability to monitor the operation:

1. Improvements in the accuracy of the azimuth guidance from the ILS localizer.

2. Development of a radio altimeter to provide very accurate height data during the final phase of approach and the flare on to the runway; a function for which the ILS glide path was not designed and which, by the nature of its design, it was inherently incapable of performing.

3. Research leading to tighter coupling between the flying controls and the inputs from the ILS and the radio altimeter.

4. Development of automatic throttles for control of speed during approach and of speed reduction during the flare.

5. Studies of the response-time of large aircraft to lateral error correction.

6. In relation with the preceding item, development of automatic overshoot ('go around again') procedures when error in azimuth close to the ground was unacceptably large in relation to the narrowness of the runway.

7. Automatic 'drift kick off'.

8. Design to ensure that no equipment failure would be catastrophic.

9. Visual approach-slope indication to pilots.

10. Extension of the high-intensity approach-lighting system already described into the runway itself to give improved visual guidance in the touch-down zone and during the ground roll.

11. Display to aircrew of the performance and functioning of the system as a whole and its key components.

By the late 1950s BLEU and the principal contractor were able to demonstrate a single-channel system which worked reliably; but, being a single system, it could not meet the requirement that no component failure would be catastrophic. There were also, at this stage, fundamental reservations about the ILS itself, which were later resolved by various techniques, including the use of wider-aperture[32] antennas for the localizer, the reduction of errors in the glide path as a result of siting problems, and improved monitoring of the performance of the ILS on the ground.

The risk of catastrophic failure in an airline service, it was thought, should be less than one in ten million landings. The unanswerable argument was that, at such a level, the risks associated with automatic landing in bad weather would be less than the risks historically associated with landings by human pilots in good weather. Given the achievable reliability of a single-channel system the overall reliability specification could be achieved in one of two ways: a 'duplicate monitored' system employing two separate systems separately monitored, with automatic change-over if the system in use failed to satisfy the monitor; or a triplex system with three completely separate channels (each channel being a complete system with its own auto-pilot, radio, etc.), all three working simultaneously, like a triumvirate in which any two members have the power to throw out any one with whom they markedly disagree. It was, not inappropriately, called a 'voting system'—but not one with proportional representation. Both systems have been employed. There are of course philosophical problems involved in the application of probability theory to probabilities of the order of one in ten million. They are implicit in a scientific approach to high safety standards of any kind, and are considered in general terms in Chapter 14.

British acceptance of automatic landing in passenger operations *as an achievable goal* was signalled in 1961 when the Air Registration Board issued a paper entitled 'Airworthiness requirements for autoflare and automatic landing'. This paper contained the classification of targeted weather conditions listed in Table 10.1, which was adopted by ICAO in 1965. The punctiliously slow march, step by step, over a period of twenty years, to the routine of automatic landing in virtually any weather is illustrated by the history of the Smiths 'autoland' system in the Trident fleet of British European Airways described in Table 10.2. In part at least, this reflects the time required to acquire a massive volume of data on automatic landings in good weather conditions; in part the unwillingness of any major airline even to appear to experiment with the lives of its passengers; in part the sheer volume of data and analysis required to satisfy airworthiness authorities that a risk is of the order of one in ten million.[33] In 1988 it was estimated that British Airways alone had performed more than 100 000 automatic

Category	Minimum decision-height	Runway visual range
1	200 ft	800 m
2	100 ft	400 m
3a	0 ft	200 m
3b	0 ft	50 m
3c	0 ft	0 m

Table 10.1. 1965 ICAO classification of weather conditions.

1962	Flight-test programme started.
1965	Category 1 certification of automatic flare.
1966	Development aircraft autoland in Category 3b conditions.
1968	Category 2 certification for passenger operations.
1972	DH 12 ft/RVR 200 m certification for passenger operations.
1974	DH 12 ft/RVR 150 m certification for passenger operations.
1979	DH 12 ft/RVR 75 m certification for passenger operations.

Table 10.2. British Airways Trident Autoland Programme.

landings in regular passenger service, although the majority were in conditions of good visibility.

Although the ILS system remained, other technologies advanced rapidly during the process. Sir John Charnley wrote:[31]

All major avionic systems in later generations of transport aircraft like the Boeing 757, 767, and Airbus make extensive use of digital technology with the well documented advantages that it offers in terms of computing capacity and speed, memory, physical space and power consumption. Additionally, in safety-critical systems, it opens up, through the software and its architecture, reconsideration of the various ways of providing the redundancy, monitoring and displays needed to meet the 'fail operational' requirement. It also offers intelligent self-test facilities and location of system faults for maintenance, re-test and validation.

Other relevant developments included higher-resolution radar and improved visual aids. After an automatic landing in low visibility the aircraft still has to be navigated to the terminal building.

Advances in electronics generally, and microwave techniques specifically, led to concurrent consideration of alternatives to ILS. By about 1970 some 50 or so proposals had been advanced. In 1978 the International Civil Aviation Organization adopted as an eventual successor to ILS a microwave landing system (MLS) working on a time-reference scanning-beam principle. MLS offers improved accuracy and stability. Furthermore, whereas the ILS offers a single flight-path defined by the localizer beam and the glide path, with MLS the pilot may select any flight-path within 40° of the centre line of the runway and up to 15° from the horizontal plane. It also provides guidance after a missed approach (see Fig. 10.16). The plan was that over the last decade of the twentieth century MLS would replace ILS internationally, though for more than a decade both would have to be carried by many aircraft.

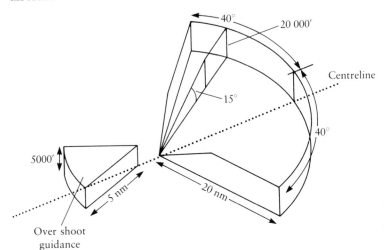

FIGURE 10.16
Guidance provided by the microwave landing system (MLS).

Meanwhile, the performance already achieved by satellite navigation systems described in Chapter 12 implies the eventual feasibility of providing position and motion data with sufficient accuracy and reliability to land an aircraft anywhere in the world by such means. At the time of writing the official position is that, despite the huge costs of world-wide MLS and the inconvenience and potential dangers arising from aircraft using both systems for more than a decade, the world-wide MLS programme is unaffected (see also Chapters 12 and 16).

From the inception of automatic landing, the desirability of improving the human pilot's ability to monitor, of keeping the human pilot in the control loop, had been stressed, particularly by pilot organizations. Over the period, there has also been a demand for capability to land in reduced weather minima from operators of smaller aircraft for which automatic landing equipment was too expensive, and from operators of all aircraft at airports where the ground equipment was not of the required standard. A key factor in meeting these demands has been the evolution of holographic head-up displays (HUDs), which require coherent light sources invented in the 1960s and introduced in Chapter 9 in the context of laser gyros. A holographic HUD enables the pilot to read a display while looking out with his eyes focused on infinity. In the 1970s it was found that a HUD developed to enable airline pilots to monitor an automatic landing permitted safe manual landings in conditions of more reduced visibility than had been thought possible earlier; but this application found little acceptance internationally. In the 1980s head-up guidance systems (HGS), with computer-generated holographic displays derived from ILS and inertial inputs, led to manual landings with 50 feet decision-height and 210 m runway visual range. The future role of the human pilot is as unresolved as the future of homing radio systems, and much more emotive. Prognosis is not within the province of this book.

All the most modern navigation systems rely heavily on the computer revolution. Chapter 4 described how the analogy between Boolean algebra and telephone switching circuits led to the realization that a circuit of relays could be a digital computer, were the electromagnetic relays then employed not so slow. The thermionic valve (or electron tube) is much faster, and made possible the digital computers which are now central to all but the simpler navigation systems. The roots of software are in Victorian pure mathematics; the roots of hardware are in twentieth-century radio.

John Mauchly and John Eckert devised for the US Army in 1946 one of the first[34] electronic digital computers, ENIAC (electronic numerical integrator and computor), which contained 18 000 thermionic valves and other switching devices besides. It weighed 30 tons. The ENIAC was less powerful than a modern desktop; but John von Neumann, the distinguished mathematician who was director of the Federal Electronic Computer Project from 1945 to 1955, could write:[35]

> [ENIAC is] a good deal larger than what is likely to be the size of the machines which will come into existence and operation in the next few years. It is probable that each one of these will consist of 2000–6000 switching organs.

Not even von Neumann could foresee the explosion of computer power fuelled by the development of semiconductors, notably the silicon integrated circuit or 'chip', which has transformed navigation (and so many other technologies) before our eyes. Even a 'desktop' today may have a capacity of 10^8 bytes. The first step was the invention of the semiconductor transistor in 1947 by John Bardeen, Walter Brattain, and William Schokley. They received a Nobel prize for it. Bardeen, who lived until 1991, is quoted as saying, 'I knew the transistor was important, but I never foresaw the revolution in electronics it would bring.'

Notes to Chapter 10

1. They used 'horns' and 'prisms' and 'lenses' of dielectric material to focus the transmission on the receiver.
2. In 1876 Alexander Bell patented the first telephone of practical use.
3. Augusto Righi at Bologna and Vincenzo Rosa at Livorno.
4. We always forget the Russians. Alexsandr Popov independently invented the earthed antenna and improved the coherer. Popov's researches at the time were directed at lightning; but, on hearing of Marconi's work, he turned to communication, and achieved a range of 30 miles by 1899. Popov's equipment installed on an ice-breaker was instrumental in saving 27 lives at sea in 1900. A suggestion in 1948 that this was the first use of radio to save life at sea was immediately challenged by a director of the Marconi company, citing an incident in 1899 in which the crew of the East Goodwin light-vessel saved their lives by signalling their distress by Marconi radio equipment. All statements that an event is the first of its class are subject to rebuttal.
5. The Italian Minister of Posts and Telegraphs had suggested that young Marconi be admitted to

a mental hospital. England seemed more fertile soil, and Marconi had English relatives who were instrumental in setting up his company. The honour of Italy was saved by its navy, with which Marconi had a mutually rewarding relationship for many years.

6. It is sometimes forgotten that Captain (later Admiral of the Fleet Sir) Henry Jackson of the British Navy communicated between ship and shore by radio two years earlier.

7. CQD was the signal. The more urgent rhythm of SOS came later. In 1903 Marconi had contracts to instal radio on 32 British ships, in addition to his government contracts.

8. Instruments aboard the satellite *Explorer IV* launched in 1958 revealed streams of high concentrations of charged particles moving along the lines of force of the earth's magnetism hundreds of miles above the surface, in the region now called the magnetosphere.

9. A widely accepted classification of radio waves is shown in the table below. Since the velocity of light is conveniently close to 300 000 000 metres per second, wavelength in metres × frequencies in cycles per second equals 300 000 000. By international convention a frequency of 1 cycle/sec. is called a *Hertz*; thus 1 MHz (1 megahertz) and 1 kHz (1 kiloHertz). Radiation at wavelengths below 10 cm is also called *microwave*.

Band	Frequency	Wavelength
Very Low Frequency—VLF	<30 kHz	>10 km
Low Frequency—LF	30–300 kHz	1–10 km
Medium Frequency—MF	300 kHz–3 MHz	100–1000 m
High Frequency—HF	3–30 MHz	10–100 m
Very High Frequency—VHF	30–300 MHz	1–10 m
Ultra-High Frequency—UHF	300–3000 MHz	10–100 cm
Centimetric	3000–30000 MHz	1–10 cm
Millimetric	>30000 MHz	<1 cm

10. The US army installed the Lafayette station for transatlantic communication near Bordeaux in 1918, with two arc oscillators rated at 1 megawatt transmitting on a wavelength of 20 *kilometres*.

11. Pierre and Jacques Curie discovered the piezoelectric effect in 1880.

12. Positive feedback in the triode application was originally termed *regeneration* (USA) or *reaction* (UK). Its importance and the intensity of competition at the time are illustrated by the fact that there were four parties to patent litigation on the matter. The US Supreme Court finally decided in favour of DeForest in 1928. Negative feedback is also widely used for different purposes.

13. Marconi was anticipated by the amateurs, who were crowded into frequency bands believed unsuitable for long-range communication. In 1921 British amateurs received a twelve-word message from an American amateur with a 1 kw transmitter on a wavelength of 230 metres. In 1923 amateurs in New York were able to talk with others in California using low-power transmitters in the 100-metre band.

14. NDBs transmit an unmodulated continuous wave in the MF band. Broadcasting on MF frequencies occupies a wider band because it is amplitude-modulated. Receivers designed only for use with NDBs can therefore be more selective, with a proportionate reduction in static, the bane of MF D/F.

15. Conversion angle is described in an *Amendment* to the RAF *Manual of navigation* in the mid–1930s. The RAF had been using D/F since its formation in 1918.

16. In a polar diagram the distance of the curve from the origin represents the relative field strength

(or sensitivity) in that direction. The signal strength across the vertical loop in direction θ relative to its own axis is of the form $A\cos\theta$, where the value of A is the same in all directions. If the output of an omnidirectional antenna is arranged to be A, and circuits are employed to make the phase the same, the combined signal strength is $A(1 + \cos\theta)$, which gives the cardioid polar diagram of Fig. 10.7.

17. It was later said that this report was (in modern jargon) disinformation to hide the fact that the Royal Navy could decipher German signals. Round's comment is not available.

18. See Best (1950).

19. In RAF equipment extensively used at this time one doubler and two triplers were employed to multiply the crystal frequency by a factor of 18.

20. The first RAF VHF D/F station was installed in October 1939, according to Smith (1947).

21. Kendal (1990).

22. When the International Civil Aviation Organization was formed most civil aviation in the world was US domestic traffic.

23. More precisely, the carrier was modulated at 9960 Hz, which itself carried a frequency modulation at 30 Hz—the reference signal. The rotation of the coil caused a 30 Hz amplitude modulation of the signal, and the phase comparison with the reference modulation determined the radial. In the Doppler VOR, which came later, the reference signal is AM and the Doppler shift caused by commutation around a ring of dipoles is FM.

24. Lorenz adapted this technology to the *Knickebein* bombing system, with which the bomber flew to its target on an extremely narrow beam by the standards of the time. Arrival over target was signalled by the reception of a narrow beam from a remote point. Any continuous wave (CW) system is easily jammed, and CW beams can be deflected. The British worked on both countermeasures.

25. R. A. Smith (1947). In both World Wars many pilots were inexperienced and short-lived. Perhaps more professional pilots would have made more of the SBA.

26. The rapid development during the Second World War of radio navigation and radio counter-navigation led to many instrument landing systems contemporary with SCS 51. At the time the advantage of a pulse system such as BABS (Chapter Eleven) over CW systems such as SCS 51 was the accuracy with which distance to go could be displayed. SCS 51 was the right one because US policy said so. Also, it was more developed than the others, and was right in the essential—visual presentation directly to the pilot of his orientation above/below and left/right of the required flight-path.

27. On approach the heading must be offset from the direction of the runway by the amount of the drift caused by the crosswind. At the moment of contact of the wheels with the runway the aircraft must be aligned with the runway. The pilot makes the correction by a kick on the rudder before contact.

28. The design of the high-intensity approach-lighting pattern was based on theoretical analyses and experimental simulations designed to discover how perception of aiming-point, position, and rate of change of position is derived from the pattern of lights seen. At the time so scientific an approach to ergonomic problems was unusual.

29. Decision-height is the height at which the pilot makes his final decision to proceed with the landing. If the landing is to be manual he must be able to see enough of the approach lighting at decision-height to provide sufficient information for a safe landing.

30. In the 1960s it was shown that autopilot coupling to a VOR could track the radial of the VOR within 0.1°, subject of course to system error of the VOR itself, which was an order higher. The best human pilots could achieve was 1°; 2° was more typical (Robinson and Thomas 1971).

31. This discussion of automatic landing relies heavily on Charnley (1989).

32. Antenna systems which can only measure the bearing of a small part of the wavefront are known as *Narrow-aperture* systems, because the total width of their elements is small in relation to the wavelength. Wide-aperture systems may employ the Doppler effect (Chapter Twelve) or use broadside arrays. Another problem was the effect of a small vertically polarized component of the transmission when the aircraft banked.

33. The time taken to certify subsequent aircraft was much reduced.

34. Although it is sometimes said that ENIAC was the first electronic computer, it was preceded in 1943 in Britain by the *Colossus*, which was employed on the famous *Enigma* deciphering programme.

35. Quoted from *The general and logical theory of automata*, reproduced in Newman (1956).

CHAPTER ELEVEN

The Seeing Quality of Radio

✠

WE cannot see through cloud and haze because dust particles and water droplets are very large in relation to the wavelength of light. Electromagnetic radiation is reflected or absorbed by objects in its path which are large in relation to the wavelength. There is little diffraction when the wavelength is very large in relation to the size of the object. When the dimensions of the object are of the same order as the wavelength, reradiation by conducting bodies is complex—some will resonate. To 'see' objects by radio in all weathers we need wavelengths which are large in relation to raindrops, but not large in relation to the size of the objects. The discrimination that is required to prevent the receiver being swamped with ground or sea returns, and to measure azimuth accurately, necessitates antenna arrays which are large in relation to wavelength, placing different upper limits on the wavelength which may be used on ground stations, ships, and aircraft.

In the mid-1930s, in the shadow of impending war and the perceived growing menace of bomber aircraft, men pondered on these matters secretly in all the great military powers.[1] Only the urgency and the secrecy were new, not the idea. In a well-publicized address in the United States in 1922, Marconi had called attention to the properties of 'very short electrical waves' and recalled that Hertz had been the first to show that 'electric waves can be completely reflected by conducting bodies'. Marconi went on to suggest a seaborne application which would 'immediately reveal the presence and bearing of the other ship'.

One wonders what Christian Hülsmeyer thought of the great man's belated bright idea. Hülsmeyer's British patent of 1904 is entitled 'Hertzian-wave projecting and receiving apparatus adapted to indicate or give warning of the presence of a metallic body, such as a ship or a train in the line of projection of such waves'. His *Telemobiloskop* was successfully demonstrated on a bridge at Cologne in May 1904. A bell rang when a ship entered the field. Hülsmeyer first took a German patent and tried to interest the Kaiser's Navy. Von Tirpitz replied[2] 'Not interested. My people have better ideas.' What they were we do not know.

The British Navy were equally uninterested. In June 1904 Hülsmeyer successfully demonstrated his equipment to eight major international shipping companies at Rotterdam; the range was several kilometres. Despite wide publicity, which extended as far as the *New York Times*, not a single order was received. Hülsmeyer was then twenty-three. Unable to finance patents in every country, he turned successfully to other things. The telemobiloskop employed a spark transmitter and a coherer receiver which were unremarkable in themselves; but the antenna arrays and other devices used to obtain relatively narrow beams, to screen the receiver from the transmitter, and to identify the reflection, employed ideas that were thirty years before their time.

After the Second World War, Hülsmeyer's daughter wrote to Winston Churchill suggesting that the radar of the victorious allies employed principles embodied in her father's British patent. Churchill's secretary emulated his master's prose. The simple reply was 'I am desired by Mr Churchill to thank you for your letter which it has given him interest to receive.' In the end, Hülsmeyer was honoured by his own countrymen. Those paying tribute on his 75th birthday, a few months before his death, included Chancellor Adenauer and many eminent German scientists. Today the plaque on the wall of his former home proudly declares Hülsmeyer to be *Der Ur Radar Erfinder*. Grudgingly, one must concede that Sir Robert Watson-Watt, who proclaimed himself to be the 'father' of *Radar*, had a point. The word is an acronym of American naval origin[3] for *radio detection and ranging*, and although Hülsmeyer could certainly detect, it seems unlikely that the method of finding range which he intended would have worked.

Although the UHF (16 cm) obstacle detector installed on the new French liner the *Normandie* in 1935 was well publicized as an iceberg detector (memories of the *Titanic* still lingered), and an important paper reporting the results of research on the reradiation properties of targets appeared in Italy[4] at the astonishingly late date of 1939, in Germany and Britain, which were to become briefly the leaders in the field, the curtain of security had already descended in 1935. There are therefore different histories of radar, although each party commenced at a similar state of the art and had some access to each other's secrets through the study of each other's radiation, espionage, interrogation of prisoners, capture of equipment, and so on.

Naturally, until the turn of the tide, German thinking was offensive and British defensive. In both countries the navy was responsible for important pioneering work; but from about 1938 neither navy had the highest priority. In Britain, the highest priority was the defence of the island against bomber aircraft; in Germany, the admirals were no match at a political level for Goering (who commanded the air force) after he had realized the potential of radar.

It has been credibly argued that the German equipment was better engineered, but that the British application to the operational requirement was more effective. In Germany, the military requirement was stated from on high with little understanding of what the scientists could do; and some promising lines of research were stopped by the edicts of high-ranking officers who did not appreciate their potential.[5] In Britain, scientists worked directly with fighting men to develop equipment. Germany also suffered from the self-imposed loss of

Jewish scientists.[6] It has been suggested that the quality of operating personnel in the field was lower in Germany.

The account below of radar is initially from a British point of view, and from an Anglo-American point of view after the gift to the USA of all Britain's radar secrets, the application of vast resources by the US government, and the entry of the USA into the war had led to an American ascendancy in the field which still endures. This is the mainstream of the history of radar. The story of the victors is usually better told than that of the vanquished. In Britain during the 1939–45 war scientists, for the first time, walked the corridors of power.[7] Neither science nor warfare will ever be the same again. The victorious scientists joined the victorious generals in writing their memoirs; but the alleged superior objectivity of the scientific vocation is not discernible.

In 1934, according to the oft-told tale, A. P. Rowe, then Assistant to the Director of Scientific Research at the Air Ministry, reviewed the files on Air Defence and concluded that Britain had no defence against the German bomber. A committee of eminent scientists, all of whom had served in the armed forces during the First World War, was formed under the chairmanship of H. T. Tizard, who had been Rector of the Imperial College of Science and Technology since 1927. The committee was told that for the detection and location of enemy aircraft the army had acoustic devices, the navy had binoculars, and the air force had the eyes of its crews. Prior to its first meeting, Robert Watson Watt, Superintendent of the Radio Research Station at Slough, had been consulted about the possibility of 'death rays'. Watson Watt had replied negatively, but thought that the detection of aircraft by their reflection of radiation at radio frequencies was realistic, despite the minute fraction of radiated energy which would be reflected back by an aircraft.

The proposal was not novel even in England. It had been advanced in 1928 by L. S. Adler while working for the Royal Navy on signal research and development. In 1931 W. A. S. Butement and P. E. Pollard of the army's Signal Experimental Establishment were allowed to work in their spare time on a pulsed system of ship detection for coastal defence. Their offer to demonstrate it was declined, on the grounds that there was no War Office requirement. Watson Watt himself was later to claim that he originally advocated radiolocation years earlier. The novelty was that, in January 1935, the perambulators of the corridors of power were listening.

The first requirement was Treasury approval for a modest budget, necessitating a demonstration of feasibility. Arnold F. Wilkins, Watson Watt's leading collaborator at the time, predicated that a bomber with a 25 m wingspan was equivalent to a horizontal dipole which would strongly reflect radiation at 50 m. As it happened, a BBC station transmitted from an array of horizontal dipoles at Daventry on a wavelength of 49.8 m. While an RAF bomber flew in the field of this transmitter Wilkins successfully demonstrated to Rowe the interference between the direct signal and that reflected by the aircraft at a receiver in a van in a field. A budget of £12 300 (excluding the flying costs of RAF aircraft employed in the experiments) was granted for one year, and British radar began.

In principle there were, in 1935, a wide variety of choices in the design of a ground-based

Rear view of the apparatus used by Wilkins on 26 February 1935 to demonstrate radio echoes from aircraft. Cathode ray tube to the upper left.

radio system to give early warning of aircraft. Years could have been spent on the evaluation of the alternatives. A fascinating aspect of the early development of British radar was the absence of feasibility studies. There was no time for research on the reflective qualities of aircraft at different frequencies. Watson Watt and Wilkins decided that a bomber was a thick horizontal conducting wire of the length of its wingspan, and that was that.

Distance measurement by radio had been addressed in the 1920s in the context of studies of the ionosphere (already mentioned in Chapter 10), geodetic survey, and radio altimetry. Assuming that there is no phase change on reflection, distance might be found by comparing the difference of phase of the transmitted and reflected radiation: 2 × distance/wavelength = phase difference/360°; but phase differences of multiples of 360° are all identically zero, so that there is ambiguity unless the wavelength is large in relation to distance: but in that case there would be virtually no reflection. One solution is to modulate the carrier wave at a very low frequency, and compare the phase of the modulation of the reflected signal. The *Normandie* iceberg detector already mentioned radiated a UHF continuous wave of 16 cm, nearly 2000 MHz, modulated by 800 Hz. CW technologies were also developed in Germany.

Alternatively, one can measure the time-interval between the transmission of a pulse and the reception of the echo: 2 × distance = speed of light × interval. There were two intrinsic limitations. The pulse recurrence frequency (PRF) must not be so high that there can be any ambiguity as to which pulse reflection is being received, so the speed of light/PRF must exceed 2 × distance, preferably by an order or more. Secondly, the duration of the pulse must be so short that it is not still being transmitted when its reflection begins to be received. In the technology of 1935 this provided a real lower limit to the range which could be measured by pulse. A pulse consists of a number of cycles. Let n be the practical minimum. Range could not be measured if n × wavelength > 2 × range. Furthermore, the precision of time-measurement is influenced by the 'steepness' of the pulse, which takes some cycles to build up. The duration of a cycle at 30 m wavelength is 0.1 microseconds, at 30 cm only 0.001 microseconds—further reasons to prefer higher frequencies.

The team went straight for pulses and stayed with them for the rest of the story. As mentioned in Chapter 10, pulse techniques were first applied to ionospheric research by Breit and Tuve[8] in the USA in 1925, and later taken up in England. Watson Watt, Wilkins, and other members of the team had been associated with this work, and were familiar with the latest state of the art. The early work on radar in Britain was an extension of a decade of study of electrical radiation in the atmosphere; and most of the relevant experience of the team was in this field.

The cathode-ray oscilloscope provided the radar *eye*. This was a familiar tool to the team. Watson Watt (together with Appleton and J. F. Herd) had patented a circuit which provided a unidirectional linear time-base in 1924. In 1933 HMSO published a monograph by Watson Watt, Herd, and L. H. Bainbridge-Bell (another member of the 1935 team) entitled 'The cathode-ray oscillograph in radio research'. The cathode-ray display, now ubiquitous in television and visual displays of many kinds, is almost as familiar to us as the wheel. In essence it is an electron tube of the form illustrated in Fig. 11.1. Electrons emanate from a heated cathode, as in all thermionic valves, and a control grid controls the density and thus eventually the brightness of the picture. Other grids accelerate and focus the beam to produce a bright spot in the centre of the luminescent screen in the absence of any signal on the deflecting plates. Instead of electrostatic focus and deflection by plates, magnetic focus and deflection may be used, employing coils around the neck of the tube. The value of the device from the early 1920s has depended on the low inertia of an electron stream, which allows rapid deflection of the spot.

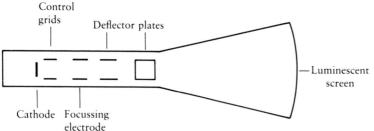

FIGURE II.I
Basic principles of the cathode-ray oscilloscope.

In the oscilloscopes of the period an internally generated signal was applied to opposing deflector plates, so that the beam oscillated to form a *time-base*. If a linear time-base is required to show ranges up to 150 km (corresponding to an interval of 1 millisecond) the beam must slowly sweep from left to right at a constant rate in 1 millisecond, and then flick very rapidly back.[9] The commencement of the sweep is synchronized with the transmission of each pulse. The reflected pulse (suitably amplified) is applied to deflector plates at right angles to those which furnish the time-base. Figure 11.2 shows a target at 75 km on a 150 km time-base.

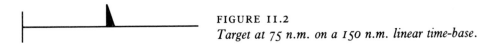

FIGURE 11.2
Target at 75 n.m. on a 150 n.m. linear time-base.

For the measurement of the azimuth of the target the entire range of direction-finding techniques evolved over the preceding thirty years were available (Chapter 10). There was an implicit choice between systems involving rotating beams and 'floodlighting' systems. A co-related choice was between monostatic working (in which the reflection is received at the source and used to determine the range, bearing, and elevation of the target) or bistatic (or multistatic) working,[10] in which reception of the target reflection at two or more locations can be used in a variety of ways to acquire the position of the target. For *Chain Home* (CH), the basic early-warning system, horizontally polarized monostatic floodlighting was chosen. The horizontal polar diagram is illustrated in Fig. 11.3. Azimuth and angle of elevation were both found by radiogoniometric techniques (Chapter 10). After 11 months there was a prototype on a wavelength of 26 m, providing detection at 100 miles accurate, in range at least, to half a mile.[11]

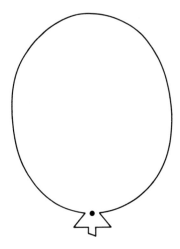

FIGURE 11.3
CH horizontal polar diagram.

Twenty CH stations and a rudimentary organization for the use of the data they provided were operational when the war started (Fig. 11.4); but they were not suitable for gunlaying, for ground control of intercepting fighters (GCI), or for surveillance of coastal waters. They

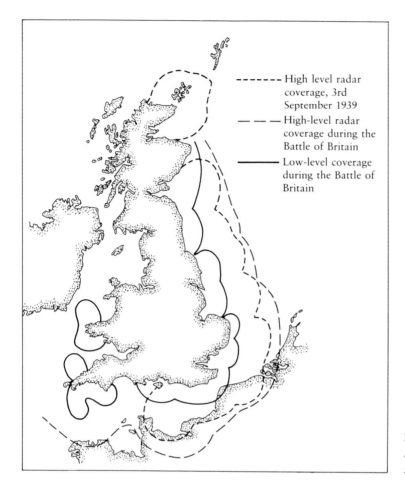

High level radar coverage, 3rd September 1939

High-level radar coverage during the Battle of Britain

Low-level coverage during the Battle of Britain

FIGURE 11.4
*Radar coverage of Britain
1939/40.*

could not detect targets below 2° of elevation. Floodlighting had its merits for early warning, but the rotating beam had two enormous advantages: there is a greater concentration of energy, and plan position indicators (PPIs) could be employed.[12] The advantage of PPI display had been appreciated in both Germany and Britain since 1935; but it was only practical at much higher frequencies with a rotating beam system. The time-base of the PPI radiates from the centre of the screen in synchronization with the beam. The target appears as a spot of light in the direction of the echo at a distance from the centre that represents the range of the echo, as in Fig. 11.5. When the immediate priority of an early-warning system was satisfied, efforts in ground radar turned to CHL (chain home low), GCI, and gunlaying systems.

Narrow beams required antenna arrays large in relation to wavelength. At the CH frequencies (and also those used by the German system *Freya*), vertical antenna arrays, 70 m and more in height, were required to obtain the necessary discrimination—in particular to avoid the swamping of the picture by ground returns. Something quite different was required for ship borne radar, to say nothing of aircraft equipment. An October 1935 statement of the

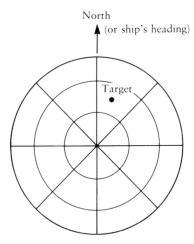

North
(or ship's heading)

Target

FIGURE 11.5
A plan position indicator.

operational requirement for naval radar specified *microwave* equipment, not only to reduce the size of the ship's antenna, but to avoid the ship's radar becoming a homing beacon for enemy bombers. The technology to home on to microwave transmissions came only a few years later.

There was nothing new about VHF: the original Hertz oscillator probably transmitted on a wavelength of about 4 metres, had he the means to measure it. In the 1920s it had been thought that ordinary thermionic valves could not operate on centimetric wavelengths, because the transit time of the electrons from cathode to anode was too long. The real, unrecognized, problem was the stability of the transit time. Several exotic microwave transmitting devices appeared, some of them producing a fraction of a watt. In 1936 the 16 cm obstacle detector on the *Normandie* produced 10 *watts*. As many *kilowatts* were sought. One important development was the *magnetron*,[13] a term used since 1921 to describe a vacuum electron tube (usually a cylindrical diode) in which plate current is controlled by magnetic fields. In the early 1930s Philips of Holland produced a magnetron which gave 80 watts on 13 cm continuous wave. A Philips magnetron was delivered to the German navy in 1933.

The difficulties due to the inability to produce power on centimetric wavelengths, and therefore to discriminate with small antenna arrays, are clearly seen in early British aircraft interception (AI) radar operating on 1.5 metres. The transmitting array was in the nose, two quarter-wavelength antennas on a wing acted as elevation antennas, and a half-wavelength dipole with director on each wing provided the azimuth array. The polar diagram is illustrated in Fig. 11.6, the display in Fig. 11.7. The signal received from the elevation antennas (after amplification) is fed to either side of the vertical display; and, similarly, the signals from the azimuth arrays to either side of the horizontal display. Thus the orientation of the target is indicated by the imbalance of the blip, about 20° below and 30–40° to the left in the illustration. There was no range scale, nor any need for one, because the ground return swamped the screen at all ranges greater than the aircraft height, which it sharply defined.

AI MK IV described above (and installed in RAF Beaufighters in 1940) is interesting also because it created a human requirement in terms of spatial visualization and quick thinking

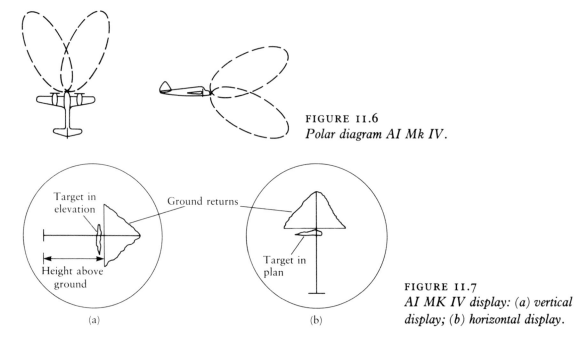

FIGURE 11.6
Polar diagram AI Mk IV.

FIGURE 11.7
AI MK IV display: (a) vertical display; (b) horizontal display.

unparalled in the history of navigation. As the armament was fixed forward, the object of the navigation was to get on the target's tail. If the target's range is allowed to exceed aircraft height, it is lost. The target's course can be inferred indirectly from the motion of the 'blip' down the time-base and the change in its shape. Assume that the Beaufighter is heading south. If the target is heading east, a sharp turn to the left is required at maximum power before the target gets lost in the ground return. If the target is heading west, the only hope is to throttle right back, drop the undercarriage to increase drag, and turn right, losing the blip temporarily, and hoping to come out of the turn behind the target and not in front of it. There are only a few seconds to decide, and, when the correct decision is taken, the enemy unkindly changes course! Only a few had the knack of it.[14]

The desperate need for powerful microwave transmitters was met by the invention of the multi-cavity magnetron at Birmingham University by Henry A. Boot and John T. Randall at the beginning of 1940. The university had been given a contract by the Admiralty to research microwave transmission, and work had concentrated on developing a high-power version of the klystron invented at Stanford University, California. Randall and Boot were assigned the less promising task of trying to do something with the magnetron. Apparently they shared the research philosophy of Watson Watt and Wilkins, for in 1976 they were to write: 'Fortunately we did not have the time to survey all the published papers on magnetrons or we would have been completely confused by the multiplicity of theories of operation.'

The story is related that Randall went back to the original experiments of Hertz and, in his mind, extended the Hertz resonant ring into a cylinder with a slit in it, as in Fig. 11.8. He then saw how this could be developed into the six-cavity figure illustrated.[15] Early in 1940 the laboratory model produced over 1 kw pulse power at a wavelength of about 10 cm.

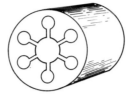

(a) Resonant ring (Hertz)   (b) Resonant cylinder   (c) Resonant six-cavity device

FIGURE 11.8
Evolution of the multi-cavity magnetron.

The first production model generated 10 kw, which was soon increased to 100 kw. At the end of the war there was megawatt power at that wavelength, and wavelengths down to 3 cm could be transmitted at less power.

That was the beginning of microwave radar as we now know it. The Royal Navy seized on the magnetron (and on related work on the klystron to provide a local oscillator for centimetric receivers) to produce the first fully operational centimetric radar in the world. From its formation early in 1941, the Admiralty Signals Establishment made major contributions to coastal and naval radar. Perhaps the improvement in AI is as dramatic an illustration as any of the potency of the multi-cavity magnetron. Ground returns could be put where they belonged, and any of the three displays shown in Fig. 11.9 were at the AI designer's disposal. In Fig 11.9(a) the display shows the target as the eye sees it, in correct azimuth and elevation, but with no indication of range, since a 2D display cannot show three independent variables. This can be supported by a second display in which range is shown against either azimuth or elevation, as illustrated in Figs. 11.9(b) and 11.9(c).[16]

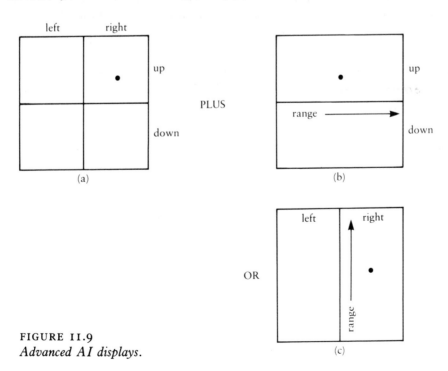

FIGURE 11.9
Advanced AI displays.

A scarcely less dramatic outcome of the magnetron was terrain-mapping radar, in the form of H_2S and later derivatives. In the early years of the war metric naval radar and ASV (aircraft to surface vessel radar) displayed coastlines, but no metric radar could effectively distinguish the features of terrain. Ten-centimetre H_2S enabled the bomber to identify cities and some topographical features of enemy territory by night or through cloud. Later 3 cm equipment gave even greater detail. Accurate altitude above terrain for precision bombing was also provided.

Shortly after the achievement of Boot and Randall all resistance to Hitler on the continent of Europe ceased. In the opinion of many, not least the US ambassador to Britain, the defeat of Britain by Germany was imminent. Certainly Britain lacked the production resources its situation needed. The USA was not to become (by courtesy of Japan) an ally for another year and a half. Churchill chose this moment to do a curious thing. On 8 July 1940 President Roosevelt received a letter from the British ambassador to Washington offering to disclose all Britain's technical secrets to the American government without reciprocal undertakings from the US; but there was an implied quid pro quo. The letter concluded: 'We for our part are probably more anxious to be permitted to employ the full resources of the radio industry in your country with a view to obtaining the greatest power possible for the emission of ultra short waves than anything else.'

The timing was perfect. Eleven days earlier Roosevelt had created the National Defence Research Council (NDRC), and one of its first acts was to establish a microwave committee. A British mission led by Tizard (Sir Henry at that date) departed on 30 August for Washington bearing, *inter alia*, the multi-cavity magnetron, described in 1946 by one enthusiastic American scientist as 'the most valuable cargo ever brought to our shores'.[17]

The word 'magnificent' appears infrequently in this book; but the American response *was* magnificent. In October the Radiation Laboratory was founded at the Massachusetts Institute of Technology (MIT), and eminent American scientists flocked to it. The Laboratory's given priorities, agreed between the Tizard mission and the NDRC, were in order:

1. microwave AI;
2. precision gunlaying radar; and
3. a fixing system requiring no response from the ship or aircraft (see Chapter 12).

In the same month the first contracts were being settled with Bell Laboratories, General Electric, Sperry, Bendix, RCA, and Westinghouse.

In December 1940, for the first time ever, radar was fitted to an American aircraft. It was a 1.5 m pre-magnetron British ASV Mk II (see below), fitted to a US Navy PBY. Only three months later an American-designed and built 10 cm radar employing magnetron technology was flying in a US B18. At that precise date (10 March 1941) the staff of the Radiation Laboratory had already reached 140. In effect, American aircraft overflew pre-magnetron radar. When the US finally became a belligerent in December 1941, its leadership in the field was assured.[18]

No small group of people ever win a major war; but sometimes quite small groups can prevent it being lost. It might be said that the group associated with ASV (aircraft to surface vessel) were in that category. ASV worked on similar principles to AI Mk IV except that only a horizontal display was required and the sea return, unlike the ground return, did not swamp the picture. The equipment did not require the special aptitude and skill required by Mk IV AI, but did require intense concentration. The early unsuccessfulness of the Mk I ASV in anti-U-boat operations has been variously attributed to the equipment itself, poor training or unsuitability of aircrew, and defects of aircraft and weaponry. In the quarter ending with February 1941 96 Allied ships were sunk by U-boats without loss. If that rate had continued, Britain would have quickly lost the war by attrition.

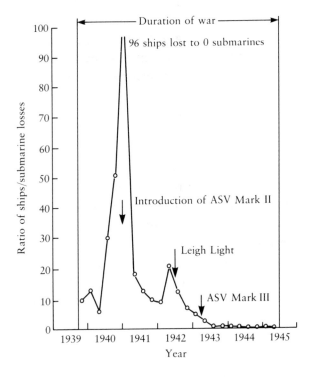

FIGURE 11.10
The war against the U-boat.

Figure 11.10 (based on Figure 6.1 of Bowen 1987) shows the effect of the introduction of ASV Mk II, which had the same 7 kW pulse output as ASV Mk I, but was better engineered and had a longer pulse and a lower PRF. Presumably improvements in aircrew, aircraft, and weaponry also played their part. The rise in Allied shipping losses in early 1942 seen in the figure has been attributed in part to the rich pickings for U-boats in American waters immediately after the USA entered the war, but was also partly due to the German development of ASV detectors and other U-boat counter-measures. The signal received at the target is of course several orders stronger than the echo signal received back at the radar transmitter. The range of receivers designed to give warning of radar surveillance may therefore exceed the range of the radar itself. German equipment to warn submarines of ASV and night bombers of AI became a technology in its own right.

After the introduction in March 1943 of microwave ASV Mk III, an H_2S derivative, the U-boat became an ineffective weapon and the coffin of its crew. During the war more than 80 per cent of all U-boat crews perished or were taken prisoner. Admiral Doenitz's speech at Weimar has often been quoted:

> . . . *the enemy has deprived the U-boat of its essential feature—namely the element of surprise—by means of radar. With these methods . . . he has conquered the U-boat menace. . . . It was not superior strategy or tactics which gave him success in the U-boat war, but superiority in scientific research.*

Doenitz may have been a little previous. The introduction in 1945 of new countermeasures against microwave ASV and of faster schnorkel-fitted electric U-boats might have restored the fortunes of the U-boat to some extent, had Germany had the means to continue the war.

The bizarre story of the interaction of British and German radar during the war would be hilarious were it not so grim. In London, against all reason, the existence of German radar was not officially accepted as proven until 1941.[19] From the beginning, both sides recognized the necessity for identification of friend or foe (IFF). The reception of the radar pulse at the friendly aircraft triggered a coded response, which might be varied and which might be on the same or a different frequency. Thus began *transponders* and secondary radar generally—now major features of air traffic control in particular. Early British IFF was unreliable. On one famous occasion two AI-equipped night fighters were sent up to intercept a returning RAF bomber. The first Beaufighter shot down the Stirling; the second Beaufighter shot down the first.

It was believed in the RAF that IFF jammed German radar. In fact the frequencies of Freya-Flammen (Freiburg II) were such that IFF enhanced the reflection and doubled the range of the German radar. Only in 1944 were RAF crews unequivocally ordered to switch off IFF over enemy territory.[20] From 1943 German night bombers were equipped to detect AI, a task made easier by the British night fighters' IFF.

Both sides were aware from the beginning of the feasibility of jamming enemy radar, but deferred its use in the belief that the inevitable retaliation would be more expensive. One British proposal of 1938 involved the jettisoning of thin wires (of a length to be determined by the German frequency) suspended on toy balloons. The eventual British measure, *Window*, consisted of millions of aluminium strips to be dropped by the bombers. In May 1942 Bomber Command obtained permission to use it; but the decision was reversed on the intercession of Fighter Command and scientists (including Watson Watt) concerned with the defence of the island. In July 1943 Churchill decided (in his words) to open the window. It was first used on a raid on Hamburg; and, according to German sources, anti-aircraft guns fired 50 000 rounds but only downed three bombers. Later, a few bombers in the stream transmitted jamming signals on German radar frequencies, naturally creating a demand in Germany for fighters equipped to home on them! Towards the end, German radar was effectively jammed, so the Germans ingeniously used British radar as a multistatic system.[21] The difference in time between receiving the transmitted pulse and the reflected pulse defines an elliptical line of position, with the two ground stations as foci. The position of the aircraft could be found by the intersection of several ellipses or, at one station, by combining the ellipse with measurement of direction.

Gee, Loran, and other wartime fixing systems which derived from radar technology are a subject of the next chapter; but radar equipment intended for the location of targets became valuable navigation aids from the beginning. The display of coastlines on naval and ASV radar has already been mentioned. Metric AI and ASV were easily adapted to the first radar beacons, which were modified IFF sets. The pulse transmitted by the ASV triggered a response (coded for identification) which appeared on the screen as a blip, like a target but at much greater range. The difficulty with Mk IV AI that the beacon would be swamped by ground returns was overcome by off-setting the frequency of the beacon's response and switching the aircraft receiver to that frequency in the navigation mode. As is illustrated in Fig. 11.7 (p. 210) the presentation of azimuth in metric AI and ASV was crude; but a beacon could be used for homing, or the ranges from two or more to fix. These beacons became so important to night-fighter navigation that when they were fitted with microwave equipment for interception purposes 1.5 m equipment was carried for navigation.[22]

The principles of these beacons were applied to the *Rebecca* (airborne)/*Eureka* (beacon) system for supply-dropping, for paratroop-dropping, and eventually on route navigation. Ultra-light Eureka beacons for use in the field weighed only 14 kg, including mast, antenna, and battery.

The success of radar beacons led quickly to the Beam Approach Beacon System (BABS) for approach to land. The dissatisfaction with SBA (Chapter 10) led to the development of BABS Mk II for Bomber Command, employing dedicated equipment. At the war's end it was no match for ILS, not least because there was no glide path; and the problem of direct presentation to the pilot of a meter display was never entirely solved.

The development of wartime radar after the first early-warning system has been illustrated by aeronautical examples because these were strictly navigation systems, and, before the multicavity magnetron, technically difficult. The Navy required early-warning systems, surface surveillance radar, gunlaying, and (on aircraft carriers) GCI; but the designers of such systems had the enormous advantages that much larger antenna arrays were feasible than on aeroplanes, especially on battleships and aircraft carriers, and there was no great requirement for miniaturization.

The story related is one of changes in perception unparalelled in the history of the application of science to navigation. Hülsmeyer demonstrated the practicality of radio detection at the very beginning of radio, before primitive radio direction-finding, and no one wanted to know about it for thirty years, while radio technology raced ahead on all other fronts and became big business at a pace only exceeded by the automobile. The British team which applied skills acquired in other fields of research in 1935/6 to produce in eleven months a prototype CH station capable of detection at 100 miles and range measurement with an accuracy of half a mile, did not exceed six persons of all grades during that period. In contrast, less than ten years later, the US Department of Defense radar R&D establishments employed many thousands of people.[23] At the peak (in early 1945) there must have been more scientists and engineers in the USA, Britain, Germany, and Japan working on the application of radio to navigation and location than all the scientists and engineers who devoted their time to location and navigation in the whole of history up to 1935. Equally remarkable is the way in which, in so few years, the motivation to acquire a defence against enemy bombers led to a revolution in navigation, from pinpointing a paratroop drop to fixing in mid-ocean (Chapter 12).

The application of wartime radar to the navigation of peaceful commerce had its own problems. One difficulty was expressed by Sir Robert Watson-Watt at the time, in his usual elegant but circumlocutory prose. He wrote in his *Foreword* to the first edition of F. J. Wylie's classic *The use of radar at sea*:

> *In the armed forces and their supply services the provider and the user could be brought into more intimate and continuing contact than can the user and provider in the diversifed arts of peace . . . The wide terraces of civil practice must, of commercial necessity, be fewer and more steeply separated than the numerous shallow steps of the staircase of specialised military provision.*

More baldly: which comes first, the system or the requirement; who is going to define the requirement; who is going to pay for the development of the system; what rate of obsolesence will the market bear?

These have been the fundamental issues in the development of civil navigation since the war. Some civil developments have been directly government-funded. The work of the Blind Landing Experimental Unit described in Chapter 10 is one example. More typical is the history of INS described in Chapter 9. All the research and basic development were done on military contracts, with submarines particularly in mind. At a certain date the contractors were allowed to apply the technology to civil use, and the airlines in particular were eager buyers. The peacetime development of marine radar has been largely manufacturer-led. Gradually the International Maritime Organization (IMO) imposed minimum standards. Today a minimum of two radars is obligatory throughout the world on all vessels over 10 000 g.r.t.

After the war, marine radar was immediately the most important peaceful application of radar. By 1953 2800 vessels on the British register alone were radar-equipped. Their centimetric PPIs displayed coasts and other ships in correct azimuth and range. The unwary might have expected a great improvement in coastal navigation and, more specifically, a dramatic reduction in the collision rate in congested waters, which was so outrageously high. In fact, the phrase 'radar-assisted collision' justifiably entered the vocabulary of marine navigation.

Part of the problem was the *International regulations for preventing collision at sea*, which had evolved over two centuries in a world without radar. These *Rules* established criteria by which both vessels could determine which should avoid the other, and imposed on the other the categorical duty to maintain course and speed. If one vessel sails and the other steams, the steam vessel must always give way, however unimaginable the prospect of a supertanker giving way to a sailing dinghy may be. There was one set of criteria when both vessels were sailing and a quite different set when both were steaming (or motoring). To confuse the simple mariner, should that mythical creature exist, there were caveats which said, in effect, 'When these rules don't work don't use them.'[24] One case for the caveats is the circumstance, of increasing importance as traffic grew, in which giving way might provoke risk of collision with a third vessel.

The vital principle implicit in these rules was that, if one ship can see the other, the other can see her, and both ships can equally and simultaneously determine which should give way and which should maintain speed and course, without the necessity of any communication between them. A vessel recognizing on radar a collision hazard without a visual sighting does not know if the other is aware of the situation, and therefore does not know what to do. There is also the point, trivial in post-war days before the proliferation of pleasure craft, that it is not even known whether the other vessel is under sail or steam. The situation cried out for IFF, and it seems strange that this was not clearly seen at the time, and that, forty years on, secondary radar is not standard, although MIDAR (microwave identity data automatic response) has been proposed. There were collisions which would probably never have occurred without radar. As a result the judges were obliged to make case law. In one early case a US court decided that the radar-equipped ship involved in a collision in a fog bank was solely to blame, because its radar was switched off. Neither ship was required to carry radar; but one, having fitted it, was obliged to employ it in the application of *Rules* for which it was never intended.

The representation of coastlines disappointed and confused some users—some features do not appear to the radar 'eye' as they appear to the human eye. There was confusion too between echoes from land, ships, and buoys. Undoubtedly in these matters, as in radar-assisted collisions, lack of skill and sheer incomprehension on the part of the user were a major problem. An authority on such matters wrote[25] as late as 1980:

> *Radar provided a means of detecting other vessels at increased range in restricted visibility and of determining their movements and the risk of collision, but these advantages were negated by the improper use of the equipment and the tendency of radar-equipped ships to maintain full speed. Investigations of collisions involving vessels using radar in restricted visibility almost invariably reveal that adequate plotting has not been carried out.*

Presumably the change of tense in the last sentence was deliberate.

The situation slowly ameliorated. The collision regulations were changed, notably in 1972, to adapt them to the modern world. Improved training, the widespread use of radar simulators, and a new generation of seamen who grew up with radar, all helped. The use of VHF voice channels to enable ships to call radar targets on their screen and co-operate with them directly, and radar surveillance of heavily trafficked channels by VTS (Vessel Traffic Services) have also been valuable. Today every vessel over 500 g.r.t. must be radar-equipped.

Every vessel over 10 000 g.r.t. must carry at least two radars and an automatic radar-plotting aid of specified form (ARPA). Racons (the microwave successors to Eureka) are increasingly deployed where they are required (there are about 1500 world-wide). Reflectors commonly extend the range at which buoys can be seen on the screen from 2 to 10 miles.

After the war there was no rush to install radar on civil aircraft. The map-reading capability of radar is largely irrelevant to navigation on airways defined by track guidance systems, and even weather radar is of limited value if one's freedom to divert from a stormy track is constrained by the presence of other traffic. Nevertheless, weather radar began to find its way on to airliners from the late 1950s. The major application of radar to civil aviation has been to air traffic control (ATC).

An important feature of civil air navigation since the war has been its subjection to ATC. Although ATC is legally an exercise of the sovereignty of a state over its territorial air space (extended by international agreement over non-territorial waters), it has been perceived in the Western world as a safety service from the beginning. As air traffic grew, the principal objectives of ATC became clear: to avoid collision in the air and to provide that sequence of landings and take-offs at busy airports which permits the maximum safe utilization of runways.

In pursuit of these objectives ATC relied heavily at first on primary radar and voice communication with pilots.[26] Specific-purpose radars evolved for airfield control, approach control, airways surveillance, even control of taxiway traffic. As traffic intensified, voice communication did not provide adequate means of identifying the blip on the controller's screen. IFF (or secondary radar) was needed. The first civil aircraft transponders were simple devices which were turned on at the controller's request to enhance and therefore to identify the aircraft's blip. The advantages of technology which became available to label blips and to interrogate the transponder directly for basic data were soon realized. Gradually data links became more sophisticated. When flight-management systems (FMS, mentioned in Chapter 9) evolved, the obvious line of development was automatic data links between the FMS and the ATC computer.

It is frustrating. There is no lack of air space; one only has to stand at the world's busiest airport and look at the sky to see how empty it is. The cost to the world of the inefficiency of ATC viewed as a collision-avoidance system exceeds the Gross National Product of many member nations of the UN. There is the cost to the airlines and the passengers of the ATC delays familiar to all. The price of the ATC service alone is of the order of pounds sterling per passenger flying hour in Europe. These are only the tip of the iceberg. Airways routeing itself adds on average 7 per cent to the great circle distance in Europe, and denies optimum route selection (Chapter 13). On many European routes, preferred flight level is refused more often than not, adding substantially to fuel consumption. Required thrust varies linearly with weight, and millions of tons of fuel are consumed annually to carry large fuel reserves for ATC contingencies, mainly unfavourable clearances and terminal area delays. Finally there is the implicit additional cost of aircraft designed to carry such fuel reserves.

In the era of GPS (Chapter 12) and low-cost high-power computers, the problem of lone vehicle navigation, if not entirely solved, is entirely soluble at the present state of the art. Radar is scarcely relevant except perhaps in terminal areas. The *unsolved* problem of civil navigation, both at sea and in the air, is the safe, efficient, and orderly flow of traffic. Radar is at the heart of the solution to this problem.

The marine and the aeronautical worlds started from diametrically opposed positions. The ship's captain was the master *under God*, and no one else told him what to do. The airline pilot was early habituated to doing as he was told in the form of cockpit drills, check-lists, and defined and detailed procedures covering every contingency management could conceive. Besides, ship radar should be sufficient to prevent collision even if it evidently does not; whereas, with speeds more than an order higher, there was no way airborne radar could prevent aircraft colliding in the air. The traffic policeman was quite unavoidable. Slowly these opposed positions are converging.

At sea, the observance of one-way traffic routes is now compulsory in some heavily congested areas. The first, in the Dover Strait, was opposed in the 1960s by some ship-owners, who saw it as an infringement of the freedom of the seas, but (signs of the changing times) was supported by the masters themselves. In response to a questionnaire circulated by the International Chamber of Shipping, to the surprise of many, only 107 of 3755 forms returned were against routeing. The word *control* is carefully avoided; but, in heavily congested areas, Vessel Traffic Services are slowly extending their role.[27]

In the air, since 1980, airborne collision avoidance systems have had an internationally accepted *name* at least. Unsurprisingly, it is ACAS. The USA is leading the field.[28] At the time of writing it is phasing in a requirement for the carriage of TCAS (traffic alert and collision avoidance system), which works by detecting other aircraft from their transponder signals. In one mode a data link is used for coordination purposes. TCAS II equipment gives commands to both aircraft in the vertical plane only: one might be constrained not to climb, the other not to descend. There is no thought to reinstate the freedom of the skies by such means. The modest intent is to avoid 90 percent of the collisions which do take place (at a frequency of about one every five years in the USA) in a controlled airspace.

Thus it seems that, at least for the rest of the century, collision avoidance by means other than the human eye will rely, at sea, on shipborne radar supported by routeing and VTS; in the air on air traffic control supported by airborne radar.

Notes to Chapter 11

1. Swords (1986) describes early independent work in Britain, Germany, the USA, France, Italy, Japan, the USSR, Holland, and even Hungary.
2. Quoted from Pritchard (1989).
3. The original British term was RDF (Range and Direction Finding or, for disinformation purposes, Radio Direction Finding). The term *radiolocation* was also used in Britain; but the American palindrome *radar* was irresistible.
4. Tiberio (1939).

5. According to Baron von Ardenne, Goering rejected a proposal to develop panoramic display equipment in 1940 on the grounds that the war was already won. Swords (1986) describes difficulties of organization of effort and communication between the military and the scientists in Japan, where seriously directed work was not initiated until 1941, by which time Germany and Britain already had extensive and successful operational experience, and the USA was racing ahead.

6. Professor W. T. Runge, Head of Development of Telefunken, later recalled that, when Hitler came to power, a Nazi in the export sales department was given responsibility for cleansing management and technical direction of 'opposing elements'.

7. The phrase is due to one of the walkers, (Lord) C. P. Snow.

8. Watson-Watt (1957) pointed out that Swan and Frayne preceded their fellow-countrymen Breit and Tuve in experimental work on radio pulses. Work on pulses in the optical range goes back to Armand Fizeau in the nineteenth century (see Chapter 4).

9. The required circuitry was known as a squegging oscillator.

10. Bistatic and multistatic systems were later to be employed in diverse tasks including missile tracking.

11. The wavelength originally proposed was 50 m, twice the span of a bomber wing; but there was interference at that frequency. It was also found, fortunately, that an aircraft is a wide-band reflector. For early warning of enemy aircraft, accurate range is more important than accurate direction, as the enemy will presumably change course frequently to obscure his intentions.

12. Cathode-ray-tube technology was advancing rapidly to meet the needs of television, especially in Britain, the US, Germany, and Holland. The BBC launched the first high-definition television broadcasts in 1936, using the EMI system.

13. Lee De Forest, the inventor of the triode, called *magnetron* a Greeko-Schenectady word. It was coined at the General Electric Research Laboratory situated in Schenectady, New York.

14. Dr E. G. Bowen, who was responsible for creating this equipment, recalls (1987) that the air gunners who were originally deployed were rarely successful, and the RAF found some of the needed talent among over-age (i.e. over 31) schoolmasters with glasses. In fact, the RAF created a category of 'radio observer', with status equivalent to that of pilots. The very existence of their job was an official secret at the time. The lack of success of British AI in the beginning was also due to the lack of a multi-seater aircraft with sufficient fire-power and speed. The requirement was met by the purpose-built Beaufighter with 20 mm cannons. In 1940 AI-equipped night fighters were destroying bombers at the rate of about 2 a month. In May 1941, Beaufighters manned by 'radio observers' destroyed 102 night bombers over British soil at night. Siemens produced a pilot-operated AI for single-seater fighters, but the Luftwaffe concurred with the RAF that it was a two-man job. Bowen, incidentally, had been one of the earliest advocates of rotating beam systems and of PPI display.

15. Figure 11.8 is based on Pritchard (1989), figure 9.2.

16. Microwave AI became operational in the RAF with the Mk VIII during the summer of 1942. It was superseded by the (American) Mk X, which differed from the Mk VIII mainly in scanning and display. Operating on 10 cm, it had a range of 8 miles, and remained standard in the RAF until 1957.

17. The magnetron was given to Germany when an H_2S was found virtually undamaged in the wreckage of an RAF aircraft shot down over Rotterdam. The Germans appropriately called their derivative 'Rotterdam'. The British decision to use the magnetron over enemy-occupied territory must have been difficult. There is a story that the magnetron was taken to Japan by U-boat—an interesting voyage at that date. It was reported much later that a multi-cavity magnetron was under development in Japan during the war.

18. The contribution to Allied radar of Australia and Canada, co-belligerents of Britain from the first day of the war, should not be forgotten. Thousands of ASV Mk II, for example, were manufactured in both countries.

19. It was suspected. The Germans clearly had the technological capability to do what the British had done and, in any case, on the fall of France, had acquired from France both French and some British technology. It was known in Britain that, at the time of the fall of France, SFR (Société Française Radioélectrique) had developed a magnetron producing 500 watts at 16 cm. Earlier, brief information on German radar had been anonymously delivered to the British naval attaché in Oslo. J. H. Beattie points out (personal communication 1991) that the Royal Navy had viewed the *Seetakt* radar on the wreck of the *Graf Spee* in December 1939. And then there were the intercepts of radiotelephone traffic between German fighters and controllers. Official British espionage services do not seem to have been organized for the acquisition of scientific intelligence until later.

20. In 1942 the Operational Research section of Bomber Command reported that IFF had no effect one way or another, but suggested that IFF should be left on for morale purposes. Officialdom was eventually convinced of the dangers of the practice by Enigma decodes.

21. The Klein Heidelberg Parasit. As range measurement was more accurate than azimuth, Germany had experimented earlier with multistatic systems to give range/range fixes. Two circles intersect in two points, and the ambiguity is said to have proved troublesome.

22. Microwave beacons (Racons) were developed in the USA and became important aids to marine navigation subsequently; but they were not available in Britain at the time. There were no tuneable magnetrons then, and there was a view that receiver band width must be unacceptably high, given the variability of the frequency of resonance of magnetrons in production at the time. By 1945 3 cm radar fitted to US naval aircraft could receive microwave beacons installed at 240 US naval air stations.

23. Nearly 4000 in the NDRC Radiation Laboratory (opened in 1940 at MIT), thousands more at the Aircraft Radio Laboratory, the US Signal Corps Laboratory, the Naval Research Laboratory, and other establishments. In Britain the peak personnel (in 1945) at the Telecommunications Research Establishment was about 3000. The Admiralty Signals Establishment reached a peak of 4700 people, but not all were employed on radar.

24.   *Art. 27.* In obeying and construing these Rules, due regard shall be had to all dangers of navigation and collision and to any special circumstances which may render departure from the above Rules necessary in order to avoid immediate danger.
    Art. 29. Nothing in these Rules shall exonerate any vessel . . . from the consequences of . . . the neglect of any precaution which may be required . . . by the special circumstances of the case.

25. Cockroft (1980).

26. In oceanic areas radar surveillance is of course impossible. In these and *Flight Information Regions* surveillance is based on aircraft reporting. Until the late 1950s communication in these areas was often by morse code through intermediate radio operators.

27. The Channel Navigation Information Service for the Dover Strait commenced in 1972. It was confirmed by Neil in 1990 that the philosophy continues to be (as it always has been) one of non-intervention. Interestingly, the six cogent reasons for non-intervention given in the reference could equally be applied to ATC at one stage; and most of them still could.

28. The US also insisted on marine automatic radar plotting aids (ARPA) in US waters before there was international agreement.

CHAPTER TWELVE

Radio, Apollonius, and Professor Doppler

✠

ABOUT 200 BC Apollonius of Perga wrote his *Treatise on conic sections* in eight books, of which four have survived in the original Greek and three in an Arabic version (it is said that Halley learned Arabic expressly to translate them), and one is lost. Eighteen hundred years after Apollonius, his treatise was still the standard work on the subject when Kepler discovered that the orbit of a planet is that conic section which Apollonius called *ellipse* (falling short). To another he gave the name *hyperbola* (falling beyond). Whereas on an ellipse the *sum* of the distance of its two foci is everywhere the same, on a hyperbola it is the *difference* in the distance of the two foci which is constant. The construction of a hyperbola from this property is shown in Fig. 12.1. If therefore we have the means, not to measure the distance from a fixed point, but the difference in the distance of two fixed points, we have a hyperbolic line of position. Two such lines cutting at a fairly wide angle provide a fix, as in Fig. 12.2, which illustrates a fundamental defect of hyperbolic systems. The accuracy of the fix, depending as it does on the spacing between the lines and the angle of cut between them, is seen to vary widely over the area covered. Hyperbolae, like astronomical position circles, may intersect in two points which are generally so far apart that there is no ambiguity in practice.

Before the technology existed to apply this geometry to radio navigation there were sonic applications. Claud Powell[1] has suggested that the idea may go back as far as 1860. If two bells suitably sited on opposite sides of a channel are actuated simultaneously by landline, the navigator is nearer the one he hears first; he is in the middle of the channel if he hears them simultaneously. Acoustic hyperbolic fixing of the position of enemy heavy artillery was studied in Austria and France before the First World War. The British system, devised by 2nd Lt. (later Professor Sir) Lawrence Bragg in 1915, employed a bank of six microphones,

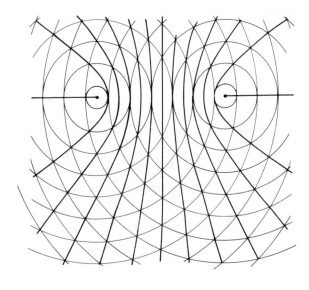

FIGURE 12.1
Graphical construction of hyperbolic pattern.

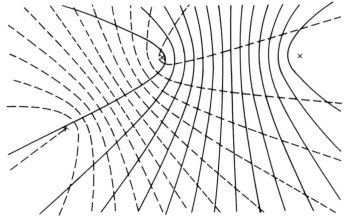

FIGURE 12.2
A hyperbolic fixing chain.

each connected by landline to one of a bank of six galvanometers photographed on a moving film, which also carried time-marks in one hundredths of a second. The time-interval between the flicker of any two galvanometers, multiplied by the speed of sound, defined a hyperbolic line of position of the gun, with the two corresponding microphones as foci. In 1923 it was proposed to apply the method to navigation. The ship would fire an underwater explosion, which would be picked up by a bank of hydrophones. The received data would then be radioed to the ship.

The earliest attempts at hyperbolic radio navigation, going back at least to a patent[2] of 1904, relied on the difference in amplitude of received signals; but although the idea remained in the air as late as 1923, it was by then quite obvious that there was no reliable relationship between distance and signal strength. As in radar, the choice is between phase comparison and pulse timing. Phase comparison came first; when it was first mooted the technology for pulse systems did not exist.

If two stations transmit in phase, the phase difference between the received signals (expressed as a fraction of a cycle) times the wavelength is the difference in the distance of the two stations from the receiver. There is an inherent ambiguity if the two transmitters are more than one wavelength apart, because the difference in the distance can exceed one wavelength. A phase difference of 360° is zero. There are therefore as many 'lane ambiguities' as there are wavelengths between the transmitters. These ideas were addressed in a French patent taken out in 1923 by H. M. A. Mottez, inventing what he called an 'interference-type radio beacon using rotating directional signals'. Two vertical omnidirectional antennas two wavelengths apart transmit in phase at equal strength. Maximum signal is received along the lines illustrated in Fig. 12.3(a), on which the signals are received in phase, that is to say on which the difference of distance is zero, one, or two wavelengths. If the transmissions are not in phase the lines are such as those illustrated in Fig. 12.3(b). The idea of Mottez, which was to prove so fertile, was to rotate the phase difference of the two transmissions 0–360° at a constant rate, with a start signal. Using a stop-watch in a manner reminiscent of the old Telefunken beacon (Chapter 10) the navigator would time the period from start to maximum signal, defining the family of curves (such as those illustrated in Fig. 12.3(b)) on one of which he must lie. Mottez proposed to resolve lane ambiguity by a technique involving transmissions on another frequency.

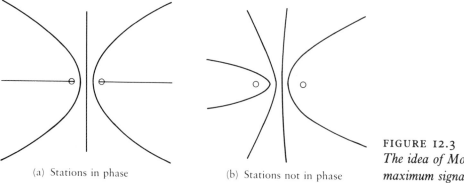

(a) Stations in phase   (b) Stations not in phase

FIGURE 12.3
The idea of Mottez. Lines of maximum signal.

Every hyperbola is asymptotic to some straight line passing through the centre of the baseline, as in Fig. 12.4. If the distance of the ship is large in relation to the length of the baseline the hyperbolae are indistinguishable from their asymptotes. As a practical matter, if the baseline is too short to be plotted on the chart in use, hyperbolic position lines are, for all practical purposes, straight lines (great circles) radiating from the centre of the baseline, and the tedium of dealing with hyperbolae dissolves. To illustrate: in the Mottez design, if the maximum signal coincides with the start signal the asymptotes are the perpendicular to the baseline (zero phase difference); lines incline to it at 60° (360° phase difference); and the extensions of the baseline (720° phase difference). Systems in which the hyperbolae are practically great circles are called 'collapsed' hyperbolic systems.

The only collapsed system to have any impact on navigation (if we except the very special case of the loop itself) was *Sonne*, already mentioned in Chapter 10. Invented in Germany

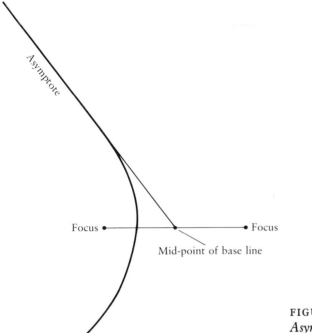

FIGURE 12.4
Asymptote as position line.

by Ernst Kramar, it became the standard German radio aid to long-range navigation during the Second World War, and was subsequently adopted by ICAO for that purpose under the name given to it by the RAF, *Consol*. The principle is as elegantly simple as Otto Scheller's course-setter so long before, and it develops the theme of Mottez.

Figure 12.5 is the polar diagram of three vertical omnidirectional antennas spaced three wavelengths apart. The solid lobes represent the case when the phase at A leads that at B by 90°, and C lags by the same amount. The dotted lobes represent the polar diagram when the phasing at A and C is reversed. If the field represented by the dotted diagram is broadcast for ½ second, and that by the solid diagram for 1½ seconds, dots will be received at points such as P_1 and dashes at P_2. On all the straight lines in Fig. 12.5, the asymptotes to the hyperbolae representing zero (multiples of 360°) phase difference between A and C, a continuous note is heard. If, in addition to the phase reversal twice in two seconds, the phases of the transmissions of A and C are rotated 360° at a steady rate over a short period, each equisignal line is rotated to the next. A navigator hears dots (or dashes) followed by a steady note from which dashes (or dots) emerge. There are 60 characters, including those lost in the equisignal. After counting the dots and dashes, compensating for those lost in the equisignal, the navigator can find his (great circle) position line by interpolating between the straight lines of Fig. 12.5, although it was normal practice to use charts with a Consol pattern overprint. Consol has no lane identification. At long range the lanes are so wide that there is no ambiguity in practice, unless the navigator is totally lost. At medium range lane can be identified by using the Consol station as an NDB. At close range, or near the line of the antennas, the station is simply used as an NDB.

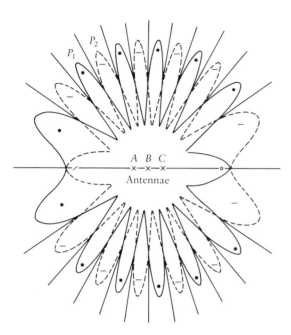

FIGURE 12.5
Polar diagram of Consol.

Consol is unique in navigational history in terms of its range and accuracy with rudimentary equipment aboard the craft. Operating in the 300 kHz band, only an ordinary receiver is required, as with the radio range, but Consol is omnidirectional except near the baseline. Operational range over the Atlantic of stations in Norway, NW Ireland, NW France, and NW Spain was as much as 1200 n.m. by day; at night ionospheric effects could increase the range to about 1500 n.m. On the normal to the baseline, at ranges of 250–1000 n.m., the 95 per cent probable error of the position line would be less than 0.4°; about double that at night. The system is less prone to error arising from atmospheric distortions than some other MF systems because, as the transmitting antennas are so close, the radiation from them follows similar paths. Although a separation of three wavelengths was mentioned above, other separations may be used. Increasing the number of wavelengths of separation increases the number of lanes, enhancing the theoretical accuracy obtainable with narrow lanes, but increasing the problem of lane identification. In its time Consol was popular with U-Boats, fishing boats, and transatlantic airliners, amongst others. New stations were still being constructed in 1970.

In contrast with the 'collapsed' hyperbolae of Consol, the base line of the *Decca* system is typically 60–120 n.m., large in relation to wavelength and significant in relation to the range at which it is used, so that the position lines appear on a conformal chart much as in Fig. 12.2, and there are many lines of zero phase difference; typically lane-width on the baseline is 300–500 metres. The basic principle was devised by W. J. O'Brien, working in the USA in 1937, and the system was developed in England during the war and first employed on a large scale in the allied invasion of Normandy in 1944. After the war the system was developed commercially by the Decca Navigator Company—the only case of a widespread fixing system provided by private enterprise. By 1970 Decca chains covered heavily trafficked coastal waters in many parts of the world; in particular, most European waters were covered from the eastern Baltic to Gibraltar.

A chain consists of a master and three slaves, all of which transmit a continuous wave signal in the 70–130 kHz band. Each frequency employed is some harmonic of an underlying frequency (f) in the region of 14 kHz. At the receiver phase is compared at the lowest common multiple harmonic of f. Thus, if the master broadcasts at $6f$ and the purple slave at $5f$, phase comparison between the two is at $30f$. The output was a visual display, the 'decometer', the rotor of which takes up a position proportional to the phase difference. The position line is then plotted on a special chart overprinted with the lattice of Decca position hyperbolae.

The equipment employed in the Normandy landings identified lane by counting and recording the number of times the vessel passed through a line of zero phase difference. This presupposed that the chain was continuously received from leaving port in a known lane. It would be useless to a vessel entering coverage at a position not known with sufficient accuracy to identify the lane. Commercial Decca therefore employed other techniques (which improved over the years) to provide positive lane identification. Area coverage is provided by a sequence of chains, often employing one site for slaves of different chains. In the nature of such a hyperbolic system, accuracy of fixing greatly depends on the position of the vessel in relation to the geometry of the chain. At such frequencies ionospheric effects reduce the accuracy at night. For a favourably placed vessel in full daylight the 95 per cent fixing error is of the order of tens of metres (less than the size of the vessel), but in the middle of a winter night perhaps a whole order higher. At a range of 300 n.m. from the transmitters error in full daylight might be 2 n.m. Thus a sufficient density of Decca chains provided fixing in coastal waters of unprecedented accuracy at a time when the increasing density of traffic was demanding more accurate and disciplined navigation.

As befits a private-enterprise system, strenuous and ingenious efforts were applied to the adaptation of the existing European chains to the navigation of commercial aircraft in the area; but, for the reasons given in Chapter Ten, they were doomed to failure. In its early form the *Flight Log* displayed the Decca fix on a chart (with airways overprinted) by a stylus which moved in response to one hyperbolic position line, while the chart itself moved in response to another. Developments in computer technology led in 1959 to *Omnitrac*, which computed from Decca inputs distance along track and across track in relation to 'way points', the latitude and longitude of which had been pre-selected by the pilot. By that date flight under IFR (instrument flight rules) in areas under Decca coverage was usually along airways defined by the radials of VOR (Chapter Ten), so the Decca equipment was seen as superfluous. Nevertheless, the essential principle of Omnitrac was to have far-reaching implications for air navigation, including the aeronautical application of another phase comparison hyperbolic system, *Omega*.

It was known that, at the very low frequencies employed for communications until about 1923, propagation characteristics are relatively stable and predictable, the surface of the earth and the lower levels of the ionosphere acting as a wave guide. From about 1947 thoughts turned to the possibility of applying these characteristics to a VLF world-wide fixing system by phase comparison, using baselines thousands of miles long. Most of the earth's surface is water, and at 10 kHz attenuation over the sea is only 2–4 dB/1000 km.[3] On a land path, phase velocity is 0.05–0.1 per cent less than over the sea; but this may be corrected. Paths over ice-caps represent a more serious problem, with attenuation an order higher. Another problem is interference between the ground wave and the first-hop E-layer reflection. Figure 12.6 (which follows Powell (1962)) illustrates the ideal case, in which they are exactly in phase; but if they are 180° out of phase and of equal strength no signal is received.

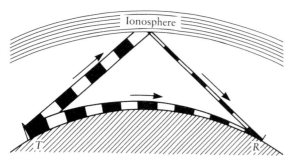

FIGURE 12.6

The skywave/groundwave relationship at the point of equal amplitude.

In 1955 Professor J. A Pierce conducted a key study, published in 1957. By comparing the phase of his stable oscillator in Cambridge, Massachusetts with that of a signal received on 16 kHz from Rugby, England, he studied the variation in the propagation time of the latter. The diurnal variation corresponds to the variation in the height of the reflecting layer from about 92 km at night to about 76 km in full daylight. The spread of 35 microseconds between total day and total night in the Pierce phase trapezium illustrated in Fig. 12.7 corresponds to a distance of about 6 n.m. if uncorrected. Pierce found that it was during the

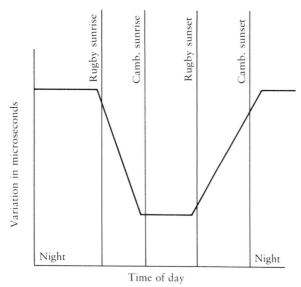

FIGURE 12.7

The Pierce phase trapezium (smoothed).

transition periods represented by the sloping lines that prediction was least reliable, suggesting that the system might be more useful to deep water mariners, who can wait a few hours for a reliable fix, than to airmen, who cannot.

In 1954 the Decca Navigator Company had published a detailed proposal for a VLF system called *Delrac*.[4] Pierce himself proposed a system called *Radux*. The system eventually adopted, *Omega*, is a US Navy development employing precisely the frequencies proposed for *Delrac*. It became effective in the 1970s although the last permanent station, Australia, did not become operational until the 1980s. The other seven permanent stations are in Argentina, Japan, Hawaii, La Réunion (Indian Ocean), Liberia, North Dakota, and Norway. Since there is no master–slave relationship[5] a position line is obtainable, at least theoretically, from any pair; but base lines of 5000–6000 n.m. are normally used. The technology of the 1970s permitted transmission and reception on very narrow frequency bands, drastically reducing background noise and so eliminating the need for very powerful transmitters which had been required for VLF communication in 1920.

The main operating frequency is 10.2 kHz, with a corresponding lane width on the base line of 8 n.m. One means of lane identification consists of the recorder's counting the number of times a line of zero phase difference is crossed (as in early Decca); but this fails whenever reception is discontinued. Signals are also transmitted on 11.3 and 13.6 kHz, the three frequencies being the 9th, 10th, and 12th harmonics of 1.13 kHz. The beat frequencies of 1.13, 2.26, and 3.4 kHz give coarse patterns with lane-widths of 72, 36 and 24 n.m. respectively on the baseline. These patterns do not provide accurate position lines; but they do resolve lane ambiguity if position is already known with sufficient accuracy to resolve 72 n.m. ambiguity.

Relatively simple marine equipment was used initially together with charts showing the Omega position lines, and tables for the correction of propagation errors. As the baseline is so long the hyperbolae are sweeping lines, which often appear virtually straight on the chart in use. With lane counters, recorders, and reasonable vigilance, problems of lane slippage could usually be eliminated. For most of the time, over most of the world, an accuracy of at least 2 n.m. might be expected; but there are many anomalies, often associated with paths over large ice-caps.[6] In the jargon, Omega is not a 'high integrity' system. In the earlier years, tables and charts for some parts of the world were inadequate.

There was a more subtle factor inimical to Omega. From the beginning of radio navigation, radio operators and navigators both at sea and in the air had coaxed the best out of their equipment; but in the 1970s people began to expect to push a button and get the right answer every time. This factor was general, but most striking in the airlines. In the 1950s specialist flight navigators exercised skill and patience in identifying first- and second-hop reflections from different levels of the ionosphere seen on their Loran A sets (see below), interpreting and correcting them to obtain usable results. When the INS-equipped Boeing 747 entered service in 1968, transatlantic navigation became the trivial business of feeding the flight-plan into the computer and letting the automatic pilot/navigator do the rest, while position in latitude and longitude, and along/across the flight-planned track, were displayed digitally to the human pilots. There was no place in airlines for systems which required charts, or careful and thoughtful interpretation.

The difficulty was only partly overcome by computer-interpreted Omega, which corrected propagation errors employing sophisticated geophysical models. The version of such equipment offered to aviation provided autopilot inputs and the desired digital display to the human pilots. Problems of occasional lane slippage and propagation anomalies remained, and the modern philosophy of flight-management precludes heuristic solutions. In many operations it was not clear what Omega contributed. The main aeronautical market became general aviation. Computer-controlled Omega offers direct interface with flight-control systems, VOR/DME, INS, Loran, GPS.

The availability at reasonable prices of 'atomic clocks', specifically the rubidium frequency-standard, accurate to $1:10^{12}$, permitted an alternative usage of Omega, the 'rho–rho' fix. The time is known with sufficient accuracy to determine the phase at the transmitter. Comparison with the phase at the receiver gives ranges, which is ambiguous in multiples of wavelength (30 km).

The idea implicit in *Differential Omega* is that, in one locality, the propagation errors are about the same. If they are measured at a shore station and broadcast, nearby shipping will get a better fix using the shore station correction than using the predicted correction. Stratton (1990) reports daytime errors of 0.5 n.m. at 500 n.m. reducing to 85 m at a distance of 5 n.m. However, 150 n.m. from the shore station in an east–west direction, the difference in local time may cause much larger discrepancies around sunset and sunrise. The application of the differential principle to more advanced systems is now of great importance.

The Omega radio compass offers an alternative means of orientation in very high latitudes. On the basis of work by Petrov and others, Kemp suggested in 1990 that the accuracy of the measurement of the bearing of an Omega signal relative to heading could be increased to about 0.2° As the bearing relative to north or any grid is determinate from the position, ship's heading is also determinate. Such a technique would have more application to a ship equipped with gyrocompass (useless near the pole) and magnetic compass (useless near the magnetic pole), or a land vehicle, than to aircraft equipped with INS or even high-quality directional gyros.

The USSR also developed a VLF fixing system contemporary with Omega (and having some advantages over it); but in the political climate of the time it was not offered for universal use.

The principal hyperbolic systems using pulses were developed originally to meet military need of the Second World War. Throughout the war British strategy was to bomb the German hinterland mainly at night;[7] but, at the beginning, the RAF was obliged to rely on astronomical navigation and DR over blacked-out Germany at night. Embarrassingly, only 5 per cent of the bombs landed within 5 miles of the target.[8] The first solution was *Gee*, which in 1940 applied existing radar technology to an idea proposed by R. J. Dippy in 1937. The essential principle is that a 'master' transmits pulses which triggers the transmission of pulses from a number of 'slaves'. The pulses are displayed on a cathode-ray tube to the navigator, who reads the time-interval between them. This requires an accurate electronic clock on the aircraft; and sufficiently stable oscillators were not practical aircraft equipment at the time.

Dippy's idea was to use, as a 'master clock', a 150 kHz high-precision crystal-controlled oscillator kept in a thermostatically controlled oven at the A (master) station. This oscillator regulated the pulse recurrence frequency of the A station. The indicator unit in the aircraft also contained a 150 kHz crystal-controlled oscillator which could be varied over a range of 45 Hz. The received PRF was used to adjust the aircraft oscillator to the exact frequency of the A station oscillator. The aircraft oscillator so stabilized calibrated the time-base of the display. Pulses transmitted by the slaves were delayed by an interval sufficient to ensure that the A pulse was always received first. The PRF of the slaves B,C was half that of A, and it was arranged that the sequence was ABAC. The time-base displayed to the navigator was split in two, so that he saw the dual picture of Fig. 12.8. When a fourth station was included in the chain it appeared as a double blip on both time-bases. The display was too small to be read with sufficient accuracy, so the operator 'strobed' the small area around each pulse, switched to an enlarged display, and by separate controls brought the B and C pulses into alignment with the A pulses on each segment of the time-base. He then selected the fine display of 150 kHz calibration pips illustrated in Fig. 12.9. Further expansion of the time-base scale was available if justified. The system was used with charts showing the Gee lattice. As in Decca, short baselines, in the region of 70 n.m., were used in order to ensure clear reception at all times of master signals at slaves. At the time it was a revolutionary advance in fixing systems, with a 50 per cent error of about 500 m in geometrically favourable areas.

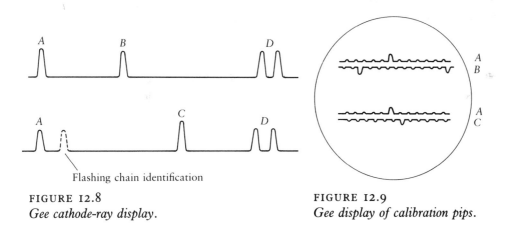

Flashing chain identification

FIGURE 12.8
Gee cathode-ray display.

FIGURE 12.9
Gee display of calibration pips.

The first Gee chain was designed to cover the Ruhr, and was employed on a large scale on the night of 8 March 1942. Immediately the percentage of bombs falling within 5 miles of assigned target jumped to 35 per cent, and survivors had less difficulty in finding their way home. Range at 15 000 feet was about 450 miles. It did not last; within months jamming started, which was countered by use of multiple transmissions on frequencies ranging from 22–85 MHz. The higher frequencies were employed in a chain designed to cover the Normandy invasion, in which Gee was very successful. At that stage it was practical to destroy the jamming stations. In 1945 Gee coverage as far as Rangoon was planned; but, although the system provided accurate area coverage overland at reasonable cost, it was abandoned.

Loran[9] (later known as Loran A or HF Loran) was developed in the USA only slightly later than Gee, and designed so that the equipment on the ship or aircraft was interchangeable with Gee. Considering the co-operation which existed between their sponsors during the development period it is unsurprising that the two systems have much in common; but whereas Gee was intended specifically for the bombing of Germany, Loran A was intended for longer-range use over the sea by both ships and aircraft. They were perceived as complementary contributions to the Allied war effort. The radio frequency employed was 2 MHz, which, it was thought, was the optimum frequency for obtaining an extended ground wave over the sea and, beyond the range of the ground wave, stable ionospheric reflection. At this frequency, ground waves are much attenuated over land; but the system was intended primarily for maritime use. Loran A operated in master–slave pairs of two stations with much longer baselines, usually arranged to be over water. At these frequencies pulses of 50 microseconds were used, compared with 5 microseconds for Gee. They were arranged to be exactly the same shape, so that, with a differential gain control, the user could fit together the ground wave from both stations. The procedure for measuring time-intervals was similar except that the scale was in microseconds, instead of in the Gee units derived from the 150 kHz oscillator.

Whereas Gee skywaves were merely a nuisance, in Loran they were essential to the long-range operation of the system. The user at night might see first- and second-hop reflections from the E and F layers, and, with experience, identify them. Charts showed the Loran lattices and corrections for skywave matching. Cross-matching between skywave and ground wave required the use of tables. The range by day of the ground wave over the sea was usually about 700 n.m.; the first-hop E wave extended at night to about 1400 n.m. Other reflections could be received at much greater ranges, but did not give an accurate position line. With some later improvements to the system the fix accuracy with good ground-wave matching was within a mile or so at best, although, as with all hyperbolic systems, much depended on the user's position relative to the geometry of the chain. Using skywave matching a skilled operator would expect a position line to be well within 10 n.m. Loran position lines were often used in conjunction with astronomical position lines. Full-scale trials of the equipment commenced in June 1942, and by the end of the war much of the oceans of the northern hemisphere was covered. The system has been described in its original form; but Loran A survived long enough to evolve into a semi-automated system, with digital read-out and automatic tracking.

During the experimental work on Loran it was discovered that at low levels of incidence the first-hop E reflection was surprisingly stable. S. S. Loran used baselines of the order of 1200 miles, the transmitters being synchronized by skywave. One pair had one station in Scotland and another in North Africa, the other pair were along the North African coast, so that the two position lines gave an excellent cut over much of Germany. A fixing accuracy of 1 n.m. over Berlin has been claimed,[10] but seems optimistic. S. S. Loran did not have the impact on the war in Europe which it would have had only a couple of years earlier because of the introduction of the microwave systems described in Chapter 11.

The advantages of these pulse systems over the phase-comparison systems are that there is no lane ambiguity and no interference between sky and ground waves provided that the pulse is short in relation to the time-interval between reception of the two.[11] Also it is possible to transmit short pulses at a peak power which would be impractical in continuous transmission. However, phase can be compared much more accurately than the interval between reception of pulses can be measured. One of the difficulties is that although engineers seek to make pulses as 'steep-fronted' as possible, the pulses do take a finite time to build up, and the receiver may not detect the pulse at its precise commencement. In contrast, phase comparison became very precise as highly stable oscillators became available. In the 1960s it was practical to compare phase with an accuracy of 1 per cent of a cycle on ships and aircraft. At 100 kHz this corresponds to 0.1 microseconds of time-interval, equivalent to a distance of 30 metres.

Loran C sought the best of both worlds by comparing the phase of pulses. At the selected carrier-wave frequency of 100 kHz, ground waves over an ocean path may be usable at 1000 n.m., and skywaves persist day and night. The pulse takes 8 cycles (80 microseconds) to reach maximum power; but the minimum delay between ground and skywave is only 30 microseconds, so it is the third cycle at which phase is compared. The technique of locking into the third cycle is sometimes called 'indexing'; and an index error of 1, analogous to lane ambiguity, corresponds to 3 km on the baseline. Instead of transmitting a single pulse, a train of 8 pulses at one-millisecond intervals is transmitted by all stations, the master transmitting a ninth for identification purposes. Some of the train are 'phase coded'. Slave transmissions are deferred by a period of the order of hundredths of a second in order to ensure that they always arrive after the master signal and its entire train of skywaves. They bear a different phase code. By the technique of 'synchronous detection' the phase of the third cycle of each of the eight pulses transmitted by the slave is compared with its counterpart received from the master.

A chain consists of a master and up to four slaves, although the original master–slave relationship has long since been replaced by atomic frequency standards. As most baselines are over the sea, their precise length is often determined by topographical considerations; but in chains intended for use over or at sea (which most of them are) 600 n.m. is typical. The first Loran C came into operation in 1957. Like the VOR, there have been major engineering developments since the system's inception. Over the decades Loran C, perhaps more than any other hyperbolic system, has challenged the ingenuity of competing manufacturers of receiving equipment to apply the latest technology to the needs of the market, in indexing and the use of skywaves for position-finding, as well as in the application of computers, which is now standard in all continuing hyperbolic systems.

Although early equipment provided a digital read-out, there was scope for users with visual monitors to exercise skills in the interpretation of skywaves and the avoidance of index error; but most modern equipment is completely automated. Basic accuracy with strong ground waves is within 0.4 microseconds, corresponding to a position-line error of 60 m on the baseline. Error when first-hop skywaves are matched is more than an order higher, and there is a greater risk of index error. Within its coverage, Loran C is more accurate than Omega; but the area covered is smaller, although much larger than that of a Decca chain. Apart from economic considerations there are not enough islands to cover the Pacific, or even the route of Columbus from the Canaries to the New World. More compact Loran C chains have been installed to provide area coverage overland with sufficient accuracy and reliability to permit non-precision approaches at some US airports. All hyperbolic systems are being rendered obsolescent by satellite systems.

It is a matter of everyday experience that a moving source of sound changes pitch as it passes, a phenomenon particularly noticeable with low-flying jet aircraft. In 1842 Christian J. Doppler, professor of experimental physics at Vienna, published a paper explaining what is called the 'Doppler effect'. In 1848 Armand Fizeau[12] gave the correct explanation in the optical case. A source transmitting continuously on frequency f is moving towards us at velocity v. The velocity of light c is relative to us (Chapter 4). The source's radiation is at the crest at time t_0 when it is distant d_0. The crest reaches us at $t_0 + d_0/c$. The next crest is emitted at $t_0 + 1/f$, when the distance is $d_0 - v/f$. It reaches us at $t_0 + 1/f + d_0/c - v/fc$. The time-interval between crests is $(1 - v/c)/f$. The received frequency f_1 is given by $f = f_1 (1 - v/c)$. This is the Doppler effect.[13] As v/c is so small the Doppler shift may be taken as fv/c or v/λ (λ is the wavelength).

In some navigational applications of Doppler the user transmits and measures the Doppler shift of the reflection to find the relative velocity of the reflector. Assuming that reflection is instantaneous and without phase change, for the first crest, time out is $d_0/(c+v)$ and time back must be the same (remembering that c is always relative to oneself): elapsed time $= 2d_0/(c+v)$. When the next crest is emitted, distance is reduced by v/f, so the echo is received after $2(d_0 - v/f)/(c + v)$. The interval between echoed crests is therefore $1/f - 2v/f(c + v) = (c-v)/f(c+v)$ and $f_1 = f(c+v)/(c-v)$. For all practical purposes the beat frequency (the doppler shift) is $2v/\lambda$.

It is immediately apparent from this equation why development of radio Doppler had to wait for a mature microwave technology, although radio Doppler patents began appearing from 1937. At lower frequencies the beat frequency is too low. The requirement for narrow beams is another compelling reason for microwave, especially in airborne equipment. There are also lower limits on the wavelength which can be used. If the wavelength is of the same order as the size of water droplets in the atmosphere, the equipment is useless, and it is found that attenuation in heavy rain rises steeply when wavelength is reduced to 2 cm. In the region of 1 cm there are also problems with absorption by gaseous molecules. Early systems operated on 3 cm, which was later reduced to about 2.25 cm.

The application of these principles to air navigation is obvious. At modern aircraft speeds the Doppler shift of centimetric radiation is of the order of 10 kHz, which can be measured accurately. Doppler shift provides valuable information to the air navigator which could not, before INS, be provided satisfactorily by any other means. The aircraft compass and air-speed indicator show the motion of the aircraft relative to the air in which it flies. Its velocity vector relative to the earth is the resultant of this and the wind velocity. DR in the air relies on prediction of wind velocity or measurement of drift and ground speed.

From the beginning of air navigation there had been instruments for measurement of drift, usually consisting of a grid which was aligned with the apparent direction of features of the terrain.[14] Some of these had cross-wires, so that the ground speed could be estimated from the time taken for a feature to pass from one to the other. Such an estimation depended on the height above the terrain, which was not accurately known before the radio altimeter. Even the drift measurement was inaccurate unless the instrument was gyro-stabilized. The equipment was useless over cloud, calm sea, or unilluminated terrain.

An aircraft moving at velocity V relative to the terrain directs a beam at the ground in a direction making an angle θ with the the velocity vector V. The component of V in the direction of the beam is $V\cos\theta$, and the Doppler shift is $2V\cos\theta/\lambda$ regardless of the angle at which it intersects the terrain. Reflections of all beams making the same angle with the vector V have the same Doppler shift and describe the surface of a cone whose apex is the aircraft—a cone which intersects the terrain (if flat) in that conic section which Apollonius would have called 'falling beyond' (unless the aircraft is in steep dive). In Fig. 12.10 B is the point where the vertical beam strikes the terrain, and C the point where some oblique beam does so. The locus of BC is a hyperbola, of which the aircraft's track is the axis. Figure 12.11 shows such hyperbolae of constant Doppler shift. If θ is too close to 90° the Doppler shift is

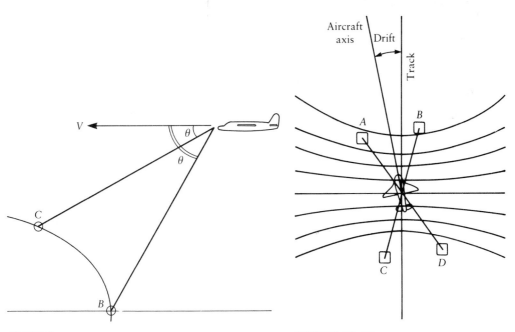

FIGURE 12.10
Locus of constant Doppler shift.

FIGURE 12.11
Hyperbolae of constant Doppler shift.

too low; but if the angle of incidence is too small, the reflection back to the aircraft is poor. Typically, beams are arranged to be at 60°–70° to the longitudinal axis of the aircraft.

Figure 12.11 also illustrates four beams symmetrically disposed about the axes of the aircraft. The Doppler shifts of A and B are different, as are those of C and D because of aircraft drift. The shifts of D and C are not the reverse of A and B because of the component of V in the direction of the aircraft's vertical axis. The components of V relative to the three axes of the aircraft are determinate given the Doppler shifts of A,B,C,D. This information, together with heading and pitch, provides track, ground speed, and vertical speed; the further input of true air speed enables wind speed and direction to be displayed.

Doppler DR navigators entered military service in 1953; the lifting of security classifications enabled public discussion from about 1958; and equipment was in airline service in 1960. The earliest equipment employed analogue computers, and displayed only drift and ground speed. Later models employed digital computers, solid-state microwave sources, and other solid-state circuits, reflecting the advancing technology of the period. The equipment first offered to airlines represented a key first step in the automation of over-ocean navigation. The pilot keyed at a checkpoint the required track and distance to go to the next checkpoint, and the equipment thereafter displayed (in addition to drift, ground speed, and wind velocity) distance off the required track and distance along it. This display was corrected at intervals by fixes, at that time usually derived from astronomical, Consol, and Loran A position lines —a cumbersome process, since the position lines still had to be plotted and translated manually into coordinates of along and across flight-planned track. Nevertheless, for the first time, the pilot had a continuous display of his position in relation to his flight-plan; the accuracy of DR was greatly enhanced as well as automated; and an adverse encounter with a jet stream was announced immediately, instead of remaining undiscovered until the next fix.

Doppler as described above suffers from two defects which are really irremediable, which is not to say that the most ingenious and strenuous efforts were not made to remedy them both. One is the sea return. A calm sea is a poor reflector *back to the aircraft*, which is, after all, contrary to the law that angles of incidence and reflection are equal and opposite. The Doppler result is also subject to the current, which, in the deep oceans, is rarely more than a knot or so. With strong winds the reflection problem is eased; but the reflecting water may itself be moving at speeds in excess of 6 kt.

The fundamental defect of Doppler as an automatic DR system is its reliance on the aircraft heading reference. Accuracy in drift measurement of 0.2° was claimed for the earliest commercial Dopplers; but there was little incentive to improve it because the accuracy of the magnetic heading reference was no better than 1°. The development of highly stable twin gyro systems was welcomed, and it was suggested hopefully in 1958 that accurate knowledge of ground speed and the miniaturization of precision gyros could overcome the long-standing objections to aircraft gyrocompasses (Chapter 9).

INS was of course a better way of applying the new technologies of gyros and solid-state digital computers. Within a decade of the introduction of Doppler by the airlines it was wiped out, as far as new aircraft were concerned, by INS; a striking example of the new competitiveness of navigation systems. At the time of writing, Doppler continues in service to meet specialized requirements, both military and civil; in obsolescent fleets; and in commercial applications for which INS is too expensive.

There is no comparable application of radio Doppler to the navigation of ships. Quite apart from difficulties due to the necessarily low angle of incidence and the low speeds involved, the information provided (were these difficulties surmountable) is the ship's velocity relative to the surface of whatever wave the beam happens to bounce off—something of no conceivable interest to the navigator.

There is another way: an illuminating example of how navigational science proliferates. Radio waves are heavily attenuated under water, and penetrate only a few metres; but sound waves propagate well,[15] and at a velocity only a millionth of that of light, so that manageable wavelengths may be used. Sonar Doppler, operating on the same basic principles as aircraft radio Doppler, can provide the same data if the water is shallow enough for the reception of good echoes from the bottom. VLCCs (very large cargo carriers), a quarter of a mile long and with hundreds of thousands of tons of inertia, presented the world with many original problems, not least the limitations of traditional human skills in judging speed, distance, and direction when berthing. The sonar Doppler docking aid illustrated in Fig. 12.12 showed the forward (or aft) speed of the ship together with the separate sideways velocity of the bow

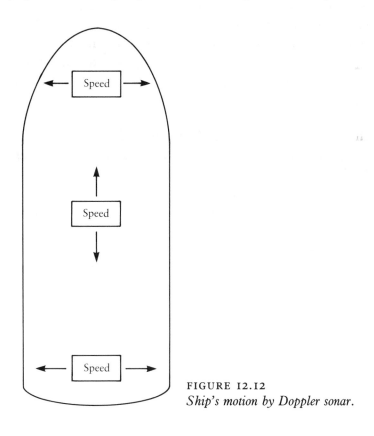

FIGURE 12.12
Ship's motion by Doppler sonar.

and stern digitally displayed in units of 0.01 kt, which is almost exactly one foot per minute. The turbulence of the water caused by propeller action in a confined space causes problems. Other berthing systems which were developed later include radio Doppler, differential GPS (see below), and electro-optical systems. Doppler logs are now widely fitted to ships.

In recent decades offshore oil operations have created a demand for the solution of the unique navigation problems of the submersibles associated with them. The inherent capability of Doppler to provide vertical as well as horizontal velocity has been particularly applicable to these problems.

On 4 October 1957 the USSR launched Sputnik I, the first man-made satellite. Within a few months scientists at John Hopkins University computed its orbit from its Doppler shift. The obvious implication was that, conversely, the measurement of the Doppler shift of a satellite of known orbit could be used to determine the position of the receiver. At the time the US Navy was seeking means to improve the capability of *Polaris* submarines to launch long-range missiles accurately in a hostile environment. Federal funding was granted to a project led by Richard Kershner of Johns Hopkins from which the US Navy navigational satellite system *Transit* evolved. Transit became fully operational in 1964, and was made available to the world at large in 1967.

The largest single uncertainty in any satellite fixing system is the speed of propagation through the atmosphere.[16] Following Newton's experiments with prisms it had been surmised by seventeenth-century adherents to wave theory that refraction was due to the slowing effect of the medium, and that it varies as the wavelength of the light; the relationship between refraction and speed of propagation was demonstrated in the nineteenth century (Chapter 4). Transit uses 400 MHz for the position-determining signal. The delay in the signal by refraction is deduced by measuring how much more a secondary signal at 150 MHz is delayed.

A unique feature of fixing by satellites is that they provide position in 3D with respect to the centre of gravity of the earth—a very different thing to latitude, longitude, and height above mean sea level. Scientific advances have an odd way of proposing answers to the questions they pose. It was only by analysis of satellite orbits and their precession that it was learned that mean sea level at the north pole is 30 m nearer the centre of the earth than at the south pole, were anyone to dig through the ice to find it.[17] Observation of satellite orbits and hence deductions as to the earth's gravitational field and shape have led to the greatest revolution in geodesy since Cassini. The accuracy is astonishing, considering the difficulties caused by refraction and extraneous factors affecting the orbit such as drag.

As was observed in an earlier chapter, there is no point in measuring with great precision the 3D position of an aircraft if it does not agree with the chart coordinates of the runway and its alleged height above mean sea level. The satellites themselves have resolved the problem they have raised: they have revolutionized surveying as well as geodesy. Fortunately surveyors can use satellites much more accurately than navigators—they may use repeated passes, and they do not require results in real time. They may use up-dated satellite position data determined after the event, and the differential techniques described in the context of Omega.

Of all the technological advances relevant to the development of navigation by satellite since the conception of Transit, the most remarkable has been in data processing, specifically in the form of the microprocessor. The first Transit receiver for Polaris submarines in 1962 filled three metres of large racks. The 1973 Magnavox commercial model weighed 190 kg; the corresponding 1976 model weighed 34 kg. At about that time the price for a commercial receiver was in the region of $80 000; within a few years $20 000 was the going rate for much improved equipment.[18] Algorithms of a complexity which would have been impractical when the Transit project was launched are now commonplace.

In principle at least, there are several ways by which data on the position and motion of the receiver can be obtained from artificial satellites which transmit or respond. Bearings are not practical; at the distances involved, an error of 0.001° would result in a position-line error of 1 km; results two or three orders better than that can be obtained by Doppler shift, range measurement, or the measurement of difference of range.

As communications satellites in geosynchronous orbit[19] became commonplace, an obvious candidate was a transponder in the Eureka tradition (Chapter 11) aboard such satellites to give ranges. The main sources of error are variations in the velocity of propagation, variations in the satellite's orbit, and delays at the satellite in amplifying the user's signal, changing its frequency, and transmitting it back. All these errors can be determined by analysis of the perceived range at five or more monitoring stations of precisely known position.[20] These data are transmitted back to the satellite so that it can describe the errors of its ways to users. Such a system has appropriately been described as a 'closed loop differential system'. A commercial venture, *Starfix*,[21] applied these principles to provide offshore oil surveyors in the Gulf of Mexico with location accurate to 5 metres on a 95 per cent probability basis. Such a system is useless in polar regions. Apart from requiring a truly global system, the military have long since learned the lesson of IFF and absolutely reject transmission by the user. Military systems must, like *Transit*, rely on satellite broadcasts.

The measurement of the difference of distance of two satellites gives a surface of position, a hyperboloid, described by the rotation of the hyperbola about the axis formed by the line joining the two satellites. A 3D fix is obtained at the point where three surfaces intersect. Fortunately modern microprocessors make light work of such matters. They, and atomic clocks of an accuracy unthinkable a few decades ago, also permit a different approach to what we may now call 'classical' hyperbolic navigation.

Suppose that when Dippy started thinking about Gee in 1937 there had been sufficiently accurate atomic clocks portable on aircraft to determine the actual time of arrival of a pulse, and the pulse was coded in some way to announce its precise time of transmission. The range is time-interval × speed of light, and only two ranges are required to fix. If the clock were not quite accurate enough, three ranges would give the traditional cocked hat. If there were no other errors the position would be the centre of the inscribed circle of the cocked hat, and clock error would be its radius/speed of light (see Fig. 12.13). Instead of the three Gee stations

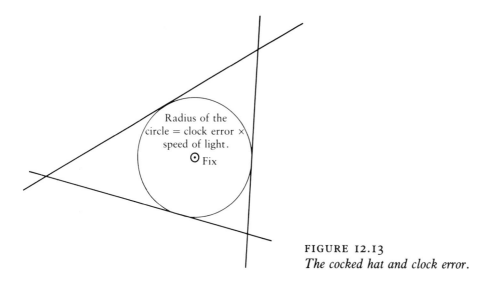

Radius of the circle = clock error × speed of light.

⊙ Fix

FIGURE 12.13
The cocked hat and clock error.

giving a fix by the intersection of two hyperbolae they would have given it as the centre of a cocked hat—and given the right time as a bonus. This is the way GPS works; but, to give position in 3D space, four satellites are necessary.

The *Navstar Global Positioning System*, widely known as GPS, was developed by the US Department of Defense to supersede Transit. To provide world-wide continuous coverage it employs 18 satellites plus spares symmetrically arranged in elliptical orbits. The satellite transmits to the user on 1575.42 MHz and 1227.6 MHz for navigation purposes and for ionospheric correction on the principles described in the context of Transit. The operational control system consists of five monitoring stations widely distributed around the world which track all satellites in view. The raw data acquired by the monitors is transmitted to a single master control station where the precise ephemerides of the satellite, its clock drift, and the propagation delay are calculated. These data are 'uploaded' to the satellite, and become part of its broadcast signal. The user's receiver generates its own identical signal controlled by its own atomic frequency standard. This signal is 'slewed' to synchronize with the received signal. The quantum of the slew determines the elapsed time of the signal and hence the 'pseudo range', that is to say the range subject to the errors of the user's atomic frequency standard. Four pseudo ranges, together with the information transmitted by the satellite enable the user's data processor to calculate position and velocity in 3D. The form of the broadcast signal employs advanced information theory to make interference with the signal 'impossible', although of course it can be jammed. The histories of cryptography and radio counter-measures both illustrate that, in this context, 'impossible' is a word to be used with caution.

The sensational consequences of GPS are due not only to the high precision and integrity of its world-wide coverage, but also to the low cost of the user's equipment, which has made GPS available to all. In 1991 single-seater aircraft spraying locusts in the Sahara desert were routinely fixing position with an accuracy of 30 metres. A small affordable box also provided track guidance and way-point facilities. Employing techniques (mentioned briefly above) not available to 'real-time' navigators, the relative positioning by GPS of points on the earth hundreds of kilometres apart with an accuracy of the order of millimetres has been reported.[22] This unique and curious moment is savoured in Chapter 16.

Notes to Chapter 12

1. The writer has relied heavily on Powell (1972, 1981, 1986) for the whole of the early history of hyperbolic navigation.

2. R. A. Fessenden took out a patent along these lines in 1904 involving an 'amplitude standard' aboard the vessel.

3. One of the problems of navigation of submerged submarines is the heavy attenuation of signals at radio frequencies under water; the lower the frequency, the less the attenuation. It was found that VLF signals could be received thousands of miles away at periscope depth. This fact was a major incentive to Omega development. Modern submarines have VLF communication and Omega antennae on the conning tower.

4. The Decca Navigator Company later proposed *Dectra*, and built a transatlantic chain employing the sites of two Decca stations of the Newfoundland chain and one of the North British chain. From 1957 there were extensive trials by shipping companies, airlines, and the military. Its superiority over other transatlantic fixing systems then in use was demonstrated, but the system was not adopted. The idea that the system could be the basis of ATC employing automatic data links was very advanced at the time.

5. By this date the development of stable oscillators had eliminated the need to synchronize transmissions continuously by having the master trigger the slave.

6. Barr and Young (1989) describe particularly large errors over Antarctica.

7. In 1940 this was a matter of necessity. If RAF Bomber Command had indulged in extended flights on a large scale over the German heartland in daylight it would have been quickly eliminated.

8. The unpublished précis of a lecture given by the Director of Navigation at the Air Ministry, Group Captain F. C. Richardson, to the RAF Staff College in 1946 gives the following percentages of occasions on which bombs dropped by the RAF on Germany were delivered within 5 miles of assigned target:

Before Gee		5%
June 1942.	Gee standard	35%
Dec. 1942	Gee jammed	25%
June 1943	Pathfinders, H₂S, and Oboe	49%
Aug. 1943	Improved techniques	55%
Apr. 1944	,, ,,	62%
Oct. 1944	Weakened German defence	82%
1945	,, ,, ,,	90%

9. Believed to be an acronym for *Long-Range Aid to Navigation*. Loran was the result of the third priority agreed for the Radiation Laboratory in October 1940 (see Chapter 11).

10. R. A. Smith (1947).

11. This proviso, which is inconsequential at Gee frequencies, invalidates the use of pulse techniques at the very low frequency of Omega, where the period of a single cycle is nearly 100 microseconds.

12. A year later Fizeau published the first reliable measurement of the speed of light by a terrestrial method, which Maxwell adduced as powerful evidence of his theory of electromagnetic radiation (Chapter 4).

13. When the effect of relativity is included the received frequency is $f\left[(1 + v/c)/(1 - v/c)\right]^{1/2}$. Even at the speed of space vehicles the difference is small.

14. One of these was invented by Gago Coutinho, the navigator of the first flight across the equatorial Atlantic in 1922. He used it with dramatic success on that extraordinary feat, which involved a rendezvous for refuelling with a sloop at St Paul's Rocks (200 m across and low-lying) after 11 hours of flight over the ocean without radio.

15. It has been well known since the early eighteenth century that water conducts sound better than air; and attempts to apply underwater acoustics to the benefit of shipping have a long history. Echo-sounding experiments go back at least to 1838, and hydrophones to detect the presence of other vessels to 1889 (Hackman 1984). Sonar gear for the detection and location of enemy submarines was extremely important in both World Wars, and presumably remains so.

16. One of the difficulties at Hopkins in computing the Sputnik I orbit was that the satellite transmitted on 20 MHz, where refraction delays were an order higher, and the means of evaluating them relatively crude by later standards.

17. King-Hele (1964).

18. Lewellen (1984).

19. A geosynchronous orbit is a circular one in the equatorial plane at such a speed that the satellite completes its orbit relative to the stars in one sidereal day. The satellite therefore appears to an observer on the rotating earth to be in a constant direction, to which the 'dishes' of satellite television viewers can be pointed.

20. Blanchard (1989) gives a straightforward derivation.

21. The Starfix division of John Chance Inc.

22. Ashkenazi and Cleasby (1991).

CHAPTER THIRTEEN

The Path of Minimum Time

✠

A COMMON object of navigation is to follow the route of least time, fuel, or cost, having regard to all the circumstances, such as winds, tides, shoals, icebergs, pirates, and so on. In modern times this is within the domain of the *Calculus of variations*, which is concerned with the identification of that curve of some class of curves at which some specified variable is a maximum or minimum. It is a calculus which becomes difficult very quickly. We intuitively perceive that the shortest distance between any two points in unconfined space is a straight line. If we are confined to the surface of a sphere it is not obvious, but it is easy to show, that the shortest distance between any two points is a great circle. If the surface is that of a spheroid, quite difficult mathematics is needed to find the geodetic, and its shape can be surprising. The nub of the matter is that in the differential calculus the function is given, but in the calculus of variations it has to be found.

One classical problem in this calculus is the determination of the shape of a rigid wire between two specified points along which a weight suspended on a frictionless pulley, as in Fig. 13.1, will descend from one point to another in the least time. If the wire is straight, the distance is a minimum; but if the wire is bent downwards a little to increase the acceleration at the beginning of the run, getting off to good start will make up for the extra distance. Finding the time taken on any curve of a given equation is a straightforward exercise in integral calculus; but which is the shortest? The question attracted so much interest that the impressive name of 'brachistochrone' was given to the curve of least time. Jean Bernoulli posed the problem in 1696. It is said that Newton received notice of it in the afternoon, and proved that the brachistochrone is a segment of a cycloid before going to bed. The minimum time-path of sailing ships and aircraft has features in common with the brachistochrone problem; but getting off to a good start is not necessarily one of them.

The navigation problem was not perceived in such terms until the nineteenth century, and at one time the calculus of variations was quite irrelevant. Until recent centuries few ships

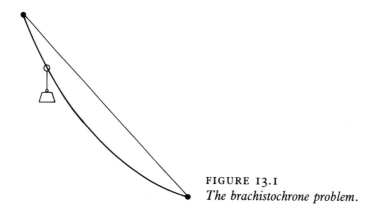

FIGURE 13.1
The brachistochrone problem.

could sail within 90° of the wind. The medieval problem was to get to the destination at all under sail. The alternative was to row; but the human body is an inefficient propulsion engine even under the discipline of the whip. Man-powered galleys dominated some naval battles from Mycenaean times until the battle of Lepanto in 1571; yet, even when there was an unlimited supply of slave labour,[1] the size of the human engine, its maintenance, and its high specific fuel consumption, precluded long-range operations. Before steam, sail was the only way.

From the earliest times one sailed with the wind and tide, employing local weather and sea lore. One waited for favourable conditions and anchored or stayed under nearly bare poles when conditions were not favourable. In coastal waters one took advantage of the semi-diurnal variation of tidal streams and land or sea breezes. One progressed as one could: a plot of most voyages would have looked liked the walk of a very drunken sailor. Long oceanic voyages in regular commerce only became possible when seamen learned enough climatology to take advantage of seasonal and spatial variations in the general wind circulation. The most famous application of this technique is the first voyage of Columbus, when he sailed down to the Canaries to cross the Atlantic with the north-east trade winds behind him, and returned with the westerlies prevailing in higher latitudes. Presumably Columbus took advantage of whatever Portuguese lore he could glean (they were naturally very secretive about it); but in this matter the Europeans were centuries behind the Arabs and the Chinese.

The route from the Persian Gulf to China may have been trafficked as early as the eighth century; but such voyages must have been exploratory, for a tenth-century Arab writer notes with awe that in his own times a certain captain had successfully completed seven voyages. The voyage of 5000 n.m. crossed the Indian Ocean from the Straits of Hormuz to Malabar (900 n.m., largely out of sight of land), down to Ceylon, across to Sumatra, through the Malacca Straits and up to Canton (see Fig. 13.2). The route was developed before the compass, for it is recorded[2] in the tenth century that the pilots had a large number of books, and acted on the directions therein. Severin writes[3]

> *Where we speak of the north-east or south-west monsoon and think in terms of broad*
> *seasons of the year, the Arab navigators wrote of a complex range of particular mawsim*

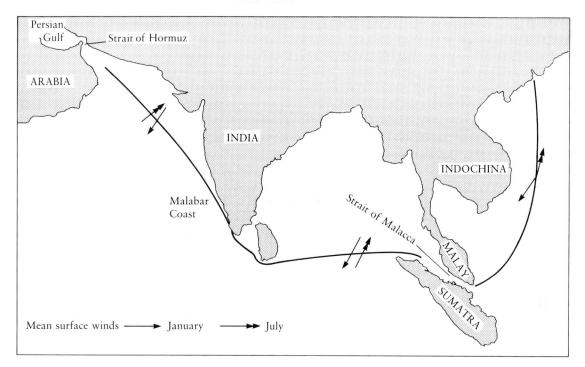

FIGURE 13.2
The Arabia–China trading route.

> *denoting specific places and dates in the calendar year, and generally meaning the day*
> *you left a particular port to head in a certain direction.*

It was both the wind required to reach destination, and the date on which it was to be expected.

Severin, who sailed an Arabian *boom* from Oman to Canton with an Arabian crew in emulation of the legendary Sindbad, writes of his best (Omani) helmsman[3]

> *. . . he knew his major stars, and could tell the coming of a squall. If I make him*
> *sound a bit like Chaucer's sea captain, it is because perhaps he was. Yet when it*
> *came to sailing a course, though there was a compass, he rarely looked at it and indeed*
> *did not position himself where he could read the card. He always sailed the vessel as*
> *well as she would go in the general direction required. When questioned about this he*
> *replied that, on a long passage, the wind might change for better or worse, and that what*
> *mattered was that Sohar sailed comfortably, whenever possible.*

That must have been the way it was. There is a season for everything. Time is *not* of the essence. Avoidable wear and tear is foolish. Why worry about the track made good today when we do not know what track we may sail tomorrow? Why hasten to make port when we may well be blown out to sea again or, reaching the coast prematurely, be shipwrecked?[4] Everything in its time and season.

As the Portuguese explored the East Atlantic they in their turn learned to use prevalent winds and currents. It seems that by 1430 they had learned to return from Africa by taking a long board into the Atlantic, having the north–east trades on the beam and expecting the westerlies of higher latitudes to bring them home. There was a conscious effort to learn and understand. As early as 1416 Gonçalo Cabral was sent by Prince Henry the Navigator to study the strong currents between the Canary Islands—a venture which has been claimed to be the first scientific expedition of its kind. By the end of the fifteenth century the Portuguese were familiar with the winds and currents in the equatorial region of the Gulf of Guinea, and knew of the symmetry of Atlantic winds on either side of the equatorial zone. Oceanic 'rutters' appeared describing optimum routeing in relation to prevailing winds and currents. The traditional coastal rutters (which go back to the *Compasso da navegare* described in Chapter 1) were extended to include the latitude and magnetic variation of places. These were valuable secrets; and, at the same time, the Portuguese caravel, with its triangular lateen sails for beam winds and square sails for a following wind, and its broad payload-carrying beam, was becoming a more efficient vehicle than earlier vessels. To protect their navigational secrets the Portuguese resorted to what one writer[5] has described as 'all sorts of trumpery' to give the impression that their success was due to their caravels' being able to sail close-hauled against foul currents in a way they in fact could not.

The Portuguese and, after Columbus, the Spaniards, perforce navigated the Atlantic much as the Arabs had long navigated the Indian Ocean; but, in the spirit of Renaissance culture, Europeans were obsessed with knowing where they were. A constant theme of passengers writing about their navigators, throughout the centuries of the Great Pursuit of the Longitude, was the way navigators asserted their position with confidence, argued among themselves about it, and were invariably wrong. A Spanish gentleman who was one of the first tourists to visit the New World marvelled at the dull wits and clumsy hands of navigators in general. Thomas Gage, who had the interesting experience of sailing with the Spanish Indies Fleet of 1625, wrote[6]

> The Captain of our Fleet, wondering much at our slow sailing . . . called to council all the pilots of the ships, to know their opinions concerning our present being, and the nearness of land . . . Here was cause of laughter enough for the passengers to hear the wise pilots' skill; one saying we were three hundred miles, another two hundred, another one hundred, another fifty, another more, another less. . . .

Samuel Pepys, who became Secretary to the Admiralty in 1673, had earlier confided to his diary after a sea voyage that naval officers would be better employed, after making landfall, discovering why they had been wrong rather than arguing who was right.

The North Atlantic was to become the most trafficked ocean on earth. Its circulation is dominated by the Gulf Stream. The clockwise flow, about 50 miles wide and 3000 feet deep, is the largest current in the world after the Antarctic circumpolar current. Its existence was surmised in the early years of exploration of the New World. In 1513 Juan Ponce de Léon, steering south with a following wind off the east coast of Florida, could see that, with respect to landmarks, he was making no headway. Two of his ships were in water shallow enough to anchor; but the current broke the ropes. Ponce de Léon only detected the current because he could see the shore. A fundamental difference in the development of knowledge of the circulation of the atmosphere and the ocean is that whereas the surface wind is immediately perceptible, and upper winds may be estimated by the motion of clouds, there was no direct means of measuring the speed (relative to the earth) of the surface of deep waters until recent decades. It is therefore not surprising that, although traffic between England and its American colonies increased steadily from the early seventeenth century, a chart of the meandering of the Gulf Stream in the North Atlantic did not appear until 1770. Whalers of the English colonies in North America seem to have been the first to understand something of the Gulf Stream in northern waters. The whales keep outside the Gulf Stream, because it is relatively empty of marine life.

Timothy Folger, a whaler captain, is believed to have been the first to chart the stream in northern waters. At the time Benjamin Franklin, in his capacity of postmaster-general of the American colonies, investigating complaints about late delivery of mail from England, found that the post-carrying packets from Falmouth took up to two weeks longer than the merchantmen from London, who should have had a longer passage. The merchantmen had learned from the whalers; the packets had not. Folger told Franklin:

'We have informed them that they were stemming a current that was against them to the value of three miles an hour and advised them to cross it but they were too wise to be counselled by simple fishermen.'

To a man of Franklin's proclivities, this was fascinating. With Folger's guidance he produced for the General Post Office in London the famous chart of the Gulf Stream, adorned by a cachet showing a colloquy between himself and Neptune. Franklin gave some indication of temperatures to be expected, and advised using a thermometer to keep in the warm water eastbound and the cold water westbound. The map, which is illustrated in Fig. 13.3, shows the stream following the coast of North America quite closely from Florida to Nova Scotia, and then veering to the east. The speed is shown as declining from 4 kt off South Carolina to 2 kt at about 40°N 50°W. East of that position the map was quite wrong, and his influential opinion that the circulation was due to the trade winds was untenable. (These were not the reasons for his dismissal by the GPO in 1774, two years before Franklin signed the Declaration of Independence.) In 1969 the mesoscaph *Ben Franklin* drifted with the stream in 31 days, at an average depth of 650 feet, from a point off West Palm Beach to a point 1400 miles away, about 400 miles east of Cape Cod. It is now known that the circulation of the Gulf Stream is complex and variable.

When Franklin was still the colonial postmaster, Constantine John Phipps was making soundings of the North–east Atlantic below 4 000 feet; but the rise of oceanography is really a nineteenth-century event: the word *oceanography* only came into use in 1883. In those voyages of exploration of the sea itself, vessels of the Royal Navy such as *Beagle*, *Erebus*, *Lightning*, *Porcupine*, and, most of all, *Challenger* played leading roles. The interests of the naturalists who accompanied them was catholic; for many, marine biology was of primary

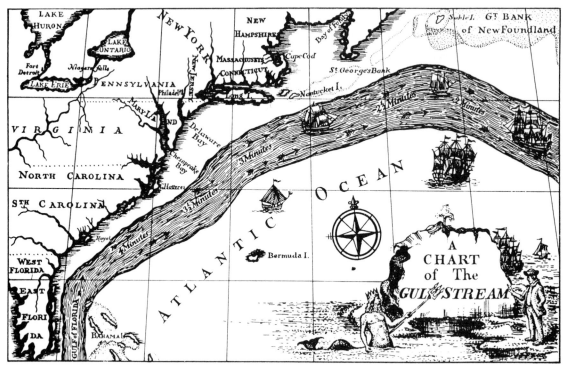

FIGURE 13.3
Franklin's map of the Gulf Stream.

interest, but they also sounded the depths and measured temperatures at different levels. Some were misled because the effect of high pressure on the thermometer was not at first understood. François Peron returned from a voyage around the world in 1803 convinced that temperature decreased indefinitely with depth, and therefore that at a sufficient depth the sea-bed was covered by ice. James Clark Ross, aboard HMS *Erebus* in 1839, reached the conclusion that the temperature of deep water was 4°C (39°F) at all latitudes. This remained a popular belief until it was found aboard HMS *Lightning* in 1868 that at 61°N 5°W the temperature at 510 fathoms was 33°F, whereas at 60°N 7°W the temperature was 47°F at 530 fathoms, naturally with quite different marine life. Some measure of the prolixity and industry of Victorian marine naturalists is suggested by the 29 500 pages of the report by the six scientists on the HMS *Challenger* voyage of 1872–6.

Alexander von Humboldt had earlier suggested that the general circulation of the oceans is sustained by differences in density caused by temperature (and salinity) variations. So it is, but nineteenth-century oceanographers did not realize that the key is the Coriolis or geostrophic acceleration described by Gustave de Coriolis in 1835, and discussed in Chapter 8 in the context of tides. All long-term, long-distance ocean currents of depth represent the dynamic equilibrium between the Coriolis acceleration and the horizontal density gradient.

The Coriolis acceleration is zero at the equator, and there are two distinct hemispherical circulations. In fact there is very little movement of water between the two hemispheres. The late development of this approach to the subject is suggested by the fact that it was only in the mid-twentieth century that H. Stommel explained the westward intensification of current in the northern parts of both the Atlantic and Pacific Oceans in terms of the variation of the Coriolis effect with latitude, and that G. Neumann showed that the lack of such intensification in the South Atlantic is related to the broad equality between the change of depth of the current system with latitude and the change in the value of the Coriolis effect with latitude.

There are two obvious reasons for this late development: one was the difficulty of accumulating data even on surface currents in deep water; the other is the complexity of the process itself. There is the influence, especially in the surface currents which concern the sailor, of winds and tides. There is viscosity and friction. There is the effect of the efflux of the fresh water of the great rivers and the melting ice-caps. There are the varying depths of the sea. Above all, the world ocean which covers most of this planet's surface is swirling about in a fantastically configured bowl which rotates once a day.

The dynamics of the atmosphere, if not more simple, are certainly more clear. Viscosity is several orders less, and air flows freely over the broad oceans. Even over great mountain ranges it is not constrained to a tortuously shaped basin. When a horizontal pressure gradient develops in the atmosphere, air tends to be sucked towards the lower pressure. Its motion is deflected by the Coriolis force until the unaccelerated stable condition illustrated in Fig. 13.4 is attained. The air is moving at right angles to the pressure gradient at a speed given by $p'/2\rho\omega\sin\phi$, where p' is the pressure gradient, ω the earth's angular velocity, ρ the air density, and ϕ the latitude. This is called the *gradient wind*. If the isobars do not follow a great circle, centripetal forces enter the equation, causing the cyclostrophic effect illustrated in Fig. 13.5, which has the effect of reducing the speed for dynamic balance in a cyclonic distribution, and increasing it in an anticyclonic one. These are the conditions for dynamic equilibrium in a static pressure distribution. The term *geostrophic wind* has been used both as a synonym for gradient wind and to describe the dynamic equilibrium wind, including the cyclostrophic effect.

In the real atmosphere, pressure distribution is usually changing, with the consequence

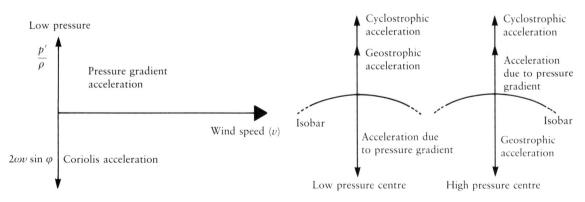

FIGURE 13.4
The gradient wind in the northern hemisphere.

FIGURE 13.5
Cyclostrophic effect on wind.

that winds tend to flow across the isobars in the direction of deepening low pressure. Near the surface the kinetic energy of the wind is dissipated in turbulence and eddies. The retarding effect of surface friction may be represented by an acceleration vector opposed to the wind. A balance between pressure gradient, friction, and Coriolis effect is illustrated in Fig. 13.6. The effect of surface friction is to reduce the speed of the wind and turn it towards the low. If the wind does no work, it follows the isobars; if work is done against friction it must be supplied by air moving down the pressure gradient. So closely does the wind follow these simple principles in temperate latitudes that in modern times, before computers took over, the contours of surfaces of constant pressure in the atmosphere were first forecast, and the forecast upper winds then deduced from them by simple rules.

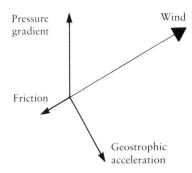

FIGURE 13.6
Friction effect on wind near the surface.

All this should have been perfectly clear to Gustave de Coriolis in 1835, yet more than twenty years later, when C. H. D. Buys Ballot, director of the Royal Netherlands Meteorological Institute, enunciated the law named after him (if one stands in the northern hemisphere with one's back to the wind, the low is to one's left and the high to one's right; and vice versa in the southern hemisphere), Buys Ballot could not say why it was so. In the nineteenth century, developments in theoretical meteorology and in the science of the dynamics of the ocean had little influence on navigation, excepting always the great achievements of the century in the field of tidal prediction (Chapter 8). The proliferation of marine naturalists found its reward in other fields, notably biology.[7] It was data collected by the navigators themselves which led to the more refined use of climatological and ocean-current data in the nineteenth century to achieve better routeing. The optimum routeing of sailing ships was the first systematic application to navigation of the statistical method which has since proved so powerful a tool in many aspects of navigation.

The dominating figure was Matthew Maury. As a young officer in the US Navy he studied winds and currents with optimum routeing in mind. He was lamed in an accident, and appointed to the Depot of Charts and Instruments[8] in 1841. In that office he issued specially designed log-books to ships' captains to systematize data collection. A prodigious worker and a prolific writer, he collated hundreds of thousands of observations to produce recommended routeings according to the season. His first wind and current charts of the North Atlantic appeared in 1847. An estimate was made in 1854 that Maury's sailing directions saved 30 days on the passage from England to California. It is claimed that the first ship to follow

Maury's routeing on the New York–Rio de Janeiro run completed the return trip in half its usual time. One modern writer suggested that Maury's work was worth $40 million a year in saving of ships' time towards the end of the century; others might demur, but none would deny that his work was epochal.

Maury's best work was done during a period in which ships were becoming significantly faster, so that a simple before-and-after comparison would be invalid. The development of the *clippers*, mainly in the US from about 1830 to 1860, was helped when the British Navigation Acts were repealed in 1849, opening the British tea trade to all comers. The tea clippers in particular became highly competitive. In one race from China to London via the Cape of Good Hope, after three months at sea on independent tracks, the two leading contenders were first sighted coming up the English Channel barely a couple of miles apart. Astonishing records were made by those splendid if unscientific practitioners of the minimum time-path. Liverpool–New York (with the prevailing westerlies and the Gulf Stream going the wrong way) in 15 days, New York–Valparaiso in 59 days, Shanghai–London in 91 days.

Maury is important in another way. He was influential at the Brussels conference of 1853 at which the leading maritime nations agreed to a co-operative system of world-wide meteorological observation and reporting—itself a historical achievement. Like Franklin a century before him, Maury was caught in a war of secession—whether it is a civil war or a war of independence depends on who wins. Maury, a native of Virginia, unlike Franklin chose the losing side. After living in Mexico and England (where he had always been greatly admired) he returned home to Virginia in his old age, despite the Yankees, as Professor of Meteorology.

Although Maury was the dominating figure in this field he was by no means alone. The British Meteorological Office by 1872 had produced charts for each month covering large parts of the ocean divided in 'squares', showing prevailing winds by month and some information on prevailing currents. The importance then attached to the collection of climatological data is suggested by the *Report* of the Meteorological Committee for that year laid before both Houses of Parliament. It listed by name the ships and their captains who fully co-operated in an extended form of reporting to the satisfaction of the committee. From a navigator's point of view, the collection and collation of climatological data was much more valuable than the development of a theory of meteorology. Before radio there was no way of advising a ship at sea of either forecasts or 'actuals'. The optimum route could only be sought on the basis of collated statistical data and what the navigator could see with his own eyes.

Sir Francis Galton is chiefly remembered today as an anthropometrist and eugenicist. He also made important contributions to statistics (he invented the correlational calculus), and to meteorology in the study of anticyclones, a word he invented.[9] In navigation he was the first to address the construction of the minimum-time path (MTP), on which he first communicated some ideas to the British Association in 1866. He developed them further during the next few years, and submitted a memoir to the Meteorological Committee in 1872. The Committee, of which he was a member, did not trouble to mention it in the *Report to Parliament* mentioned above.

One problem is to know the motion of a ship *through the water*, given the speed and direction of the wind relative to the ship's head. Galton knew perfectly that this depends on the build of the ship, the load, and the rig she carries. For the purpose of his memoir, after taking the advice of unnamed naval authorities, he assumed the performance of the imaginary 'Beaufort' ship, which he showed in his Table 1, transcribed here as Table 13.1. The first column showing corresponding wind speeds has been added by the present author. The original only showed the Beaufort Scale[10] of the wind, which was the scale in which all the wind reports were made. The table is intrinsically interesting as a contemporary assessment of the performance of large sailing ships when they reached their acme.

Wind speed (mph)	Wind force, Beaufort Scale	Speed of a Beaufort ship in mph				
		Points off the wind				
		0	4	8	12	16
17–21	5	2.6	3.7	9.6	10.8	8.4
12–16	4	1.6	2.2	5.8	6.6	5.2
8–11	3	1.0	1.4	3.7	4.2	3.3
4–7	2	0.4	0.6	1.6	1.8	1.4
2–3	1	0.2	0.3	0.5	0.6	0.5

Table 13.1. Part of Galton's Table 1

From the centre of each 2° 'square' Galton laid off the average current vector for eight hours. From the point so found he laid off the progress the ship would make in eight hours through the water on each of the eight points of his Table 1 on the basis of the prevailing wind for the square. The envelope of these eight points, representing the distance the ship would sail in eight hours in any direction, he called the 'isodic' curve. Its radius in any direction is the 'isod'. For any given track he interpolated between isodic curves of adjacent 'squares' by the method illustrated in Fig. 13.7. Cc is the progress a Beaufort ship will make on the track XY with an average wind. Galton thought that the current vector could be printed on the charts for all ships, and the isodic curves drawn for each 'square' for any desired type of vessel. Well and good, but what does the navigator do when the wind he experiences is at marked variance to the wind on which the isodic curve is based; and which is the MTP anyway? Galton had a partial answer to both questions which only provokes others. He wrote:

> *Another application of the principle of isods is to draw curves having ports for their points of convergence. Then the captain of a vessel, making for any of these ports, having such and such a wind, and making such and such a forecast of coming weather, may be enabled to decide what course to shape, that when the time during which he relies on his own prediction of the weather shall have passed by, he may be within as few isodic intervals as possible of the port he is seeking.*

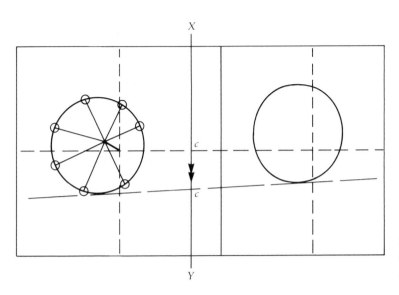

FIGURE 13.7
Galton's construction of an isodic curve and interpolation method.

As steam prevailed, such interest as there was in Galton's isods declined, but was revived after some decades by lighter-than-air dirigibles. It is sad that they appropriated the term *airship*, which would have described perfectly the modern airliner. As the speed of the wind could exceed the air speed of airships they could find themselves in the predicament of Ponce de Léon in the Gulf Stream. The airship R 34, which was the first aircraft to cross the Atlantic westbound (in July 1919) took 108.2 hours from East Fortune near Edinburgh to Mineola near New York City, equivalent to an effective ground speed on the great circle of 26 kt. In 1919 there was the organization and the means of communication to plot synoptic charts, and a meteorology sufficient to use isobaric charts and deduce the geostrophic winds over Europe from them; but the data available over the Atlantic were too scant for effective wind forecasting. The seven officers of the operating crew of the R 34 on its epochal flight included a meteorologist, and a subsequent paper[11] by its commander, Major G. H. Scott, shows his awareness of the problem.

The nature of the MTP of an aircraft is simpler than that of a sailing ship. The isod is simply the resultant of two vectors, the air speed/heading and the wind velocity. The isodic curve is found by laying off from the source the wind vector and, from its extremity, drawing a circle of radius the airspeed as in Fig. 13.8. There is an analogy between the MTP of an aircraft and the path of light through a medium of varying refractive index which had first been considered in the seventeenth century. Ph. Frank may have been the first to notice the analogy in 1918; but M. A. Giblett in 1924 was the first to develop it.[12]

Giblett used a construction which goes back to Huygens and the early wave theory of light. In Fig. 13.9, A is the departure point. The isodic curve, which we must now learn to call the first *time-front* or *isochrone*, is drawn as in Fig. 13.8. From the points on it, B,C,D,E, which are in the general direction of desired progress, the winds for the next hour appropriate to each zone are laid off, BP,CQ,DR,ES. Centre P,Q,R,S, arcs of radius = air speed are drawn. The envelope FGHK is the time-front for the second hour. Time-fronts for suc-

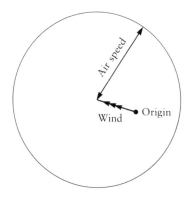
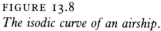

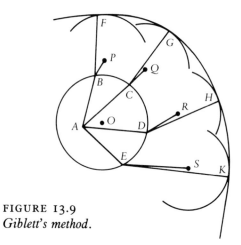

FIGURE 13.8
The isodic curve of an airship.

FIGURE 13.9
Giblett's method.

ceeding hours are similarly drawn in the general direction of the destination until it is encompassed. The tracks ABF, ACG, ADH, AEK, are necessarily MTPs to somewhere and the MTP to destination is sketched in by visual inspection. Since, by construction, the heading on an MTP is always perpendicular to the time-front, the complete flight-plan— time, ground speed, tracks, required heading—can be read directly.

Giblett illustrated his theme with isobaric charts of northern Europe from which he deduced the geostrophic winds. One example, perhaps unwittingly, illustrates the hopelessness of airship scheduling; from a point in Norfolk equidistant from Edinburgh and Paris, MTP flight time to Edinburgh is four hours, but to Paris ten hours. Another example illustrates the curvature of the MTP over even short distances. The MTP from Biarritz to Hamburg starts due north, passes over London in a north-easterly direction, and rotates overall, relative to local north, about 80°. Giblett's demonstrations were on isobaric charts of northern Europe where meteorological reporting was relatively dense and communications relatively good; but the great advantage of the MTP was on long flights, and some of those monsters could stay in the air for a week. Over the world as a whole, and especially over the oceans where data were most needed, they were in scant supply. In 1929 a joint study by the British Meteorological Office and the RAF showed the enormous time-savings which might be possible. In one example based on a reconstructed 'actual' isobaric chart, the MTP offered a 40 per cent time-reduction compared with the great circle from Bedfordshire to New Jersey; but there were, at the time, insufficient reports from the Atlantic to forecast the MTP with confidence. Discussion was reduced to silence by the airship disasters of the 1930s, from which the vehicle never recovered.[13]

At about the time of the *Hindenburg* disaster (which effectively terminated the use of the airship as a passenger-carrying vehicle), Ernest Zermelo, a mathematician who had distinguished himself for many years in set theory, glanced at the MTP problem and in 1939 published a note cryptically entitled 'Über die Navigation in der Luft'. He gave an elegant expression for the MTP which effectively states that at any point on an MTP the rate of change of heading equals the rate of change of tailwind component with distance in the direction of the time-front[14] (i.e. at right angles to the heading). People's minds were turning to other things at that date.

Shortly after the subsequent World War, interest focused on the MTP of *aeroplanes* flying the North Atlantic in rapidly growing numbers. There was far more information on wind and pressure distribution than there had been before the war, notably from Ocean Weather Ships which, by international agreement, were stationed at meteorologically strategic locations in the ocean. There was also a much expanded reporting net, including stations in Newfoundland, Greenland, and Iceland; there were reports from ships and the aircraft themselves. It became possible to forecast upper winds over the area 12 hours in advance with some confidence.

Another factor was the radar altimeter. As aircraft maintain flight level by reference to a pressure altimeter, an aircraft in level flight is really flying on a surface of constant pressure. The radar altimeter was used over the sea in two ways: by comparing actual and forecast height of the pressure level (and temperature), the upper air forecast could be monitored and modified; and by determining the slope of the surface of constant pressure in the direction of flight, the cross-component of the gradient wind could be calculated.[15]

In an important review[16] of the state of the art in 1949, J. S. Sawyer showed that in December 1946 the average flight-time of a 200 kt aircraft flying from London to New York at the 500 mb level would have been 20 hr 20 min. on the great circle and 17 hr 48 min. on the MTP. Few aircraft of the period had that endurance; but all had a wide choice of refuelling points in Eire, the Azores, Iceland, Newfoundland, and Labrador. He also showed that the MTP is the average drift path (that on which the heading but not the track follows a great circle) when wind varies along track but not at right angles to it. Sawyer thought Giblett's construction of the MTP was too time-consuming, and proposed a method of his own based on Zermelo's equation, as did others.

The transparent template illustrated in Fig. 13.10 was popular in the airlines at that time. The upper air forecast consisted of charts each showing the predicted contours of a particular pressure level. At any latitude the slope of the surface varies as the gradient wind.[15] The parallel lines X, Y on the template are spaced so that when they are laid parallel to the contours on the forecast chart the gradient wind in knots is one-tenth of the difference in height between them in feet. By elementary geometry, if the lines are laid parallel to the track instead of to the contours, the headwind component is read instead of the wind itself.

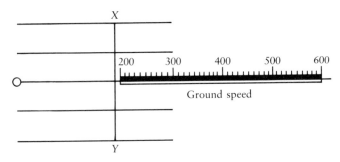

FIGURE 13.10
A wind template for flight planning.

Applying the component to the planned air speed to obtain the ground speed, hourly progress along any track can quickly be marked off through the slit with a distance scale shown in the figure. This device enabled a heuristic approach which worked very well. In a few minutes a practised navigator could compare flight-times on several tracks which his experience suggested might be close to the optimum, considering also the risk of icing or turbulence, the proximity of on-route alternates, etc. As in all MTP work, it is important not to define precisely an MTP (which is hypothetical because of forecasting error), but to follow a path on which the forecast time does not substantially exceed that on the forecast MTP, and on which the navigator will not be embarrassed if the forecast is all wrong.

In 1953 H. M. De Long and F. C. Bik of KLM showed that Giblett's construction need not be time-consuming. They produced an ingenious drawing instrument which enabled time-fronts and MTPs to be drawn quickly on the upper air forecast chart. They were usually drawn on two forecast charts at different flight-levels, assisting selection of optimum flight-level. The method suffers from the defect of all solutions to a problem which are valid only if all the assumptions prove to be correct, and which give no weight to the probable error of the assumptions. The KLM method showed the forecast MTP, but gave no indication of its merit. For example, it would be silly to fly 200 extra miles for a *predicted* time-saving of five minutes—less than the probable error of the forecast. The heuristic methodology described in the preceding paragraph was more consistent with sound tradition.

Navigation of aircraft has always been a 3D matter, and the effect of vertical wind shear on optimum altitude was always considered; but it was not the major consideration in the piston-engined era. Before pressurization, carriage of passengers above 10 000 feet had to be avoided. The minimization of turbulence and icing was imperative. Each succeeding generation of pressurized airliner was marketed on its 'above the weather' capability. One could hardly fly in the 'soup' to minimize headwind. The last piston-engined generation, flying in the region of 20 000 feet or slightly higher, encountered some of the effects of the jet stream; but it was the Comet 1, cruising in the region of 35 000 feet, which discovered that winds of 200 kt are not rare at that altitude. This discovery might have been anticipated on theoretical grounds. The rate of change of pressure with height at any level varies directly as air density. It follows that if two columns of air in proximity have quite different temperatures up to the tropopause, and pressure at the surface is broadly similar, there must be a huge horizontal pressure gradient just below the tropopause. Figure 13.11 is a typical vertical cross-section through the jet stream, which can encircle the globe at temperate latitudes.

The Britannia 310, a long range turboprop, focused attention on 3D navigation. Optimum techniques are most rewarding, as they were in the days of airships, when air speed is low in relation to the speed of the wind and its shear in horizontal and vertical planes, and the sector is long. The Britannia flew at jet-stream altitudes at about 300 kt, only two-thirds of the speed of the jets which replaced it, on the London–New York route, with marginal range capability in the headwind case. In broad terms, such an aircraft[17] flies further per unit fuel near its ceiling with zero winds or tailwinds; but, with vertical wind shears which are not uncommon, the altitude for maximum range in headwinds could be reduced by 10 000

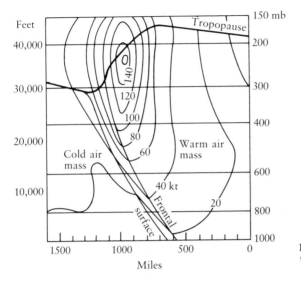

FIGURE 13.11
Wind speeds in a typical jet stream.

feet and still be above the weather. The aircraft could also fly faster relative to the air at the lower level. Temperature too has its effects.

In any defined 3D field of temperature and wind, for any permissible fuel consumption, there is an optimum flight-plan describing paths in the horizontal and vertical planes and the programme of power settings. If the quantity of fuel which may be loaded is not a limiting factor, fuel and time both have their several values, and one can be spent to save the other. There is therefore an optimum trade-off between them, and a unique minimum-cost flight-plan. These matters were addressed by Williams[18] in the context of the Britannia 310. His equation of the minimum-cost flight-plan, like Zermelo's equation for the 2D MTP eighteen years earlier, could only be applied indirectly to flight-planning in real atmospheres (regarded as 3D fields of wind and temperature) before computers. Williams evolved graphical methods of combining the MTP in the horizontal plane with the optimum in the vertical plane. At that time there was no other traffic on the North Atlantic at the altitudes normally favoured by the Britannia, and they could plan flight as they pleased. Computers, Doppler, and INS were on the horizon, and the unwary might have hoped that, at last, the calculus of variations might be properly applied to navigation.

In fact, from 1959, the airlines switched in concert from piston engines to turbojets, all seeking the same tracks and altitudes. Traffic boomed and, with the separation criteria then in use, congestion ensued. Aeroplanes slogged across the Atlantic on fixed tracks like so many trams, and only Concorde went across the Atlantic whither it wished. In the age of powerful computers, optimum flight-planning techniques have been applied in a sophisticated manner that was not foreseen in 1959 when the trouble started. The tramlines across the North Atlantic are now varied from day to day on the basis of the atmosphere forecast to permit the most expeditious and economic flow of traffic in both directions.

As steam replaced sail, the original incentive towards optimum routeing, power to the sails, disappeared;[19] but, in the first half of the twentieth century, some progress was made on the traditional lines pioneered by Maury. For example, there were significant improvements in routeing within the southern and more vigorous reaches of the Gulf Stream. More generally, ships followed routes which were likely to avoid bad weather, icebergs, and other perils. Passenger ships in particular avoided heavy seas; but for a while there was little attempt at formal analysis comparable with work on the MTP in the air from 1924 onwards.

The main reason was the required term of the forecast: aeroplanes only needed a forecast for 12 hours ahead; ships would have needed as many days. Another reason was the complexity of the parameters which determine the optimum route of a ship, and the peculiar difficulty of forecasting them. Obviously the dynamic pressure of the wind on the surfaces above the water-line either aids or opposes the propulsion of the ship; but this is almost trivial compared with the action of the waves in high seas on the motion of the ship, causing dissipation of energy in pitch and roll. Figure 13.12 shows the effect of waves on ship performance at constant power in the case of a medium-sized type of vessel common in the 1950s.[20] The figure is an oversimplification; the effect of rough seas also depends on wavelength, the worst effect occurring when there is resonance between the period of the wave and the period of oscillation. It is normal practice to reduce speed in heavy seas, especially in passenger ships or those carrying heavy deck cargo, complicating the expression of the optimum still further; but it seems there are also rare circumstances in which a small ship should increase speed to avoid resonance.

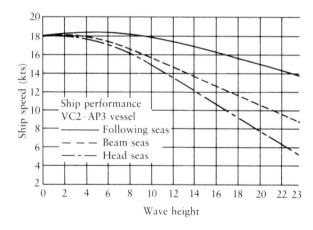

FIGURE 13.12
Ship-performance curves.

The forecast optimum route of a motor vessel therefore depends more on wave forecasting than on wind forecasting, and waves are inherently more difficult to forecast, because they depend on past as well as present weather. Efforts were made to forecast waves during the latter part of the Second World War in the context of amphibious operations. Small Infantry Landing Craft are not suitable for operation at sea in large waves, to say nothing of the assault on the shore. With the benefit of work done then, the US Hydrographic Office pioneered[21] wave forecasting in the mid-1950s. They used synoptic 'actual' wave charts (based partly on reports from ships) and forecast weather charts prepared by the US Weather Bureau, which, at the time, forecast five days ahead. In simplistic terms 'actual' wave data was used to predict swell, and the wind forecast was used to predict wind waves.

In the late 1950s the US Hydrographic Office applied their forecasts to optimum routeing, using the method Giblett had applied to aviation a quarter of a century earlier. Time-fronts at daily intervals were constructed on the basis of the wave forecast and performance data curves of the type illustrated in Fig. 13.12. The construction is illustrated by Fig. 13.13 for an eastbound transatlantic voyage. Since the time-fronts are limited by the forecast to the fifth day, the MTP is interpolated from the origin to the point on the fifth time-front nearest Fastnet.

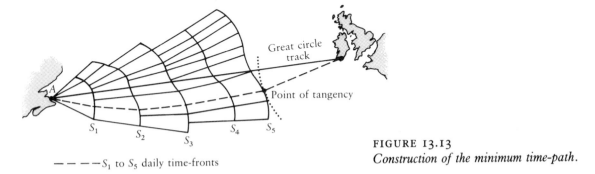

FIGURE 13.13
Construction of the minimum time-path.

$- - - - S_1$ to S_5 daily time-fronts

Of course, if forecasting had permitted the extension of the time-fronts to the eighth day, the MTP might have been a very different curve; for that matter, Fastnet might not have been the preferred turning-point. The difficulty was exacerbated over the Pacific, where tracks over open water are much longer. It was only partially overcome by daily updates, always projecting the track five days ahead. It was claimed by Hanssen and James in 1960 that in a sample of 1000 ocean crossings by the US Military Sea Transportation Service, the service provided caused an average time-saving of 14 hours, greater safety, and more consistent schedule-keeping. Consistency of schedule-keeping in such operations determines the utilization of ships and crews which may be planned, and affects the efficiency of the overall operation in other ways. It is frequently a more important figure of merit than the *average* voyage time.

There is a fundamental difference between the marine and aeronautical cases. In the latter, although temperature has some influence, the MTP is primarily a matter of air currents, which may, or may not, take the aircraft into better weather. In the marine case, because the MTP of motor vessels is primarily concerned with the avoidance of heavy seas, it is usually in unison with the pursuit of safety and comfort. It was fully understood from the beginning of optimum routeing at sea that, particularly for passenger vessels and those with heavy deck cargo such as container vessels, *optimum* routeing may attach greater weight to the avoidance of heavy seas than to the mere consideration of the effect of sea conditions on performance, and hence on the MTP.

The other point is that the merits of the aircraft MTP are compared with the great circle, whereas the study cited compared 'optimum' routeing on the basis of wave forecasts with 'standard' routeing. Some of these standard routes were very long: that from San Francisco to Yokohama went south of the rhumb line. Some significant time-savings occurred primarily because forecast conditions permitted a shorter route than the standard route based on average conditions by criteria which were not necessarily refined.

It is still not clear (to this writer at least) to what extent the improvement derived from modern optimum routeing techniques is due to reliance on forecasts rather than climatological statistics, and to what extent it derives from a more analytical and rational approach to the whole subject. As Verploegh pointed out in 1963, 'The long experience of mariners in practising their methods of weather navigation and the customary practices which resulted from this experience have never been analysed in a systematic way.'

That is no longer relevant. Over the past thirty years there has been a great surge of interest in a scientific approach to the optimum routeing of ships, and there is now a substantial literature on the subject. Since the pioneering work of the 1950s there has been, in the wake of the computer, much sophistication in the mathematical approach to the subject, which is now highly technical. 'Dynamic programming', originally developed by Bellman, has provided an instrument well suited to the intrinsic nature of the problem.[22] At the same time there has been a closer scrutiny of what we really mean by *optimum*. Obviously comfort, safety, least time, and least fuel (and schedule-keeping in scheduled operations) are all desiderata which may conflict to some extent.

Specialists in ship performance and naval architecture continue to stress the complexity of the effect of sea conditions on speed at given power, emphasizing the importance of wave-length and wave period, which are more difficult to forecast than wave height and direction, on which the early work was exclusively based. There have been several new approaches to wave forecasting. Scepticism has been expressed on the value of reports of actual wave conditions (the seaman has no means of measuring wave height); and alternative means have been sought to predict the swell element of the sea condition. Work has been done on forecasting wave state exclusively by inferences drawn from the dynamics of the atmosphere up to 500 mb in the days immediately passed; the wind of the past few days powers the swell of today.

Although in the air, the principal restraint on optimum 3D routeing is now the ATC service, which provides protection against collision, at sea it is still the unresolved problem of forecasting sea state reliably for the period of duration of transoceanic voyages; hence the stress on dynamic programming in the marine case. The possibility has been raised that, at sea also, free-ranging optimum routeing might provoke collision; but the density of transoceanic traffic is still so low outside the congested areas where there are mandatory routeing procedures that sound radar and visual watch-keeping practice should suffice. In an age where facsimile machines and computers are commonplace aboard ship, the debate whether routeing is best done on board, or by shore-based teams of mariners and meteorologists, continues. A compromise by which the actual routeing is done on board, but with more informed advisory services from ashore, should not be excluded.

International concern about energy conservation, and much higher fuel prices in the mid-1970s, led to a small revival of interest in sail-assisted motor vessels. The optimum routeing of such vessels, employing modern technology, is a fascinating problem,[23] and one quite different to the problems of motor vessels and aeroplanes.

Notes to Chapter 13

1. French galleys were still operating at the end of the reign of Louis XIV and, until the French Revolution, convicts were called *galèriens*.
2. By the geographer Bashari Mukaddasi.
3. The writer has relied heavily on Severin (1987) and sources quoted by him for material on medieval Arab navigation of the Indian Ocean.
4. The dangers of premature arrival are a recurring theme throughout the centuries of sail. Richard Norwood, who measured the arc and linear distance between the Tower of London and York Minster very creditably in 1635 (Chapter 6), proposed a length of 6120 English feet for the nautical mile, which he later reduced to 6000 feet so that the sailor should 'fall not in with a place unexpected'. One welcomes the sentiment; but reducing the length of the nautical mile by 2 per cent does not have the desired effect.
5. Michael Richey (personal communication).
6. Gage (1928), also quoted in Severin (1987).
7. The Theory of Evolution derives from Charles Darwin's voyage as a naturalist on HMS *Beagle*.
8. From which the US Naval Observatory and the US Hydrographic Office later emerged.
9. In 1911, when the word *anticyclone* had passed into general usage, the objection was raised that it is 'pedantic in conversation, impossible in verse, whose end is stormy, while its prefix is loaded with suggestions of conflict'. The word *halcyon* was proposed instead; but *anticyclone* has passed its centenary.
10. Admiral Sir Francis Beaufort was a most influential nineteenth-century hydrographer. He drew up his scale in 1806, and it was adopted by the Royal Navy in 1838, and by the International Meteorological Committee in 1874. Before the anemometer there was no means of measuring wind speed; and, in any case, in a moving vessel the indicated wind is relative to the vessel. The Beaufort scale is defined in relation to the visible evidence of wind, mainly the condition of the sea; but force 12 is that which 'no canvas can withstand'. All the reports of wind received by the Meteorological Committee, and the charts and tables, were necessarily expressed in these terms, which is why Galton expressed his ship's speed in m.p.h., but his wind speed in the Beaufort scale. The wind speeds assigned to the scale in Table 13.1 were agreed internationally in 1939. Earlier British and American equivalents are different.
11. Scott (1921). Despite his rank, Scott was never in the army. A naval officer, he was transferred to the newly formed RAF, which briefly used army ranks.
12. Giblett (1924).
13. The dirigible has a long history in relation to its slight impact on navigation and civilization as a whole. In 1851 Henri Giffard was the first to fly a powered lighter-than-air craft; but, as its air speed was only about 10 km/hr, it was only *dirigible* on a windless day. In 1884 Renard and Krebs completed a circuit in *La France* which qualifies it as the first dirigible. The action moved from France to Germany, where David Schwarz built the first rigid dirigible in 1897. Count Ferdinand von Zeppelin, who had served the Union side in the US Civil War as a balloon

observer, conceived the idea of enveloping a number of balloons in a streamlined structure. He was enormously influential throughout the future development of the airship. Zeppelins bombed London during the First World War, and, as noted in the text, a British airship (based on a Zeppelin design) crossed the North Atlantic from Scotland to New York against the prevailing westerlies in 1919. In 1929 the *Graf Zeppelin* flew non-stop from Friedrichshaven to Tokyo. Goodyear (of Akron, Ohio) acquired the patents and processes of Zeppelin; but both the *Akron* and the *Macon* were lost and not replaced. British interest in airships virtually ceased in 1931, following the loss of the R 101 and the lives of many leading figures in British aviation. The final blow was the conflagration of the *Hindenburg* on landing at New Jersey, which was shown in all its horror on every movie screen, and ended the history of the airship in regular passenger-carrying service. The airship has its revivalists; but how slowly moving vehicles are to be accommodated by ATC is not explained.

14. The equation as described is strictly valid for a plane earth. If θ is the grid heading, u the tailwind, n an element of distance along the time-front, A the air speed, and S the scale factor of the chart on which grid reference lines with respect to which θ is measured are parallel, the full equation is

$$\frac{d\theta}{dt} = \frac{\partial u}{\partial n} + \frac{A + u}{S} \cdot \frac{\partial S}{\partial n}$$

15. The geostrophic wind equation is $2\rho\omega V\sin\phi = dp/ds$ where dp/ds is the rate of change of pressure with horizontal distance (called p' in the text), ρ the air density, and ω the earth's angular velocity. Figure 13.14 illustrates contours on a surface of constant pressure. On elementary hydrostatic principles the difference in pressure between Q_1 and Q_2 is $\rho g.dh$. So ρ drops out of the wind equation, which becomes $2\omega V\sin\phi = g.dh/ds$. If the slope is measured in some direction PR_2 making a horizontal angle α with PQ_2, V is reduced by a factor of $\cos\alpha$ to give the component of the wind at right angles to PR.

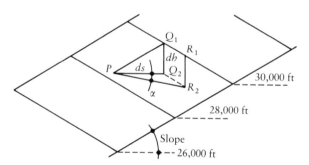

FIGURE 13.14
The geostrophic wind on an isobaric surface.

16. Sawyer (1949).
17. The Canadair CL 44D, employed as a freight carrier a few years later, was the only other *long-range* aircraft with similar characteristics. The same techniques were employed, ATC permitting.
18. Williams (1957).
19. Nevertheless, a steamer captain, James Hayes, wrote to the Meteorological Committee in support of the 1872 wind charts described earlier in this chapter in the following terms: 'I am sure such a plan as the present Chart must be useful even to steamers. In the tropics steamers want a beam wind as much for improved draught to their fires and ventilation for passengers, as to aid with sails.' In navigation there is always something else to consider.
20. Figures 13.12 and 13.13 are based on illustrations in Hanssen and James (1960).

21. In the United States commercial weather forecasting companies also offered weather routeing services from about 1953.
22. Bellman's principle of optimality states that an optimum policy has the property that whatever the initial state and initial decisions are, the remaining decisions must constitute an optimum policy with regard to the stage resulting from the first decision. That, one would have thought, has always been the principle of good navigation; the novelty lies in the algorithmic applications of the principle.
23. The problem is addressed in Hagiwara and Spaans (1987).

CHAPTER FOURTEEN

A Game of Chance

✠

THE last chapter was nominally about the path of minimum time; but—from the medieval Arab navigators to the modern optimum-routeing scientists—the idea has been continually insinuated that there is some other optimum path, or as John Dee put it, 'the shortest *good* way'. Dee was an eminent mathematical practitioner of Elizabethan England, and wrote[1] in 1570

> *Navigation, which demonstrateth, how, by the Shortest good way, by the aptest direction, and in the shortest time: a sufficient shippe, between any two places (in passage navigable) assigned, may be conducted: and in all stormes and naturall disturbances chancing, how to use the best possible meanes, to recover the place first assigned.*

In this he spoke for navigators of all ages but our own. Within living memory, the world was willing to make subjective and amorphous judgements about the *good* way, the *aptest* direction, and the *best possible means*, without examining too closely the meaning of the words italicized. Judgements depended on the cultural background, experience, and sense of the judge, and on service traditions. What might be dashing and admirable in a naval commander might be contemptibly foolhardy in the captain of a merchant ship.

A novel feature of modern culture is that we seek precise quantitative figures of merit by which we can measure and compare 'good' and 'better'. We know that to find such measures we must go back to the beginning, and ask what the navigation is for. Sometimes it is simple. On some early voyages of exploration the navigation was a success if the navigator returned alive, and a failure if he did not. The navigation of a surface-to-air guided missile is a success if there is a hit, and a failure if there is not. Usually however, the object of the navigation is a mess of conflicting aims. The fundamental problem of navigation is now seen as the optimum resolution of that conflict.

The problem is illustrated by the case of an airliner in scheduled service—not dissimilar to that of a ship in scheduled service mentioned briefly in the chapter preceding this. When the pilot assumes command, the payload and the revenue to be earned are settled matters; so normally is the future schedule of aircraft and crew. All the pilot can do is provide the best possible product to his passengers at the least cost to his employers within externally imposed constraints. These constraints are in three categories: air traffic control to provide safe and expeditious flow of air traffic generally; operational limits and procedures designed to protect the safety of the pilot and his crew and passengers; and noise-abatement procedures designed to limit the nuisance the flight causes to people on the ground. The seven desiderata are listed in Table 14.1. A distinction is made between quickness and regularity, because although the programme of least time has some intrinsic merits, premature arrival may cause congestion and inefficient deployment of ground facilities and personnel. The pilot's task is to optimize these seven desiderata.

Desiderata of the navigation	Affects product quality	Affects production costs	Affects pilot's interests	Imposed by regulation
Safety	yes	yes	yes	yes
Comfort	yes	—	yes	—
Quickness	yes	yes	yes	—
Regularity	yes	yes	yes	—
Fuel-saving	—	yes	—	—
Low wear	—	yes	—	—
External noise-abatement	—	yes	—	yes

Table 14.1. The seven desiderata of airline navigation

Every one of the desiderata listed conflicts with at least one other. There is an obvious conflict between fuel conservation and quickness, and if too much weight is attached to quickness it may also adversely affect wear and tear and comfort and safety. If tailwinds are carrying the flight ahead of schedule, quickness conflicts with regularity. Noise-abatement may adversely affect fuel and quickness; carried too far it would also be unsafe. Some desiderata affect product quality, and some operating costs; some are imposed by the external constraints. Only safety is required on all three counts—four, if we include the pilot's personal interest. Catastrophe reduces the perceived quality of the product to zero, and costs the airline and its insurers hundreds of millions of pounds. If we were to subscribe to the doctrine that the customer is always right, and deduce the value he places on his life from the way he drives his motor-car, we would conclude that the high cost to airlines of accidents is the principal motive for high safety standards, and wonder that the safety of such operations is regulated by authorities to such an extraordinary and unprecedented degree.[2]

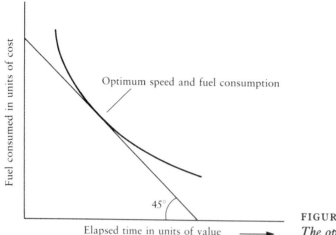

FIGURE 14.1

The optimum motorway speed.

If we have two conflicting desiderata we can determine the optimum compromise if, and only if, we can express both of them as a function of some common scale of value. Figure 14.1 plots fuel consumption against journey-time on an open motorway cruising at constant speed. The speed limit being the cut-off point, all speeds lower than the limit are taken to be safe. If the graph is expressed in units of fuel and time we have no means of determining the optimum point. If the graph is drawn with axes the *cost* of fuel and the *value* of time at a common scale, the optimum point is that at which the tangent cuts both axes at 45°; if one (*y*) can be expressed as an algebraic function of the other (*x*), it is the point at which $dy/dx + 1 = 0$.

The airline pilot has seven conflicting desiderata, so this graphical construction is not possible; but the equation of the optimum flight programme may be written in terms of partial differential coefficients if the value functions are known. As a practical matter, airlines have no idea how to express value functions of product-quality desiderata—even the cost functions present problems; but such difficulties are minor compared with one overwhelming philosophical difficulty. For six of the desiderata the only possible common scale is money; but there is no scale on which we can measure the benefit of avoiding pain, suffering, and unnatural death. The dilemma is not peculiar to either navigation or the aeroplane. Our society licenses many artefacts, from motor cars to plastic bags, which are occasionally lethal; and we pay for the amenity of the many with the agony of a few, while striving to minimize the incidence of the latter. Of course our airline pilot will use what Dee called 'the best possible means' to be safe. Comforting though this may be, it does not begin to address the logical difficulty.

Politicians, journalists, pilots' unions, and even, to their shame, airline chairmen, are fond of saying that safety is paramount. This is pernicious and dangerous nonsense. It is easy to show that however many steps are taken in that direction, there remain an infinity of finite steps which have not been taken. If we really mean that safety is paramount we would stay at home. If we are ever to take off, either we must accept that the optimum flight programme is an intrinsically insoluble problem, or we must arbitrarily assign an acceptable probability of catastrophe. *Rational* navigation is *necessarily* a game of chance.

One reason for basing this example on an airline rather than a shipping company is that it was in aviation that the international community first accepted the inevitability of this dilemma, originally in aircraft design, but later in air navigation. The criterion of one catastrophic failure in 10 million landings for automatic landing systems has already been mentioned in Chapter 10. When ATC developed internationally after the Second World War, separation criteria were subjective. Criteria were adopted which were thought to be 'safe' by ill-defined notions, with one eye on what was practical in contemporary traffic densities. Techniques developed in the 1960s by which a risk–separation relationship was identified by mathematical analysis. In the early 1980s traffic-separation criteria were adopted on the North Atlantic which, it was thought, gave a risk of nominally zero separation[3] of two per hundred million flying hours in each of the three dimensions of separation. A similar approach to other aspects of safety of navigation is gradually becoming commonplace not only in the air and at sea, but even on land—for example in the formulation of speed limits for motorways.

The application of science to the creation of the instruments of warfare goes back at least as far as Archimedes and the defence of Syracuse against the Romans in the third century BC. In Renaissance times both Leonardo da Vinci and Michelangelo worked as military engineers; but the application of scientific method to the actual conduct of operations was not undertaken on a significant scale much before about 1940. In Britain, the inventors of radar (Chapter 11) extended their brief to the design of operating systems. It is claimed that it was A. P. Rowe himself who devised the term *operational research*[4] to describe what *Webster's dictionary* would later define rather primly as 'the application of scientific and especially mathematical methods to the study and analysis of complex problems that are not traditionally considered to fall within the field of profitable scientific enquiry'. Today there are few complex problems which are not considered to fall within the field of profitable scientific enquiry, so if we accept the *Webster* definition, operational research is necessarily dying on the vine of its fruitfulness. Since the practical object of any operational research is always to improve the quality of management of some process, it has come to be subsumed from about 1950 within management sciences as these have developed.

As always when one seeks to find the beginning of an idea, it is presaged earlier than one would expect. During the First World War F. W. Lanchester,[5] better remembered today as a pioneering aeronautical and automotive engineer, published a remarkable book in which he reached such conclusions as 'the fighting strengths of opposing forces are equal when the squares of the *numerical strength* multiplied by the fighting *value* of the individual forces are equal' and 'when the components differ among themselves, as in a fleet which is not homogeneous, the measure of the total of the fighting strength of a force will be the square of the sum of the square roots of the strengths of the individual units'. As Lanchester himself pointed out, some of the brilliant commanders of history had fought their battles on principles congruent with those of Lanchester; but one imagines that they would have wondered what he was talking about.

Whoever invented its name, operational research was in the air around 1940, and its practice was not confined to the teams of scientists who were recruited to address the operational conduct of war, in some cases with phenomenal success. It was also spontaneously practised by young combatants who had never heard of operational research. They were more likely to have a little scientific training than their fathers had when they went to war in 1914, and more likely to ask *why*.

An isolated RAF Beaufighter squadron based in the Libyan desert in 1942/3 was required to provide air escort to small Malta-bound convoys from first light to last light. They had no radar, and strict radio silence was enjoined. Occasionally the convoy was not sighted at the estimated time of arrival overhead it, and the standing order in that case was to do a square search of the form illustrated in Fig. 14.2, where v is the estimated visibility. These occasions nearly always occurred at first light, when the visibility was bad and the convoy had not been under recent surveillance by the squadron itself for some hours. By careful analysis of their own flight logs the aircrews concluded that although the nearly total darkness of scheduled first light was a difficulty (about which they could do nothing, since their schedule was controlled by planners hundreds of miles away), the convoys did in fact depart from plan during the night on occasions. The aircrews evolved the searches illustrated in Fig. 14.3, which they used whenever it was thought that the convoys were more likely to be found in one direction than another. They knew convoys were rarely ahead of schedule, as this had been planned for the fastest speed of the slowest ship. It is all rather obvious, and such searches were developed simultaneously by others; but they were not in the training manuals, and these young men, some under twenty-one, were using their brains in a way that was less natural to the older officers who constituted the organization.

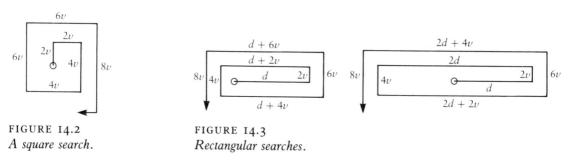

FIGURE 14.2
A square search.

FIGURE 14.3
Rectangular searches.

At about this time scientists serving the US Navy Operations Research Group were also considering searches.[6] By simple analysis of statistics about submarine contacts on enemy merchant vessels by area, and intelligence on the density and distribution of such vessels, they were able to assess the effectiveness of submarine watch-keeping by area, the extent of enemy anti-submarine activity by area, and the success of the enemy in evading submarines. From such assessments they were able to propose a more efficient deployment of submarines in terms of tonnage sunk (product quality) and submarine losses (cost).

Comparable simple analytical techniques were applied to aircraft search for enemy submarines, which also led to identification of the areas in which search was most profitable and warning of changes in U-boat tactics. Aircraft had previously been directed at an area where most sightings occurred. It had not been realized that the large number of sightings in the area was due to the concentration of patrols in the area! The study also revealed the inefficiency of watch-keeping on long patrols. The average aircrew could expect to sight a U-boat once every several hundred hours. It had not been appreciated previously that scanning the sea systematically for hours without expecting to see anything requires enormous concentration and special training. Most combatants were not professionals, and were inadequately trained in some functions. The group were able to show that in one case 'a diversion of ten per cent of the operational effort into carefully planned practice can increase the overall effectiveness by factors of two to four'.

Operational research played at least as important a part in the war of the RAF against the U-boat in the Bay of Biscay. AM (1963) describes how fruitfully it was applied to tactics and strategms of all kinds, even to the optimum duration of an ASV operator's watch. Admiral Doenitz's famous tribute to the contribution of British scientists to the U-boat war (which is quoted in chapter 12) should be taken to apply to operational research as well as radar.

These are only a few examples of the successes of operational research during that war. It influenced the theory of air and naval combat, the principles of evaluation of systems, techniques of gunnery and bombardment, convoy methods, the deployment of tankers, and many other things. As Jacob Bronowski wrote[7] (in 1951) 'the field of opportunity (for the methods of operational research) will never again be quite so blank, so simple and so lavish'. Fears were expressed that, in peacetime, operational research would become a painstaking combination of cost accounting, job analysis, time and motion study, critical-path analysis, and so on. It could not be foreseen in 1950 that computers would open new worlds of application for the mathematical ideas associated with operational research: linear programming, dynamic programming, queueing theory, game theory, information theory, and so on.

Rational analysis of our objectives leads us inexorably to a probability approach to the optimization of navigation and, in particular, to the assignment of a finite value to the desired level of safety, but probabilities of the order of 10^{-7} present difficulties. Some philosophers have had problems with probability in general. The probability we assign to an event varies depending on what we know about it. The probability that an unspecified person will die in the next year is simply the number of annual deaths in the country divided by its population. Each item of further information about the person—age, sex, occupation, smoking and other habits, diet, state of health, and so on—changes the probability. Some modern mathematicians wash their hands clean of the epistemological question by saying that mathematical probability is primitive, beyond definition, and distinct from the philosophical concept.

When we say the probability of a tossed coin coming up heads is 0.5 (or 50 per cent), two totally different meanings may be ascribed to the statement. One, which Keynes called 'The Principle of Indifference', is a statement of ignorance. Given the information that the coin must come up either heads or tails and no other information, each event is equally probable.

The other, the statistical or actuarial meaning, is that coins have been tossed millions of times and, by and large, they come up heads as often as not. The mathematical probability (as demonstrated by the principle of indifference) and the statistical or actuarial probability (the historical frequency of the event) are the same, but it is only when the sample is large that probability is a reliable basis for prediction. If the coin does in fact have a head and a tail, the probability that it will come up heads on between 49 per cent and 51 per cent of occasions is only 0.16 if the coin is tossed 100 times; if it is tossed 10 000 times the probability is 0.95.

Mathematical probability has its origins in attempts by Renaissance mathematicians to develop a theory of games of chance; but Jakob Bernoulli, whose *Ars conjectandi* was published posthumously in 1713, is usually regarded as the founder of probability theory. The study of statistics has other origins. Risk-taking as a business is seen in the marine insurance which flourished in Italian maritime cities from the late Middle Ages. It is thought to have been introduced into England by Lombard bankers much later. John Graunt seems to have been the first, in 1662, to extract significant statistics from records of births and deaths or, as he put it, 'Natural and Political Observations made upon the Bills of Mortality'. He was a shopkeeper; but, with the encouragement of Charles II, was elected a Fellow of the Royal Society. Another pioneer in this field was Caspar Neumann, a clergyman of Breslau, who studied the records of births and deaths in that city. It was Neumann's statistics which were the basis of that work of Halley which is the subject of the next chapter.

An important feature is the analysis of frequency distribution. After Newton's Binomial Theorem it became clear that the probability of a number of occurrences of an event of probability p on n occasions is given by the binomial expansion of $(p+q)^n$, where q is the probability of the non-event ($p+q=1$). Thus the probability that the event will occur x times is

$$n! \ p^x \ q^{(n-x)}/x! \ (n-x)!.$$

If an automatic landing system with a failure probability of 10^{-7} is used on 10^7 occasions there are virtually equal 36.8 per cent probabilities that the system will fail once or not at all, an 18.4 per cent probability that it will fail twice, and about an 8 per cent probability that it will fail more than twice,[8] including the remote probability that it fails on all ten million occasions. Of course, as a practical matter, there is absolutely zero possibility that the system would survive so long. We really do not believe in the actuality of very remote possibilites.

Except for the safety problem, the application of probability to navigation is largely concerned with the distribution of error rather than the occurrence or non-occurrence of events. Error, like many things with which the navigator is concerned, such as position, direction, and speed, is continuously variable. From about 1800 Gauss and Laplace developed the 'normal' distribution, which in mathematical terms is a limiting case of the binomial expansion. Poisson and others developed different distributions which correspond to particular cases. To a remarkable extent it is possible to fit many types of statistical data to mathematically derived distribution curves.

A normal distribution, the typical bell-shape of which is illustrated in Fig. 14.4, is completely defined by the *mean* and the *standard deviation* (SD),[9] both of which can be calculated from a series of observations. The normality of the data is tested by other criteria. The probability that a normal error will not exceed one SD is 68.2 per cent and the probability that it will not exceed two SD is 95.4 per cent, which is why the errors of navigation systems have been frequently described in previous chapters in terms of 95 per cent probability; the '95 per cent error' is simply twice the SD if the distribution is normal. Laplace showed in 1812 that if an error is the result of a large number of elemental errors, each of which are equally probably positive or negative, the distribution of the resultant error is normal. Normal distributions are frequently found in nature. The distribution of deviation of actual temperature from the mean for the time of day and date at many places follows a normal distribution quite clearly, as if nature tries to keep to the mean temperature, but every day misses the mark by a normally distributed error.

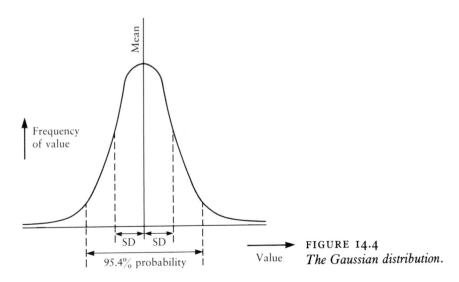

FIGURE 14.4
The Gaussian distribution.

Not all errors are normally distributed or even distributed in any systematic way. If a large number of small children not practised in such work add 1987 to 3654, each child is as likely to make an error in one column as in another. We cannot expect to see any relationship between the quantum of the error and the frequency of its occurrence, still less a normal one; but the error is bounded, in that it is unlikely to exceed 10 000. This example enables us to make the somewhat simplistic distinction between 'ordinary' error, which, even if it is not perfectly normal, has the quality that any large error is less probable than any smaller error, and 'blunder', which has the markedly different characteristics illustrated in Table 14.2. A typical case of blunder in modern navigation is the insertion of way points into a navigation computer; an error of 10° is as likely as one of 1'. The equivalent of blunder in

Characteristic	Error	Blunder or Fault
Presence	Always	Infrequent
Frequency distribution of magnitude	Any large error less frequent than any smaller error	Within limits any magnitude as likely as another
Effect of improvement	Reduces magnitude of error	Reduces frequency of blunder

Table 14.2. The characteristics of error and blunder

machines is *fault*. Each instrument may have its own systematic error; it is subject to random error, which may follow approximately a normal pattern; and it is subject to occasional failure.

When one seeks to quantify navigation errors with probabilities of the order of 10^{-7} or so, one difficulty is at once apparent. It has been known since the 1950s that 'ordinary' navigation errors do not precisely fit a normal distribution. We would expect as much, since the proof that they do requires them to be the resultant of an indefinitely large number of elemental errors, all of which are equally probably + or −, which is not generally the case. Actual distributions can be determined from analysis of a large number of observations; but we do not have anything like the number of observations to predict empirically the shape of the tail of the distribution curve in the 10^{-7} region. At the time that a mathematical approach to North Atlantic air-traffic separation was being developed, evidence was growing that track-keeping errors of 2, 3, and even 4 standard deviations were occurring far more frequently than their *normal* probabilities of 4.56 per cent, 0.27 per cent, and 0.006 per cent respectively.[10] Large quantities of data can only be accumulated over a long period, and navigation is changing too rapidly for that. Then there is the problem of blunders, which follow no distribution pattern at all.

Mathematicians of our own time have not shied away from these difficulties. A formula for collision risk in terms of normally distributed error and limited blunder was published[11] in 1958; and in the 1980s it was shown how 'ordinary' error which is not precisely normal and blunder could be combined in double-double exponential distributions.[12] The problem remains, and is exacerbated by the automation of navigation and the improved quality of navigation systems. Large 'ordinary' errors are being almost eliminated, so that catastrophic failure of navigation is due increasingly to blunder or fault. If a state is reached such that aircraft collision can only be caused by blunder or fault rather than error, and, within limits wider than nominal separation, any magnitude of blunder is as likely as any other, the only sense in which a large nominal separation between aircraft is safer than a smaller one is that if separation criteria are high there are less obstacles for an errant aircraft to bump into.

There are few aspects of navigation which have been more influenced by the ways of thought, largely developed over the past half-century, with which this chapter is concerned than the assessment of position from inconsistent, inaccurate, or inadequate data. In 1982

Michael Richey, addressing the Royal Institute of Navigation on the occasion of his retirement as its director, said, 'Ideas, by and large, dominate events . . . Thirty years ago navigational errors were regarded as a lapse in performance; today every navigator recognizes that the world is black and grey, not black and white, and that the treatment of navigational errors lies at the root of navigation.'

If what is written reflects what was thought, before the 1940s it was thought that navigational information was either 'about right'—and therefore good; or wrong—and therefore unusable. The skilled navigator detected the latter by criteria which the writers did not define too closely. In Fig. 14.5 an aircraft was able to pinpoint its position at A. At a time when the DR position based on the estimated wind is D, the position line BC is obtained. Drift measurements suggest the true track is AE. One of the (rightly) most admired books of the 1930s on air navigation tells its readers to assume the position X, the intersection of AE and BC, rejecting D. As the author was an eminent and highly intelligent practitioner, one wonders if secretly he did not, in practice, adopt the position Y, giving just a little weight to the estimated wind.

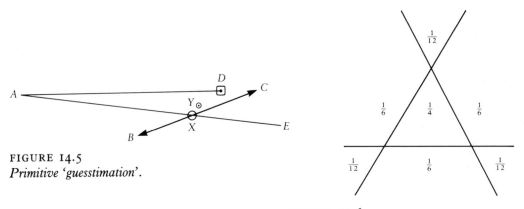

FIGURE 14.5
Primitive 'guesstimation'.

FIGURE 14.6
The probability of being within the cocked hat is 1/4.

Fig 14.6 is the cocked hat formed by three position lines. If no information is available on the distribution of error the probability of being in each of the seven zones defined by the cocked hat is as shown in the Figure. The proof is so simple that an outline of it is given in Note 13; but the writer is unaware of any text likely to be read by mariners or airmen of the period which even suggests that the true position is probably outside the cocked hat. It is correct to adopt the centre of the triangle as what came to be called in the 1940s the most probable position (MPP) only if there is no information on the relative probable error of the different position lines. Very often there is such information. If the sides of the cocked hat are bearings (radio or visual), and there is no reason to believe that the angle measured in each case is any less accurate than any other, the probable linear error of each bearing is proportionate to the range of the object. Even when the cocked hat is astronomical, the

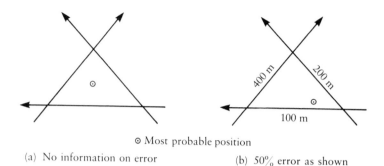

⊙ Most probable position

(a) No information on error   (b) 50% error as shown

FIGURE 14.7
Most probable position given three lines.

navigator may have reason to give more weight to one than another. Figure 14.7 illustrates the MPP in a cocked hat: (a) when there is no information on the relative probable error of the position lines: (b) when the probable error is in the ratio 4:2:1. Such matters were not addressed, although they would have been child's play to eighteenth-century mathematicians.

The change in attitude of navigators to which Richey referred was all part of the new analytical approach from the 1940s described earlier in this chapter. Navigators were taught, for example, how systematic errors were eliminated when bearings (or azimuths in the astronomical case) were 120° apart, but not when they were 60° apart, although the cocked hat appeared to be the same. An Institute of Navigation monograph[14] published in 1956 showed how the normal distribution curve of error of one observation could be extended to a 3D 'Gaussian heap' to represent two observations with different but normally distributed errors, as in Fig. 14.8. A horizontal section is the ellipse of probable error, the dimensions of which correspond to the uncertainty of position. The monograph went on to show how position ellipses could be combined. The case illustrated in Fig. 14.9(c) might correspond to a circumstance in which the smaller ellipse is based on two present observations, and the larger ellipse on earlier observations, the ellipse being enlarged by the passage of time rather than errors inherent in the observations on which it is based. Although of little practical consequence at the time, the notion that the estimation of present position should be based on consideration of past as well as present observations was to prove of great importance when computer technology permitted the application of complex algorithms to navigation.

Despite the famous dilemma of Captain Sumner in the nineteenth century (Chapter 7), in

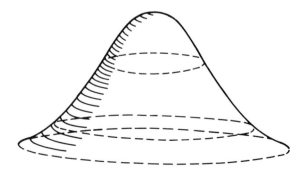

FIGURE 14.8
A Gaussian heap.

274

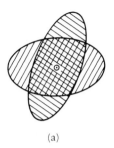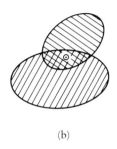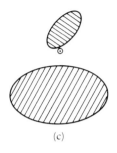

(a)   (b)   (c)

FIGURE 14.9
Most probable position from two position ellipses.

modern times it was the airman rather than the seaman who was most frequently troubled with the question of what to do with a single position line. When the sun is visible, the seaman on an ocean voyage could happily rely on his DR for as long as it takes for the azimuth of the sun to change enough to give him a good 'cut' between two sun lines in the manner which Sumner himself proposed. The airman on the same route could not wait. It was the navigation over water of transport and patrolling aircraft by day which led to the first primitive approach to a statistically most probable position.

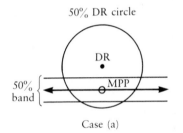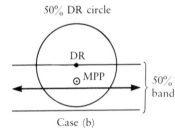

FIGURE 14.10
Most probable position with one position line.

The RAF actually developed MPP 'drills'; those applying to a single position line are illustrated in Fig. 14.10. The DR position is surrounded by a circle of such a radius that (it is estimated) there is a 50 per cent probability of the position's being within it. The position line shown is surrounded by a band whose width is the estimated 50 per cent probable error. The drill was: in the case of Fig. 14.10(a) adopt as the position the foot of the perpendicular from the DR position to the position line; in the case illustrated in Fig. 14.10(b) adopt as the position the centre of the segment formed by the DR circle and the boundary line of the position line which cuts it. All this begs a number of questions, of which the most obvious is the assumption that the area of probability around the DR position should take the form of a circle. The assumption implies that track error in radians × ground speed = ground speed error. Even if the assumed wind vector is as likely to be in error in one direction as another, the implied relationship between the errors of the compass and of the air-speed indicator had no basis in fact.

The enlightenment of navigators in these matters must have improved the quality of navigation; but the benefit of such drills, of drawing ellipses and so on, may be doubted. At first sight, an obvious application of such techniques was the South America–Europe air route of the late 1940s; the ocean crossing between Brazil and West Africa was often flown in daylight, and the only radio aids were short-range in the terminal areas. During the 8–9 hour crossing the sun's azimuth changed anything up to 180°, but usually too slowly to transfer position lines as Sumner did (Chapter 7). It was necessary to conserve in some way the different information provided by earlier sun lines when the azimuth was different. A procedure often adopted was simply to drop a perpendicular from the DR position on to each sun line to define an MPP, to restart the plot from it as if it were a fix, and to use the implied wind velocity as a factor in estimating the DR position at the time of the next sun sight. Commonly more than a dozen sun lines would be drawn during the course of the flight; but, for clarity, Fig. 14.11 shows a flight in which only two sights were taken and this method was employed. A third of the way across, the sun provides a track check at X, and two-thirds of the way across it provides a progress check at Y. At that point it does not matter in the least whether the adopted position at X was widely in error along track, because there is up-to-date distance-to-go information; the navigator is conserving the information gained at X to reduce the reliance of his track-keeping on DR by a half. The more sophisticated MPP techniques of the period mentioned above added nothing to the efficiency of navigation to the destination, but it could be argued that they would improve the quality of position-reporting on route—a matter of importance if there were conflicting traffic or a situation of distress arose.

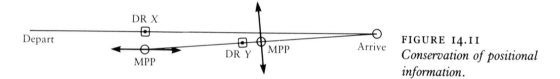

FIGURE 14.11
Conservation of positional information.

The practical results of a heuristic application of elementary probability theory of navigation were modest. The great value of the principles outlined above was only realized by powerful mathematical techniques employing data-processing machinery. One interim step was the development of small computers, intended primarily for yatchtsmen, which provided automatic reduction of astronomical sights and the computation of the most probable position from them.

From the 1950s scientists developing more advanced navigation systems had a problem. How to measure the accuracy of advanced equipment under trial when it was more accurate than the conventional means of determining position or velocity as the case might be? Stokes and Smith have described trials in 1964 of an INS with an accuracy approaching one nautical mile per hour on a UK to Newfoundland route employing Loran C and Doppler plus Decca in the coastal regions at both ends of the route. Clearly a Loran fix in itself, or a Doppler-based DR position in itself, would provide little indication of the performance of the INS; but a continuous record of position and velocity according to Loran, according to Doppler, and according to the INS system under test, enabled the effect of random errors in the Loran and DR (Doppler error plus heading reference error) to be smoothed.

Errors which were consistent from flight to flight could be identified and corrected. Another part of the analytical process was the correlation of the results with the known pattern of error of the three systems. The authors wrote:

> Data processing was done in stages. In flight the Doppler/heading system gave one version of position, the Decca and/or Loran C a second version, and the IN itself a third version. All the data were recorded twice a minute on punched paper tape. Post-flight this was processed to provide plots of the differences in latitude and longitude between the various systems as functions of time, and these plots were smoothed by curve-fitting using a least-squares method.
>
> The IN error plot was often used to correct the position data obtained from the Doppler and the radio aids. For example, it was found that Loran C had a systematic error which was a function of position and grew to significant levels near Newfoundland. This was detected by the IN error plot having a form unlike typical IN errors, and being consistent from flight to flight. This form of error could be allowed for, and was incorporated into the analysis on subsequent stages of data processing to produce the aircraft datum position.

Such a process is labour-intensive, and is not navigation, since the analysis was necessarily after the event. To apply such principles to navigation, both computers and the new kind of mathematics which has evolved with them were needed. The early work on most probable position suggests that if DR and past and present observations are subject to normally distributed errors, each having a known variance, the problem of making the best estimate of position reduces to one of minimizing the variance. This approach was developed by R. E. Kalman and R. S. Bucy at the beginning of the 1960s, and their 'filter' was first employed operationally in 1963 in the course of the Apollo space project.

The Kalman filter is a complex algorithm which, in effect, enables the process outlined in the preceding paragraph to be carried out continuously in real time. As applied to navigation using dead reckoning and a single sensor of position, it would continuously assess present position, basing itself on the present data, the historical data, and the known pattern of error of the navigation system—a process analogous to the deduction of an MPP from a dubious position line and an even more dubious DR position, but far more subtle and complex.

In fact, Kalman filters are used to assess present position and velocity employing virtually continuous inputs from all available navigation aids, giving a weighting to each aid according to the programmed error characteristics, and some weight to the historical data. In effect they are continuously predicting a DR position and modifying it by the present inputs on the basis of their presumed error distributions. This technology leads to the concept of the *Integrated Navigation System*. It underlines the view expressed in Chapter 9 that the computer, not the INS, is the heart of the modern flight-management system, which might track a VOR radial with little regard for the input from the VOR itself. In the beginning, radio was an aid to navigation, and has always been so at sea. In the air, the radio range, and later the VOR, made it a means of navigation. In the most modern aviation systems it is an aid once more.

Kalman filters so employed may be regarded as a technique in 'Multisensor Data-Fusion', the term now given, particularly in the military field, to the process of creating a complete picture from a mass of data from a large number of sources having different characteristics. Of course many animals (including ourselves) have inborn algorithms to achieve instinctively multisensor data-fusions of exquisite complexity; and we have no idea how we do it. The novelty lies only in the logical analysis of the process and its mathematicization.

The most complex navigation problem (in mathematical terms) which the writer has been able to discover is the navigation of London taxis; and it is precisely the one which the twentieth-century developments described in this chapter have quite passed by. The life of the navigator of a London taxi is a continuous search for higher probabilities of success in achieving complex objectives. Careful observation suggests that many of them understand their art very well, although they may not express it in analytical terms. A London taxi-driver is usually a self-employed businessman, whose business is to maximize his net revenue over the working day. Many taxi-drivers rent their cabs at a rate which is inclusive of insurance and maintenance, so that they are not overly concerned with wear and tear. For simplicity it will be assumed that net revenue is maximized if the total of fares receivable less the cost of fuel consumed is a maximum over the working day. The operation is conducted within two constraints: the driver's perception of what is safe, and his perception of the risk of penalty for contravention of traffic regulations.

The fare, which is fixed by the Home Office, is determined by a meter which incorporates time- and distance-measuring equipment. The next fare increment is triggered when either the time or distance which is bought for a fare increment is exhausted. In Fig. 14.12, O is a point at which a fare increment is triggered. If the next increment is triggered by distance run (s), the taxi is on the line AB, if it is triggered by elapsed time (t) it is on the line BC. It is convenient to use s and t as unit distance and time respectively, and the amount of an individual fare increment (p) as the unit of money; s/t is the unit velocity, which is, in fact,

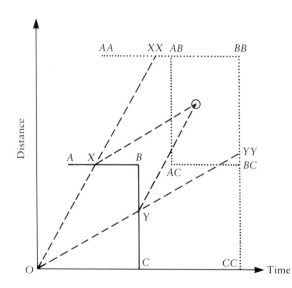

FIGURE 14.12
OX, a vector v > 1, OY a vector v < 1. If OX, OY occur in succession the vector is said to rotate (about the axis OBB). Motion from O in one fare segment: to AB if 3 > v > 1; to BC if 1 > v > 0. Motion from O in two fare segments: to AA.BB if 3 > v > 1, both v; to BB.CC if 1 > v > 0, both v; to area AB.BB.BC.AC. with fare segment vector rotation.

about 10 m.p.h. If the scale of Fig. 14.12 is selected so that the slope of OB, corresponding to unit speed, is 1, and a speed limit of 30 m.p.h. is enforced, the slope of OA is 3. The progress of the taxi during the fare increment is represented by a vector such as OX if the average speed $v > 1$ and the length of the vector is $(1 + 1/v^2)^{1/2}$. If $v < 1$, the progress is represented by a vector such as OY of length $(1 + v^2)^{1/2}$. This method of metering produces a strange result when two consecutive fare increments are considered. If $v > 1$ in both segments, position is on the line AA. BB; if $v < 1$ in both segments, position is on the line BB. CC; but if $v > 1$ in one segment and < 1 in the other, the position is anywhere in the area AB. BB. BC. AC. It may be said that this effect has been achieved by vector rotation about unit velocity.

Vector rotation only occurs when traffic conditions require, or seem to require, an average speed of less than 1 for a period of 1; but before considering the navigator's tactics in these conditions it is convenient to consider the tactic if there are no limits on v. It is easy to show that the speed of maximum profit V is given by $[A/f'(V)]^{1/2}$ where A is the value the navigator assigns to his time and $f'(V)$ is the increase in (fuel cost per unit distance) per unit increase in speed, a function of the performance of the taxi. If the navigator is objective, A is the opportunity cost, that is to say the value of time saved by fast driving in terms of revenue to be generated by future customers.[15] The rate of gross revenue generation when on hire is a minimum of unity when $v < 1$, but it can exceed 10 bowling down the motorway to London Airport, taking into account the surcharge for longer runs. The taxi-navigators seeking to assign a value to A have no idea how long they must wait for the next fare, nor at what rate it will generate revenue; but, willy nilly, a value must be assigned to V. Observation suggests that a value of 50–70 m.p.h. is commonly assigned by practitioners. They do not pay undue attention to 30 m.p.h. and 40 m.p.h. speed limits when conditions permit violation, but very rarely exceed a 70 m.p.h. speed limit significantly.

Reverting to the stop/go conditions of London traffic and Fig. 14.12, if it is assumed that the maximum v in such conditions is 3, and V is in the region of 5–7, the preferred position of the navigator over the two segments illustrated is AA. The passenger's preference is the same if he places a positive value on his own time. If he is concerned only with cost, he desires to be on the line AA. BB, but he is indifferent at what point, so there is no divergence of interest. If the line AA. BB cannot be attained and position is necessarily within the rectangle AB. BB. BC. AC, there is a divergence of interest; for example the cost to the passenger per unit distance is twice as much at AC as at AB; but the taxi-driver prefers AC, because he is earning at the same rate, using less fuel, and has his revenue-generating customer for longer. The navigator's interest is served by the maximum amount of vector rotation if unit speed cannot be sustained over a period. The object is jerkiness in phase with the meter. The point is illustrated in Fig. 14.13. If the driver maintains unit speed for two units of time he progresses two units of distance and earns 2p. If he maintains a speed of 2 for unit distance, is stopped for unit time, and then again drives at a speed of 2 for unit distance, he earns 3p instead of 2p for the same time and distance.

The navigator is restrained from the perfect practice of such techniques by traffic conditions

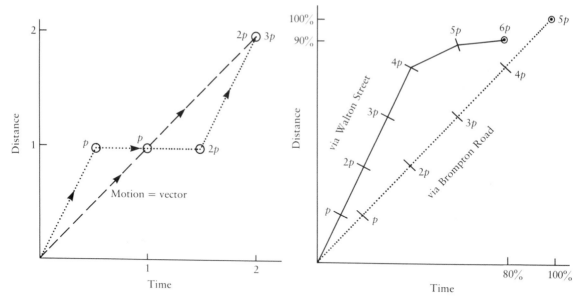

FIGURE 14.13
Increasing revenue by jerkiness.

FIGURE 14.14
The Walton Street tactic. In these hypothetical conditions the skilled navigator reduces distance by 10 per cent, time by 20 per cent, fuel cost by 15 per cent, and earns 20 per cent more revenue.

and the reactions of other drivers and his passengers. He lacks instrumentation (he cannot even see the meter without turning his head); but he does what he can. He selects the route to achieve the maximum number of high-speed spurts, resigning himself to periods during which time drives the meter at great cost to the passenger and little profit to himself. Figure 14.14 is a hypothetical example of a reduction of distance by 10 per cent, time by 20 per cent, and fuel cost by 15 per cent, and an *increase* in fare of 20 per cent. Along the route he enhances the probability of inducing a large vector rotation by driving up to a red light or a traffic jam at the highest prudent speed. Any observer with the time and patience can see for himself how excellently many, but not all, London taxi-drivers understand these principles.

A taxi-driver may spend a third of his day off hire, and the search for a profitable customer involves complex considerations of probability. At an elementary level, a cab cruising for hire should drive at that speed which is the optimum compromise between sweeping the largest area in the least time, fuel conservation, and efficiency of search-watch while driving in traffic. So well are these principles understood that an observer can tell whether a cab is for hire or not by the way it is driven; in particular the taxi for hire does not race up to red lights. The navigator must also consider the merits of joining a cab rank, and conserving fuel and his own energy. If he cruises for hire he must choose the optimum route. The search is not simply for any customer, but for a profitable one. Waiting at the rank of a west-end hotel has a high probability of profitable fares to airports at certain times; at others the probable fare is to local theatres or restaurants, and relatively unprofitable. The notorious difficulty of finding a cab at a west-end hotel at theatre time is evidence that this principle too is well understood.

The taxi-navigator has no data on the probability functions other than his own experience, and no data-processing capability other than his own brain. As navigation at sea and in the air becomes more and more a science-based process, the London taxi becomes more conspicuously an example of navigation as an art. Careful observation suggests that it is an art practised with great skill by many drivers.

Notes to Chapter 14

1. Quoted from 'The Groundplat of my MATHEMATICALL Preface: annexed to Euclid (now first) published in our Englishe tongue. An. 1570. Feb 3.' The ground plate lists and defines 19 'sciences and artes mathematical', of which navigation is one. The most charming is *Musike* —Which demonstrateth by reason, and teacheth by sense, perfectly to judge and order the diversitie of Soundes, high and low.'

2. There is nothing comparable at sea. In part this may be justified by the inherent dangerousness of the heavier-than-air flying machine. It is right that the risk of collision on airways should be many orders more remote than that between ships in the English Channel, because such collisions are likely to be three orders more catastrophic in terms of human life. However, the real reason for the remarkable difference between the regulation of safety of marine and air traffic is political. Since the repeal of the Navigation Acts in the nineteenth century marine traffic, other than cabotage, has been open to all comers. Shipping may operate under flags of convenience. Following principles defined after the war by the Chicago Convention and the Bermuda Pact, scheduled air services between any two countries are limited to carriers designated by one or the other or 'fifth freedom' carriers approved by both. The political means to enforce regulation therefore exists in the air, but not at sea to the same extent.

3. Nominal zero separation is dangerous, but not necessarily catastrophic. If aircraft are separated laterally and that separation breaks down they will only collide if they are at precisely the same altitude, the pilots do not see each other in time, and there is no ACAS system in operation. For the original mathematical analysis see Reich (1966); for a general description of the rationale see Booker and White (1979).

4. The term *operations research* is usually preferred in the United States.

5. The book was called *Aircraft in warfare*, but the subject-matter was much wider than the title suggests. Frederick William Lanchester was an entrepreneurial engineer in the age which produced Sperry and Marconi. A paper he wrote on the stability of aeroplanes six years before the first flight was awarded the Gold Medal of the Royal Aeronautical Society about thirty years later. Lanchester motor cars were in production from 1900.

6. The work is described in Morse and Kimball (1951), which is quoted in the next paragraph. Of the two authors, Morse was an academic physicist who served as director of the US Navy Operations Research Group, and Kimball, an academic chemist, served as Deputy Director, Operations Evaluation Group, US Navy.

7. In a review of Morse and Kimball (1951) for the *Scientific American*.

8. Given that n is very large and the reciprocal of p, the probability of failure on zero or one occasion is each the reciprocal of e. If x is a few, the probability of occurring on x occasions is $1/e.x!$ This is a special case of Poisson's exponential series often applied to remote probabilities.

9. The standard deviation of a set of n observations of x is given by $(SD)^2$ = sample variance = $\Sigma\, y^2/n$, where y is the residue of an observation after deducting the value of the mean. If the distribution is normal, the mean and the variance define it precisely. Tests involving the third and fourth power of residuals provide criteria for assessing the normalcy of the distribution of the observations made. In probability theory the term standard deviation has a consistent meaning.

10. J. B. Parker writes (personal communication 1991) 'The main reason why the Gaussian distribution breaks down in air separation studies is that many different navigators are involved. I have never met any evidence that a single navigator's errors (apart from blunder or fault) are un-Gaussian.'

11. Parker (1958).

12. See for example Hsu (1980).

13. If there is no information on the distribution of probable error, a position line of any shape simply divides the earth's surface into two domains, and the position is as likely to be in one as in the other. We may arbitrarily denominate them the + domain and the − domain, and we choose to do so by nominating the enclosed area of the cocked hat the 3+ zone. Every zone bounded by a side of the triangle is a 2+, 1− zone, and each zone at a vertex of the triangle is a 1+, 2− zone. The 3− minus zone is conspicuous by its absence. If the true position were in the minus zone of each and every position line as they have severally been labelled, the cocked hat would necessarily be shaped in the form of its mirror image, and the position would be within it. The fact that the cocked hat has taken the form it has tells us that the position is in the + domain of at least one position line. Given that we are in the + domain of one position line and may equally be in either the + domain or the − domain of two other position lines, out of four there is one chance that the position is in the 3+ zone, two chances that it is in a 2+, − zone, and one chance that it is in a 1+, 2− zone. The probability of being in each zone is therefore as shown in Fig. 14.6.

14. Anderson and Parker (1956). Figures 14.7, 14.8 and 14.9. are based on illustrations contained in this paper.

15. The problem is similar to that of the optimum speed of a fishing vessel returning with its catch, or that of a tramp vessel.

CHAPTER FIFTEEN

On The Price of Annuities

☩

DURING the centuries in which commerce impelled navigation,[1] it involved little capital investment. Only a century ago, the navigation equipment on a well-found ship consisted only of a few compasses, chronometers and sextants, charts, drawing instruments, tables, almanacs, and the like. The establishments ashore which provided supporting services: hydrographic and cartographic, tables of tides and almanacs, marine lights, etc., cost a negligible part of the Gross National Product. From the 1930s, warfare or, more generally, that preparation for war we call *defence*, has been the driving force behind the extraordinary revolution in navigation—at enormous cost. The trend spilled over the boundary between military and civil, especially in aviation. In 1968 when the Boeing 747 entered service, it was said to be the first airliner on which the navigation equipment cost more than the engines, and the first civil craft of any kind on which the cost of standard navigation equipment exceeded one million dollars. We can only guess at the total real cost, subsuming all research and development, of the navigation equipment of a nuclear submarine or of the *Navstar* (GPS) system.

The approximate cost of terrestrial installations of radio aids to navigation can be estimated, however. The precise figure of total annual cost depends on the estimated operating life over which the costs of purchase and installation are amortized, and the interest rate paid to fund that capital expense, but it is in the region of a billion dollars a year.[2] In 1984 about 80 per cent of these costs were incurred by point-source aeronautical systems, only 1 per cent by marine beacons of various kinds, and the remainder by area aids (mainly Loran C and Omega)[3] used by both seamen and airmen. It is on the navigation of aeroplanes and submarines, rather than that of surface vessels, that the money has been spent in this explosion of the cost of navigation.

The new status of navigation has been accompanied by a diversification of means to achieve any desired end. For the civil user the choice of goods on display is difficult enough; for the military user it is much more complex. To achieve their ends the military must frequently fund research and development with no certain knowledge either of the eventual cost of the product or its effectiveness. When the proliferation of the means of universal destruction made superior military navigation literally *priceless*, the means of funding it remained finite. Of necessity, *cost-effectiveness* became the battle cry of the warriors.

Looking at cost-effectiveness with the fresh eyes of Voltaire's *L'ingénu*, but a numerate *ingénu* with a late-twentieth-century mind, the first thing one would observe is that for the expression to have any meaning at all it must be possible to express cost and effectiveness in the same units. The measure of cost is money, so effectiveness must be translatable into money. For a civil user buying packaged goods, this is relatively straightforward. If a shipping company or an airline is unable to determine its gain from a defined improvement in navigation, the indicated solution is to change the management; but how does one determine in dollars the value of the superiority of Navstar over Transit to the defence of the United States of America? That is certainly not a question for the ingenuous to address.

Our *ingénu* then observes that the problem is heavy with overtones of probability. The military, when initiating a research and development programme, cannot know exactly how effective the result will be, and 'cost-overruns' are notoriously common. Even the civil purchaser of a proven package is uncertain of its productive life. The ubiquitous example in modern commerce is the computer. Corporations in every field of business bought data-processing systems on a cost–effectiveness calculation based on a productive life of n years. The progress in data-processing technology has been so unexpectedly rapid that, typically after about $\frac{1}{2}n$ years, it could be convincingly argued that it would be cost-effective to scrap the lot and buy new gear. Such convincing arguments were of course based on over-optimistic estimates of the life of the new gear; and so it went on. Ironically, the extraordinarily rapid development of this technology was only realizable commercially because the market was willing to scrap yesteryear's wonder, and with it the assumptions on which the decision to purchase it was based.

Finally, the *ingénu* perceives that even when the difficulties of translating effectiveness into money and of expressing probability in numerical form have been overcome (or more frequently glossed over), the figure of merit is not the simple expression [benefits − costs]. We (or someone else) must sow before we can reap. It is a universal truth that some costs of a project are incurred before any benefits can be realized. The timing of costs and benefits must be included in some way in the figure of merit. We are all constantly exhorted by moneylenders to 'buy now, pay later', the moneylender charging a fee, quaintly called *interest*,[4] for this convenient deferral. Apprised of this service, the *ingénu* realizes that, by including interest in the cost, costs may be made concurrent with benefits, so that a perfect comparison is possible. Warming to his theme, the *ingénu* sees that the method is equally applicable if the investor in navigation in fact has surplus cash; the only difference being that the interest rate to employ is that which the investor would otherwise have enjoyed on the cash he has invested in navigation. The point is of theoretical interest only. Almost all governments, shipping companies, and airlines, at almost all times, are net borrowers. From whatever pocket they take the cash to invest in navigation, as a practical matter it simply increases their net debt; and their particular borrowing rate is the one to apply.

Ignorant of the primitive mathematics used in finance, the *ingénu*, assuming that the amount of the interest varies as the amount of the debt, concludes that, for the purpose of deferral of expense, the debt grows at a rate proportionate to its size, a function well known to scientists and engineers. He might write, in Newton's notation, $\dot{x} = kx$, where x is the accrued debt and k is the interest rate. The solution to this equation, which has been known for about three centuries, came as no surprise at the time because, with hindsight, it is an implicit corollary of Napier's work a few generations earlier, although he did not go quite so far (Chapter 3). The solution of course is $x = x_0 e^{kt}$, where x_0 is the amount of the initial loan and t is the time elapsed; but although moneylending may not be the oldest profession in the world, it is certainly far older than exponentials and logarithms. Old habits died hard in the world of finance.

In a primitive moneylending transaction the sum x is loaned for a fixed period, at the end of which the borrower must repay $x(1+i)$, i being the interest rate for the period, not per annum, and expressed as a decimal, not as a percentage (i per cent $= 100i$). If, at the end of the period, borrower and lender so agree, the debt and interest due may be refinanced, and, if the interest rate is unchanged, the debt due at the end of the second period is $x(1+i)^2$. More generally, if there are no payments, the debt at the end of n periods is $x(1+i)^n$. xe^{it} is the limiting case of this expression, as $1/n$ tends to zero, that is to say as the period tends to zero. For clarity, i will be used only in the sense of interest rate per period throughout this chapter, although financiers always speak of an annual interest rate: thus the rate quoted for a three-month loan is $4i$. It is clear from the foregoing that this is imprecise; $i' = (1+i)^4 - 1$, where i' is the annual rate equivalent to a quarterly rate of i.

Many financial instruments have evolved from the simple loan. Those which have some relevance to the funding of investment in navigation systems include:

> *Floating-rate bonds and roll-over loans.* At the end of each period the interest is paid and a new rate (based on market conditions) is set for the next period. These are the instruments preferred by bankers, who borrow short-term to lend long-term. They are less attractive to borrowers, whose difficulties in analysing the cost-effectiveness of the proposed investment are compounded by not knowing what the interest rate will be.[5]

> *Fixed-rate bonds and loans.* These are attractive to lenders (usually bond-purchasers) who do not fund their loans in the market-place and seek a fixed income. The advantages to the borrower are obvious. An important part of the financier's art is the devising of instruments which are attractive to specific classes of borrowers and lenders. The periodic payment, p, (the *coupon* in the jargon of the bond market) need not equal the market rate of interest. If it is less, the bond sells at a discount; if p is greater than the market i, the bond sells at a premium. The extreme case is the zero coupon bond, which sells at a price,

expressed as a percentage of face value (i.e. the sum to be repaid on redemption), of $100 (1+i')^{-n'}$, where i' is the market annualized interest rate for a debt of a term of n' years. In the general case in which p is not zero, and y is the amount finally redeemed,

$$x = \sum_{r=1}^{r=n} p(1+i)^{-r} + y(1+i)^{-n}.$$

It is a tedious business to determine i manually from this equation, given $x, p, y,$ and n. Most businessmen making financing decisions did not know how to do it, and financiers employed people to do little else. Mainframe computers were used from the late 1950s; and about 1970 pocket financial calculators appeared which were programmed at the touch of five buttons and the requisite numerical keys to provide any unknown in the above equation given the other four variables. One of the financier's most cherished mystiques became available to all.

Fully amortized loans, lease-purchase, and hire-purchase. These are the special case in which y in the formula above is zero. Principal and interest are fully repaid in the course of the periodic payments. In the case of lease-purchase and hire-purchase, title remains with the lender–owner until the last payment is made. The best-known application of these instruments is the retail financing of consumer goods; but they are also used to finance ships and aircraft when the credit of the operator is not of the highest. They also seem to have been used in a disguised form to finance ground-based navigational aids where there is a political risk. The great merit of the self-amortizing loan (whatever the structure of the lender's security) is that payments may be made to coincide with benefits, and (sometimes) with the cash flow which those benefits bring.

The name of Edmond Halley has appeared frequently in preceding chapters as navigator extraordinary, astronomer, physicist, mathematician, and hydrographer. He also invented actuarial science, created the basis of investment analysis, and—had he known it—described precisely the correct method of assessing the cost-effectiveness of a navigational system. How could he have known it? Nearly a century was to elapse before the high cost and great benefit of the chronometer first raised the question of the cost-effectiveness of a navigational instrument. His embarkation on this work seems to have been due to two fortuitous circumstances.

The German city of Breslau had long kept detailed records of births and deaths, including age at death. A clergyman of the city, Caspar Neumann, had analysed some of them to disprove popular superstitions relating mortality to phases of the moon and the like. He sent his work as a matter of possible interest to the great German philosopher and mathematician Gottfried Wilhelm Leibniz, from whom it passed, via a Mr Justell, to the Royal Society. It is said that Halley had promised unspecified material to help fill the *Philosophical Transactions* published by the Royal Society; and thus there appeared in volume XVII for the year 1693 *An Estimate of the Degrees of the Mortality of Mankind, drawn from Curious Tables of the Births and Funerals at the City of Breslaw; with an Attempt to ascertain the Price of Annuities upon Lives. By Mr E. Halley.*

Halley knew of Graunt's *Observations made upon the Bills of Mortality*, published in 1662 and based on records of births and deaths in London (Chapter 14); but he thought Neumann's data, covering the five years 1687–91, were far more significant, partly because they included age at death, but also because of the 'great and casual Accession of Strangers' who die in London. Breslau, he thought, was the kind of place where people die where they were born. His entire thesis is based on this assumption. His first step was to calculate, or estimate by interpolation, the number of people who died on average at each age; from this, with some smoothing of the data, he determined Table 15.1, the model for mortality tables ever since. If it is assumed that mortality rates remain constant (no wars, plagues, or improvements in medical practice) and there is neither emigration nor immigration, it follows that, for example, of a thousand babies who live until their first birthday, 855 will live until their second birthday, and 20 until their 84th birthday. Halley was aware of the dangers of taking only a five-year sample of a single Silesian provincial town; but he was concerned more with method than with the significance of his sample.

Age	Persons	Age	Persons	Age	Persons	Age	Persons
1	1000	22	586	43	417	64	202
2	855	23	579	44	407	65	192
3	798	24	573	45	397	66	182
4	760	25	567	46	387	67	172
5	732	26	560	47	377	68	162
6	710	27	553	48	367	69	152
7	692	28	546	49	357	70	142
8	680	29	539	50	346	71	131
9	670	30	531	51	335	72	120
10	661	31	523	52	324	73	109
11	653	32	515	53	313	74	98
12	646	33	507	54	302	75	88
13	640	34	499	55	292	76	78
14	634	35	490	56	282	77	68
15	628	36	481	57	272	78	58
16	622	37	472	58	262	79	49
17	616	38	463	59	252	80	41
18	610	39	454	60	242	81	34
19	604	40	445	61	232	82	28
20	598	41	436	62	222	83	23
21	592	42	427	63	212	84	20

Table 15.1. Halley's mortality table

Then we come to the nub of the matter, the calculation of the price of annuities. The first step is the calculation of the *Present Value* of future receivables, discounted at an assumed interest rate of 6 per cent per annum. He uses the term *Present Value* in precisely the sense in which it is used by financial analysts today. Halley's table is shown in Table 15.2. It is a tabulation of 1.06^{-n}, where n is the number of years. Thus, for example, the present value of £1 receivable in 12 years is £0.4970, because that is the sum which would grow to £1 in 12 years if put out at 6 per cent interest compounded annually. Halley tells us that he used six-figure logarithms to calculate this table. His logarithm of $1/1.06$ is correct to six decimal places; but inevitably small rounding errors occur in a few places in a four-figure table of the result.

Years	P.Value	Years	P.Value	Years	P.Value	Years	P.Value
1	0.9434	14	0.4423	27	0.2074	40	0.0972
2	0.8900	15	0.4173	28	0.1956	45	0.0726
3	0.8396	16	0.3936	29	0.1845	50	0.0543
4	0.7921	17	0.3714	30	0.1741	55	0.0406
5	0.7473	18	0.3503	31	0.1643	60	0.0303
6	0.7050	19	0.3305	32	0.1550	65	0.0227
7	0.6650	20	0.3118	33	0.1462	70	0.0169
8	0.6274	21	0.2941	34	0.1379	75	0.0126
9	0.5919	22	0.2775	35	0.1301	80	0.0094
10	0.5584	23	0.2618	36	0.1227	85	0.0071
11	0.5268	24	0.2470	37	0.1158	90	0.0053
12	0.4970	25	0.2330	38	0.1092	95	0.0039
13	0.4688	26	0.2198	39	0.1031	100	0.0029

Table 15.2 Halley's Present Value Table (£1 discounted at 6 per cent p.a.)

To calculate the price of an annuity for life of £1 payable in arrears and purchased at the age of 35, Halley, in effect, reasons as follows: from Table 15.1, of every thousand babies who attain the age of 1 year, 490 survive to be 35; assume they all buy the annuity; then from Table 15.1, £481 will be paid at the end of the first year, £472 at the end of the second year, and so on until they are all dead. The sum of the present value of all these sums equals the cost of 490 annuities of £1. Halley divides that sum by 490 to produce what he calls 'Years' Purchase', i.e. the factor by which a desired annuity must be multiplied to determine its price. His result, which is given in Table 15.3, he described as 'the short result of a not ordinary number of Arithmetical Operations'. Understandably, they are not quite so accurate as Table 15.2. Even with a programmable financial calculator the calculation is tedious.

Halley then turns to the price of an annuity on two lives of different ages, that is to say an annuity payable until both are dead. His method is equally applicable when different reduced annuities are to be paid to the survivor. Let a be the amount of the annuity while both live, b the amount if only the elder is alive, c the amount if only the younger is alive—

Age	Years' Purchase	Age	Years' Purchase	Age	Years' Purchase
1	10.28	25	12.27	50	9.21
5	13.40	30	11.72	55	8.51
10	13.44	35	11.12	60	7.60
15	13.33	40	10.57	65	6.54
20	12.78	45	9.91	70	5.32

Table 15.3 Halley's table of 'Years Purchase' (=cost of annuity/annuity)

a practical arrangement, perhaps, for a married couple. Halley takes the example of persons of 18 and 35 proposed. From Table 15.1 there are 610 × 490 = 298 900 possible couples, and 6 of the younger and 9 of the elder die before the first annuity is payable, so on the first anniversary of the purchase no annuity would be payable to 6 × 9 = 54 couples, a would be payable to 604 × 481 = 290 524 couples, b would be payable to 481 × 6 = 2886 elder survivors, and c to 604 × 9 = 5436 younger survivors. The present value of $290 524a + 2886b + 5436c$ is then calculated, and the process repeated for subsequent years until all are dead. The sum of all present values is divided by 298 900 to determine the price of the joint annuity.

Halley goes on to explain how to determine the price of an annuity on three or more lives, but, understandably, gives no examples, as the number of possible combinations becomes cumbersome without data-processing machinery (other than an abacus).

It is immediately apparent how we may apply Halley's method to a decision whether to invest in an improved navigation system. For simplicity it is assumed that the price is known and the benefits are annually in arrears from purchase date and constant. There is however some uncertainty as to the quantum of the benefits, the ongoing costs of operation and maintenance, and how long it will be before the equipment becomes obsolete. These uncertainties are expressed in the table of probabilities shown in Table 15.4, where the term 'net benefit' is used to mean the annual benefit less the ongoing annual costs of maintenance and operation. It is considered that the equipment will have no residual value when it is obsolete.

Life (years)	Net Annual Benefit					Sum of annual benefits	PV of SUM
	110	120	130	140	150		
			% probability				
5	5	6	7	8	7	4350	15680.8
6	6	7	8	9	8	5000	20557.0
7	5	5	6	7	6	3810	17387.9

Sum of 100 present values = 53625.7
Probable present value = 536

Table 15.4. The probable present value of future benefits

The purchase would be funded from existing bank lines of credit, and the borrowing rate is 12 per cent.

Each percentage point of probability is taken to be a unit member of a population of 100. In each row the sum of the net annual benefits received by all units is calculated, and the present value of the flow of such a sum of benefits for 5, 6, or 7 years (as the case may be) is computed. The sum of these present values is the present value of all the benefits received by the population of 100 as Halley would have calculated it. The result divided by 100 is the probable present value of the benefits of the acquisition to be compared with its price. Cost-benefit analysis is often regarded as an esoteric and essentially modern field of study. It has been with us, virtually unchanged except for the data-processing machinery, for three hundred years; and the man who discovered it was also a distinguished navigator.

Notes to Chapter 15

1. Although many of the voyages of exploration were of a military nature, and competition between rival nations often found military expression, the underlying motivation was usually commercial.
2. Pearson (1986) calculated a figure of $721 000 000 p.a. based on 1984 figures, including depreciation at a constant rate over 15 years; but not the interest element of amortization.
3. Based on data contained in Pearson (1986).
4. The evolution of moneylending has been complicated by the fact that in both the Christian and Mohammedan religions usury is a sin, and in both cultures at some times and places moneylending at interest has been a crime. Since it is economically desirable that those who have a temporary surplus of cash should place it at the disposal of those who have a temporary need for it, and reasonable that the lender should be paid for his service, ingenious devices were employed to circumvent religious principle for the social good. A popular instrument was the bill of exchange payable in a different currency and in a different place, and therefore necessarily at a different time. Standard journey-times evolved. A Florentine banker might buy for florins a note payable in Bruges in local currency. In theory at least, the banker's branch or correspondent in Bruges after an agreed interval bought the note in exchange for one payable in florins in Florence, again at a later date. On expiry this note, naturally for a larger sum than the purchase price of the original florin note, is presented to the original borrower, and, if both parties agree, the note can be recycled. The banker's profit comes not from moneylending but from exchanging money, which was not sinful or criminal. Then as now, banks do not borrow money, they 'accept deposits', and the *interest* payable to the depositor was an equity interest, a profit participation in a perfectly respectable exchange business. Popes had no difficulty in placing their surplus cash at interest with bankers while abhorring and punishing usury. When the usury laws were relaxed, the word *interest* acquired its present artificial meaning. In Italian, a promissory note with no connotations of currency exchange is still called a *cambiale* (note of exchange). The writer was told by an Arab banker that almost identical techniques were employed by Muslim merchants trading in the Indian Ocean in those days; but he was quite silent on the question as to how such matters are handled today in countries which strictly enforce Islamic law.
5. During the 1980s, floating interest rates in both £ and $ varied by a factor of about 2:1.

CHAPTER SIXTEEN

Past, Present, and Future

✠

THE pace quickens. When Hipparchus invented the coordinate system of latitude and longitude, the latitude could be found, at least on land, with an accuracy of perhaps ¼°. About another two thousand years elapsed before the longitude could be found at sea with the same accuracy. During the nineteenth century great strides were made in the perfection and compensation of the pivoted needle compass, in nautical astronomy, in cartography and surveying, in oceanography and meteorology, in tidal prediction, in marine lights. Yet the fact remains that, a century ago, the only means of navigating a ship across the ocean were, as they had been for so many centuries, the heavens, the magnetic needle, and the log. Out of range of coastal radio navigation aids, that was still the case in many merchant ships fifty years ago.

The quickening of pace has continued to the present. The developments from the experiments of Hertz in the 1880s to radio-navigation as it was practised in the 1930s seem modest compared with the developments of the last fifty years. Only thirty years ago, over much of the earth's surface, the only fixing system available to ships and aircraft alike was still the sextant and chronometer. Ground-based radio systems have marvellously evolved to perform many diverse functions, ranging from global VLF fixing systems to the highly local function of precision landing systems at airports. Equally, the development of the gyrocompass in the first half of the twentieth century seems slow compared with the achievements of inertial systems in more recent decades. The optimum routeing of ships has taken greater strides since the middle of this century than it had then taken since the days of Maury. The diversity of development has been as remarkable as its speed. Many systems of the past fifty years have not been mentioned in preceding chapters. There has been no space, for example, for correlation techniques. An application to low-level strike aircraft enables the computer to navigate by correlating the map in its memory with what the radar sees. There are also marine and submarine applications of correlation techniques. Implicit in all the changes of recent decades is the computer revolution. How can this acceleration continue?

We are at a unique moment in the history of navigation. We have within our grasp the means of determining location and velocity by satellite anywhere in the world with sufficient accuracy for the most exigent demands of commercial *en route* navigation both at sea and in the air. We can see that satellite systems which are already possible, employed in a differential mode, could provide sufficient accuracy to dock a supertanker or land an airliner, and so provide in a single world system all the navigational needs of all users engaged in peaceful commerce or the pursuit of pleasure. All the land-based systems developed over the century could become obsolete.

Both GPS and the comparable Russian system *Glonass* are superb achievements; but they were designed to meet military requirements, and may properly be regarded as military systems of their owners. However benevolent the passive intentions of the owners in peaceful times, it is intrinsically unsatisfactory for the world at large to place the safety of human life entirely in the hands of someone else's weapon system. A system dedicated entirely to peaceful commerce could now provide greater accuracy at less cost. It has been estimated that 80 per cent of the GPS cost was due to the stringent military specifications.

Low cost Magellan GPS receivers.

There are many proposals, many contenders and volunteers; but there is no immediate prospect of an international consensus on what such a system would be, who would pay for it, who would manage it, and how the management of so great a responsibility would be supervised and controlled. A difficulty which is rightly stressed is the horrific consequence of the failure of a system on which the navigation of the whole world relies at all times. Perhaps for this reason alone, total reliance on satellite systems, for aircraft landing at least, is not presently foreseeable, however much the satellite system is duplicated, triplicated, and made 'fail-operational'.

The need for ground-based systems of lesser precision, especially when their reliability is not critically important to human lives, is not obvious. One study in 1991 concluded that Europe could be provided with satnav coverage, broadly of Loran C standards, at the cost of a single Loran C chain.[1] At the time further Loran C chains in Europe were envisaged; even the proponents of Decca had not abandoned their case.

The application of differential techniques (Chapter 12) to GPS (known as DGPS) is already being vigorously pursued, although the full constellation of GPS satellites will not be operational until about a year after this book is published. Stations ashore already compute the correction for satellite ranges and broadcast them to ships in their immediate vicinity. The obvious media are the existing MF marine radio beacons. It is claimed[2] that the first DGPS system to use marine radio beacons in this way is a Magnavox system provided for the Swedish Maritime Administration and the Finnish Board of Navigation to cover the narrow channels leading to Stockholm and Helsinki. Accuracy of the order of 5 metres is claimed. The case for land-based radio aids to marine navigation, except perhaps for docking purposes, is becoming tenuous.

Notwithstanding the caveats widely expressed about automatic landings by DGPS, NASA and Honeywell, and also Telefunken reported[3] in 1991 successful experimental Category 3 (see Chapter 10) automatic landing by 'inertially-smoothed' DGPS; which presumably means applying Kalman filter techniques to the outputs of the DGPS and the aircraft INS. Some-where, someone must be studying the inclusion of the output of existing ILS installations (Chapter 10) with INS and DGPS in a Kalman filter to provide safer and more accurate automatic landing. Despite the official position of international (and some national) organisations, it must be doubted that all of the hundreds of millions of sterling pounds required for the world-wide implementation of the MLS programme (Chapter 10) will ever be spent. Studies of the application of DGPS to taxiway guidance, and the navigation of aircraft on the ground generally, were also being reported frequently in 1991. Papers describing the very high accuracies being obtained using GPS in the interferometric or phase-tracking modes also appeared in that year.[4] Determination of aircraft attitude in flight with respect to all three axes with an accuracy of 6' and position with an accuracy of one metre were reported.

It was the chronometer which first introduced economics to navigation. Its high initial cost discouraged its usage for decades. From the introduction of radio and the gyrocompass, the cost of navigation/communication equipment continued to escalate, eventually reaching $ 1 000 000 in the first INS-equipped Boeing 747s of the late 1960s. All the more sophisticated systems of navigation and communications were beyond the reach of users of modest means. The most extraordinary feature of the GPS and computer revolutions is, in the absence of user charges for GPS, a total reversal of the long-established trend. In late 1991 the smallest yacht could be GPS-equipped for £500. It was mentioned in Chapter 12 that in 1991 single-seater pest-spraying aircraft in the Sahara desert were routinely fixing position by GPS with an accuracy of 30 m. In this they were ahead of the airlines, which were equipped at the time with VOR and DME and, where appropriate, Loran C and Omega, which provided area coverage of a lower accuracy. Spraying aircraft, during the locust plagues in the same area in the late 1980s, had only their compasses and their maps to guide them over terrain which often lacked clear features. It is in such low-cost operations that the impact of GPS has been most immediate and most dramatic. The military share these serendipitous benefits.

Navstar GPS Satellite

For the first time the infantryman has a universal fixing system which does not rely on a map,[5] an application which can scarcely have been envisaged when satnav systems were first perceived as a possible solution to the nuclear submarine's navigational problem.

For millennia navigation was of ships. Within the life-span of the very aged it has been applied successively to submarines, aircraft, and space vehicles. Quite suddenly, from the mid-1980s, land-vehicle navigation equipment became a booming market, a consequence of the low cost of data storage, processing, and display, rather than of GPS. Ironically, the only vehicles, other than wholly submerged submarines, which cannot navigate accurately by satellite are vehicles in the deep canyons of some modern cities. Land-vehicle navigation systems may guide the driver of the vehicle or provide automatically vehicle-position data to a central control. An obvious market for the latter kind of system are the police, who might find it useful for spotting a highway patrol snoozing in a lay-by in the early hours of the morning, as well as for the more efficient tactical management of the pursuit of crime. The great diversity of systems currently offered responds to the great diversity of land-vehicle needs. For the car-driver finding his way in an unfamiliar city a DR system updated by signals installed on strategically placed traffic-lights might be attractive; but an entrant in the Paris–Cape Town race should choose GPS: suitable equipment in late 1991 cost £300. Indeed, it was reported[6] in 1991 that, despite the blockage and reflection of satellite signals by buildings, the Dallas Area Rapid Transit Authority has ordered GPS to equip some 1600 vehicles with an integrated system of voice communication and data-links, automatic vehicle location, monitoring, and computer-aided dispatch.

It is clear that we are only at the beginning of the exploitation of the potential of satellite navigation and communication for the benefits of civilisation as a whole. In the course of it, navigational science, in the widest sense, will be of practical value far beyond its traditional fields of ships and aeroplanes. There is a widening of the application of the navigational sciences to the needs of society, and a parallel integration of navigation and communication technologies in systems of guidance, command, and control. Previous chapters describing the burgeoning of navigational sciences over 23 centuries have been history. This chapter, in so far as it describes the present, is journalism, soon to be as irrelevant a curiosity as an old newspaper.

The question, 'how can the acceleration of the rate of progress continue' has been posed and left unanswered. The history of airliners since the Second World War suggests an analogy. Typically, the DC4 was used at the beginning on the North Atlantic. It was unpressurised, and therefore constrained to fly in the worst of the weather; the passenger cabin was very noisy; and engine vibration was palpable. It cruised at 180 knots, and could manage Shannon (W. Ireland) to Gander (Newfoundland) against headwinds with about 40 passengers. Airlines which remained loyal to the Douglas *marque* replaced the DC4 with the DC6, which was pressurised, and thus flew above the worst of the weather; it cruised at 240 knots, was larger, and had greater range. The DC6 was replaced by the DC7, larger, faster, quieter, higher-flying, and with even greater range; but still piston-engined. Airlines which continued their loyalty to the Douglas *marque* replaced their DC7s with DC8s rather their contemporary rivals the Boeing 707s. Both types were turbojets cruising at 460 knots at unprecedented altitudes, relatively vibrationless and (in the cabin) silent, and carrying much more than a hundred passengers non-stop between the capitals of Western Europe and New York. In one typical airline this total transformation from DC4, via DC6 and DC7, to DC8 *took only ten years*.

That was 34 years ago. From the passenger's point of view nothing much has changed since then:[7] the same six-abreast tube, and broadly the same speed and cruising altitude. Even the Boeing 747, the largest and still the dominant wide-body aircraft, has been with us for nearly a quarter of a century. From the point of view of the pilot, the engineer, the airline accountant, and people who live near airports, the rate of progress has been unabated in terms of reliability, safety, all-weather capability and system integrity generally, fuel consumption, payload-range capability and performance generally, operating cost, and external noise. It is the *direction* of progress which has changed rather than its *rate*. Perhaps it will be like that with navigation in the coming decades.

Addressing the question 'what do we want from future progress in navigation technology' in respect of maritime and aerial commerce, we find that the technology to remedy the greatest navigation problems of the present already exists. Our failure is extrinsic, it lies in other directions.

In maritime commerce the most important navigational problem is the avoidance of collision with other vessels and with such solid objects as rocks. The consequences of such incidents, in terms of loss of life, destruction of valuable property, and ecological disaster, are at an unacceptable level. It is incomprehensible, given the present state of the art of radio-communication, that every year some merchant ships simply disappear. The perceived remedy is the Global Maritime Distress and Safety System (GMDSS), which will include satellite communication in oceanic areas. All the disasters in recent years which have been extensively reported and analysed were avoidable. In some cases, poor visual and radar watchkeeping, or the incompetence or negligence of ship's officers, were clearly a factor. The low standards of operational skills and discipline on some ships may be traced back to the repeal of the Navigation Acts in the early nineteenth century, and thus, in our times, to the proliferation of large vessels on flags-of-convenience. Under such flags high operational standards are not enforced. We are fortunate that there is no corresponding licence in the air. Subject to the 'fifth freedom' exception, the right to carry aerial traffic between two states is limited to carriers nominated by one or the other of them and, in highly developed countries at least, the legal means, and the infrastructure necessary, are rigorously employed to ensure compliance with high standards.

Ships which maintain the highest standards of professionalism are not equipped for collision avoidance to a level which is clearly within the present state of the art. Although secondary radar has been with us since the IFF of the Second World War (Chapter 11), the officer of the watch has no direct means of identifying a vessel which he sees on his radar screen. The avoidance of collision by communication and co-operation between ships in potential hazard is haphazard. Although an automatic radar plotting aid (ARPA, Chapter 11) is now mandatory, the state of the art is not fully exploited. However, the neglect of safety at sea is not limited to navigation. Large ships with a single propulsion system and a single steering system are still allowed everywhere.

In aerial commerce the problem is not the collisions which do occur; they are very rare, and usually involve a light aircraft with a pilot not qualified to professional standards. The problem is the high total costs of the air traffic control service which maintains these enviable standards. The anatomy of these costs (outlined in greater detail in Chapter 11) extends beyond the user charges (of the order of £s per passenger hour) to the consequences of delays, clearance at unfavourable flight levels or on unfavourable routes, and the consumption of millions of tons of fuel annually *merely to carry* the weight of the reserve fuel required for unfavourable ATC clearances and delays in flight. Of all inadequacies of navigation this is the most expensive to the world as a whole at present.

Today, the queue to join the queue to land at New York starts on the ground at London and elsewhere. The reason is that in oceanic areas (where aircraft cannot be seen by ground radar) control is based on verbal position reports by pilots. Each aircraft is deemed by ATC to occupy a block of space 2000 feet high, 60 n.m. wide, and 10 minutes (more than 60 n.m.) long, and any invasion of that space is regarded as potentially hazardous. There are just not enough blocks of that size in the oceanic airspace. Acceptable lateral and longitudinal criteria are a function of the frequency, accuracy, and reliability of the pilot reports, and of the capability of ATC to process data and execute control functions. Even if the pilots know their position and velocity with the precision which satnav has made possible, the present inadequacies of communication and ATC data-processing capability would not permit the reduction of these criteria to acceptable levels. In some airlines today a passenger may chat comfortably with his wife 10 000 miles away using international satellite telephone links, while the pilot struggles to reach ATC on single-side-band HF. He would do better if he knew his controller's telephone number! The perceived solution is ADS (automatic dependent surveillance), which, employing two-way reliable data-links via satellites, will provide ATC with automatic position and velocity vector reports at intervals as low as 10 seconds. Voice channels for tactical communication will also be provided.

In European airspace, with radar surveillance, better communication by conventional means, and ground-based navigation aids, separation criteria are much lower, but capacity is often determined not by physical separation of the aircraft, but by the sustainable workload of the controllers. ATC was originally an exercise of sovereign right and duty over a nation's airspace, and national boundaries have no place in an efficient ATC system. Nowadays *Eurocontrol* has impressive offices; but we still have British, French, German, etc., ATC, each with its own ideas, management, and willingness or not to spend. A decade or so ago it was recognised that advances in precise flight-management systems which enable aircraft to maintain an exact flight-plan, automatic data-links, and improved data-processing could lead eventually to a precisely timed pre-cleared slot, for example, from a gate at London (Heathrow) to a gate at Paris (Charles de Gaulle); but progress in most directions is far behind the state-of-the-art of the navigational, communications, and data-processing sciences.

Suddenly, after all these centuries, perfection of navigation beyond the dreams of only a few decades ago is technically within our grasp; but, before we weep that there are no more worlds for navigational science to conquer, let us not forget that radio waves cannot reach deeply submerged submarines. They no longer have to surface to recharge their batteries; but, so far as published information goes, they still have to approach the surface to update their INS from time to time. It is ironical that the very vehicle which triggered the satnav revolution is the one with the big unsolved problem. Perhaps correlation techniques will provide an answer.

Throughout the ages, experienced human navigators, aware of their subjection to error, blunder, and ignorance, developed a sense of smell, an innate heuristic means of perception that something is wrong. Machines have no sense of smell, and evidence is growing that people who navigate by keying machines have lost theirs. Perhaps the last frontier lies in that direction.

Notes

1. Quoted in COMMENT *Navigation News*, (September/October 1991), vol. 6, issue 5, p. 1.
2. News item in *Navigation News* (September/October 1991), vol. 6 issue 5, p. 19.

3. News item in *Navigation News* (November/December 1991), vol. 6, issue 6, p. 3.
4. Report of USION 47th Annual Meeting in *Navigation News* (September/October 1991), vol. 6, issue 5, p. 2.
5. Some hand-held GPS receivers were sold out during the Gulf War. It was reported that mothers of soldiers in the Gulf were buying them and shipping them to their sons.
6. News item in *Navigation News* (November/December 1991), vol. 6, issue 6, p. 3.
7. Excepting Concorde, a distinguished if irrelevant engineering achievement. Its impact on air transport proved negligible.

References

✛

AM (Air Ministry, London) (1963). *The origins and development of operational research in the Royal Air Force*, Air Publication 3368. HMSO, London.

Anderson, E. W. and Parker, J. B. (1956). Observational errors. *Journal of Navigation*, **9**, 105–35.

Ashkenazi, V. and Cleasby, C. (1991). *GPS as a tool for engineering applications of geodesy*. First International Symposium on the Applications of Geodesy to Engineering, Stuttgart.

Barr, R. and Young, K. B. (1989). Omega navigation in the shadow of Antarctica. *Journal of Navigation*, **42**, 236–47.

Bellman, R. (1957). *Dynamic programming*. Princeton University Press, New Jersey.

Best, F. P. (1950). Use of direction finding at sea. *Journal of Navigation*, **3**, 332–5.

Blanchard, W. F. (1989). Civil satellite navigation and location systems. *Journal of Navigation*, **42**, 202–22.

Booker, P. and White, F. A. (1979). Minimum navigation performance specifications in the North Atlantic region. *Journal of Navigation*, **32**, 357–74.

Boot, H. A. and Randall, J. T. (1976). Historical notes on the cavity magnetron. *IEEE transactions*, **ed. 23**, 389–97.

Bowen, E. G. (1987). *Radar days*. Adam Hilger, Bristol.

Bronowski, J. (1951). [Book review.] *Scientific American*, October, 1951, 75–7.

Burton, S. M. (1951). *Nautical tables*. Burton's Navigational Publications Ltd, Alva, Scotland.

Cameron, I. (1965). *The lodestone and evening star*. Hodder & Stoughton, London.

Castlereagh, D. (1971). *The great age of exploration*. Aldus Books, London.

Chamberlin, E. R. (1974). *The fall of the house of Borgia*. Temple Smith, London.

Charnley, Sir J. (1989). Navigation aids to aircraft all-weather landing. *Journal of Navigation*, **42**, 161–86.

Clarricoats, J. (1967). *The world at their fingertips*. Radio Society of Great Britain, London.

Cockroft, A. N. (1980). The compulsory fitting of seaborne radar collision avoidance systems (a discussion). *Journal of Navigation*, **33**, 389–91.

Cotter, C. H. (1968). *A history of nautical astronomy*. Hollis and Carter, London.

Crone, G. R. (1966). *Maps and their makers* (revised edn). Hutchinson, London.

Crowther, J. G. and Whiddington, R. (1947). *Scientists at war.* HMSO, London.

Davenport, W. W. (1978). *Gyro.* Scribner, New York.

Durant, W. (1936). *The life of Greece.* Simon & Schuster, New York.

Fanning, A. E. (1986). *Steady as she goes.* HMSO, London.

Forbes, E. G. (1965). The foundations and early development of the nautical almanac. *Journal of Navigation*, **18**, 391–401.

Forty, G. M. (1983). Sources of latitude error in English sixteenth century navigation. *Journal of Navigation*, **36**, 388–403.

Forty, G. M. (1986). The backstaff and the determination of latitude at sea in the seventeenth century. *Journal of Navigation*, **39**, 259–68.

Gage, T. (1928 [1648]). *The English American: a new survey of the West Indies, 1648* (ed. Sir E. Denison Ross). Routledge, London.

Galton, F. (1872). *Memorandum on the construction of 'isodic charts'.* Minutes of the Meteorological Committee, December 2, 1872, London.

George, F. (1956). Hariot's meridional parts. *Journal of Navigation*, **9**, 66–9.

Giblett, M. A. (1924). Notes on meteorology and the navigation of airships. *Meteorological Magazine*, **59**, 1–17.

Gingerich, O. and Wether, B. L. (1983). *Planetary, lunar and solar positions AD 1650–1805.* The American Philosophical Society, Philadelphia.

Gould R. T. (1923). *The marine chronometer.* The Holland Press, London.

Grant, G. A. A. and Klinkert, J. (1970). *The ship's compass*, (revised edn). Routledge and Kegan Paul, London.

Hackman, W. (1984). *Seek and strike.* HMSO, London.

Hagiwara, H. and Spaans, J. A. (1987). Practical weather routeing of sail-assisted motor vessels. *Journal of Navigation*, **40**, 96–119.

Hanssen, G. L. and James, R. W. (1960). Optimum ship routing. *Journal of Navigation*, **13**, 253–72.

Hawking, S. W. (1988). *A brief history of time.* Bantam Press, London.

Herbert, A. (1985). *Quantum reality.* Anchor Press/Doubleday, New York.

Hibbert, C. (1974). *The rise and fall of the house of Medici.* Allen Lane, London.

Hine, A. (1968). *Magnetic compasses and magnetometers.* Adam Hilger, Bristol.

Hsu, D. A. (1980). Further analyses of position errors in navigation. *Journal of Navigation*, **33**, 452–74.

Hughes, T. P. (1971). *Elmer Sperry, inventor and engineer.* Johns Hopkins Press, Baltimore.

Hutchins, H. L. and May, W. E. (1952). *Lodestone to gyrocompass.* Hutchinson, London.

Jessel, A. H. (1948). The range and accuracy of consol. *Journal of Navigation*, **1**, 241–56.

Kemp, J. F. (1990). An omega/VLF radio compass. *Journal of Navigation*, **43**, 118–24.

Kendal, B. (1990). The beginnings of directional radio techniques for air navigation. *Journal of Navigation*, **43**, 313–30.

King-Hele, D. G. (1964). The shape of the earth. *Journal of Navigation*, **17**, 1–16.

Koestler, A. (1959). *The sleepwalkers.* Hutchinson, London.

Lanchester, F. W. (1916). *Aircraft in warfare.* Constable, London.

Lecky, S. T. S. (1881). *Wrinkles in practical navigation.* George Philip and Son, London.

Lewellen, G. (1984). *Transit user equipment for marine navigation.* Proceedings of the Royal Institute of Navigation Conference on Global Civil Satellite Navigation Systems.

Malin, S. R. (1985). The international prime meridian conference. *Journal of Navigation*, **38**, 203–6.

May, W. E. (1955). Alexander Neckham and the pivoted compass needle. *Journal of Navigation*, **8**, 283–4.

May, W. E. (1960). The last voyage of Sir Clowdisley Shovel. *Journal of Navigation*, **13**, 324–32.

May, W. E. (1981). Were compasses used in antiquity? *Journal of Navigation*, **34**, 414–23.

Morison, S. E. (1942). *Admiral of the Ocean Sea*. Little, Brown, New York.

Morse, P. M. and Kimball, G. E. (1951). *Methods of operations research*. Wiley, New York.

Motte, R. and Calvert, S. (1988). Operational considerations and constraints in ship-based weather routeing procedures. *Journal of Navigation*, **41**, 417–33.

Motzo, B. R. (1947). *Il compasso da navegare*. Università, Cagliari, Sardinia.

Neil, H. J. (1990). The channel navigation information service for the Dover strait. *Journal of Navigation*, **43**, 331–42.

Newman, J. (1956). *The world of mathematics*. Simon and Schuster, New York.

Ordnance Survey (1967). *History of the retriangulation of Great Britain*. HMSO, London.

Parker, J. B. (1958). The effect of blunders on collision risk calculations. *Journal of Navigation*, **11**, 29–33.

Pearson, M. G. (1986). The cost-effectiveness of terrestrial radio-navigation. *Journal of Navigation*, **39**, 424–38.

Pierce, J. A. (1957). Intercontinental frequency comparison by very low-frequency radio transmission. *Proceedings Institute of Radio Engineering*, **45**, 794–803.

Pledge, H. T. (1939). *Science since 1500*. HMSO, London.

Powell, C. (1962). The use of VLF transmissions for navigation. *Journal of Navigation*, **15**, 277–86.

Powell, C. (1972). Historical hyperbolae. *Journal of Navigation*, **25**, 107–8.

Powell, C. (1981). Hyperbolic origins. *Journal of Navigation*, **34**, 424–36.

Powell, C. (1986). Radio navigation in the 1920s. *Journal of the Institute of Electronic and Radio Engineers*, **56**, 293–7.

Pritchard, D. (1989). *The radar war*. Patrick Stephens, Wellingborough, Northants.

Proudman, J. (1973). *Tides*. Encyclopaedia Britannica, Vol. 21, (14th edn), 1125–37. Encyclopaedia Britannica Inc.

Raper, H. (1890). *The practice of navigation and nautical astronomy* (19th edn). J. D. Potter, London.

Reich, P. G. (1966). Analysis of long range air traffic systems. *Journal of Navigation*, **19**, 88–98, 169–86, 331–47.

Richey, M. W. (1983). The province of the Institute. *Journal of Navigation*, **36**, 1–20.

Robinson, R. S. and Thomas, G. (1971). Chapter 9 in *Navigation systems*. Van Nostrand Reinhold, London.

Sawyer, J. S. (1949). *Theoretical aspects of pressure pattern flying*, MO 496C (Meteorological Office Publication 496C). HMSO, London.

Scott, G. H. (1921). Airship piloting. *The Aeronautical Journal*, **25**, 47–71.

Severin, T. (1987). Early navigation: the human factor. *Journal of Navigation*, **40**, 1–18.

Smith, R. A. (1947). *Radio aids to navigation*. Cambridge University Press.

Smith, S. G. (1986). Developments in inertial navigation. *Journal of Navigation*, **39**, 401–15.

Stokes, R. F. and Smith, S. G. (1983). Integrated navigation systems for aircraft. *Journal of Navigation*, **36**, 359–78.

Stratton, A. (1990). Differential omega as a worldwide navigation aid. *Journal of Navigation*, **43**, 88–104.

Sun Guang-Qi (1989). A brief history of ancient Chinese sailing directions. *Journal of Navigation*, **42**, 11–30.

Swords, S. S. (1986). *Technical history of the beginnings of radar*. Peter Peregrinus, London.

Taylor, E. G. R. (1950). Five centuries of dead reckoning. *Journal of Navigation*, **3**, 280–5.

Taylor, E. G. R. (1956). *The haven-finding art*. Hollis and Carter, London.

Taylor, E. G. R. (1960). Mathematics and the navigator in the thirteenth century. *Journal of Navigation*, **13**, 1–12.

Taylor, E. G. R. (1967). *The mathematical practitioners of Tudor and Stuart England*. Cambridge University Press.

Taylor, E. G. R. and Richey, M. W. (1962). *The geometrical seaman*. Hollis & Carter, London.

Taylor, E. G. R. and Sadler, D. H. (1953). The doctrine of nauticall triangles compendious. *Journal of Navigation*, **6**, 131–47.

Tiberio, U. (1939). Misura di distanze per mezzo di onde ultracorte (radiotelemetria). *Alta Frequenza*, **8**, 305–23.

Turnbull, H. W. (1951). *The great mathematicians* (4th edn). Methuen, London.

Verploegh, G. (1963). The weather routing of merchant ships. *Journal of Navigation*, **16**, 399–413.

Vigneras, L. A. (ed.) (1960). *The journal of Christopher Columbus*. Orion Press, London.

Waters, D. W. (1956). Plane sailing or horizontal navigation. *Journal of Navigation*, **9**, 454–61.

Waters, D. W. (1989). The English pilot: English sailing directions and charts and the rise of English shipping, 16th to 18th centuries. *Journal of Navigation*, **42**, 317–54.

Watson-Watt, Sir R. (1957). *Three steps to victory*. Odhams Press. London.

Whitehead, A. N. (1925). *Science and the modern world*. Macmillan, London.

Williams, J. E. D. (1950). Loxodromic distances on the terrestrial spheroid. *Journal of Navigation*, **3**, 133–40.

Williams, J. E. D. (1957). Navigational aspects of turboprop operation on the North Atlantic. *Journal of Navigation*, **10**, 31–49.

Wrigley, W. (1977). The history of inertial navigation. *Journal of Navigation*, **30**, 61–8.

Wylie, F. J. (1952). *The use of radar at sea*. Hollis & Carter, London.

Acknowledgements

✠

The author and publishers are grateful to the following bodies and individuals for permission to reproduce certain photographs in this book and for assistance in providing prints.

Commander A. E. Fanning: photographs appearing on pp. 89, 129, 136, 137, 138, 140.

Magellan Systems Corporation, San Dimas, California: photograph appearing on p. 292.

National Maritime Museum: photographs appearing on pp. 14, 17, 23, 25, 29, 31, 38, 82, 101.

Quadrant Picture Library: photograph appearing on p. 57.

Ann Ronan Pictures at Image Select: frontispiece

The Royal Institute of Navigation: photographs appearing on pp. 122, 156, 294.

Science Museum Library: photographs appearing on pp. 36, 99, 113, 118, 121, 150, 178, 184, 205.

The author provided the photograph appearing on p. 50.

Index

✠

Page numbers in italics refer to figures.